Kramer

THE PROTO-ELAMITE
SETTLEMENT AT TUV

Ilene M. Nicholas received her B.A. degree in anthropology and history from the University of Arizona. She obtained her Ph.D. in anthropology from the University of Pennsylvania. She has taught at the University of Pennsylvania and the Temple University Center City Campus, and is currently Associate Professor of Anthropology at Hobart and William Smith Colleges. She has excavated at Grasshopper Pueblo (Arizona); Daniel's Village (Connecticut); Malkata (Egypt); Tell Leilan (Syria); and Hasanlu Tepe and Tal-e Malyan in Iran. In 1985 she co-directed a special Fall Term Abroad program in Cairo, Egypt, for Hobart and William Smith Colleges. Her current field research is being conducted in association with The University Museum's Baq'ah Valley Project (Jordan), for which she undertook a program of mapping and test excavation at the Early Bronze Age site of al-Qesir during the summer of 1987. Her research interests have focused on the study of evolutionary theory and of protohistoric urbanism in the ancient Near East and on methods for the construction of functional profiles of ancient communities.

University Museum Monograph 69

MALYAN EXCAVATION REPORTS
William M. Sumner, Series Editor
VOLUME I

THE PROTO-ELAMITE SETTLEMENT AT TUV

Ilene M. Nicholas

Published by

THE UNIVERSITY MUSEUM
of Archaeology and Anthropology
University of Pennsylvania
Philadelphia
1990

Design, editing, typesetting, production
Publications Department, The University
Museum of Archaeology and Anthropology

Printing
Science Press
Ephrata, Pennsylvania

Library of Congress Cataloging in Publication Data
Nicholas, Ilene M.
   The proto-Elamite settlement at TUV.

   (Malyan excavation reports ; v. 1) (University
Museum monograph ; 69)

   Bibliography: p. xxx
   1. Anshan (Ancient city) 2. Elam—Antiquities.
3. Excavations (Archaeology)—Iran.   4. Iran—
Antiquities.   I. Title.   II. Series.   III. Series: University
Museum monograph ; 69.
DS262.A57N53   1988   935   88-4786
ISBN 0-934718-86-5

Partial support for this publication was provided by Ohio State
University and the Metropolitan Museum of Art.

This book is dedicated to my grandmother, Helen G. Nicholas,
with love, affection, and gratitude
for her support all these years.

Table of Contents

Tables

Illustrations

Figures

Plates

Acknowledgments

Robert H. Dyson, Jr., then Curator of Near Eastern Archaeology at The University Museum, initiated The University Museum, University of Pennsylvania sponsored excavations at Tal-e Malyan in 1971. William M. Sumner was appointed project director and five field seasons (1971, 1972, 1974, 1976, and 1978) were completed by 1978. Additional support and participation in the Malyan excavations was provided by the Boston Museum of Fine Arts, Harvard University, the Metropolitan Museum of Art, the National Geographic Society, the National Science Foundation (BNS79-5860, BNS76-06455, SOC75-1483), the Ohio State University, the University of California (Los Angeles), the University of Oregon, the University of Michigan, and the Smithsonian Institution.

The particular work summarized in this volume would not have been possible without the efforts of a great many people. A special acknowledgment must be made here to Michael Nimtz, who began the major excavations at TUV in 1974. Tragically, Michael was killed in the collapse of the Tehran airport roof at the end of that season. His efforts at TUV are not forgotten.

Major thanks are due to all the people who helped supervise the excavations on the TUV mound: Peter Farries and Marjorie Weishaar at Test Trench F in 1971, Linda Jacobs and Matthew Stolper at the TUV operation proper in 1974, and Samuel Mild and Holly Pittman who worked with me at TUV in 1976. Thanks are also due to the representatives from the Iranian Center for Archaeological Research in those seasons: Aschar Mir Fattah, Jaffar Nikkah, and Mohammed Mavedat. Naomi Miller and Melinda Zeder were of great assistance in the implementation of a program of screening and flotation of selected deposits, and carried out specialized studies on the botanical and faunal remains, respectively. Obviously this excavation could not have been accomplished without the skillful help of the residents of Malyan Village, especially that of two talented pickmen, Khodaram and Sohrab Meeri.

Special attention must also be drawn to the valuable work of the laboratory staff in processing the materials collected at TUV: Jack Balcer, photographer, 1976; Carol Beeman, registrar, 1974 and 1976; M. James Blackman, geologist, 1976; Kathleen MacLean, registrar, 1976; Janet Nickerson, artist, 1974 and 1976. It is also appropriate to point out here the special epigraphic study of the TUV tablets carried out by Matthew Stolper, analysis of evidence for copper-base metallurgy by Vincent Pigott, and study of the seals and sealings by Holly Pittman.

Although I can not name them all individually, I also wish to thank the other members of the Malyan project staff for their inspiring conversation and aid in formulating ideas, as well as the numerous assistants, work-study students, and volunteers who labored on TUV material at Ohio State University. In the latter connection special mention must be made of Kathleen MacLean, for without her help in working with the computer register and indices for TUV, the analysis of that mound could never have been completed. Special thanks are also due to Elise Auerbach for her assistance in organizing TUV materials in Philadelphia.

Analysis of the TUV materials was initially undertaken as my dissertation project in the Department of Anthropology, University of Pennsylvania. The first phase of analysis was partially supported by a study grant from the Near East Research Fund of The University Museum.

My involvement with TUV can be traced back to the help and encouragement of Robert H. Dyson, Jr. He initiated my involvement with the Malyan project, became my dissertation advisor, and patiently listened to me talk about my efforts in both my depressed and excited moments.

In the writing of my dissertation Jacques Bordaz acted as a major stimulus to my thought. His careful criticism and many hours of discussion of my manuscript helped shape the initial phase of the TUV analysis. The further analysis of TUV presented in this volume moves beyond that developed in the dissertation, but I have tried to build on the critical foundation inspired by our earlier discussions.

I should also like to acknowledge the help and encouragement of many other friends and colleagues over the years I have been studying the TUV material, in particular John Alden, Wendy Ashmore, Virginia Badler, Betty Starr Cummin, Ayse Gursan, Mary Virginia Harris, Elizabeth Henrickson, Susan Howard, Norton Kent, Eleanor King, Shapur Malek, Gregory Possehl, Mitchell Rothman, Maude de Schauensee, Glenn Schwartz, Brian Spooner, Gil Stein, Karen Vellucci, and Mary Voigt, as well as my colleagues at Hobart and William Smith Colleges, especially Judith-Maria Buechler, Richard Dillon, and James Spates. Thanks are also due to Hobart and William Smith Colleges for summer research funds and sabbatical leave, part of which were used in the preparation of the current manuscript reflecting the second stage of the analysis of TUV materials.

Last, but far, far from least, I wish to thank William Sumner. Although I did not become a member of the Malyan project staff until 1975, William Sumner made me feel a valued member of his research team from that very first moment, and has provided constant encouragement, criticism, and friendship ever since. We have engaged in endless conversations and arguments about the issues involved in the TUV analysis. Quite simply, it is the inspiration of those debates which led me to significantly rework my dissertation along the lines of the present monograph.

Responsibility for any errors in the present volume remains mine alone.

Foreword

The development of American archaeological research in Iran, initiated in 1931 and interrupted for nearly a decade after 1940, flourished in the years after 1957, the first season of The University Museum, University of Pennsylvania, excavations at Hasanlu under the direction of Dr. Robert H. Dyson, Jr. (Dyson 1983). Dyson's students, trained at Hasanlu and the University of Pennsylvania, were soon engaged in a variety of archaeological projects characterized by a strong anthropological perspective and interdisciplinary organization.

The Malyan project is in the second generation of this tradition. I arrived in Shiraz in the autumn of 1967 to conduct a regional survey of the Kur River basin as dissertation research under Dyson's supervision. Field survey and ceramic studies continued, mainly in autumn and winter, for two years, with time off in the summers for excavation. Robert Dyson and Mary Voigt introduced me to the art of excavating and recording mud brick architecture and cultural deposits at Hajji Firuz Tepe and Dinkha Tepe in 1968. In the following summer I was invited to join the excavation staff at Godin Tepe under the direction of T. Cuyler Young, Jr., who exposed me to variations on the excavation and recording system developed by Dyson at Hasanlu. My theoretical perspective and methodological concerns were first formed by these experiences and then developed and refined through interaction with the Malyan staff as we confronted the problems of archaeological research in an ancient urban context. The excavation and recording practices that evolved and were used at Malyan are described in the introduction and chapter 1 of this monograph.

Although this is not the place for an historical essay on the Malyan project, it is appropriate to relate how the site was selected for excavation and why the TUV mound was chosen for extensive exploration in 1974 and 1976. My first visit to Malyan was on March 27, 1968. I was astonished at the size of the mound, unmatched by any of the sites previously visited, not excepting Persepolis or the Sasanian city of Istakhr. I walked across the site, taking note of topographic features such as the city wall embankment, the contrasting mounded and flat areas within the wall, the presence of two qanats, and evidence of abandoned archaeological excavations. Banesh, Kaftari, Qale, and late historic ceramics were identified in the surface assemblage but no comprehensive survey was undertaken at the time. It turned out that the excavations noted had been conducted by the Archaeological Department of Fars Province in 1960/61 but the excavation records are reported to have been damaged and lost as a consequence of a leaky roof in the reconstructed "harem" building at Persepolis.

Early in 1970 Dr. John Hansman showed me an aerial photograph of a small eroded salt plug, located on the right bank of the Kur River about 25 km southeast of Bande Amir, that he thought might be Anshan. His analysis of historic evidence had convinced him that Anshan should be found in central Fars. After eliminating the salt plug as a possibility, I described Malyan to Hansman, since the site fit his requirements exactly. Hansman obtained aerial photographs and visited the site in the late summer of 1970 before completing his paper arguing for the identification of Malyan with Anshan (Hansman 1972). At about this time I discussed the site with Robert H. Dyson, Jr., then curator of the Near Eastern Section, and he suggested that I write a proposal for trial excavations under University Museum sponsorship. This proposal was approved by the Expeditions Committee of The University Museum Board of Managers in December 1970 and the first season was planned for the following summer.

A fragmentary examplar (mf 0002) of the Hutelutush-Inshushinak brick (Lambert 1972) was discovered on the surface during a visit to the site in the company of Pierre and Battya de Miroschedji on March 5, 1971. This brick, along with other fragments collected later that year, allowed Erica Reiner (1973) finally to demonstrate that Malyan is the location of Anshan.

An important objective of the initial season in 1971 was to determine the chronological range of the site and to locate areas where deposits of various periods could be efficiently explored. Systematic surface survey suggested that Banesh deposits, representing the earliest extensive occupation of the site, were everywhere covered by considerable later overburden, except on a small mound located within the northeast corner of the city wall embankment. The surface assemblage of this mound, which later came to be called "the TUV mound," is almost exclusively composed of Banesh ceramics; and a small test trench (TT-F), excavated in 1971, confirmed the presence of undisturbed Banesh deposits immediately below the surface. The decision to excavate a single large operation rather than several smaller openings, the specific location of the operation, and the general excavation and recording procedures are my responsibility but the authority to supervise daily work routines and make tactical excavation decisions was delegated to senior graduate students. It should be noted that the TUV operation was tied to the Malyan datum (the southwest corner of operation A) by tape and compass. The resulting error of several meters has no significant analytical consequence since TUV is isolated from the rest of the site by a considerable open distance without cultural deposits.

In 1974 excavations were conducted at TUV from August 28 to November 23 under the supervision of Michael John Nimtz, a graduate student in Anthropology at the University of Pennsylvania, who had excavated Banesh levels at the ABC operation in 1971 and 1972. Nimtz's proposal for a dissertation based on data from TUV was approved before the 1974 season. Building Levels I and II were essentially completed in 1974 and a small sounding was excavated into Level III.

Michael Nimtz was killed in a tragic accident when the roof collapsed at Tehran airport on December 5, 1974. After three seasons of his quietly amiable, industrious presence, Michael was sorely missed by us all. He was later granted a posthumous Ph.D. in Anthropology by the University of Pennsylvania.

The final season of work at TUV, from August 22 to November 20, 1976, was devoted to an expansion of the opening in Building Level III under the supervision of Ilene Nicholas. By the end of the 1976 season three building levels had been exposed, providing the data for Dr. Nicholas' dissertation, completed in 1980. The present monograph is an extensively revised version of that dissertation incorporating new analysis, additional descriptive detail, and revised interpretations. Proceeding from a functional classification of finds, Nicholas identifies and studies the spatial organization of various activities using a set of key concepts adapted from the work of Stanley South (1977, 1978, 1979). These concepts: site content, site structure, and site function, form the basis for an interpretation of the TUV institutional context on several levels. This explicit functional analysis, unique in scope and detail, constitutes an important theoretical and methodological advance in Near Eastern archaeology.

The position of the Banesh Proto-Elamite settlement at TUV in the local settlement system is discussed in chapter 9. The evolution of Proto-Elamite civilization in Fars has been discussed in preliminary fashion elsewhere (Alden 1979, 1982 a, 1982 b; Amiet 1979; Sumner 1986) and here it suffices to place TUV in a general chronological and regional context. The prehistoric and early historic chronology of central Fars is divided into ten phases: Achaemenid Phase, 600-300 B.C.; Possible hiatus; Shogha-Teimuran Phase, 1600-800 B.C.; Qale-Middle Elamite Phase, 1600-1000 B.C.; Kaftari Phase, 2200-1600 B.C.; Possible hiatus; Banesh Phase Late, 3000-2600 B.C.; Banesh Phase Middle, 3250-3000 B.C.; Banesh Phase Early, 3400-3250 B.C.; Lapui Phase, 3900-3400 B.C.; Bakun Phase, 4500-3900 B.C.; Shamsabad Phase, 4800-4500 B.C.; Jari Phase, 5500-4800 B.C.; Mushki Phase, 5900-5500 B.C.

This listing glosses over complications, such as the coexistence of stylistically distinctive phases in the late second millennium B.C. (Shogha-Teimuran to the east; Qale-Middle Elamite to the west), the possibility that the two hiatuses indicated may not exist, problems in defining boundaries between phases, and considerable uncertainty about the calendrical dates assigned. Nevertheless, the general configuration is secure and the dates of TUV, which falls in the Middle Banesh Phase, are firmly established by a consistent series of eight low standard deviation radiocarbon determinations (table 1; also cf. Voigt and Dyson n.d.:Table 2).

The most notable regional trend is the gradual increase in the number and average area of sites until a population maximum is reached sometime late in the Bakun Phase. A disproportionate amount of this growth is concentrated in the central part of the plain, irrigated by water diverted from the Kur River, where settlement density is very high by Bakun times. The unfavorable consequences of agricultural intensification become apparent in the Lapui Phase, when the Kur River irrigation system is gradually abandoned due to salinization and a new settlement pattern focused on natural pastures emerges. The number of settlements, already reduced in the Lapui Phase, continues to decrease in the Banesh Phase, partly as the result of an increasingly nomadic pastoral adaptation, partly due to growth of the city at Malyan, but also possibly because of real population loss due to excess of deaths over births or emigration from the valley. Thus, we understand that the TUV settlement existed during a critical moment in the history of Iran, at the end of the great demographic cycle following the Neolithic Revolution and at the beginning of a second cycle associated with the rise of Sumerian and Elamite civilization. Dr. Nicholas gives us the most substantial and detailed account yet available of the conditions of life at this turning point, a contribution that is sure to enhance our effort to understand the causes and processes involved in the evolution of social and economic complexity.

William M. Sumner
Columbus, Ohio
December 19, 1986

Introduction

The Cultural Context of the Banesh Occupation at TUV, Tal-e Malyan

The excavations reported on in this volume uncovered portions of three building levels occupied during the late fourth millennium B.C. These excavations were located on a small outlying mound of Tal-e Malyan (ancient Anshan), a large urban site in the Kur River Basin of highland Iran (Figure 1).

The original chronological and contextual framework for the archaeology of the Kur River Basin rests on the surveys and soundings of Vanden Berghe (1959). Vanden Berghe, however, found no cultural assemblage representing the late fourth millennium B.C. (Sumner 1972a:28-32). The discovery of such an assemblage awaited the gathering of ceramic surface collections during Sumner's extensive survey of the area, begun in 1967. Sumner (1972a) designated this new assemblage as Banesh, and considered the phase of settlement characterized by this ware to be broadly contemporaneous to the Jemdet Nasr phase in Mesopotamia.

At first, the Banesh phase in the Kur River Basin was little understood, for sherds of this assemblage had been found on only 26 sites in the entire survey area, and often only in very small quantity (3-4 diagnostic sherds per site). When excavation began at Tal-e Malyan, however, it was rapidly learned that Banesh phase occupation of that city had been extensive, covering about 50 hectares. Furthermore, the discovery of Proto-Elamite tablets in both the ABC and TUV operations linked Malyan to a whole group of sites in Iran from which numerical and/or pictographic tablets had been or were being discovered. These sites were Susa, Chogha Mish, Tall-i Ghazir, Godin Tepe, Tepe Sialk, Tepe Yahya, and Shahr-i Sokhta.

The time during which Proto-Elamite tablets were being written is a tantalizing one for Near Eastern archaeologists; the late fourth millennium B.C. lies at the beginning of the historic era in Mesopotamia and its borderlands, at an important juncture in the evolutionary development of early urban systems (Redman 1978). Tal-e Malyan, for example, was first extensively occupied during this time period. The era was also one of "internationalization," with sites such as Farukhabad (Wright 1972), Godin (Weiss and Young 1975) and Yahya (Beale 1973) beginning to participate more extensively in long distance trade networks. The manner in which the sites characterized by possession of Proto-Elamite tablets interacted among themselves and with sites that apparently did not use tablets, such as Farukhabad, Iblis, and Bampur, as well as with the larger Jemdet Nasr "Oikoumene" postulated by Caldwell (1968), has been one of the major concerns of Iranian archaeologists in the last decade (see for example Alden 1982a, Amiet 1979, Lamberg-Karlovsky 1978, Potts 1977, Sumner 1986).

The designation Proto-Elamite Period is sometimes used as a convenient label for the range of Iranian prehistory in which Proto-Elamite tablets are found. Strictly speaking, however, Proto-Elamite is a linguistic designation. The label was first applied to a pictographic script found at Susa in the province of Khuzistan, southwestern Iran (Scheil 1905; Brice 1962). Although no one could actually read the script at that time, it was called Proto-Elamite for geographic and stratigraphic reasons. Susa was known to be the historic capital of the kingdom of Elam, and numerous records written in Elamite had been recovered from the upper levels of that site. It was therefore inferred that the crude pictographic tablets coming from the lower levels at Susa represented early attempts at writing made by the ancestors of the later Elamites; accordingly, the pictographic script was designated as *Proto-Elamite*. It has not been proven, however, that the authors of the tablets were the direct forerunners of the Elamites.

Furthermore, it is clear that the rubric "Proto-Elamite tablets" is generally applied to *two* distinct categories of tablets. The earlier group consists of numerical notation tablets; it is not clear whether these

TABLE 1

RADIOCARBON DATES FROM BANESH PHASE MALYAN (ABC AND TUV OPERATIONS)

Provenience	Sample #	Date	MASCA-corrected date
ABC B.L. IV	TUNC-31	4671 ± 88 B.P.[a]	
ABC B.L. IV	P2334	4460 ± 70 B.P.[b]	3310-3210 ± 80 B.C.
ABC B.L. IV	P2336	4630 ± 260 B.P.[b]	3450-3390 ± 270 B.C.
ABC between B.L. II and III	P2335	4390 ± 90 B.P.[b]	3160 ± 90 B.C.
TUV B.L. IIIA Room 284	P2333[c]	4150 ± 250 B.P.[b]	2900-2800 ± 250 B.C.
TUV B.L. IIIA Trashpile 241	P2985		3210-3310 ± 60 B.C.[d]
TUV B.L. IIIA Area 375	P2986		3380 ± 70 B.C.[d]
TUV B.L. IIIA Room 258	P3050		3230-3340 ± 60 B.C.[d]
TUV B.L. IIIA Area 338	P3061		3320-3330 ± 70 B.C.[d]
TUV B.L. IIIA Room 250	P3063		3180 ± 70 B.C.[d]

These samples suggest a date of about 3200 B.C. for TUV B.L. IIIA.

[a] Bovington et al. 1973:594.

[b] Fishman and Lawn 1978:225-226.

[c] Sample was undersized.

[d] Dates taken from a MASCA date list of March 30, 1982.

should be regarded as an independent development distinct from the appearance of numerical tablets in Mesopotamia (see Schmandt-Besserat 1981). The later group includes tablets with distinctly Proto-Elamite (as contrasted to Sumerian) pictographs.

Clearly there are ambiguities even with the use of Proto-Elamite as a linguistic designation. Unfortunately the term is also used to mean a people and a material culture, although the ethnicity of the tablets' authors and the degree of identity or diversity of the cultural assemblages accompanying the tablets are still far from being adequately understood.

Given this confusing situation, each new piece of information that can be brought to shed light on these matters is extremely important, for the sample of material excavated in association with Proto-Elamite tablets is still frustratingly small.[1] The ABC and TUV operations at Malyan add considerably to this data base, especially since Malyan fills in an important geographic gap between the sites in the lowlands of Khuzistan and the eastern Iranian sites of Yahya and Shahr-i Sokhta.

The Malyan evidence is also important for the light it sheds on the evolution of early urban systems in the Near East. Banesh phase Malyan is an example of a site in its initial urban growth phase. The ABC operation samples the main portion of the settlement; TUV samples an adjacent ancillary settlement (Figure 2).

The TUV mound appears to have been closely tied to the main community at Malyan via participation in

1. Sialk (Ghirshman 1938) and much of Susa (MDP series) were unfortunately excavated without the benefit of present day advances in archaeological field techniques. This greatly limits the utility of the evidence from those sites. For summaries of the limitations of the earlier work at Susa, see Le Breton 1957:80; Dyson 1966: chapters III-IV. Fortunately Ghazir, Chogha Mish, Godin, Yahya, Shahr-i Sokhta, and (recently) the Acropolis and Ville Royale at Susa have been well excavated, but the levels with Proto-Elamite tablets have been exposed in relatively small amounts. Available reports on the levels with Proto-Elamite tablets include: Ghazir—Whitcomb 1971; Chogha Mish—Delougaz and Kantor 1972, 1975, Kantor 1973, 1974, 1975, 1979; Godin—Young 1969, Weiss and Young 1975; Yahya—Lamberg-Karlovsky 1971, 1972, 1976, 1977, 1978, Potts 1975, 1977; Shahr-i Sokhta—Amiet and Tosi 1978; Biscione, Salvatori and Tosi 1977, Lamberg-Karlovsky and Tosi 1973; Susa—Le Brun 1971, 1978, Steve and Gasche 1971, Vallat 1971, Carter 1974, 1978, 1981.

a shared information-processing network. A number of Proto-Elamite tablets and fragments were found in Banesh phase levels at both ABC (20 finds—Sumner 1974, 1976, and personal communication) and TUV (21 finds).

Four Banesh phase building levels with multi-room structures are known from ABC (Sumner 1974, 1976, n.d.a). The architecture can be described as generally somewhat larger scale than that found at TUV. The effective exposure of the Banesh levels at ABC was about 390 m^2 for B.L. II (B.L. I is dated to the Kaftari phase[2]), about 383 m^2 for B.L. III, about 220 m^2 for B.L. IV, and about 177 m^2 for B.L. V (W. Sumner, personal communication). The area under excavation in the ABC operation was reduced with increasing depth for safety reasons.

The three Banesh phase building levels with multi-room structures from TUV are the subject of the present report. The effective exposure of these levels was about 200 m^2 for B.L. I, 455 m^2 for B.L. II, and 247 m^2 for B.L. III.

In addition to the major horizontal clearances of Banesh deposits at operations ABC and TUV, Banesh sherds were found at Malyan in a number of smaller operations. None of these other deposits produced Proto-Elamite tablets, however.[3]

When the cultural assemblage from TUV is compared to those from other sites with Proto-Elamite tablets, a relative date for the TUV Banesh is readily obtained. The Banesh occupation at TUV appears to be relatively *later than* Susa 17, the earlier part of the Ghazir "Proto-Elamite Period," Protoliterate Chogha Mish, Godin V, and the late Uruk phase in Mesopotamia. The TUV Banesh can be regarded as *broadly contemporaneous with* Susa 16-14B, the later part of the Ghazir "Proto-Elamite Period," Sialk IV, Yahya IVC, Shahr-i Sokhta I, and the Jemdet Nasr phase in Mesopotamia (Nicholas 1980a:65-97).

The absolute dating of TUV should also be considered. Table 1 provides the available carbon dates for Banesh levels at both the TUV and ABC operations at Malyan. Six radiocarbon samples from B.L. IIIA at TUV have now been dated. These samples suggest a (MASCA-corrected) date of c. 3200 B.C. for this level. Note that the ABC dates suggest that ABC B.L. IV may have been slightly older than TUV and ABC B.L. III-II roughly contemporary to the buildings at TUV.

In summary, then, the TUV operation represents a relatively large horizontal exposure of late fourth millennium B.C. date. The material from this operation is relevant both to Proto-Elamite questions and to investigation of the growth and functioning of early urban systems in the Near East. The latter theme has been especially central to the TUV research, as this volume illustrates.

---

2. Kaftari is the phase following Banesh in the Kur River Basin sequence. The Kaftari phase is dated to the second half of the third millennium and the early second millennium B.C.

3. The character of these operations can be briefly described as follows (W. Sumner, personal communication).

Operation BY8 was designed to investigate the Malyan city wall. This operation consisted of a northern area of 9 x 4 m and a narrow southern trench of 21 x 2 m. Two phases of building for the city wall were found near the south end of this operation. Late Banesh sherds were recovered from a deposit of bricky trash (incorporating ashy lenses) that sloped up against the eroded face of the earlier construction phase of the wall.

Operation EE16 was a 5 x 20 m trench which produced Banesh sherds (as well as sherds of other phases) but no distinct Banesh occupation levels.

Operation F26 was a 10 x 10 m square which produced a hard, bricky-melt Kaftari deposit overlying a Banesh deposit of similar character. No architecture was preserved and find density was low.

A small deep sounding in square H5 of the GHI operation provided stratified material which appears to be transitional between the Banesh and the Kaftari ceramic phases. The lowest level of the sounding contained Banesh ceramics, in a deposit including strata of secondary origin.

Operation XX was a 10 x 10 m square which contained stratigraphically inverted trash deposits of Banesh and Kaftari date.

Operation Z46 was a 10 x 10 m square which produced Banesh sherds *mixed* with sherds of other phases.

I

Method and Theory

Method and theory are indubitably intertwined in the conduct of archaeological research, but neither is a static entity. Both method and theory evolve as data collection and analysis proceed. This volume, an interpretation of the TUV operation at Tal-e Malyan, Iran, reflects the reality of ten years of developments in the method and theory applied to this material. No attempt is made herein to disguise certain inconsistencies and inadequacies in the TUV research which have arisen as a result of these changes in method and theory. Similarly, no claim is made here that the interpretation offered is the best possible explanation of the remains at TUV. What *is* offered is intended to be a full and complete description not only of the remains discovered at TUV, but also of the excavators' and analysts' reasoning behind the conduct of the research.

The Research Context of the TUV Operation

Tal-e Malyan lies on the Iranian plateau in Fars province, about 46 km north of Shiraz and the same distance west of Persepolis (Sumner 1974:158). The site, consisting of about 200 hectares bounded by an ancient enclosure wall (Figure 2), has been identified on epigraphic evidence (Reiner 1973) as the Elamite city of Anshan (cf. Hansman 1972).

A number of preliminary articles on the Malyan project have already been published (Sumner 1972b, 1973a, b, c, 1974, 1975a, 1976, 1985, 1986; Reiner 1972, 1973, 1974; Carter 1975; Carter and Stolper 1976; Janet Nickerson 1977; Alden 1978; Balcer 1978; Blackman 1981, 1982; Nicholas 1981; Zeder 1984; Stolper 1985) and several dissertations have been written in conjunction with the project (Alden 1979; Nicholas 1980a; Miller 1982; John Nickerson 1983; Zeder 1985). Holly Pittman is finishing a dissertation on Proto-Elamite seals and sealings.

A future volume of the *Malyan Excavation Reports* will discuss the research strategy at Malyan in detail. The Malyan Project can be briefly described here as having grown out of a settlement pattern survey of the Kur River Basin (Sumner 1972a). Malyan was chosen for excavation because its great size suggested that it had been the major urban focus for the Kur Basin in antiquity. The goals of the initial seasons at Malyan were:

First: To establish a chronological framework as a prerequisite for all further work.
Second: To begin an investigation of culture change during the early urban period lasting from the mid-third through the second millennium B.C. and,
Third: To begin an investigation of variability within the city during several periods of occupation (Sumner 1980:1).

The excavation and surface survey program at Malyan rapidly established that the earliest extensive occupation of the site lay within the Banesh phase of the late fourth millennium B.C. It soon became clear that in most areas of the site, Banesh levels were covered by extensive younger deposits. Luckily there also existed at Malyan a small (3 hectare) mound in the flat northeastern part of the site, within the enclosure wall but separated from the main mounded zone by an area lacking in cultural deposits. A sounding, Test Trench F, was placed in this small mound during the 1971 season.

Test Trench F was a small sounding, 2 x 5 m in area, 1.5-1.75 m in depth. The trench lay at the southern end of the small mound. At the time that it was established, the master grid for Malyan had not yet been laid out; it can now be estimated that Test Trench F lay approximately 10 m southwest of U166.

Test Trench F was initially opened by Peter Farries and completed by Marjorie Weishaar. Fifteen lots of material were recovered, part of a mud-brick wall was intersected, and one small pit was discovered. No other significant features were uncovered. There were three identifiable strata: a top, trashy stratum, a middle stratum with bricks and bits of ash, and the bottom stratum with clay and a bricky-melt deposit. Banesh phase sherds were found throughout.

The importance of Test Trench F lay in its confirmation of the surface indications that the northeastern mound was probably not occupied after the Banesh phase.

The first two seasons at Malyan also established that the Banesh occupation of the main mounded area had been extensive, perhaps covering nearly 50 hectares. In the ABC operation, Proto-Elamite tablets were discovered in association with large-scale Banesh phase architecture (Sumner 1974, 1976, n.d.a). Following the initial discovery of Banesh material at ABC, it became one of the goals of the Malyan Project to go back to the vicinity of Test Trench F and open up a larger horizontal exposure on the small northeastern mound. The intention behind this new excavation was to sample a different segment of the city, in the hope that intra-settlement functional variability could be investigated for the earliest occupation phase of the city.

The TUV operation was begun in 1974 to pursue that goal.

The 1974 supervisors at TUV were Michael Nimtz (T166, T168, U164, U166, U168, V164, V168, X168), Matthew Stolper (U168, W168), and Linda Jacobs (U168, V166, W168). These individuals directed excavations which uncovered large portions of two Banesh phase building levels, and established the existence of a third building level with a small test pit.

The 1974 season at TUV revealed a rich but puzzling Banesh occupation. The operation produced Proto-Elamite tablets and numerous seal impressions, yet the architecture was quite small-scale, and there were a number of apparently domestic features such as hearths and ovens. The general appearance of TUV was clearly quite different from that of the ABC operation on the main mound.

During the 1976 field season, work at TUV was accordingly directed toward continued investigation of Banesh phase intra-settlement variability by excavating a portion of the third building level mentioned above. Another major concern of the 1976 season was the collection of data for use in methodological investigations of variation in depositional processes. The 1976 supervisors were Ilene Nicholas (T168, U168, V166, V168), Holly Pittman (U166) and Samuel Mild (V168).

General Theoretical Orientation

Much of the theoretical background for the TUV excavation lies within the general framework of the settlement pattern approach, a vigorous branch of archaeological analysis with direct links to the primary spatial dimension built into all archaeological data.

Largely due to the stimulus provided by Adams (1965; Adams and Nissen 1972), *regional* settlement pattern studies had become a major focus of effort among Near Eastern archaeologists by the early 1970s. The settlement pattern approach, however, also calls for analysis of spatial patterns at *intra-site* and *intra-structure* levels of observation (Trigger 1968). Despite the fact that the individual structure and the individual site have been standard units of analysis in the Near East ever since archaeology began there, scholars have (until recently) generally not paid much explicit attention to systematic testing of spatial patterns at these levels. Exceptions to this general lack of consideration include discussion of the distribution of artifacts at Sakeri Sughir (Wright 1969) and Farukhabad (Wright 1981), discussion of the localization of economic activities within the sixth millennium village of Hajji

Firuz (Voigt 1976, 1983), and treatment of the "social context" of trash disposal at Hierakonpolis (Hoffman 1974). At Malyan, a concern with investigation of intra-site functional variability was evident from the beginning, as discussed above.

The present author became affiliated with the Malyan Project in 1975, taking over at that time the responsibility for analysis of the TUV operation. The initial results of this analysis were presented as a dissertation (Nicholas 1980a). That report on TUV was strongly influenced by the work of Stanley South (1977a, 1977b, 1978, 1979) on method and theory in American historical archaeology. The concepts of *site content, site structure, site function*, and *functional class* were adapted from South's work and applied to the TUV analysis.

As presented by South (1979), the first three concepts were defined in terms of the site level of settlement pattern analysis, but they can also be applied to smaller subunits of a site, such as the TUV operation. *Site content* consists of all the immoveable and moveable elements of the archaeological record, i.e., strata, architecture, features, artifacts, and other moveable finds. *Site structure* consists of spatial patterns recognized among fixed and moveable elements of site content. *Site function* refers to the role that the site played within a larger cultural system.

Functional classes (South 1977a) are an analytic device, allowing the grouping of elements of site content which are presumed to be related to one another in function. The functional classes established for the TUV material served as a bridge between discussion of site content and analyses of site structure and function in the initial report on TUV. These concepts are retained in the present work but set within a personal view of archaeological form, function, and process that the author has developed over the past four years (Nicholas 1983a, 1983b).

FORM, FUNCTION, AND PROCESS

The key issue in archaeology is here regarded as being the discovery of the relationships between (a) the material *forms* observed in the course of archaeological research and (b) the *processes* which operated in the past (Schiffer 1976, 1983) to give the archaeological record its particular character. Archaeologists are ideally searching for the *organizational properties* of the archaeological record (Binford 1981a).

How does the concept "function" fit into this equation? In current archaeological theory, investigation of function is widely held to be quite distinct from investigation of process. Function is a somewhat amorphous theoretical concept floating uneasily somewhere between the material forms we dig up and the processes we reconstruct. Much more attention has been paid in the literature to the consideration of style as a factor in cultural process than to the consideration of function. (See for example Hodder 1978, Sackett 1977, 1982 on style; Dunnell has written several important papers [1978a, b] on function.) Similarly, typologies of artifact form tend to be largely morpho-stylistic in nature, with minimal dependence upon functionally related criteria.

As a result of this lack of theoretical consideration, functional reconstruction is commonly regarded as equivalent (at best) to a static description of synchronic relationships within a particular cultural system. Processual investigations, on the other hand, are viewed as dealing with the dynamics of system changes through time.

Function is thus frequently considered to be best understood through excavation of broad horizontal exposures at a particular site, while process has been generally studied via survey projects covering broad spans of space and time. But while excavation and survey are clearly traditionally recognized as valid complementary *methods* in the archaeologist's repertoire, at the level of *theory*, functional explanations are frequently viewed as inherently less satisfying than processual ones. For example, Wenke (1981:81) says

> Functional explanations are *descriptive* in that they refer to how one element in a system functions in relation to other elements in that system, and how one can predict the states of particular elements from knowledge of the states of other elements....This is to be contrasted with evolutionary explanations that attempt to account for *why* something came to be. (First emphasis added.)

Statements such as this overlook the fact that functional studies are also addressing "why" questions. Both functional studies and processual studies are analytical interpretations of the inherently static data obtained in research, and both function and process have explanatory potential. Functional questions basically ask *why* a given cultural system was able to maintain itself (however briefly) in equilibrium; processual questions ask *why* a cultural system was *not* able to maintain itself in such equilibrium. Surely it is equally important to identify and understand the mechanisms of negative feedback as it is to discover positive feedback mechanisms leading to changes in system states. Phrased in such terms, the distinction between function as static description and process as dynamic explanation collapses.

The archaeologist's task, then, is to move from static observations of data (site content) via analysis to an understanding of the natural and cultural formation processes which have structured the archaeological record. From an understanding of this site structure the archaeologist can then move on to modeling the mechanisms influencing the stability of a past cultural system and to an interpretation of site function.

To guide this analytical task, a mediating hierarchy of conceptual units would seem useful. These analytical entities might include the utilized item, the activity, the institution, the community, and the cultural system. Some possible material correlates of these entities respectively include artifacts, features, buildings, sites, and regions, though a simple one-to-one correspondence between analytical entity and material correlate is probably more an exception than it is the rule (see the next section below).

Ironically, of these analytical levels, that of the institution has been the most neglected in archaeological research, yet it is precisely at the institutional level that the unity of function and process can be most clearly seen. In many ways, the institutional level is the keystone of the analytical hierarchy being proposed here. Institutions include such familiar entities as the family, secular government, and religion, but more generally refer to all agencies of societal control or coordination of activity. Interplay among the decision patterns of several institutions creates in turn recognizable community and cultural patterns. The stability (smooth functioning) or instability (processual change) in past cultural systems can thus conveniently be regarded as being most directly affected by institutional level factors in the analytical hierarchy. Both function and process in large part result from the cumulative effects of institutional decision-making.

THE FUNCTIONAL HIERARCHY OF ANALYTICAL UNITS

Notions of hierarchy are well embedded in archaeological theory (e.g., Clarke 1968, Trigger 1968, South 1977b: Figure 1.1). The hierarchy proposed in this volume is designed to facilitate analysis of the functioning of past cultural systems by replacing static material entities with more dynamic conceptual ones. The intent is to free the analyst from the tendency to expect a rigid one-to-one correspondence between *things* dug up and their ancient *roles* in the cultural system. As ethnoarchaeologists have repeatedly cautioned, one artifact may be used in several different ways, one room for several different purposes. The converse is true as well. Archaeologists are also well aware of this problem. Writing of lowland Maya settlement pattern studies, for example, Ashmore (1981:12) notes

> The pivotal problem is the lack of a strictly one-to-one correspondence between forms and functions: some activities may be carried out via a formally varied set of features, and many features serve multiple functions. Given this lack of direct translatability, a number of people have advised against reification of formal types for use in functional discussions...[yet] we must have some basis for making functional assessments of settlement patterns.

Attempts to model site structure and function thus often become confused when material entities are thought of as composing the system. A system is more easily understood if one concentrates on the functions of the elements. The hierarchy proposed here does just that.

The lowest level of the hierarchy is that of the *utilized item*. The material correlates of this level are artifacts, raw materials, by-products, etc. A utilized item is defined as an element which has been employed in a particular way. One material artifact may easily be counted in analysis as two or more utilized items (cf. Dunnell 1978a:55). In the TUV analysis, for example, impressed sealings are counted twice, as items used in

the act of storing or packaging goods, and as items used in the act of conveying information.

Utilized items of similar functions can be grouped into functional classes (defined above). These functional classes serve as a bridge to the next level of the hierarchy, that of the activity.

An *activity* refers to a set of related actions undertaken with a specific aim in mind. Some activities may be very simple (such as wearing pins and beads to decorate the person) and others very complex (such as copper-base metallurgy). Activities may or may not have material correlates in the form of features or fixed work places. Many activities are free-floating with respect to such material correlates, but can be studied by analyzing the characteristics of the functional class markers.

The next level in the hierarchy is that of the *institution*. As noted in the last section, an institution refers here to agencies of societal control and coordination of activities. Institutions may sometimes have distinctive buildings as material correlates, but again a regular one-to-one correspondence of institution to building is unlikely. It is argued here that institutions may be studied via their *functional profiles*. Such profiles result from the composite traces of the suite of activities under the jurisdiction of an institution. Such an approach is inherently less static than the typological approach to architectural classification which has long been a favorite of Near Eastern archaeologists. Crawford (1977), for example, properly recognizes the difficulties involved in accurate functional characterization of a structure, and the dangers inherent in assuming that the boundaries between such things as politics, economics, and religion were then as ours are now (1977:31). She fails to pursue these points, however, and focuses instead on the recognition of particular architectural plans and the assignment of known excavated third-millennium temples and "palaces" to these types. With such an approach, it is very difficult to break away from the rigid one-to-one equation of institution with building.

Above the institutional level is that of the *community*. The material correlate of a community would generally not be a simple site, but rather a site plus its hinterland with subsidiary households, work places, and so forth. In any complex community, a number of institutions such as the family, church, and state interact. The archaeological record produced as a result of this interaction is an extremely complex palimpsest of institutional profiles.

Finally, the highest level in this analytical hierarchy is that of the *cultural system* itself. From the functional viewpoint, a distinctive cultural system can be viewed as being formed by the interaction of a number of communities. In the material realm, the cultural system may be viewed as encompassing a region(s), plus spatial offshoots representing the presence of traders, colonists, armies, and so forth.

As with analytical hierarchies in general, all five functional levels operated concurrently in the past when the cultural system under study was actually in existence. Each level of function must have affected, and been affected by, the others in the hierarchy. The breakdown of function proposed here is designed to help the analyst model the almost overwhelming complexity of any cultural system by directing attention to one aspect of function at a time. By doing so, it is

hoped that a more fully articulated model of the cultural system can be built, and the mechanisms affecting the stability of that system delineated.

In the case of the present study, it must be recognized that the TUV operation excavated only a small part of the area utilized by the ancient TUV community. Therefore the analysis in this volume is most concerned with the three lowest levels of the functional hierarchy (utilized items, activities, and institutions). Consideration of community and overall cultural system is reserved for chapter 9.

Methodology

Methods, either in excavation or in analysis, can not safely be divorced from theory if successful attainment of a project's goals is to be achieved. This section attempts to trace some of the connections between the general theoretical orientation reviewed above and the specific tactics employed in conducting the research at TUV.

EXCAVATION METHODS

GENERAL EXCAVATION STRATEGY

The details of overall Malyan Project strategy and tactics will be discussed in another volume of the *Malyan Excavation Reports*. A brief summary of methods employed at TUV is given here. Many of the digging tactics were similar to those used widely in the Near East. The size of the standard excavation square, for example, was a 10 x 10 m grid unit. The entire area within the enclosure wall at Malyan was covered with a master grid plan of such squares. The TUV operation takes its name from the grid designations for the contiguous squares placed on the south end of the small Banesh mound. The operation was initially laid out to cover a relatively broad horizontal area (900 m^2) in order to obtain a large enough sample from each level to make functional analysis feasible. (The subsequent smaller effective exposure of each building level was affected by the presence of eroded zones on this portion of the mound.)

How appropriate was the general excavation strategy used at TUV? Representative sampling is usually desired in archaeological research, but all researchers face the difficult choice of selecting the sampling strategy most appropriate to the nature of the specific questions under investigation. Sometimes judgmental rather than random sampling techniques are more appropriate.

The TUV operation was judgmentally sited on the southern end of the TUV mound for reasons explained in the first portion of this chapter. This operation is unlikely to constitute a truly representative sample of the entire TUV mound, yet viewed in retrospect, the excavation strategy carried out at TUV continues to appear appropriate to the particular problem under investigation there.

It must be remembered that the TUV operation constituted one sample unit within the universe of potential sample units comprising the site of Malyan (as defined by the enclosure wall). The first five seasons of the Malyan Project were planned by Sumner to be a preliminary exploration of this very extensive urban site. It was realized from the outset that it would be impossible to obtain a statistically valid sample of Malyan during this initial phase of excavation, due to the heterogeneity of functional areas normally characteristic of urban communities. Sumner (1975b) specifically discussed sampling issues at a meeting of the American Anthropological Association in San Francisco. One of the main issues he explored there was the size excavation units must be if they are successfully to sample material on the scale of internal socio-complexity at which a large urban center is characteristically organized.

The Malyan Project as a whole constitutes an important methodological test case of alternative sampling strategies for initial exploration of a large, ancient urban center. The Banesh phase of c. 3200 B.C. was investigated primarily through the strategy of broad horizontal exposures (the TUV and ABC operations), while the Kaftari phase (c. 2000 B.C.) was explored using a series of more widely scattered operations, many of which consisted of a single 10 x 10 m square. Evaluation of the relative merits and problems of these alternative approaches awaits the final completion of data analysis from Malyan.

It is still valuable to consider TUV alone, however, with reference to the operation's specific goals of understanding the structural organization of activities and functional change through time in this one sector of the urban system. It would appear that the allocation of our time and money into excavation of a relatively broad horizontal exposure was far more valuable than the alternative strategy of scattering 10 x 10 m squares randomly over the TUV mound would have been. Pragmatically, it would seem that there is a critical size of excavation unit which must be opened if an archaeologist is to understand the stratigraphic and cultural complexities of the deposits being exposed. In a Paleolithic site, with much greater relative homogeneity of deposits, it may well be practicable to excavate in much smaller scale units than on a village, town, or city site.

The TUV operation was conducted on a small mound immediately adjacent to a large city site. To meet the expressed goals of functional analysis in such a situation, it was necessary to retrieve through excavation (at a minimum) major room-blocks of structures. Structural complexes in fact proved to be very large at TUV. For each building level we essentially recovered only one structural complex and portions of its peripheral areas.

It would seem that the right choice of excavation strategy was made at TUV. Any of the excavated grid squares taken alone would have failed to constitute a meaningfully large segment of a structural complex. Furthermore, even basic stratigraphic interpretation of some of the grid squares (such as B.L. III in V168) would have been fraught with extreme difficulty in the absence of data from adjacent squares.

If one is seeking to understand site structure and function, it is imperative that the archaeological contemporaneity of excavated units be demonstrable on a very fine scale. Working within contiguous squares allows one to achieve this direct continuity; working with units of information derived from squares *scattered* over the mound would not, for cross-dating or seriation would be unlikely to result in the necessary precision of temporal control. A similar point has been made by Braidwood (1974:68, 73-74), who found analytical difficulties in utilizing data collected at Jarmo in a series of non-adjacent 2 by 2 m squares. He found that stratigraphic relationships could not be extrapolated effectively from square to square.

With the TUV operation as it was in fact conducted, it is possible to reconstruct changes over time in the functional nature of that segment of the TUV mound. Such a temporal sequence could not have been derived from an equal amount of excavation put into scattered squares.

Ideally the TUV operation would have been supplemented by additional small tests placed elsewhere on the mound. Such a program might have been able to assess the relative homogeneity of structure and function throughout the mound, but would be able to do so without resorting to broad horizontal exposures only because the research could draw on the understanding of depositional variation and functional variation derived from the original broad operation. Unfortunately such further research is presently impossible at Malyan.

The implication of the preceding comments is that the TUV operation can not honestly be taken to be representative of the TUV mound as a whole. The interpretations presented later in this volume are intended rather to represent the internal structure and function of simply those parts of the TUV community which lay within our area of excavation, and of those other areas which may have contributed to the production of the trash discarded there. It is recognized that different activities will doubtless have characterized the other, unexplored, sections of TUV, but the fact that these areas were not explored does not invalidate our interpretations of the section that was excavated. The TUV operation analysis stands as a case study of utilized items, activities, and institutional profiles for the southern end of the TUV mound.

TACTICS AND RECORDING

Excavation within each grid square was done by a crew of local workmen under the supervision of a staff archaeologist. Excavation was done stratigraphically, following the *lot* system of provenience control. "A lot is an arbitrary or natural subdivision of any natural or cultural Stratum or Feature (sic). Thus, a stratum or feature will ordinarily contain several lots, but no properly excavated lot will be in more than one stratum or feature" (Sumner 1978:2, emphasis deleted). All material removed from the mound was assigned a reference number (consecutively within individual grid squares) which ideally carried clearly stated horizontal and vertical boundaries. Bulk finds (sherds and bones) were bagged by lot units.

All other artifacts, small finds and samples removed from the TUV operation were registered by the Malyan Project staff. Registration numbers took the following form: mf 5290. There was one master registration list for all of Malyan; thus the TUV finds do not occur in a discrete or continuous sequence of mf numbers.

The entire Malyan register has been entered into a computer data bank. There are 1515 registration entries for TUV material. A number of these reference numbers, however, refer to more than one item. In such cases, the mf number is followed by a, b, etc. if it is necessary to quote the identification number.

Immoveable elements of the archaeological record were designated as *features*. The practice followed by the Malyan Project was to assign all walls, doors, rooms, areas, pits, hearths, and other features reference numbers in a consecutive list for each separate operation. TUV's squares taken together constitute such an operation. Thus there is only one wall 2 at TUV, and reference number 2 is not applied to any other feature there (i.e., there will be no hearth 2, or room 2). A feature that lies within several grid squares bears the same reference number in all squares.

One of the major innovations in Malyan Project methodology proved central to the research at TUV. That innovation was the Malyan Deposit Code System, a recording system which greatly facilitated functional analysis of the TUV operation. The whole question of the functional significance behind observed patterns in archaeological remains within a site is intertwined with the broader question of the formation processes, both natural and cultural (Schiffer 1976, 1983), which produced the site as a whole. The Malyan Deposit Code systematized the manner in which field observations were recorded with respect to this depositional history. When only narrative notes are taken, it is not uncommon for a site supervisor to be somewhat vague in his/her description of the character of a matrix being excavated. Using deposit codes in addition to written descriptions was intended to make the supervisors more aware of the range of possibilities to be considered for any given matrix, and to introduce an element of consistency, helping to tie together the observations of many different supervisors into an overall picture of the history of the site.

The Malyan Deposit Code, then, was an advantageous method to use when conducting research into the past function of TUV, as it allowed a more rigorous discrimination of those items actually contemporaneous in use with each building level (see chapter 2). This system was employed in both the 1974 and 1976 field seasons, as was a program of screening and floating selected samples of excavation units. Generally at least a portion of every floor and surface, trash deposit, pit, well, and special feature was screened, plus occasional control samples from bricky fill or other tertiary deposits. Flotation samples were also taken, from the material passing through the screen. Additional flotation samples were obtained directly from unscreened hearths and ash pits. In addition to the screen and float samples, 39 pollen and phytolith samples were collected (the great majority of these were from B.L. III contexts). Unfortunately, very little preserved botanical remains were discovered despite this extensive sampling program. Faunal remains, on the other hand, were extensively recovered, both from hand-collected and screened contexts.

There were some differences in methods between the 1974 and 1976 seasons. The present author had joined the Malyan Project staff in 1975, assumed responsibility

for the TUV research, and modified the immediate research goals. Seeking further illumination of formation processes became a major goal at TUV. Although this aim was rather indistinctly conceptualized at the time, it seemed reasonable to investigate the density characteristics of different deposit types. In 1974, only diagnostic sherds had been saved from each lot, and not much of an attempt had been made to obtain volumetric estimates of deposits. To meet the new goal, in 1976 *all* sherds were counted and weighed, and a more determined effort made to define lot boundaries strictly so that volumes of deposits could be calculated.

ANALYTICAL METHODS

Ideally, a detailed research design is developed before any excavation is begun; this design should be specifically related to the questions under investigation and thus to the specific kinds of analyses in which the data will be used. In practice, research designs evolve and change as excavation and analysis progress. In 1974, the aim of the TUV work had been the exposure of a broad area of Banesh phase occupation, in order to establish a data set of architecture, finds, and ceramics that could be contrasted with the finds from the ABC operation at Malyan. By 1976, emphasis had shifted more to understanding TUV as a coherent unit in and of itself, and our research design was modified to allow for greater attention to delineation of depositional processes and intra-site patterning at TUV. In conducting post-excavation analysis, an attempt has been made to understand B.L. I and B.L. II (both excavated in 1974) in terms of these issues, even though the 1974 data had not been collected with these questions of internal variation specifically in mind.

A further serious analytical problem existed because the present author had not participated in the 1974 field season. Utilization of the information derived from that season's work accordingly took on many aspects of classic archival research. It proved more difficult than had been naively expected to apply the previously collected data to the questions of interest to the present analyst.

In the 1974 season, no quantitative information was collected on the body sherds, so this information was not available to serve as a check on the depositional character of poorly described lot units within the upper two building levels. More critically, certain units of diagnostic sherds were discarded (without description) for unexplained reasons, creating unsystematic gaps in the ceramic record for B.L. I and B.L. II. Certain other categories of material, such as mineral samples, grinding stones, and other ground stone tools, may not have been consistently collected in 1974.[1]

Perhaps the most serious weakness in the TUV excavation as a whole is the inconsistent availability of a volumetric record for each provenience lot. Other than for a small number of screened lots, exact dimensions of provenience units were very difficult (often impossible) to reconstruct from the 1974 field notes. In 1976 a more consistent effort was made to provide accurate horizontal dimensions for each lot on a daily plan, and to include depth measurements in the narrative record, but still errors of omission occurred. This lack of consistent volumetric data has been one of the major difficulties in analysis of TUV. As a result, the initial report on the operation (Nicholas 1980a) presented an interpretation founded largely on non-volumetric analyses. The general trend of these analyses was checked by using a subset of deposits with known volumes. Since 1980, intensive further work with the TUV field notes and plans has led to the calculation of volumes for additional deposits and to the estimation of upper volumetric range limits for many other lots. This has made the analysis of deposit signatures (chapter 2) more securely based.

Deposit signature analysis helps the researcher to determine which elements of site content can be properly used in the reconstruction of site structure and function. Once these elements have been recognized, the researcher can proceed to an investigation of utilized items (chapter 5) by study of the shape, condition, and material of the finds. Activities (chapter 6) can be studied by grouping utilized items into functional classes and examining the ubiquity, concentration, and structural position of these items in the archaeological record. Investigation of higher level function can be approached by the investigation of structural patterns of association among different classes of items (chapter 7) and by the development of functional profiles (chapter 8).

All of these analyses have been influenced by the general theoretical orientation outlined above. The interpretation presented in the initial TUV report was couched in relatively static terms (i.e., in terms of the three levels of site content, structure, and function). The interpretation presented here is based on that foundation with the addition of substantial further analysis intended to create a more dynamic model. Insofar as site structure and function are properly understood, so do we begin to grasp process in past cultural systems.

---

1. There are several brief references in the field notes from the 1974 season to grinding stones discovered in B.L. II which were never brought in from the site to be registered. Record photographs have been used to confirm the existence of a second grinding stone in room 102 and four fragmentary grinding stones in room 43. These artifacts have been added to the register *ex post facto*.

II

Stratigraphy and Depositional Processes

Several major methodological approaches are interwoven in the functional study of the archaeological remains at TUV. The first of these approaches, acquisition of detailed control over variation in the depositional processes which created the TUV mound, is the central theme of the present chapter. The master stratigraphic sequence at TUV is summarized as a prelude to the detailed examination of depositional processes.

The Major Depositional Layers in the Stratigraphic Sequence of TUV

The TUV operation was located at the southern end of the TUV mound, as illustrated on Figure 2 and Plate 1. Work was conducted in a series of contiguous excavation units laid out on a 10 x 10 m grid. The designations of these provenience units are shown on Figure 3A; it should be noted that T166 and T168 were half squares only. Squares W168 and X168 yielded no preserved architectural levels, and are omitted from subsequent maps.

The TUV stratigraphic sequence is summarized in Figure 4. These layers (numbered from top to bottom with arabic numbers) represent *major* stratigraphic continuities, including construction levels, that can be traced over extensive sectors of the TUV excavation. Detailed variation in the nature of the matrix *within* these strata was coded by the Malyan Project's system of deposit codes, discussed in the second half of this chapter.

In different portions of the TUV operation, parts of this sequence have been eroded away, disturbed, or excavated to varying degrees (cf. Figures 5 and 6 which illustrate representative sections for the TUV operation). The horizontal extent of each major layer in the stratigraphic sequence is described below along with a discussion of the stratigraphic numbering system employed throughout this report. In this initial discussion the layers are described from the top down; subsequent descriptions of site content and analyses of that content will be treated from the bottom up, reflecting the order in which deposition occurred.

STRATUM 0: PRESENT-DAY SURFACE

The surface of the mound had a fairly dense scatter of pebbles (stones up to 20 cm in diameter), a light sherd scatter, and numerous shallow pits (4-5 cm deep, 10-15 cm in diameter) resulting from the digging of plants by local inhabitants. There were no architectural remains or features of any kind visible on the surface of the mound in the area of the TUV operation.

The surface of the TUV mound beyond the limits of the TUV operation has been studied by Alden in the course of an extensive survey of Banesh phase sites in the Kur River Basin. (In that survey, the TUV mound was designated 8F8-A.) Alden found (1979:Appendix B) that

Sherd density drops off quickly beyond the edge of the mound, but a large *jube* to the north provides additional information about this mound. First, Banesh sherds appear in the *jube* backdirt all the way to the city wall in the east. Sherds are visible in section as high as 0.3 and as low as 1.5 meters below the ground surface, indicating that a significant area of occupation has been buried by alluviation.

Second, the *jube* cuts two double rows of stone foundations identical to the wall foundation excavated in ABC B.L. IV. These are well beyond the edges of the mound and indicate that the 8F8-A settlement was once considerably larger and surrounded by a double defensive wall. The eastern portion of the mound may have been dug away to build the city wall of the later Kaftari occupation.

STRATUM 1: TOP EROSION LAYER

The character of the soil (soft, loose, sandy, unconsolidated, loamlike) in this topmost layer reflected current and past weathering conditions. The thickness of this erosional layer varied considerably over the TUV operation, in places being only a few centimeters thick, in others over half a meter in thickness. It was the topmost stratum in all excavated squares.

On the higher points of the mound, there were some fragmentary architectural remains and features of unknown date in stratum 1 (shown on Figure 7). In addition to these excavated remains, bricks of a building phase higher than the pebble surface of stratum 2 were also visible in the east and south balks of V168.

Although the great majority of sherds from the surface of the TUV mound and from stratum 1 were identifiable as Banesh phase in date, later intrusions did occur. Among the registered finds were an inscribed Middle Elamite brick (mf 1182), various iron objects (mf 1138, 1486, 3579) and glass fragments (mf 1291, 1314, 7093, 7096). Burial 283, which originated from stratum 1, was clearly Sassanian in date (Balcer 1978). Thus it is possible that the fragmentary architectural features of stratum 1 may in part be attributable to occupation on the TUV mound after the Banesh phase.

In the lower sectors of the mound, where B.L. I and B.L. II have been eroded away to varying degrees, stratum 1 is to be interpreted as an extremely mixed level, presumably consisting in the main of redeposited Banesh materials which washed down from higher parts of the mound.

STRATUM 2: PEBBLE/COBBLE STRATUM

The size of the stones composing this stratum was generally about 20 x 10 cm, with smaller ones interspersed. This stratum was not found everywhere throughout the TUV operation (cf. Figure 3B), but there was nothing particularly regular about the preserved pattern. It was decidedly an artificially deposited layer of stones, for there is no manner in which these large pebbles could have been deposited naturally in this position on the highest uneroded segments of the mound, well above the general plain level

(J. Blackman, personal communication). Rather, the pebble layer must have been deliberately constructed, though the reason for such activity is unknown. Perhaps the stone layer was intended to serve as a foundation for a building. If anything was ever built *directly* on top of the TUV pebbles, however, no trace of it now remains, with the exception of feature 210. This linear alignment of large stones, set among the pebbles of stratum 2 in southeastern U168, may represent the footing for a mud-brick wall which has totally eroded away. Also in stratum 2 were casual hearth 361 (U168) and feature 80 (U166), a pottery concentration.

STRATUM 3: BRICKY FILL

This was a generally thin stratum, consisting of bricky fill sealed over by stratum 2, but above the definable architecture of stratum 4. It most likely represents the eroded upper portions of B.L. I. (Note that for the Malyan Project "fill" does *not* indicate a deposit deliberately dumped on a surface to level an area, but rather is used synonymously with "matrix.")

This stratum could be sharply distinguished only under the protective capping of stratum 2. Where the pebble layer had eroded away, stratum 3 blended indistinctly into the main erosion layer of stratum 1 (see Figure 4).

STRATUM 4: B.L. I DEPOSITS

This stratum consisted of varied deposits between the walls and above the floors of the first definable construction level encountered in the excavation. B.L. I was clearly datable to the Banesh phase. The extent of B.L. I is shown schematically on Figure 3C. A detailed map and description of the architecture of this level is given in chapter 3.

STRATUM 5: B.L. I WALLS AND FLOORS

This stratum designation refers to the actual material (which often had sherds, bones, or other finds incorporated into its matrix) composing the walls, features, and prepared floors of B.L. I.

STRATUM 6: BRICKY FILL

This stratum consisted of the matrix lying below the bottom of the walls of B.L. I but above the definable architecture of the next construction level, B.L. II. The amount of time that elapsed between the abandonment of B.L. II and the construction of B.L. I is not clear (see chapter 3), but stratum 6a most likely represents the eroded upper portions of B.L. II. A distinct break in utilization of this area is thus implied. (Where B.L. I was eroded away, stratum 6a merged without a sharp break into stratum 1, as shown on Figure 4.) Stratum 6a was generally very thin. In one small sector of V166 there was a distinct intermediate surface under the 6a fill; this surface was designated stratum 6b.

STRATUM 7: B.L. II DEPOSITS

This stratum consisted of the varied deposits between the walls and above the latest floors of the second major Banesh building level that was excavated at TUV. B.L. II (Figure 3D) was more extensively preserved than was B.L. I. The architecture of B.L. II is discussed in chapter 3.

STRATUM 8: B.L. II WALLS AND FLOORS

This stratum had four subdivisions, labelled a-d.

Stratum 8a applied only to cases of B.L. II rooms having two floors, and refers to the material comprising the higher of the two floors (*not* to the fill above the floor).

Stratum 8b also applied only to those rooms having two floors, and refers to the deposit between the higher and lower floors.

Stratum 8c was applied to the walls and original floors of B.L. II.

Stratum 8d was applied to deposits below the last identifiable B.L. II floors but not yet below the bottom of the B.L. II walls.

STRATUM 9: BRICKY FILL

This stratum consisted of varied deposits lying below the base of B.L. II walls, but above the definable architecture and features of B.L. III. In most of the operation, this stratum was very thin. There is convincing stratigraphic evidence (discussed in detail in chapter 3) indicating that only a very short interval elapsed between the final abandonment of the core of B.L. III and the construction of B.L. II.

STRATUM 10: B.L. IIIA DEPOSITS

This stratum consisted of the varied deposits between the walls and above the floors in use during B.L. IIIA, the younger phase of B.L. III. B.L. III, also datable to the Banesh phase, was excavated in a smaller exposure

than were B.L. I and B.L. II (see Figure 3E). The architecture of B.L. IIIA and IIIB is discussed in chapter 3.

STRATUM 11: B.L. IIIA WALLS AND FLOORS

This stratum designation was applied only to the actual matrix comprising features, walls, or floors built during the construction of B.L. IIIA.

STRATUM 12: B.L. IIIB DEPOSITS

This stratum consisted of varied deposits below distinct B.L. IIIA phenomena but above the latest floors of B.L. IIIB.

STRATUM 13: B.L. IIIB WALLS AND FLOORS

This stratum had four subdivisions, labelled a-d.

Stratum 13a was applied only in those cases of rooms having two floors, and refers to the material comprising the higher of the two floors (*not* to the fill on that floor).

Stratum 13b also was applied only to cases of rooms having two floors. It refers to the deposits between the higher and the lower floors.

Stratum 13c was used for the walls and original floors built during the construction of B.L. IIIB (many of which continued in use through B.L. IIIA as well).

Stratum 13d was applied to deposits below the last identifiable B.L. III floors but not yet below the bottom of the B.L. III walls.

STRATUM 14: BRICKY FILL BELOW B.L. III

It is clear that B.L. III was not the bottom cultural stratum of the TUV mound. In a few places excavation penetrated down below the bottoms of B.L. III walls into underlying cultural deposits, which were designated stratum 14. It is not known whether stratum 14 is or is not related to a fourth Banesh building level.

COMMENTS ON THE SEQUENCE

1. The alert reader has noticed that the stratigraphic numbering system defined above has an apparent flaw. When a mud-brick building collapses, fallen debris fills up the spaces between such wall stubs as remain standing. As erosion continues, a "bricky melt" deposit forms, covering the wall stubs and blending into the fallen debris in the rooms. The stratigraphic numbering system used at TUV thus has the slight disad-

vantage of assigning essentially contemporaneous tertiary deposits within rooms and above wall stubs to two *different* strata.

2. Where does the material from Test Trench F (discussed in chapter 1) fit in the TUV sequence? There is no direct stratigraphic connection between Test Trench F and TUV, as the excavated areas were not contiguous. Given the erosion slope of the mound, however, one suspects that the top layer of trashy material in Test Trench F *may* be connected with B.L. III of the TUV operation.

Recognition of Variation in Depositional Processes

Depositional or formation processes are the natural and cultural forces which create an archaeological site. Such processes cause both the physical condition and the spatial distribution of the various elements comprising the archaeological record. Interest in formation processes has recently become explicit among many American archaeologists. Schiffer (1983) traces the background of this concept and discusses various properties of artifacts and deposits which might be indicative of formation processes.

One of the major methodological concerns of the Malyan Project has been the identification of depositional processes. In the following pages, the system employed by the Malyan Project to classify deposits during excavation is briefly discussed. The nature of deposition at TUV is examined and a method by which the classification of deposits in the field can be cross-checked through simple, post-excavation analysis is described. The implications of these depositional variations for functional analysis are then considered.

DEPOSIT CODES

Obviously, formation processes in the broadest sense were not continuously uniform throughout the history of occupation at TUV, for as just described in the stratigraphic overview, both occupation levels and periods of erosion occurred in the sequence. Furthermore, deposition *within* many of these major strata was varied in character. In order to understand the complex manner in which TUV (or any site) was formed, it is necessary to identify and interpret all such depositional variation. The Malyan Deposit Code was designed to facilitate recognition and classification of such variation.

In the Malyan Deposit Code (Sumner 1978), deposits are classified as primary, secondary, or tertiary; there are several subdivisions within each category (Table 2). Primary deposits are those in which finds are thought to remain in the positions in which they were last used; such deposits are very rare at Malyan (and indeed at most Near Eastern mounded sites). Secondary deposits consist of various sorts of trash accumulation. Tertiary deposits are those where the artifactual content of the deposit has lost practically all relationship to both its original locus of use and its locus of discard, loss, or abandonment. Examples of material in tertiary deposition include elements incorporated into the matrix of mud bricks used in the construction of walls, and finds in bricky fill resulting from the erosion of such walls.

Primary and secondary codes are thus indicative of formation processes which were basically cultural in origin. Most tertiary codes are labels for deposits transformed in part by natural processes. Some tertiary codes, however, reflect purely cultural processes, such as the purposeful redeposition of material to level uneven spots in a surface in preparation for building. In either case, the *finds* incorporated in such deposits have been removed from their original primary or secondary context, and hence have little utility for structural or functional analyses.

The Malyan Deposit Code was based on *visual* and *tactile* criteria. Each excavation supervisor at Malyan was instructed to assign the appropriate code to each deposit encountered, based largely on visual assessment of the characteristics of that deposit during excavation. Tactile assessment played a smaller but still important role (e.g., distinguishing bricky from non-bricky fill is often as much a matter of "feel" as it is a matter of vision).

About 79.6% of the excavated deposits at TUV were identified in the field as tertiary, 18.9% as secondary, and only 1.5% as primary (Table 3). These figures are expressed as percentages of the total number of lots rather than as volumetric percentages of the TUV operation, for actual volume of some deposits was not recorded (see chapter 1). Any discrepancy in the gross percentages introduced by volumetric differences in provenience units would probably increase rather than decrease the percentage of the mound seen to be composed of tertiary deposits.

TABLE 2

THE MALYAN DEPOSIT CODE

Deposit Code: This is a 2-digit code which will indicate the nature of the deposit within which a lot occurs.

1. **PRIMARY DEPOSITS**
   * 11   Undisturbed floor deposit. Very rare, artifacts abandoned on the floor where they were last used. Plan and photograph all finds *in situ*.[a]
     12   Undisturbed surface deposit, courtyard, open area. Plan and photograph all finds *in situ*.
   * 13   Burial deposit (each burial should have a separate lot number). Plan and photograph *in situ*.
     14   Cache. Plan and photograph *in situ*.
     15   Cluster: a group of objects apparently deposited together, not on a surface or floor.
     16   Collapsed second-story floor deposit.
   * 17   Artificially deposited pebble/cobble layer; i.e. TUV stratum 2.
     18   to be assigned
     19   to be assigned

2. **SECONDARY DEPOSITS**
   * 21   Trash deposit on a floor or surface, unlike code 11, this is the result of bad housekeeping, not sudden abandonment. Trash accumulation occurred before the room was abandoned as a habitation. Deposit is probably compacted and relatively level. Not sloping much at the sides. Use careful judgment on whether or not to plan and photograph *in situ*.
   * 22   Trash in a pit or well, boundaries of pit or well must be clearly defined.
   * 23   Amorphous trashy deposit, boundaries must be difficult to establish.
     24   Disturbed burial.
   * 25   Disturbed floor or surface deposit. Use this code only if deposit is extensively disturbed, otherwise use code 11.
   * 26   Trash deposit which accumulated on a surface within a room after that room was abandoned as a habitation. Difficult to identify; probably sloping against walls. See definition for code 21.
     27   Ceiling collapse.
   * 28   Kiln, hearth or oven contents, or other container (see code 52).
   * 29   Removal of floor or living surface. Actual material the floor or surface is made of.

3. **TERTIARY DEPOSITS**
   * 31   Surface pick-up.
   * 32   Disturbed topsoil.
   * 33   Rodent burrow
   * 34   Amorphous bricky fill, *associated wall not identified.*
   * 35   Bricky fill below tops of identified walls.
   * 36   Feature removal; this refers to the actual material a feature is made of, the bricks in a wall, the clay of a hearth, etc.
   * 37   Arbitrary floor cleaning lot composed of bricky or other fill which cannot be identified as having a trash component.
   * 38   Balk removal. Use only if balk was not removed stratigraphically.
     39   Dump
   * 40   Unknown
   * 41   Clean-up
   * 42   Non-bricky fill within identified walls (without obvious trash component)
     43   Rocky-trash fill *not associated* with mud-brick walls.
     44   Surface wash.
     45   Sandy fill, probably water laid product of steep erosion from well.
     46   to be assigned
     47   Mixed fill with some brick component *not within* identified walls.
     48   Mixed fill with some brick component within identified walls.

TABLE 2—*Continued*

*	49	Redeposited material. Material which was removed and then redeposited in antiquity; i.e. material from a burial pit.
	50	Sterile natural soil deposit.
*	51	Brick packing
*	52	Contents of pot, drain or other container. If there is a strong reason to believe the contents are a secondary deposit, use code 28.

* Deposit types observed at TUV

[a] The only example of a code 11 at TUV is a large ceramic vessel set up in a pit dug into the floor of B.L. II.

How accurate were site supervisors in their assignment of deposit codes? It is clear that during excavation in both 1974 and 1976, site supervisors at TUV experienced difficulty in recognizing and coding consistently the character of certain deposits. Most troublesome were deposits lying below the tops of defined walls but somewhere above floors and lacking such visual significata of trash as numerous charcoal flecks, stains of organic debris, and immediately apparent richness in bone or artifact density. Many such deposits, although not distinctively trashy, did not clearly represent collapse deposits either. Furthermore, supervisors could not resolve these ambiguous cases by the *type* of artifactual material found within a deposit. The sherds incorporated within the bricks used at TUV were of the Banesh phase, the same ceramic phase as that in which TUV was occupied. Thus a sherd in tertiary collapse deposition at TUV was not obviously out of place in the assemblage of ceramics known from the secondary trash deposits.

Faced with such an ambiguous situation, the site supervisor had a choice of three possible codes: 35, 37, or 42. Code 42 in theory was applied to deposits which were both non-trashy and non-bricky. Code 37 was intended for deposits which appeared to be brick collapse but immediately overlay floors. Code 35 covered all other brick collapse within standing wall stubs.

In theory, these codes represented three different tertiary depositional situations. In reality, however, site supervisors applied them to both undoubtedly tertiary and ambiguous deposits. Supervisors also were inconsistent in choosing from among the three codes. The visual/tactile boundary between non-bricky deposition (code 42) and apparent collapse (codes 35, 37) was hazy; these depositional types appeared rather to intergrade.

What are the implications of this situation for the functional analysis of TUV? Only material in primary or secondary deposition can be justifiably interpreted as contemporaneous with the occupation of the site. Tertiary deposits, on the other hand, are excluded from functional analysis as the artifactual material within those deposits has lost all relationship to its original place of deposition.

About 38% of the deposits excavated at TUV were given a code 35, 37, or 42 in the field. Does this then mean that all such lots should be automatically excluded from the functional analysis? Given the ambiguities of classification discussed above, such automatic exclusion might well lead to the removal of certain important secondary material from the data set. What is needed is some method of *checking* the subjective assignments of deposit codes. It seemed possible that such a technique might be found by investigating find density, fragmentation, and diversity in various deposit types. The results of the density tests are most relevant to the present discussion, and are briefly reviewed here.

DENSITY SIGNATURES[1]

Do different types of deposit as identified by deposit codes have distinctive signatures as measured by the density of finds within these deposits? One would theoretically expect secondary deposits to contain higher densities of material items than tertiary deposits. Four lines of evidence are available for investigation of this question. These are (1) number of diagnostic chaff-tempered sherds per cubic meter of deposit, (2) number of diagnostic grit-tempered sherds per cubic meter of deposit, (3) bone count and bone weight per cubic meter of deposit, and (4) number of registered finds per cubic meter of deposit.

---

1. An initial (and cruder) attempt to check the subjective assignments of deposit codes was presented by Nicholas (1980a:107-126) using the concept "lot content profile." The lot content profile was essentially a simple quantitative summary of the artifacts, sherds, and bones found in a given deposit. Average lot content profiles were calculated for different deposit types, with values expressed as the number of items *per average lot* (not in terms of a given volume of deposit, although these profiles were checked against a small sample of lots for which volumetric data were then available). Since 1980, re-study of the TUV field notes and plans has led to the calculation of volumes for additional deposits and to the estimation of probable volume ranges for most of the remaining deposits at TUV. In this monograph a volumetrically based analysis is presented, and the more appropriate term "density signature" replaces the cumbersome "lot content profile."

TABLE 3

DEPOSITIONAL VARIATION WITHIN MAJOR STRATA AT TUV, TABULATED BY NUMBER OF LOTS

Deposit codes Stratum	11	13	17	21	22	23	25	26	28	29	31	32	33	34	35	36	37	38	40	41	42	47	49	51	52	Total[a]
0	-	-	-	-	-	-	-	-	-	-	1	8	1	-	-	-	-	-	-	-	-	-	-	-	-	(10)
1	-	1	-	-	8	3	-	-	-	-	-	26	1	23	-	1	-	-	3	-	-	1	5	-	-	(72)
2	-	-	6	-	-	1	-	-	-	-	-	-	-	-	-	1	-	-	-	-	-	-	-	-	-	(8)
3	-	-	-	-	1	-	-	-	-	-	-	-	-	3	-	-	-	-	-	-	-	-	-	-	-	(4)
4	-	-	-	-	20	3	1	-	-	-	-	-	-	-	12	1	19	-	-	-	1	-	-	-	-	(57)
5	-	-	-	-	-	-	-	-	-	-	-	-	-	-	-	16	-	-	-	-	-	-	-	-	-	(16)
6a	-	-	-	-	-	-	-	-	-	-	-	-	-	9	-	-	3	1	-	-	-	-	-	-	-	(13)
6b	-	-	-	-	-	-	-	-	-	-	-	-	-	-	-	-	-	-	-	-	-	-	-	-	-	(0)
7	1	-	-	3	8	-	12	-	5	-	-	-	-	-	42	-	53	-	2	-	2	-	-	-	2	(130)
8a	-	-	-	-	-	-	-	-	-	-	-	-	-	-	-	-	-	-	-	-	-	-	-	-	-	(0)
8b	-	-	-	-	1	-	1	-	-	-	-	-	-	-	2	-	11	-	-	-	-	-	-	-	-	(15)
8c	-	-	-	-	-	-	-	-	-	14	-	-	-	-	-	50	-	-	-	1	-	-	-	-	-	(65)
8d	-	-	-	-	-	-	-	-	-	-	-	-	-	-	5	-	-	-	-	1	-	-	-	-	-	(6)
9	-	2	-	-	3	2	-	-	2	-	-	-	-	26	-	7	-	-	3	-	-	-	-	3	-	(48)
10	-	-	-	4	7	9	-	5	7	-	-	-	-	21	58	3	18	-	-	2	10	-	-	27	1	(172)
11	-	-	-	-	-	-	-	-	-	-	-	-	-	-	-	11	-	-	-	-	-	-	-	-	-	(11)
12	-	1	-	2	6	-	-	3	-	-	-	-	-	-	14	-	10	-	-	-	4	-	1	-	-	(41)
13a	-	-	-	-	-	-	-	-	1	-	-	-	-	-	-	-	-	-	-	-	-	-	-	-	-	(1)
13b	-	-	-	2	-	-	-	-	-	-	-	-	-	-	3	-	2	-	-	-	-	-	-	-	-	(7)
13c	-	-	-	-	-	-	-	-	-	1	-	-	-	-	-	7	-	-	-	-	-	-	-	-	1	(9)
13d	-	-	-	-	-	-	-	-	-	-	-	-	-	-	2	-	-	-	6	1	-	-	-	-	-	(9)
14	-	-	-	-	-	-	-	-	-	1	-	-	-	-	-	-	-	-	2	-	-	-	-	-	-	(3)
Totals	1	4	6	11	54	18	14	8	15	16	1	34	2	82	138	97	116	1	16	5	17	1	6	30	4	(697)

[a] Total lot units in each stratum; some may be mixed. In addition to the lots shown on this table, 21 additional lots of material were collected during the excavations at the TUV mound, for which no stratigraphic assignment can be made, such as balk straightening lots.

Chaff- and grit-tempered ceramics are the two major ware groups in the TUV Banesh assemblage (see chapter 4). Chaff-tempered ware is noticeably less durable than grit-tempered ware. Chaff-tempered sherds and grit-tempered sherds might thus have been differentially affected by post-depositional processes. These categories were therefore treated separately in the deposit signature analysis.

For both wares, only diagnostic sherd count was used as a measure. Diagnostic sherds include all rims, bases, decorated sherds, spouts, handles, and other sherds providing comparable clues to the shape or temporal placement of the vessel. Counts of non-diagnostic sherds and sherd weights were not available for the deposits excavated in 1974. The use of only diagnostic sherds in the density signature analysis probably does not reduce the reliability of the test results.

Bone count and bone weight figures for certain lots from both seasons were available, through the work of M. Zeder, the Malyan Project's faunal analyst. Bone fragmentation patterns are extremely variable, so both counts and weights were utilized in the density signature tests.

Registered finds (see chapter 5) include all other moveable items recovered during the TUV operation and deemed worthy of registration; 1803 such finds were registered, including whole and fragmentary artifacts, waste-products (e.g. debitage), by-products (e.g. copper slag), raw materials, charcoals, and other samples.

The densities of these four kinds of material were first examined in selected unambiguous deposit types (i.e., those clearly classifiable on visual and tactile criteria). From least to most reworked, these deposit types were codes 21/22B/23B, 25, 26/23A, 36A/51, 34. Only unmixed lots with known volumes were used in these tests.

It was expected that density signatures for deposit codes would overlap, but that there should be a trend toward *decreasing* density in the more "reworked" deposits. Reworking (tertiary) processes may a) disturb originally concentrated clusters of trash, spreading them over larger areas, b) contribute to the weathering and disintegration of included material, and c) often introduce new matrix material from exterior sources, thereby increasing the volume of the deposit.

To test our theoretical predictions, scatter-plots of volume/count were originally prepared for grit-ware, chaff-ware, and bone. For clarity of publication, alternative graphs were generated using StatView 512+ (Figures 8, 9, and 10). On these, density/cubic meter was plotted directly on the horizontal axis of each graph, with the percent of lots having that density in each deposit category plotted on the vertical axis.

Our basic expectation on the characteristics of tertiary versus secondary deposits was met, but overlap of deposit signatures occurred to a greater degree than we had envisioned, and details of the trend were slightly different from what we had predicted. We had recognized type 34 deposits (bricky melt and collapse) as more reorganized than type 36A deposits (mud bricks in intact walls), and had predicted that type 34 deposits should thus be less dense in finds than type 36A deposits. Our graphs and scatter-plots revealed that these signatures overlap markedly and that sometimes the trend is reversed. This is most probably to be explained by the following process. When a mud-brick wall collapses/erodes away, it is likely that some of the original mud in the bricks will be completely carried away by erosion, while the heavy finds originally incorporated in the bricks will be redeposited in a bricky matrix of lesser volume. If this process is the cause of the observed overlap and reversal in density signatures for type 36A and type 34 deposits, we would expect the trend reversal to be most marked for heaviest items (i.e., grit-tempered sherds) and less marked for lighter, more easily transportable items. This is the pattern shown on our plots. It is also possible that additional items may have entered the type 34 deposit by loss or discard. Such introduction of new material seems especially likely to occur when type 34 deposits are produced through deliberate human agency, such as the razing of an abandoned structure and subsequent levelling of the ground in preparation for a new episode of construction.

The relative sturdiness of grit-ware, chaff-ware, and bone may also explain why the overlap between secondary and tertiary signatures is greatest for grit-ware and least for bone.

The density of registered finds per deposit type has not yet been discussed. For this category of material, the density trend is clearer, and can be shown in tabular format (Table 4). Find density in secondary deposits is about double the find density in tertiary deposits (for both the screened and unscreened series).

The density signatures established by studying unambiguous deposits can be used to evaluate those deposits coded 35, 37, and 42 in the field. For deposits of known volume, find densities can be graphed, and those deposits with density signatures falling beyond the characteristic range of tertiary deposits can be identified. Such deposits are unlikely to have formed through purely tertiary processes; their high find densities suggest that material has been added by loss or discard. Such deposits might thus appropriately be labelled *tertiary with secondary admixture*.

For those deposits whose exact volume is not known, it has generally proved practicable to estimate upper volumetric limits (and in many cases, lower volumetric limits as well). Using the range of estimated volume for each deposit, it is possible to evaluate the remaining code 35, 37, and 42 deposits in a manner similar to that explained above. Deposits with tertiary signatures can again be separated from those with signatures suggestive of secondary admixture.

What is the value of this procedure for functional analysis of TUV? Quite simply, this procedure gives us a better knowledge of how the site was formed, by distinguishing areas of simple wall collapse and erosion from those deposits formed by more complicated mixes of erosion and admixture.

The procedure also gives us a chance to achieve a more refined analysis of site structure and function. Prior to this density signature procedure, the cultural material from TUV could be sorted into only two basic categories, that in tertiary deposition and that in secondary/primary deposition. Only the latter could be used in functional analysis, as only the latter could be demonstrated to be contemporaneous with the occupation and use of the site. The density signature test divides the former tertiary category into two parts, tertiary and tertiary with secondary admixture. Thus a new category has been created, one with analytic potential somewhere between that of the purely tertiary and the purely secondary. For any given deposit recognized as tertiary with secondary admixture, it is of course generally not possible to specify *which* items were introduced into the deposit in non-tertiary ways. Taken together, however, the *series* of deposits falling into this new analytical category can clarify the functional analysis of the site.

Chapter Conclusion

This chapter has summarized the major stratigraphic continuities discovered in the TUV operation. Deposit codes and density signatures have been shown to improve our understanding of the varied depositional processes which created TUV. Such identification of formation processes is critical in assessing which deposits are suitable for use in functional analysis. Before such analysis can be understood, however, it is also necessary to present a morphological description of the data base; this is the task of the next three chapters.

TABLE 4

FIND DENSITY[1]

Deposit code (see table 2)	Number of such deposits	Total volume	Mean volume in m^3	Total # of finds	# of finds per m^3
Selected Screened Lots					
21	5	1.791	0.358	43	24
22B (trash pits)	13	2.126	0.164	86	40
22A (other pits)	11	0.878	0.080	13	15
23B (trash piles)	2	1.384	0.692	11	8
25	5	0.472	0.094	13	28
26	5	0.992	0.198	40	40
37	26	4.422	0.170	54	12
42	2	0.200	0.100	2	10
Selected Unscreened Lots					
21	2	0.090	0.045	2	22
22B (trash pits)	2	0.025	0.125	5	20
23A (amorphous trash)	5	2.260	0.452	16	7
23B (trash piles)	5	4.376	0.875	21	5
25	2	2.360	1.180	4	2
42	5	3.460	0.692	29	8
37	10	11.090	1.109	28	3
35A	10	14.310	1.431	26	2
35B (those just above a code 37)	16	14.200	0.888	48	3
34	36	37.346	1.037	77	2
36	39	17.510	0.449	61	3

[1] This table presents data on the density of *registered* finds in different types of deposits at TUV. The density of bulk materials is not considered here, but rather on figures 8, 9, and 10.

III

Architecture and Features

The first portion of this chapter reviews the architecture of the three Banesh building levels excavated in the TUV operation. These levels are discussed in the order of oldest to most recent. In the latter portion of the chapter a typological description of features is presented. Such morphological description of architecture and features is a necessary prelude to functional analysis; it is these elements of site content which comprise an immoveable architectonic framework against which the spatial distribution of moveable finds can then be examined.

Architecture at TUV

Method of Construction

BRICK-LAYING PATTERNS

The TUV walls were built with sun-dried mud bricks. B.L. III was constructed of rectangular bricks 40 x 20 x 8 cm and square bricks 20 x 20 x 8 cm in size. B.L. II and B.L. I, however, were constructed with different standard brick sizes; bricks of 36 x 36 x 8.5 cm and 18 x 36 x 8.5 cm were used in both those levels.

Details of wall construction are summarized in Tables 5, 7, and 9 below. All brick-laying patterns are illustrated on Figure 11. These course patterns as drawn are slightly idealized. The builders of the TUV architecture did not always follow course patterns with total consistency. Odd patches of irregular brick segments periodically occur in many wall courses dissected at TUV.

PLASTER

Plaster is a protective coating used to cover walls, floors and features. There were four kinds of plaster found at TUV: mud plaster, white lime plaster, painted plaster, and "cement" plaster.

Mud plaster (*kagel*) was a pastelike mixture of clay, water and straw applied to wall faces in layers up to several centimeters in thickness. This was the most common type of plaster found at TUV; most walls probably had *kagel* coats when in use, although such plaster was not always preserved. The distribution of mud plaster *in situ* on walls is summarized on Tables 5, 7, and 9. *Kagel* was also used to plaster room floors and the sides of many features such as hearths.

A thin white plaster was occasionally applied over *kagel*-plastered faces. Such white plaster was called *gatch* by our workmen. *Gatch*, however, is technically gypsum plaster (Wulff 1966:126). The white plaster at TUV appears rather to have been made from marly or chalky limestone (Blackman 1982). Lime plaster was found both *in situ* on wall faces (see Tables 5, 7, 9) and as fallen fragments in room fill. Possible evidence for the production of lime plaster at TUV is summarized under functional class 5, chapter 5.

In painted plaster, pigment has been applied over a white lime plaster base. Both red and black painted plasters occurred at TUV, but not *in situ* on wall faces.

Only one example of red painted plaster was observed, on one of the bricks used to pack room 219 prior to the construction of B.L. II. This brick retained no clear relationship to its original architectural location.

The black-painted plaster fragments retained more significant associations with architecture. Most of these fragments were found in bricky deposits within room

225 of B.L. III, and clearly had fallen from (or been knocked down with) the upper wall(s) of that room. Many small and scattered pieces of both black painted and uncolored lime plaster were recovered from the matrix just above the main level of packing bricks in this room. One fragment preserved a small segment of a step-design in black and white.

Fragments of black-painted plaster also occurred in the fill of room 215 of B.L. III, in association with uncolored lime plaster.

Much more extensively preserved Banesh wall paintings were found in the ABC operation at Malyan (Nickerson 1977). Elaborate step, stripe, and swirl motifs were created by the application of pigments over white lime plaster. These pigments have been tentatively identified as hematite for red, limonite for yellow, and organic carbon for black and gray.

Discussion of possible pigment production at TUV is given under functional class 5, chapter 5.

The term cement plaster is used here to describe an exceptionally hard floor material found exclusively in structure 315 of B.L. IIIB. This plaster consisted of numerous small pebbles firmly held together by an unidentified binder, which (together with effects of heat from the burning of this structure?) gave the floor an extraordinary cementlike hardness. Unfortunately it has not been possible to have the chemical composition of this substance analyzed.

Building Level III

OVERVIEW

B.L. III was the lowest and best preserved of the identified Banesh building levels at TUV. The main exposure of this level covered about 225 m^2 (U168, T168, three-quarters of V168, the east half of U166 and the southeast quadrant of V166). The room and two associated trash pits discovered at the western end of V164 during the 1974 season probably should also be assigned to B.L. III; this was an exposure of at most an additional 20 m^2. Finally, a small sounding (about 2 m^2) in the northeast corner of T166 also penetrated B.L. III deposits.

Preservation of this building level was generally very good. Walls remained standing sufficiently high to preserve built-in features and to allow the identification of doorsills. Only in the southeastern portion of T168 were weathering and soil conditions particularly hampering to excavation. In that area there was an exceptionally dense percolation of ground salts which gave the matrix a uniform hardness and created many root casts.

The general orientation of B.L. III was slightly different from that of the two higher building levels, running somewhat more directly north-south and east-west. Neither the walls nor the room corners, however, were oriented exactly to the cardinal points.

For analytical purposes, B.L. III has been divided into B.L. IIIB and B.L. IIIA (see Figure 12). The walls and floors originally constructed in this building period are designated B.L. IIIB. Some walls and floors continued in use unmodified until the final abandonment of the level. Certain other sectors, however, were significantly remodelled prior to abandonment; the walls and floors in these zones of major reconstruction are termed B.L. IIIA.

The chronology of deposition within the architectural units of B.L. III is different from the chronology of simple construction just reviewed. Deposits on B.L. IIIB floors in unremodelled areas must have been laid down either towards the end of occupation of those rooms (in the case of most trash) or after the final abandonment of the level. These deposits must thus be viewed as contemporaneous with similar deposits lying on B.L. IIIA floors, and assigned to level IIIA. The only deposits (other than walls and floors themselves) assigned to IIIB are (1) deposits in rooms/areas which were abandoned and sealed over by IIIA walls or floors; (2) deposits on lower floors in rooms with multiple floors.

B.L. IIIB
(Figure 13, Tables 5, 6)

Much of the recovered plan constituted a complex of architecturally contiguous rooms, here called structure 1.

In the initial construction phase of this complex, the structural framework for the building (major weight-bearing walls, solid enough to have supported substantial roofing) was established. These walls are 294[1] on the west (Plate 3a), 286 and 304 on the south, and 213, 230, 239, 243, and 248 in the center and east. Possibly the narrow partition walls (211, 212, 270, 280, 293, 297, 342) were constructed at the same time, but this can not be demonstrated because B.L. IIIB was not dismantled

---

1. Wall 294 is the only wall at TUV demonstrated to rest on a *substantial* stone foundation. Some of the other walls of B.L. III structure 1 might also rest on such footings, but this possibility was not investigated. Wall 24 of the B.L. II north unit did, however, rest on a simple linear alignment of stones (feature 332).

and removed; therefore we lack bonding/abutting and it remains possible that in the initial construction phase of structure 1, the entire western sector of the complex may have been a large courtyard, connected by door 224 to the eastern half of the building. When the partition walls were constructed, direct access between the west unit and the east unit of structure 1 was lost.

In addition to the west and east units of structure 1, there were also room-blocks lying to the north and south. It is not known when these units were built; they may have been constructed at the same time as the core weight-bearing walls defined above, or after that framework but prior to the partitioning of the west and east units, or even at a subsequent time.

THE WEST UNIT (rooms/areas 258, 282, 284, 306, 309, 313)
(Plate 2)

There are a number of problems in our understanding of the architectural relationships among the rooms within this sector. Most of these difficulties stem from the existence of the U166/U168 balk, which was not removed. In addition, an intrusive Sassanian burial in pit 196 (Balcer 1978) has disturbed part of the original architectural plan.

Description of the west unit begins with its southwest corner. It is possible that "wall segment" 295 was actually a blocked doorway or a high doorsill, through which access to structure 1 was obtained from exterior area 308. North of "wall" 295 was a small room or foyer, 309. From that room one could either move north into large room or courtyard 306, or turn east and proceed along narrow corridor 313. Here the balk intrudes into our reconstruction of possible circulation patterns within the west unit. The excavated walls suggest (but only removal of the balk could prove) that corridor 313 was a zigzag passage, leading one first northward into space 282 and then eastward into room 284.

Room 284's fill was disturbed by pits 199 (dug from stratum 4) and 220 (dug from stratum 9). Some bits of white lime plaster were found in the fill of the northwest portion of this room, but none was found *in situ* on any of the wall faces.

The nature of the access between area 282 and room 258 is unknown, for this zone was thoroughly disturbed by a Sassanian burial in pit 196. Only a small stub of the original southern wall (280) of room 258 remained, plus some traces of a hearth/bin complex (273/281) built into or adjacent to that wall. Cobble feature 276 lay at the north end of room 258.

No doorways connecting rooms 258 and 284 to rooms of the east unit were discovered. This may imply

that following the construction of partition walls 211, 212, and 270, the west unit of structure 1 functioned as an independent entity.

THE EAST UNIT (rooms/areas 215, 219, 225, 242, 247, 250)
(Plates 2, 7a, 7b)

Room 225 was central to this unit, having the highest degree of accessibility of any excavated room in B.L. IIIB. This room was bounded on all four sides by thick walls that could have supported solid roofing. The mud plastered floor of this room was in excellent condition and was the hardest, most level floor in the entire building level. Some remnants of white lime plaster were found on the floor in the northwestern corner of the room.

Considerable traces of lime plaster were also found *in situ* on all four walls of the room. Furthermore, during excavation of the fill in room 225, fallen bits of both white- and black-painted plaster were recovered directly under the bricks of the B.L. II floor which had been laid across this levelled zone. It appears that the upper portion of at least one wall of room 225 had been decorated in two colors (probably a step pattern).

Built into the middle of its east wall (243), room 225 had the most elaborate example of a raised-box hearth (227) excavated at TUV (Plate 7a).

From room 225 it was possible at one time to move west through doorway 224 into room 219; at some point prior to the abandonment of B.L. III, however, doorway 224 was partially blocked and made into a white lime plastered niche opening into room 225.

Room 219 was connected by doorway 216 with room 215 to the south. These two rooms were formed by the addition of narrow partition walls to major structural wall 213. The walls of this annex could probably only have supported light roofing. There does not appear to have been any connection between either annex room and the west unit of structure 1.

The floor of room 219 was disturbed by pit 195 (intrusive from stratum 4) and by Banesh burial 278, interred at some point between abandonment of the room and the construction of B.L. II.

From the northwest corner of room 219 came the only evidence of red-painted plaster at TUV. This paint, however, occurred on a packing brick used in partially filling the room after abandonment; thus the red paint was not necessarily applied to the walls of room 219. A small bit of white lime plaster was found next to, but not adhering to, the east face of wall 270. The floor of room 219 also had remnants of white lime plaster on it.

Room 215 was in many ways a smaller version of room 225, although it could be reached through only one doorway rather than three. The standing walls on

TABLE 5
WALLS OF B.L. III, TUV OPERATION

Reference #	Unit (room-block)	Grid reference	Orientation	Areas separated	Known doors?[a]	North or east end[b]	South or west end[b]	Total width (cm)	# courses preserved	Mud plaster?[a]	Lime plaster?[a]	Brick sizes reported in notes (pattern)[c]	Comments
166	IIIB?	V164	E-W	164/165	n	M	M	40	--	--	n	--	
167	IIIB?	V164	N-S	164/163	384	door	M	40	--	--	n	--	
211	IIIA E	U168	N-S	258/215	n	jogs to w.270	meets 212	30	--	y	y, in 215	--	
212	IIIA E	U168	E-W	215/284	n	meets 213	meets 211	30	--	y	y, in 215	--	
213	IIIA E	U168	N-S	215-219/225, 284/250	224	meets 340	meets 286-304	70-90	--	y	y, in 215, 225	quarter bricks	domed oven 214
230	IIIA E	U168	E-W	225/234	n	M	meets 213, 238, 340	80	--	y	y, in 225	quarter bricks	
238	IIIA E	U168	E-W	265/219	n	meets 340, 213, 230	meets 270	30	--	--	n	--	
239	IIIA E	U168	E-W	225/250	256	M	meets 213	85	--	y	y, in 225	quarter bricks	
243	IIIA E	U168	N-S	225/242	381	door	meets 248	95	--	y	y, in 225	quarter bricks	hearth 227
248	IIIA E	U168	N-S	247/250	317	meets 243	door	80	--	y	n	quarter bricks	
262	IIIB N	V168	N-S	west side of 265	n	M	meets 238	30	-- (1)	--	n	--	drain 261 cuts this wall
270	IIIA E	U168	N-S	258/219	n	meets 238	jogs to 211	30	--	y	possible-- traces in 219	--	
280	IIIA W	U168	E-W	258/282	n	abuts 211	M	30	--	--	n	--	largely destroyed by pit 196
286	IIIA W	U168	E-W	284/outside	n	becomes 304	M	60?	--	y	n	--	S face was slightly cut into during construction of feature 315
293	IIIA W	U166/8	N-S	306/258	n	M	abuts 297	35	(42 cm)	y thick on W	n	--	
294	IIIA W	U/V166	N-S	307/306-309	n	meets 337	abuts 295	80	6	y, esp. thick on W	n	K/J 30x19-20	Substantial stone foundation; partly disturbed by pit 345
295	IIIA W	U166	E-W	309/308	see comment	abuts 296	abuts 294	40	1	y, on S	n	C 40x19-20	'wall' 295 may be a doorsill
296	IIIA W	U166	E-W	313/308	n	M	abuts 295	40+	--	y	n	C 40x19-20	plus unclear pattern to S of the 'C' row

TABLE 5—*Continued*

Reference #	Unit (room-block)	Grid reference	Orientation	Areas separated	Known doors?[a]	North or east end[b]	South or west end[b]	Total width (cm)	# courses preserved	Mud plaster?[a]	Lime plaster?[a]	Brick sizes reported in notes (pattern)[c]	Comments
297	IIIA W	U166	E-W	306/313	385	M	door	35	--	n	n	--	
303	IIIB	U/V166	N-S	W side of 307	n	meets 337	M	?	--	y	n	headers along E face	W face not excavated E face steps in
304	IIIA E	U/T168	E-W	250-247/320-326	n	M	becomes 286	175	--	y	n	--	appears to be a double wall for part of its length
316	315	U/T168	cir-cular	outside/315	n	--	--	20	1-3	y	n	variable chunks of brick	
319	IIIB S	T168	N-S	outside/320	n	meets 304	M	90	--	y	n	--	partly disturbed by pit 299
322	IIIB S	T168	E-W	320/325	n	meets 324	meets 319	35-40	--	y	n	--	
324	IIIB S	T168	N-S	320/326	329	door	meets 322	125?	--	y	n	--	very difficult to define— see text
337	blocks N end of 307	V166	E-W	338/307	n	meets 294	M	50	--	--	n	--	
340	IIIB N	U/V168	N-S	265/234	n	M	meets 213	30	--	y	n	some vertically set bricks	
342	IIIA W	U168	N-S	313/284	--	ends in 282	M	?	--	--	n	--	
383	IIIA E	U168	E-W	219/215	216	meets 213	meets 211-270	30	--	y	y, 215 side	--	

[a] n = no, y = yes

[b] M = missing data, generally because a balk intrudes

[c] The B.L. III architecture was not removed in order to excavate deeper; consequently walls were not dissected to determine brick-laying patterns except in a few special test cases. In retrospect it is realized that more attention should have been paid in the 1976 season to collection of architectural details. It can be said that the major walls of B.L. III were constructed of quarter-sized bricks (c. 20x20 cm) and plastered heavily with kagel. Smaller walls are 1 to 2 bricks thick and also mud plastered. For explanation of letter codes, see Figure 11.

all four sides of room 215 had white lime plaster *in situ* over the mud plaster on the wall faces. The upper portion of at least one wall may have been decorated in bichrome; in the upper fill of the room, north of wall 212, bits of both white- and black-painted plaster were recovered. A hearth (domed oven 214, Plate 7 b) was built into the middle of the east wall. Two floors were identified in room 215, with the lower showing traces of partial resurfacings.

Returning to room 225, note that it was also possible to move eastward through door 381 into (it is inferred) area 242. Unfortunately no floor was identifiable during the excavation of the latter area. One small piece of fallen white plaster was found in the fill there, but none remained *in situ* on the walls.

Returning yet again to room 225, one could move toward the south, through doorway 256 into room 250. The fill of room 250 was partially disturbed by intrusive pit 197 from stratum 1. (See the discussion of cobble feature 252 on page 49.)

Door 317 connected room 250 with room 247 to the east. No features were found in room 247.

Within the limit of excavation, there were no doors connecting the east unit of structure 1 with the west, north, or south. It must therefore be concluded that access into the east unit, at least after annex 219-215 was built, was via zones to the east beyond the bounds of our work.

THE NORTH UNIT (rooms/areas 234, 265, 373, 376)

Preservation of the original architecture of the north unit was very poor; this part of the complex (unlike the units previously described) was abandoned early and converted to a quite different use in B.L. IIIA. It is not known how many rooms this north unit originally contained. Our excavations uncovered clear traces of only two, 234 and 265, in northeastern U168 and the southeast quadrant of V168.

Rooms 265 and 234 were built directly against walls of the east unit, but there were no doors through those walls within our area of excavation.

Area 234 lay north of wall 230, and was bounded on the west by a flimsy, poorly constructed partition wall, 340. The northern and eastern bounds of the area were unclear. It appears that the north wall collapsed in antiquity and was preserved only as a brick fall (feature 260) in U168 and V168. Fragments of fallen white lime plaster were found in association with this brick fall. The eastern wall of area 234 most probably lay beyond the limits of our excavation. (Although feature 259 was at first thought to represent the east wall of area 234, there were problems with that conclusion. Feature 259 consisted of mud bricks set side-by-side on end, mud plastered to form a western face, with a thin coat of white lime plaster over the mud plaster. The orientation of feature 259 was distinctly different, however, from that of B.L. IIIB walls, and the top of the feature was level with the floor of area 234. It was concluded that feature 259 was the top of a B.L. IV feature immediately underlying area 234.)

West of area 234 lay room 265. The south wall of this room was wall 238. Traces of its east wall (340) and its west wall (262) were discerned for a considerable distance north into V168 but the room's original north boundary was not definable. The walls of this room were almost completely obliterated (except for the south wall, which was not disturbed) by B.L. IIIA remodelling.

Small fragments of area 376, west of room 265, and area 373 to the east were excavated as well, but relatively little could be determined about the character of these areas in B.L. IIIB. The northern wall of area 376 was probably wall 398. Burial 274 was dug into area 373 at this time.

In the southwest and northeast quadrants of V168, B.L. IIIB surfaces were not reached.

THE SOUTH UNIT (rooms/areas 320, 325, 326)

Knowledge of this unit is limited by both the relatively small exposure in this zone and the relatively poor preservation of walls and floors here. This area was very near the present southern edge of the TUV mound; erosion and weathering effects were thus greater here than to the north. There also appear to have been inordinately high amounts of ground salts percolating through the fill of this zone, resulting in the formation here (but nowhere else in the TUV operation) of many root casts, some of considerable size. These percolating mineral salts may also have been responsible for the extreme difficulty experienced in this area in differentiating mud brick from the surrounding matrix.

In spite of these difficulties, it was possible to define one room (320) and to postulate the existence of two others within this unit.

Cobble feature 327 and casual hearth 328 occurred above the floor of small rectangular room 320, which had good walls on three sides, but a problematic wall (324) on the fourth (east) side. This poorly defined wall lay within the zone of uniform matrix hardness discussed above. During excavation of this area, however, mud-plaster lines delimiting all four sides of room 320 had been briefly visible. The existence of wall 324 was further confirmed by differential drying of that area after a very hard rain. There also appeared to be a doorway (329) through wall 324, connecting room 320 with area 326 to the east.

Area 326 and area 325 (which lay south of room 320) may represent additional rooms within the south unit of structure 1, but floors were not identified in those zones.

This sector of structure 1 also received major remodelling in B.L. IIIA.

EXTERIOR AND PERIPHERAL AREAS OF B.L. IIIB

Southwest of structure 1 was exterior zone 308. Feature 315 was constructed in this zone, evidently sometime after the erection of wall 286, for the south face of that wall was partially destroyed by the building of feature 315.

Feature 315 (Plate 3b) was a free-standing, circular structure with two superimposed very hard "cement" floors containing numerous small pebbles. These floors were bounded by a narrow mud-brick wall, 316. The entire structure exhibited the effects of heat (a striking red discoloration and increase in hardness) but these effects were most intense in the northwestern arc of the building. There the mud bricks of the wall were exceptionally hard; consequently the wall stood to a greater height there than elsewhere and the beginning of doming was evident.

Area 307 led directly from exterior zone 308 north along the west face of wall 294 (Plate 3a). The long, narrow configuration of area 307 plus its conjunction with an exterior zone combine to suggest that area 307 may have been an alleyway. The exceptionally thick mud plaster on the west face of wall 294 may have reflected an exterior exposure.

If area 307 was an alley, then wall 303 which bounded it on the west can be inferred to be the eastern facade of an architectural complex (structure 2) distinct from structure 1. Only the east face of wall 303 lay within our zone of excavation; this wall stepped inward twice as one moved northward along the alley (see Figure 13).

The northern end of alley 307 was blocked by wall 337. Time did not allow the dissection of walls 337,

TABLE 6
ROOMS AND AREAS OF BUILDING LEVEL III, TUV OPERATION

Feature #	Structure and room-block	West wall[b]	North wall[b]	East wall[b]	South wall[b]	North-south dimensions	East-west dimensions	Grid reference	Floor identified?[a]	Comments[c]
164	IIIB?	M	166	167	M	2.75+	1.50+	V164	y	area
215	IIIA E	211	383	213	212	2.65	1.75	U168	2 floors	room
219	IIIA E	270	238	213	383	1.80	2.00	U168	y	room
225	IIIA E	213	230	243	239	4.15	2.60	U168	y, with lime plaster traces	room
234	IIIB N	340	260	(259?)	230	1.25?	1.55?	U168	y	room
242	IIIA E	243	M	M	239	3.75+	1.90+	U168	none id	area
247	IIIA E	248	239	M	304	1.80	2.50+	U168 U/T168 balk	y	room
250	IIIA E	213	239	248	304	2.90	2.80	U168 U/T168 balk	y	room
258	IIIA W	293	M	270/211	280	4.50?	1.80-2.20	U168	y	room
265	IIIB N	262	M	340	238	4.00+?	2.55?	U/V168	poor surface	room
282	IIIA W	293	280	211	297	1.00?	2.30?	U168/6	y	may = end of corridor 313
284	IIIA W	211/342	212	213	286	2.90	2.25	U168	y, possibly resurfaced	room
306	IIIA W	294	M	293	297	5.60+	2.60?	U/V166	y, plus part of a lower floor	room
307	Exterior	303	337	294	none	8.65	1.15-1.65	U/V166	y	alley
308	Exterior	M	295-6	316	M	3.50+	4.25+	U166	none id	open space
309	IIIA W	294	none	none	295	1.55	1.30	U166	y	foyer?
313	IIIA W	open	297	M	296	0.75	1.60+	U166	y	corridor, may = 282
315	free-standing	circular wall 316	316	316	316	diameter 3.45-3.55	diameter 3.45-3.55	T168 T/U168 balk	2 'cement' floors	oven?
320	IIIB S	319	304	324	322	1.55	2.30?	T168	y	room
325	IIIB S	319	322	M	M	1.75+	3.50+	T168	none id	area
326	IIIB S	324	304	M	322?	1.70?	1.45+	T168	none id	area
338	unknown	M	M	M	337	1.75+	2.50+	V166	none id	area

[a] y = yes

[b] M = missing data (generally because a balk intrudes)

[c] On this chart, the designation "room" is applied only if at least three walls are known; if less than 3 walls are known, the space is here called an "area."

303, and 294 to determine the nature of the temporal relationships among them. It would appear logical that originally alley 307 led on northward, but subsequently was blocked by wall 337, turning alley 307 into a cul-de-sac.

North of wall 337 was area 338. Only a small portion of this area was included in our excavation, and it is not known how it related to other B.L. IIIB structures.

Finally, two walls (166 and 167) found during the 1974 season in the southwestern quadrant of V164 can be assigned on stratigraphic grounds to B.L. IIIB, although it was not possible to determine the exact architectural relationship of these walls to the B.L. IIIB structures. The V164 group may have been a portion of structure 2.

Walls 166 and 167 appear to have formed two sides of a room (164). There was probably a doorway through wall 167 to the east. Trash pit 165, north of wall 166, is also assigned on stratigraphic grounds to B.L. IIIB.

B.L. IIIA
(Figure 14, Tables 5, 6)

During B.L. IIIA, the west and east units of structure 1 continued in use in their original architectural forms. (See the discussion "final abandonment of B.L. III" below.) Other sectors of the complex were extensively remodelled, as the present section discusses.

THE NORTH UNIT

At some time after the north unit of structure 1 was built, its rooms were abandoned and their walls almost totally torn down to make room for new construction. During this remodelling, the north unit was converted from interior to exterior space. In the center of the area, a large mud-brick platform (263) was constructed. The bricks used measured about 20 x 20 x 8 cm, a standard B.L. III size, different from the brick sizes used in B.L. II construction. The space needed for sunken oven 223 was carefully created during the erection of the platform; most of the remainder of the platform was built with rather irregularly laid mud bricks set both horizontally and vertically. There is no doubt, however, that feature 263 was a planned architectural feature; the south edge of the platform was neatly aligned and the north face, though less straight, was mud plastered.

Between the south edge of platform 263 and the north face of wall 238, a series of rather ephemeral surfaces were laid down during B.L. IIIA. These surfaces were also traced in the southwest quadrant of V168.

North of platform 263, a probable exterior surface was traced in the northeast quadrant of V168. Trash dump 241 was found on this surface.

THE SOUTH UNIT

During B.L. IIIA, the entire south unit of structure 1 and the adjacent but free-standing feature 315 were levelled. This sector became an exterior zone contiguous with area 308. Plastered sherd concentration 302 (Plate 8b) was built on a B.L. IIIA surface south of walls 286-304 and trash pit 299 was dug.

AREAS 308-307

Two features found in area 308, i.e. trash dump 301 and trash pit 285, are considered on stratigraphic grounds to have been used during the B.L. IIIA occupation. Miscellaneous feature 321 was probably deposited in alley 307 at this time.

V164 GROUP

Trash pit 163, east of wall 167, can be considered B.L. IIIA for purposes of analysis. Room 164 itself does not appear to have been altered in any way.

FINAL ABANDONMENT OF B.L. III

At least some portions of the west and east units of structure 1 were used right up to the time of construction of B.L. II. No intermediate stratum 9 surfaces or features intervened between most rooms of these units and the surface on which B.L. II was built. (The exceptions are the 215-219 annex to the east unit and room 284 of the west unit. The blocking of doorway 224 indicates the abandonment of the annex rooms at some point prior to the abandonment of room 225. Furthermore, burial 278 was deposited in room 219 prior to its closure or at the moment of general levelling of B.L. III. Burial 221 is a stratum 9 feature in the uppermost fill of room 284.)

Room 225 was never allowed to fill up with trash. It was kept spotlessly clean until the moment when it was filled neatly and completely with packing bricks and the upper portions of its walls knocked down to create a level surface on which to build B.L. II. (Some of the packing bricks had burned faces, but the lack of consistent orientation of these indicates that these faces were not burned *in situ*.)

Although only room 225 was completely filled with packing bricks, scattered sets of packing bricks were used to help level the remainder of the area occupied by the east and west units of B.L. III. Two ceramic vessels were found smashed flat on top of such packing in the east unit, just under the bricks of the B.L. II floor (lots U168-80, 95). Alley 307 was also filled in with haphazardly laid packing bricks at this time. It would thus appear that B.L. II dates to a time *immediately* following the occupation of B.L. IIIA.

Building Level II

OVERVIEW

Building Level II (Figure 15; Tables 7, 8) was the largest architectural level exposed at TUV. A continuous mazelike arrangement of rooms was found in T166, T168, U164, U166, U168, V166 and V168, covering an area of about 415 m^2 (not counting balks). The free-standing round structure (feature 169) in V164 and an associated surface south of that building (totaling c. 40 m^2) are also attributable through stratigraphic analysis to B.L. II.

The main B.L. II complex has a rectilinear plan with room corners consistently oriented to the cardinal points. (This change from the orientation of the B.L. III architecture persists into B.L. I as well.) Substantial weight-bearing walls divide the main B.L. II complex into three units here designated east, north, and southwest.

The east and north units were built at the same time. Walls 20, 21, and 264 were completely bonded at their juncture; thus the two major walls of the east unit were not only contemporaneous with one another but also with an important wall of the north unit. Preplanning of the form of these units is also indicated by hearth 29 of the north unit. Space had been carefully left for this feature in the west side of east-unit wall 21.

It is possible, however, that not all the rooms of the north unit were defined at this time, for no partition walls or other features in the north unit were bonded with wall 21.

Construction of the southwest unit apparently followed the construction of the east and north units. No walls of the southwest unit were bonded with either wall 91 of the north unit or wall 21 of the east unit. It is impossible, however, to determine from this observation the length of time which elapsed between the building of the first two units and the abutment of the walls of the southwest unit against them. The lag could have been only that of a day or so, or one of years. The former alternative seems more likely, given that all three units are built in part on the specially levelled and brick-packed areas of B.L. III.

Preservation of this building level was generally very good. Many features such as hearths and storage bins were discovered; many doorways were identifiable. Intrusive trench 76 (Plate 10b), however, seriously disturbed a number of rooms in the north and southwest units.

UNIT BY UNIT DESCRIPTION

THE EAST UNIT (rooms/areas 30, 174, 175, 178, 188; 183?)
(Plate 8a)

The east unit of B.L. II lay east of wall 21, the longest continuous stretch of wall uncovered at TUV. Although this wall was well preserved to a height above that of any feasible doorsill, there are no known doors through it. Unless there was a door in a balk or in the zone disturbed by intrusive Sassanian burial pit 196, wall 21 effectively divided the east unit from the other two units of the main complex.

The major room within the east unit, area 30, was the only definite example of a courtyard at TUV. It was the largest bounded space uncovered at the site. From its size and from the characteristics of its surface, it must be interpreted as having been unroofed. The courtyard contained only one feature, at the middle of its southern end: cobble feature 288. Burial pit 196 (from stratum 1), well 195 (from stratum 4) and well 199 (from stratum 4) were intrusive.[2] It is not known how entry was made into this courtyard. Doors must either lie in the balks or in the unexcavated northeastern corner of the room.

South of courtyard 30 lay room 174, which contained no built-in features. No doorways were identified for this room, but its bordering walls (except for those it shared with room 30) were not preserved to a substantial height; doorsills would not be identifiable.

Room 175, area 178, and area 188 were probably corners of small rooms in the east unit. Area 188 contained plastered sherd concentration 182 (Plate 8 a).

It is probable that area 183 (east of wall 179 and north of wall 180) was not part of the east unit but rather an exterior zone. This conclusion is supported by the large amount of medium-sized rocks piled up in a strip about 30 cm wide and buttressing against the east face of wall 179. Such reinforcement against erosion presumably would not be necessary had area 183 been an interior zone.

No features were found in area 183, other than a few fragmentary wall stubs (184, 185, 186) near the east margin of T168. The purpose of those walls was not clear. Traces of a very badly preserved second (later) surface within area 183 were also observed in T168.

---

2. It is tempting to speculate, though, that wells 195 and 199 were *first* dug from B.L. II, given their appropriate locations with respect to courtyard 30. See the description of these wells in the second half of this chapter.

THE SOUTHWEST UNIT (rooms/areas 102, 103, 104, 118, 126, 127, 128, 129, 138, 139, 141, 143, 386)
(Plates 4a, 11a)

This unit consisted of an enigmatic warren of rooms, including a series of segregated spaces so small that it is difficult to imagine the functions for which they might have been intended. Most of the walls of the unit were not preserved to a height great enough to allow identification of doorsills.

Nothing can be said about the nature of area 143, at the extreme west of the unit, not even whether this was an interior or an exterior space, for this area was seriously affected by erosion along the western slope of the mound.

The westernmost definite room in the southwest unit was room 141, which had no associated built-in features. East of that room was a series of five small and very narrow rectangular spaces (areas 127, 128, 129, 138, 139). A pebble-hearth feature (137) with an associated plastered bin opened off the southernmost cubicle.

Room 126, east of the cubicles, was long and relatively narrow; it may have been a corridor providing access to the partitioned zones. It contained no built-in features.

Three squarish rooms lay east of room 126. The northern room (118) and the southern room (104) contained no features; the middle room (103) had a storage bin (131) at its north end and a cobble feature (353) on the floor in front of the bin (Plate 11a). There was a narrow doorway from room 126 into room 104.

Room 102 was the easternmost room of the southwest unit. It contained no built-in features, but pit 132 was associated with the lower of two floors in this room.

Finally, enigmatic area 386 (west of room 118 and north of the cubicles) contained pit 130 and several low, narrow partitions.

No doorways are known to exist between any room in this unit and either the north or east units.

THE NORTH UNIT (rooms/areas 25, 26, 27, 31, 32, 33, 36, 38, 39, 43, 45, 47, 69, 71, 75, 109, 115, 362, 363, 364)
(Plates 4a, 5, 6a, 9b, 10b)

The north unit consisted of a complex arrangement of small rooms created by the erection of many narrow partition walls. This unit differed from the other units of B.L. II by the higher incidence of built-in features (e.g. hearths, bins) found there. Unfortunately the whole western tier of rooms (109, 362, 363, 364) was seriously disturbed by intrusive trench 76 (Plate 10b).

In reviewing the north unit, discussion will begin with the south end and move generally northward.

Room 109 (Plate 4a) spanned the full width of the north unit at its south end. There was a low bench around much of this room, but the room contained no other features. It is not clear how entry was made into the room, although there may have been a door in the northeast corner where the bench did not appear to be present.

If there were a door in that area, one could have passed through it into room 115, a small, squarish room with a domed, raised-box hearth (344) built into the west end of its north wall.

It is not possible to determine where the other doors of room 115 were located. There may have been a door into either or both of rooms 31 and 71.

Room 31, north of both room 115 and room 71, had no built-in features. In both rooms 31 and 115, however, a double layer of small rocks (9-20 cm in diameter) was found stacked directly against the west face of wall 21 at its base.

Room 71 was west of room 115, south of room 31, and connected to the latter room by a doorway. Room 71 also had no built-in features.

One could leave room 71 to the west through doorway 392 into a larger room, 69. This room had an elaborate hearth installation (68) built into the middle of its west wall. (Hearth 68 was a double hearth, also opening into room 363.)

West of room 69 lay a tier of three rooms (362, 363, and 364) which were considerably destroyed by intrusive trench 76. The southernmost room (362) was smaller than the others and may have been an alcove. The center room, 363, contained the second part of hearth 68 (see above) in the middle of its east wall. Room 364, the northernmost room of this tier, contained hearth 73.

Returning to room 69, one could exit via a wide doorway (72) north into a small, square room (75). This room contained no features. The V166/168 balk prevented the identification of other doors for this room. Movement may have been possible into either or both of rooms 45 and 27 from room 75.

Room 27, southeast of room 75, contained hearth 51, segregated from the remainder of the room by low mud (brick?) dividers.

East of room 27 lay two small alcoves. Area 25 was a small space containing storage bin 28, formed by low mud (brick?) curbings. Area 26 lay north of alcove 25 and contained hearth 52, similar to the hearth found in room 27.

North of alcove 26 was yet another alcove, feature 33. This entire space was an elaborate cobble hearth. The west wall (37) of the space may have had air vents built into it.

Immediately west of feature 33 was a small partitioned zone (32) with no associated features.

North of area 32 was room 36, which in contrast was very rich in features (Plate 5). Alcove 38, in the southeast corner, contained a storage vessel set into a

TABLE 7
WALLS OF BUILDING LEVEL II

Reference number	Unit (room-block)	Grid reference	Orientation	Areas separated	Known doors[a]	East end[b]	West end[b]	Total width	Number of courses preserved	Mud plaster[a]	White lime plaster[a]	Brick sizes[c] (pattern?)	Comments
20	E	V168	NW-SE	39/30	n	Balk	bonds 21	70	5-6	n	n	O/P 18 x 36; 36 x 36; 35 x 35 x 9	
21	E	V168 U168 U166 T166	SW-NE	N & SW units/ E unit	n	bonds 20	?	70	4-5	y	n	O/P 35x35x8½ 18x35x8½	
22	N	V168	W-E	26/25	n	abuts 21	abuts 23	18	1	n	n	A 18 x 36	
23	N	V168	SW-NE	27/26-25	n	bonds 34	abuts 24	36-54	2	--	n	X 36x36; 18x36; 18 x 18; chineh	
24	N	V168	NW-SE	27/31	n	Balk	Balk	30-31	2-5	y	n	F/E 37 x 31 x 8½	possible foundation of stones and packed mud
34	N	V168	NW-SE	45/75 43-32/27 33/26	n	abuts 21	Balk	36-37	2	--	n	F/E 36-7 x 19-20	bonds 23 in middle
35	N	V168	NW-SE	36/32 38/33	n	abuts 21	bonds 382	30	2	y	n	H/E 35 x 30; 18 x 30; 18 x 18?	
37	N	V168	SW-NE	32/33	n	abuts 35	abuts 34	75	4	y	n	complex rows of bricks with air vents	
40	N	V168	NW-SE	36/38	n	abuts 21	abuts 390	40	--	--	n	B 18 x 36	
41	N	V168	SW-NE	45/43	n	abuts 264	bonds 34	40	--	--	n	B 18 x 36	
44	N	V168	SW-NE	43/32	n	abuts 35	abuts 34	36	--	n	n	C 18 x 36	
49	N	V168	SW-NE	47/39	391?	M	abuts 264	36	--	--	n	E 18 x 36 36 x 36	door 391 is alluded to in field notes but does not appear on plan
56	N	V168	SW-NE	75/27	n	abuts 34	M	36	--	--	n	D 36 x 36	
62	N	V166	SW-NE	outside/ 109-362-363-364	n	M	abuts 91	54	--	--	n	I 18 x 36	
66	N	V166	SW-NE	362-363-364/69-75	n	M	abuts 113	?	--	--	n	(?) 18 x 36 36 x 36	seriously disturbed by trench 76
70	N	V166	SW-NE	69/71-31	392	abuts 343	bonds 113	36	2	--	n	D 36 x 36	

TABLE 7—*Continued*

Reference number	Unit (room-block)	Grid reference	Orientation	Areas separated	Known doors[a]	East end[b]	West end[b]	Total width	Number of courses preserved	Mud plaster[a]	White lime plaster[a]	Brick sizes[c] (pattern?)	Comments
91	N	U166	NW-SE	N/SW units	n	abuts 21	abuts 62	36	5	y in room 118	*	D/B 36 x 36 18 x 36	bonds 106 in middle, also 105
105	SW	U166	SW-NE	104-103-118/102	n	bonds 91	M	36	1	y, in 118	*	F 18 x 36 36 x 36	middle bonds 117
106	SW	U166	SW-NE	126/104-103; 386/118	393	bonds 91	M	36	--	y, in 118	*	D 36 x 36	
107	SW	U166	NW-SE	104/103	n	abuts 105	abuts 106	36	--	--	n	D 36 x 36	
108	SW	U166	SW-NE	127-128 129/126	n	abuts 121	M	54	--	--	n	N 18 x 36	
110	N	U/V166	runs around interior of room 109		(NE corner ?)	abuts 113	abuts 91, 62	54	2	--	n	L/M 18 x 36 36 x 36	Bench
113	N	U/V166	NW-SE	362-69-71-115/109	(SE?)	M	abuts 62	36	2-3	--	n	F/G 18 x 36 36 x 36	
114	N	U166	SW-NE	71/115	n	M	abuts 113	36	3	--	n	F/E/D 18 x 36 36 x 36	
117	SW	U166	NW-SE	118/103	n	bonds 105	abuts 106	36	3	y	*	F/E/D 18 x 36 36 x 36	
119	SW	U166/64	NW-SE	128/129	n	abuts 108	abuts 136	36	--	--	n	G 18 x 36	
120	SW	U166	NW-SE	128/127	n	abuts 108	M	36	--	--	n	C 18 x 36	
121	SW	U166/64	NW-SE	141-127-126/386	n	abuts 106	M	54	--	--	n	I 18 x 36	
122	SW	U166	NW-SE	within 386	n	abuts 106	M	18	--	--	n	A 18 x 36	line is interrupted by pit 130
123	SW	U166	SW-NE	within 386	n	abuts 124	abuts 122	18	--	--	n	A 18 x 36	
124	SW	U166	NW-SE	within 386	n	abuts 123	M	18	--	--	n	A 18 x 36	
133	SW	U164	NW-SE	138/129	n	M	bonds 136	54	--	--	n	J 18 x 36	
134	SW	U164	NW-SE	139/138	n	bonds 145	abuts 136	36	--	--	n	B 18 x 36	
135	SW	U164	NW-SE	139/?	n	bonds 145	abuts 136	18-36	--	--	n	B + A 18 x 36	
136	SW	U164	SW-NE	141/139, 138, 129, 128, 127	n	M	M	54	--	--	n	I 18 x 36	bonded in middle to wall 124

TABLE 7—*Continued*

Reference number	Unit (room-block)	Grid reference	Orientation	Areas separated	Known doors[a]	East end[b]	West end[b]	Total width	Number of courses preserved	Mud plaster[a]	White lime plaster[a]	Brick sizes[c] (pattern?)	Comments
140	SW	U164	SW-NE	143/141	n	abuts 121	M	36	--	--	n	B 18 x 36	
145	SW	U164	SW-NE	139/?	n	bonds 134	M	36	--	--	n	B? 18 x 36	
154	round bldg.	V164	curves	157-158-159/162	n	M	M	70	3	--	n	Q/R/S 28 x 28 28 x 14	
160	round bldg.	V164	SW-NE	158/157	n	M	bonds 154?	42	2	--	n	L/M 28 x 14 28 x 28	
161	round bldg.	V164	SW-NE	157/159	n	M	bonds 154	42	2	--	n	L/M 28 x 28 28 x 14	
172	E	T166 T168	NW-SE	30/174	n	abuts 179	M	54	--	--	n	K 18 x 36	
173	E	T166	NW-SE	174/175-178	n	M	abuts 21	36	--	--	n	D 36 x 36	
176	E	T166	SW-NE	175/178	n	abuts 173	M	36	--	--	n	D 36 x 36	
179	E	T/U168	SW-NE	30/183 174/188	n	M	M	72	5	y	y	O/P 36 x 36 18 x 36	middle bonds 180
180	E	T168	NW-SE	183/188	n	M	bonds 179	54	2	--	n	M/L 18 x 36 36 x 36	
184	E	T168	SW-NE	within 183	n	M	M	18	1	--	n	A 18 x 36	
185	E	T168	NW-SE	within 183	n	M	bonds 184 in middle	18	1	--	n	A 18 x 36	
186	E	T168	NW-SE	within 183	n	M	M	72	1	--	n	T 18 x 36 36 x 36	
207	N	U168	NW-SE	31/115	n	abuts 21	M	36	1	--	n	C 18 x 36	
264	N	V168	NW-SE	47/45-43 39/36	n	bonds 20	M	36	--	--	n	B 18 x 36	
335	N	V166	NW-SE	31/71	394	bonds 114	door	36	3	--	n	? (stub) 36 x 36	
343	N	V166	NW-SE	75/69	72	abuts 70	bonds 66	36-54	2	--	n	C/L 18 x 36 36 x 36	upper course appears narrower than basal course
382	N	V168	SW-NE	43/36	n	abuts 264	bonds 35	18	--	--	n	A 18 x 36	

TABLE 7—*Continued*

Reference number	Unit (room-block)	Grid reference	Orientation	Areas separated	Known doors[a]	East end[b]	West end[b]	Total width	Number of courses preserved	Mud plaster[a]	White lime plaster[a]	Brick sizes[c] (pattern?)	Comments
387	N	V166	NW-SE	363/362	n	M	abuts 62	36	--	--	n	D 36 x 36	
388	N	V166	NW-SE	364/363	n	M	abuts 62	36	--	--	n	D 36 x 36	
389	N	V166	NW-SE	364/?	n	M	M	36	--	--	n	D 36 x 36	

* The room 118 plaster was described as gray; it may have been weathered lime plaster over *kagel*.

[a] n = no, y = yes.

[b] M = missing data (generally because a balk intrudes).

[c] For explanation of brick laying patterns, see Figure 11.

plastered pit (Plate 9b). In the northeast corner was cobble hearth 29, with pit 53 immediately to its west. The northwest corner held domed oven 54, while casual hearth 55 lay in the southwest portion of the room.

Room 43 (Plate 6a) was a partitioned area west of room 36. Storage bin 42 was found in the southwestern part of room 43. This room contained two floors, separated by about 15 cm of fill. When the lower floor was in use, rooms 43 and 36 had been one continuous space. Wall 44 was built on the higher floor of room 43.

Room 45, west of room 43, contained raised-box hearth 48, which was probably built into the (unexcavated) southern wall of the room.

North of rooms 45, 43, and 36 were two areas which are difficult to interpret. Area 47 was very strange, for it had a layer of cobbles covering its entire surface. The fact that its south wall, 264, was very thin does suggest that area 47 may also have been part of the north unit of the B.L. II complex.

A doorway was discovered in the wall separating area 47 from area 39 to its east. Area 39 may have been an exterior zone, but unfortunately this cannot be proven. Erosion has removed any continuation of B.L. II phenomena to the north into W168 and X168.

THE V164 ROUND STRUCTURE (feature 169) (Plate 4b)

The round building in the northeast corner of V164 was a free-standing structure, assigned to B.L. II through stratigraphic analysis. An erosion gully ran through the area between feature 169 and wall 62 (the west wall of the north unit of the main complex).

The round structure contained three rooms (157, 158, and 159) separated by narrow walls. There were no associated built-in features in any of these rooms.

ABANDONMENT OF B.L. II

In contrast to the abandonment of B.L. III, no B.L. II rooms were filled with packing bricks after abandonment. The architecture was levelled, apparently largely by erosion, before B.L. I was constructed. It is not known how much time elapsed in the interval, but a longer interval is implied than that between B.L. IIIA and B.L. II. When built, B.L. I had the same orientation as B.L. II but a totally different ground plan.

Building Level I

OVERVIEW

Architectural remains of B.L. I (Figure 16; Tables 9, 10) were preserved only in U166, U168, V168, and the southeast corner of V166, covering no more than 200 m² when balks are excluded from the calculation. Preservation of this level coincided closely with the preserved extent of stratum 2, the pebble layer (see Fig-

TABLE 8
ROOMS AND AREAS OF B.L. II, TUV OPERATION*

Reference number	Unit (room-block)	West wall[a]	North wall[a]	East wall[a]	South wall[a]	NW-SE dimensions	SW-NE dimensions	Grid reference	Floor identified	Comments[b]
25	N	23	22	21	24	1.30	0.65-1.25	V168	y	alcove
26	N	23	34	21	22	1.30	0.80-1.50	V168	y	alcove
27	N	56	34	23	24	2.75	2.35	V168	y	room
30	E	21	20	179	172	4.75	16.80	V/U/T/168 U/T166	2 floors	courtyard
31	N	70	24	21	207	4.50	2.10	V166/8 U168	--	room
32	N	44	35	37	34	1.75	0.95	V168	y	alcove
33	N	37	35	21	34	0.60	0.90	V168	pebble layer	alcove this may be an oven—see text
36	N	382	264	21	40-35	1.90, 3.60	2.20 0.95	V168	y	room
38	N	390	40	21	35	1.40	0.90	V168	--	alcove contains a vessel set in a pit
39	outside? N?	49	M	M	264-20	5.60+	2.50+	V168	possibly 2 surfaces	area
43	N	41	264	382-44	34	1.15	3.40	V168	2 floors	room
45	N	M	264	41	34	2.10+	3.50	V168	y	room
47	N	M	M	49	264	3.50+	2.50+	V168	pebble surface	area
69	N	66	343	70	113	2.25	4.20	U/V166	2 floors	room
71	N	70	335	114	113	1.35	1.75	V/U166	floor	room
75	N	66	34	56	343	2.30	2.35	V166/8	2 floors	room
102	SW	105	91	21	M	2.05	8.50+	U/T166	2 floors	room pit 132— lower floor
103	SW	106	117	105	107	1.70	2.35	U166	y	room
104	SW	106	107	105	M	1.70	2.40+	U166	y	room
109	N	62	113	21	91	8.50	0.90-1.40	U/V166	y	room partly disturbed by trench 76; contains benches 110, 111
115	N	114	207	21	113	2.80	1.75	U166/8	--	room
118	SW	106	91	105	117	1.70	2.20	U166	y, mud plastered	room
126	SW	108	121	106	M	1.15	5.00+	U166	--	corridor?
127	SW	136	121	108	120	2.75	0.65	U166	y	cubicle seriously disturbed by trench 76
128	SW	136	120	108	119	2.75	0.70	U164/6	y	cubicle seriously disturbed by trench 76
129	SW	136	119	108	133	2.75	0.65	U164/6	--	cubicle

TABLE 8—*Continued*

Reference number	Unit (room-block)	West wall[a]	North wall[a]	East wall[a]	South wall[a]	NW-SE dimensions	SW-NE dimensions	Grid reference	Floor identified	Comments[b]
139	SW	136	134	145	135	2.10	0.75	U164	--	cubicle
141	SW	140	121	136	M	2.15	5.15+	U164	y	room
143	SW	M	121	140	M	?	4.60+	U164	traces close to wall 140	area
174	E	21	172	179	173	5.10?	2.90	T166/8	y	room
175	E	21	173	176	M	1.70	1.45+	T166	y	room
178	E	176	173	M	M	1.35+	1.05+	T166	y	room
183	outside	179	M	184?	180	4.25?	13.20+	U/T168	2 floors	area
188	E	179	180	M	M	1.85+	1.25+	T168	y	area
362	N	62	387	66	113	1.50+	1.05	V166	--	room severely disturbed by trench 76
363	N	62	388	66	387	1.50+	2.85	V166	--	room severely disturbed by trench 76
364	N	62	389	66	388	1.35+	2.25	V166	--	room severely disturbed by trench 76
386	SW	M	91	106	121	5.60+	2.25	U166	--	room? contains strange partitions and pit 130

[a] M = missing data (generally because a balk intrudes).

[b] On this table, the designation "room" is applied only if at least three walls are known; if less than three walls are known, the space is here called an "area."

ure 3B-C). Elsewhere erosion removed all traces of B.L. I walls and surfaces.

The general orientation of the architecture in B.L. I was identical to that of B.L. II. Room corners were oriented toward the magnetic cardinal points. Most of the walls formed part of a building (structure 1) which was separated on the northeast by alleyway 16 from a second building (structure 2) represented by two fragments of rooms.

To simplify discussion, structure 1 has been divided into three units: northwest, south, and east. These designations are not intended to represent discrete constructional units. All of structure 1 may have been built at the same time. This could not be established, however, because preservation of this level was poor. Walls were preserved only to a height of one or two courses, making study of bonding patterns difficult. Doorsills could not be identified, and any features which may

have originally been built into the upper walls have vanished. Wells 195 and 199, however, are associated with this level.

UNIT BY UNIT DESCRIPTION

THE NORTHWEST UNIT OF STRUCTURE 1 (rooms/areas 9, 10, 11, 12, 65, 87)

This unit was enigmatic, containing a number of relatively long and narrow rooms (10, 11, 12; 9 may have been the corner of another such room). Most of rooms 9 and 65 had been removed through erosion. The western limits of this unit are thus not known. The recovered portion of the plan somewhat resembles the layout of a storage magazine.

TABLE 9
WALLS OF BUILDING LEVEL I

Reference number	Unit (room-block)	Grid reference	Orientation	Areas separated	Known doors[a]	East end[b]	West end[b]	Total width (cm)	Number courses preserved	Mud plaster?	Lime plaster?[a]	Brick sizes[c]	Comments
2a	NW, E	V168	NW-SE	16/9-10-11-12-13-204	n	M	M	72	2	--	n	O/P 18 x 36 36 x 36	Wall 2 is a double wall with a north of b
2b	NW, E	V168	NW-SE	16/9-10-11-12-13-204	n	M	M	90	2	--	n	Q/U 18 x 36 36 x 36	
3	NW	V168	SW-NE	10/11	n	abuts 2	M	36	2	--	n	B 18 x 36	
4	NW	U/V168	SW-NE	11/12	n	abuts 2	M	36	2	--	n	D 36 x 36	
5	NW	U/V168	SW-NE	12/13	n	abuts 2	abuts 85	36	2	--	n	D + B 36 x 36 18 x 16	
7a	structure B	V168	NW-SE	16/355-356	n	M	M	72-108	1	--	n	O + V 36 x 36	wall 7 is also a double wall
7b	structure B	V168	NW-SE	16/355-356	n	M	M	72	1	--	n	O 36 x 36	
8	NW	V168	SW-NE	9/10	n	abuts 2	M	36	2	--	n	C 18 x 36	
57	NW	V166	NW-SE	?/65-11	n	M	M	36	1	--	n	D 36 x 36	
58	NW	V166	SW-NE	65/11	n	abuts 57	abuts 85	54	--	--	n	M 18 x 36 36 x 36	
81	S	U166	NW-SE	87/88-89-90	n	M	M	36	1	--	n	B + D 36 x 36 18 x 36	
82	S	U166	SW-NE	89/90	351	door	abuts 84	36	1	--	n	D 36 x 36	
83	S	U166	SW-NE	88/89	n	abuts 81	abuts 84	36	1	--	n	D 36 x 36	
84	S	U166	NW-SE	88-89-90/exterior?	n	abuts 86	M	108*	--	--	n	W* 18 x 36 36 x 36	* this wall's south edge is partly eroded
85	NW E	U168 V/U166	NW-SE	65-11-12-202/87-181	n	abuts 205	M	36-54	1	--	n	D + L 18 x 36 36 x 36	
86	S	U166	SW-NE	90/181?	n	M	abuts 84	36	--	--	n	D 36 x 36	
200	E	U168	NW-SE	202/203	n	abuts 205	abuts 5	36	--	--	n	D 36 x 36	
201	E	U168	NW-SE	13-204/203	n	abuts 205	M	54	--	--	n	L 18 x 36 36 x 36	
205	E	U168	SW-NE	181-202-203-204/354-357	n	M	M	54	--	--	n	I 18 x 36	
206	E	U168	SW-NE	13/204	n	M	abuts 201	18	--	--	n	A 18 x 36	

TABLE 9—*Continued*

Reference number	Unit (room-block)	Grid reference	Orientation	Areas separated	Known doors[a]	East end[b]	West end[b]	Total width (cm)	Number courses[b]	Mud plaster?	Lime plaster?[a]	Brick sizes[c]	Comments
349	E	U168	NW-SE	354/357	n	M	abuts 205	36	--	--	n	B 18 x 36	
350	structure B	V168	SW-NE	355/356	n	M	abuts 7	36	--	--	n	D 36 x 36	

[a] n = no

[b] M = missing data (generally because a balk intrudes).

[c] For explanation of brick-laying patterns, see Figure 11.

The northwest unit was separated from the south unit by another long and narrow room, 87. The field supervisor who excavated this room felt that it was a corridor opening into room 181 on the east. Unfortunately this could not be positively demonstrated due to the presence of the balk and an intrusive Sassanian burial pit (196) at the point where the corridor and room 181 met.

There may have been small pilasters mid-way along the preserved length of corridor 87. A fragmentary mud brick projected north from wall 81, while opposite it another fragmentary brick projected south from wall 85. The field supervisor described the space between these fragments as a doorway (352). Given the poor state of preservation of the architecture, and the occurrence of these partial bricks in a line representing the continuation of the line of wall 83, it is possible that the corridor may originally have been blocked at this point. There was simply not enough brick preserved to assess this question adequately.

A very well preserved floor was traced on both sides of the possible doorway for the entire length of area 87. Pit 101 originated from this floor just west of the "doorway," making the corridor interpretation less likely. (A pit at the end of a room near a blocking wall seems more logical than one in a passageway.) The distinction made here (to simplify discussion) between the northwest unit and the south unit may thus be a totally artificial distinction with no functional basis in reality.

THE SOUTH UNIT OF STRUCTURE 1
(rooms/areas 88, 89, 90, 181)
(Plate 9a)

From west to east, the south unit consisted of rooms 88, 89, 90 and 181. Part of room 88 was removed by erosion, and it is thus not known whether that room was the westernmost in the complex. Rooms 89 and 91

were connected by doorway 351, which had no doorsill. No other doorways were identified in this unit. Only room 181 contained a feature, well 199 (Plate 9a).

THE EAST UNIT OF STRUCTURE 1 (rooms/areas 13, 202, 203, 204, 354?, 357?)

North of room 181 was the east unit. Rooms 202 and 13 were small, while 204 was only an alcove. None of these areas contained any preserved features. Room 203 was larger, roughly square in shape, and contained well 195.

East of wall 205 the plan of the building was lost through erosion. A small wall stub (349) separated area 354 to the north and area 357 to the south, but it could not be determined if both these zones were necessarily interior spaces.

STRUCTURE 2 AND ALLEY 16

Rooms 355 and 356 were part of structure 2, which lay mostly beyond the bounds of our excavation to the northeast. Part of structure 2 may have originally existed in W168 and X168. Erosion has removed all traces of standing walls in that zone, but some brick fall possibly derived from B.L. I was recovered in W168.

Rooms 355 and 356 (which contained no features) can be interpreted as distinct from structure 1 because of the character of their shared southern wall (7). Wall 7 was an exceptionally thick "double" wall, two separate brick units constructed back to back with mortar between them.

Lying south of wall 7 was a long, narrow space (16) which also had a "double" wall forming its other side. This latter wall (2) appears to be the northern boundary of structure 1. The long and narrow space between the two very thick "double" walls (area 16) can thus be interpreted as an alleyway between two buildings (Plate 6b).

ABANDONMENT OF B.L. I

No B.L. I rooms were filled with packing bricks after abandonment. A period of substantial erosion (represented by stratum 3) appears to have destroyed all but one or two courses of the B.L. I walls. After an unknown lapse of time, this erosional episode was ended with the deposition of the pebble/cobble layer, stratum 2.

Features at TUV

Overview

The various types of features found at TUV are discussed in this section. For each type, the best example is described in detail and additional occurrences of the category summarized. Discussion in this chapter is limited to morphological description plus consideration of the general category of activity with which each feature type might be connected. The features are discussed as part of site structure in chapter 7. The feature categories are:

1. pyrotechnic features   [possible functions]
   a. raised-box hearths   [heating, cooking]
   b. gravel hearths
   c. plastered
      concentrations
   d. cobble hearths
   e. casual hearths
   f. domed ovens
   g. sunken oven
   h. ash pits
   i. hearths of unclear
      type

2. pits
   a. wells   [water procurement; followed by trash disposal]
   b. plastered pits   [storage; followed by trash disposal]
   c. trash pits   [trash disposal]
   d. burial pits   [burial]
   e. miscellaneous pits   [?]
3. drainage features   [drainage]
4. foundation trench   [architectural construction]
5. bins   [storage]
6. cobble features not
   associated with
   burning   [?]
7. trash dumps (on
   exterior surfaces)   [trash disposal]
8. burials   [disposal of the dead]
9. miscellaneous features   [?]

Pyrotechnic Features

(Figure 17)

This general category includes all those features which appear to have been connected with the use of fire. This category was the most numerous of all TUV feature types, and has been subdivided here into a set of constructional varieties.

RAISED-BOX HEARTHS

Hearth 227
(Plate 7a)

Hearth 227 (built originally in stratum 13c of B.L. IIIB) was the best preserved example of the five raised-box hearths excavated. This feature was set into the middle of room 225's east wall (243) and had three construction phases.

The earliest construction phase was also the most elaborate. The hearth consisted of a raised box (58 x 48 cm) with a lower, flat, mud-plastered surface in front and to the right of the box. The raised box slanted down slightly towards the room; incised in the central anterior portion of its top was a very slight channel reaching the box's front edge at a point directly above a cruciblelike cup. This cup was built partly into the lower surface, directly against the front wall of the raised box. This channel-cup arrangement suggests that some substance was heated on the surface of the raised box and a run-off product collected in the cuplike feature below.

The original phase of hearth 227 was not sectioned by excavation. There is no evidence indicating where the fire was built in this type of hearth; it may be that the fire was built on top of the raised box and, once the box was thoroughly heated, the ashes then were swept off onto the lower surface and the box top used as a griddle. Both the raised box and the lower surface were plastered with a hard mud plaster but neither showed

THE PROTO-ELAMITE SETTLEMENT AT TUV

TABLE 10

ROOMS AND AREAS OF B.L. I, TUV OPERATION

Reference number	Room-block	West wall[a]	North wall[a]	East wall[a]	South wall[a]	NW-SE dimensions	SW-NE dimensions	Grid reference	Floor identified?	Comments[b]
9	NW	M	2	8	57?	0.70+	0.60+	V168	y	area
10	NW	8	2	3	57?	1.90	3.00+	V168	y	room
11	NW	58-57-3	2	4	85	4.15,1.50	2.35,6.70	U/V166 U/V168	y	L-shaped room
12	NW	4	2	5	57	1.40-1.50	6.70	U/V168	y	room
13	E	5	2	206	201	2.50	1.45	U/V168	y	room
16	outside?	M	7	M	2	11.25+	1.90	V168	--	alley between structures IA and IB
65	NW	M	57	58	85	0.90+	2.25	V166	poor surface	room
87	--	M	85	?	81	7.50+	1.10	U/V166	y	corridor(?) between NW & S units of IA
88	S	M	81	83	84	3.50+	3.25	U166	y	room
89	S	83	81	82	84	1.40	3.15	U166	--	room
90	S	82	81	86	84	1.50	3.10	U166	--	room
181	S?	86	85	205	M	3.70	5.00+	U166/8	y	room contains pit 199
202	E	5	200	205	85	3.60	1.20	U168	y	room
203	E	5	201	205	200	3.55	3.05	U168	y	room contains pit 195
204	E	206	2	205	201	0.85	1.45	U168	y	alcove
354	outside? E?	205	M	M	349	--	--	U168	--	area
355	IB	M	M	350	7	3.70+	2.50+	V168	--	area
356	IB	350	M	M	7	1.55+	2.25+	V168	--	area
357	outside? E? S?	205	349	M	M	--	--	U168	--	area

[a] M = missing data (generally because a balk intrudes).

[b] On this table, the designation "room" is applied only if at least three walls are known; if less than three walls are known, the space here is called an "area."

signs of discoloration from burning. Hearth 227 may have been domed over, with a chimney, but nothing remained of the upper portions of wall 243; thus it is not possible to say definitely what the upper portion of this hearth was like.

In the second phase of hearth 227, the lower surface was packed with cobbles and sherds. A new flat, continuous, mud-plastered surface was created at the level of the original raised-box's top. The function of the feature during this phase is not clear. The elaborate construction of the packing, however, suggests that

heat-retaining properties were desirable. Rocks of about 6 x 10 cm or 10 x 10 cm were placed directly on the lower mud-plastered surface of the first phase. Above the rocks were found (from lowest to highest) layers of medium-sized pebbles, sherds and small pebbles, red-colored earth, and a hardened mud-plaster coating.

In the third phase of hearth 227, the raised box/lower surface arrangement was re-established. A new raised box was built above the hard plastered surface of the intermediate phase, while the remainder of that surface

TABLE 11

RAISED-BOX HEARTHS[a]

Feature number	Stratum	Location	Comments
48	8c	probably west wall of room 45, B.L. II	projecting from balk so placement in wall not directly observed
68	8c	built in wall 66 of B.L. II	double hearth—opens into rooms 69 and 363
273	13c	probably south wall of room 258, B.L. III	largely destroyed by pit 196
344	8c	wall 335, north wall of room 115, B.L. II	part of doming preserved; lies partially within the balk

[a]Hearth 227 is discussed in the text.

served as the lower surface in the new arrangement, although it was eventually re-plastered to repair worn areas. The raised box in this phase was rectangular in shape (35 x 61 cm). Sectioning of this box revealed a layer of cobbles placed directly on the intermediate phase surface and covered by a layer of flat sherds and black grit. The top and sides of these layers were mud plastered to create the finished box.

The other four examples of raised-box hearths at TUV (Table 11) did not have the top channel found in the first phase of hearth 227; nor were they remodelled.

GRAVEL HEARTHS

A gravel hearth is a small discrete area of artificially deposited gravel (very small pebbles) that has been affected by burning. There were only two examples (features 290 and 292) at TUV, both from stratum 10 fill (that is, not directly on the floor) in room 284 (B.L. III west unit). These features appear to have been burned in the locations where they were discovered.

PLASTERED SHERD CONCENTRATIONS
(Plate 8a-b)

Two examples of plastered sherd concentrations were found at TUV: feature 182 from area 188 (B.L. II east unit, stratum 8c) and feature 302 from B.L. IIIA (stratum 11).

The better preserved of the two was feature 182 (Plate 8a), first exposed in the 1974 season but sectioned and removed in 1976. The top surface of the feature was very hard mud plaster; the hardness of the plaster may well have resulted from heat associated with the use of this feature. Because feature 182 was located in the southwest corner of T168 and extended into both the south and west balks of that square, the plan of the fea-

ture is incompletely known. The portion recovered had an irregular oval shape (c. 90 x 95 cm) and sloped up slightly (a rise of 1-2 cm) toward the northwest. The edges of the feature appeared broken and unplastered.

Cross-sectioning of feature 182 revealed the following construction: on the top, 1.5 cm of hard mud plaster with blackened undersurface; in the middle, 2-2.5 cm of earth containing much fine gravel and some pebbles up to 1 cm long, with part of this layer also being blackened; on the bottom, a layer of large flat sherds about 1 cm thick. Generally these sherds did not overlap but lay in a relatively even plane with small spaces between them. The sherds lay not on a deliberately prepared surface but on relatively soft soil.

The entire plan of feature 302 (Plate 8b) was recovered: it was roughly circular in outline (115-120 cm in diameter) and its edges were not plastered. The appearance of the sherd layer in feature 302 suggests that large body sherds had been placed on the ground and smashed flat, creating an arrangement of many small pieces like a jig-saw puzzle.

The plastered sherd concentrations have been assigned to the pyrotechnic category of features for the following reasons: (a) the hardness of the mud plaster covering the features; (b) the black discoloration; (c) the altered nature of the ware of the sherds in these features compared to sherds from other contexts at TUV. The ceramic fabric seems to have been affected through re-exposure of the sherds to heat (personal communication, Bari Hill).

It is not clear, however, whether these features served solely as prepared surfaces on which fires could be built. It is possible that they were intentionally hardened through exposure to fire, and then utilized for another purpose, perhaps as small raised storage platforms.

COBBLE HEARTHS

This category includes all areas of cobbles (large pebbles) that were associated with traces of fire. Unburned cobble features are treated later in this chapter.

There were six burned cobble features at TUV. Each example was different so all will be individually described. In addition, another area of cobbles, feature 353, should be noted here. The 1974 field notes allude to the existence of a "hearth" in room 103 of the B.L. II southwest unit, and an area of cobbles was shown in that position on the plan of B.L. II. However, the failure of the notes to cite evidence for burning associated with this feature has led the present author to defer discussion of feature 353 to the later section on unburned cobble areas.

Hearth 29

This feature (about 85 x 80 x 5 cm) lay in the northeast corner of room 36 (B.L. II north unit) and was inset into wall 21. The feature consisted of a number of fire-cracked stones and black earth fill located within an open-ended rectangle of burned mud plaster overlying the bricks of walls 264, 21, and 40.

Hearth 33

This feature occupied a small alcove of the north unit of B.L. II (stratum 8c). Small cobbles filled a rectangular area (95 x 65 cm) formed by major wall 21 to the east, partition walls 35 and 34 to the north and south respectively, and "wall" 37 to the west.

The construction of "wall" 37 was very peculiar. It was not a wall of solidly laid brick, but had what were apparently air passages left through the brickwork. This suggests that the feature was indeed some kind of an oven or furnace.

The cobbles of the feature were set in a matrix of very soft earth with occasional intermixed lumps of hard, burned clay. Some sherds were also mixed into this matrix. A hard, burned mud-plastered surface was found against the north face of wall 34.

It was not clear how access was gained to feature 33. Wall 21 was preserved to a height sufficient to establish that access from the east was very unlikely. The other three sides of the feature were not preserved to a comparable height. Although the area north of feature 33 was obstructed by feature 38, an access opening could have been built into either the west or south side of the feature.

Hearth 137

This feature opened out of area 139 (B.L. II southwest unit). It consisted of an open-ended square formed by three cut stones; inside this frame of about 55 x 55 cm there were a pebble surface and a number of sherds, with a burned area to the south of them. A plaster bin was also associated with this feature.

Hearth 144

The complete plan of this feature is not known, for it lay in the extreme northeast corner of U164, covered at least 70 x 20 cm, and ran into the east and north balks of that square. It was within area 386 of the B.L. II southwest unit. Hearth 144 was only briefly described in the 1974 field notes, but its construction involved large cobbles and a mud-plastered surface.

Hearth 305

This feature has been assigned to B.L. IIIA stratum 10, for it lay on a concentration of broken mud bricks in the middle of alley 307, well above the stratum 13c surface. The feature consisted of a group of at least 50 large cobbles (15 to 30 cm in diameter), many of which were broken in half. The stones occurred in a single layer intermingled with sherds and some bone. This material was packed into an area of 90 x 70 cm adjacent to the west face of wall 294. Burning, as evidenced by ash, was present throughout the feature, but was most intense in the northeast corner.

Hearth 346

This large cobble feature was in stratum 9, adjacent to the south balk of V168. It consisted of a prepared surface of sherds and cobbles covering 3.5 x 1.8 m and overlain by a hard layer of mud plaster. Many of the stones were blackened and cracked, presumably from heat.

CASUAL HEARTHS

A casual hearth (Voigt 1976) is a large irregular area of burning or ash that is *not* bounded by any structural device such as mud bricks or stones. Although horizontally these burned patches are relatively large, their depth is consistently shallow. Casual hearths presumably result from such activity as the lighting of a brush fire for one or several days on an open patch of ground, just as the TUV workmen lit fires of camel thorn on cold mornings prior to the start of work. Such a patch of ash was called *ja-e atesh* ("place of fire") by the workmen, who did not use this phrase for other kinds of hearths.

A casual hearth is differentiated from an ash pit (in the TUV feature typology) by the definition that the latter has a relatively smaller horizontal extent but a greater vertical depth than a casual hearth.

Very ephemeral ash lenses and pockets were not designated as features in the field, though the presence of such traces was noted in the daily log.

There are 17 casual hearths known from the TUV operation (Table 12).

DOMED OVENS
(Plate 7b)

These flat-bottomed hearths were built into or set against walls and had no raised-box component. These features were definitely domed; an enclosed chamber was thus created in which presumably baking could be done. (It is quite likely that all of the raised-box hearths were also originally domed; certainly hearth 344 was.)

There were only two examples of this kind of pyrotechnic feature at TUV. The first was feature 54 (c. 30 x 20 cm), built on the floor in the northwest corner

TABLE 12

CASUAL HEARTHS

Feature Number	Stratum	Location	Horizontal dimensions	Thickness of burnt residue	Comments
55	7	southwest corner room 36, B.L. II	20 x 30 cm	---	against faces of walls 44 and 35
152	1	southeast V164	55 x 55 cm	---	reddened area
240	10	southern V168 B.L. IIIA	40 x 80 cm (B)[a]	3-6 cm	ash, charcoal, lumps of dark brown clay
254	10	northwest room 250, B.L. IIIA	20 x 12 cm	2.5 cm	reported as in the fill
255	10	southeast V168 B.L. IIIA	50 x 15 cm (B)[a]	2-3 cm	irregular shape
267	12	southwest room 265, B.L. IIIB	20 x 15 cm	---	on an ephemeral surface
268	9	northwest U168	---	---	between levelling B.L. III and laying of B.L. II floor
272	7	central courtyard 30, B.L. II	14 x 23 cm	"shallow"	irregular
314	10	southeast room 306, B.L. IIIA	40 x 40 cm	---	on a poor surface
328	12	north room 320, B.L. IIIB	---	---	under cobble feature 327
331	10	east side of room 258, B.L. IIIA	55 x 55 cm	---	adjacent to wall 270 on floor
341	10	south room 258, B.L. IIIA	"small"	---	in fill? at edge of disturbance created by pit 196, north of hearth 273
347	10	southwest V168 B.L. IIIA	---	---	just south of burial 336
359	1	V168	50 x 60 cm	---	on a compacted surface; reddish with small stones along western margin
360	1	V168	45 x 56 cm	6 cm	below level of 359
361	2	U168	45 x 65 cm	---	irregular; among the cobbles
399[b]	12	southeast quad, V168 B.L. IIIB	70 x 60 cm	3-4 cm	destroyed eastern part drain 261

[a] B = feature continues into a balk so actual dimensions are unknown.

[b] This hearth was discussed as the northern portion of hearth 266 in Nicholas 1980.

of room 36 (B.L. II north unit) against the south face of wall 264 and the east face of wall 44. Portions of the arched dome of this oven were discovered slipping away from the south face of wall 264.

The second example of a domed oven was feature 214. This hearth (c. 66 x 68 cm) was built into the middle of the east wall (213) of room 215 (B.L. III east wing annex). It contained a basal layer of sherds over which plaster had been spread, which in turn was overlain by a layer of small pebbles and another layer of plaster.

SUNKEN OVEN

There was only one example of this feature type at TUV, feature 223 (B.L. IIIA stratum 10, V168). Oven 223 was built into platform 263 when the latter was constructed. The bricks of the platform had been placed to create the oven compartment. For example, on the south side of the oven three bricks were placed in an arc and then given a 3 cm thick coat of mud plaster, providing a smooth inner oven wall. Stones were also used in creating the oven sides.

The oven itself was an oval, tublike area, 52 x 46 cm, c. 25 cm deep, with hard (burned) 3 cm thick clay walls. The tub was subdivided by the insertion of a 10 x 30 x 25 cm brick and a 10 x 10 cm brick fragment, standing on their sides. Two compartments were thus created; the larger (west of the brick divider) contained soft, light tan, ashy soil. The smaller eastern compartment contained soft, dark, ashy fill. A lens of gray ash covered the tops of both compartments and the brick divider. Some particles of charcoal were also found during the excavation of this feature.

The ash fill of the oven continued underneath the brick divider, indicating that the oven had been used prior to the insertion of the partition.

No air vents were detected in the extant sides of the oven. Presumably air must have been directed into the oven from above.

ASH PITS

Ash pits have more sharply defined boundaries than do most casual hearths, and generally have less horizontal extent but more vertical accumulation of ash (within a depression). There were only four such features at TUV (Table 13).

HEARTHS OF UNCLEAR TYPE

Three hearths can not be assigned to a more specific category of pyrotechnic feature.
Hearth 51
This hearth was located in room 27 (B.L. II north unit) against the south face of wall 34. No details are available about the shape of this feature or the materials used in its construction. A record photograph suggests, however, that it might have been a burned area 40 cm long, confined by mud-brick (or packed-mud?) dividers on two sides (25 cm apart), with its south end open.
Hearth 52
This hearth was located in alcove 26 of the B.L. II north unit, against the south face of wall 34 and the east face of wall 23. The notes report evidence for burning but no associated sherds, bone, or charcoal fragments. A record photograph suggests that this feature may, like hearth 51, have been demarcated by low mud-brick (or packed-mud) dividers (30 cm apart, 40 cm long) with an open south end.

TABLE 13

ASH PITS

Feature number	Stratum	Location	Horizontal dimensions	Thickness	Comments
233	9	southeast V168	25 cm diameter	9 cm	
244	9	southeast V168	46 x 50 cm	22 cm	also contained some fire-cracked rock, sherds, and bone
245	10	near west end of wall 235 of B.L. IIIA	30 x 25 cm	18 cm	
266[a]	14	southeast V168	30 cm diameter	10 cm	runs *under* wall 262 of B.L. IIIB; bowl-shaped depression of burned clay

[a]The phenomenon discussed in Nicholas 1980 as the northern portion of feature 266 is discussed here as casual hearth 399.

Hearth 52 was excavated in 1974. The notes describe hearth 52 as being immediately adjacent to a "potential pot-stand" (a stone having a central depression) set into the floor of alcove 26. The record photograph suggests that the "pot-stand" lay 50 to 75 cm east of hearth 52. Erosion between the 1974 and 1976 seasons destroyed hearth 52 and covered over the stone entirely with bricky wash. When uncovered in 1976, the stone (mf 6274, Plate 27j) was identified as a mortar set in a mud-plastered depression. When first rediscovered, the stone was thought to belong to stratum 9. Plotting of its location on the plans, however, places it exactly where the record photograph places the alcove 26 "pot-stand."

Hearth 73

This feature was built into the north end of wall 62 (B.L. II north unit). In use, it may have been associated with room 364. Stones were involved in the construction of this 55 x 55 cm feature, but there were no signs of burning, no adjacent bin, and no use of plaster. No further details are available about the nature of this feature. While the hearths at TUV had no consistent format, the fact that this feature was *in* wall 62 suggests that hearth 73 may have been a raised-box hearth or domed oven.

Pits
(Figure 18)

In this section, the various pits found at TUV are summarized. Simple rodent burrows are not included in this review. Small pits filled with ash have already been discussed in the section "ash pits" above. One highly unusual pit that seems to be connected with drainage is discussed in a later section of this chapter.

WELLS

Pit 195

This pit originated from stratum 4, from the floor of room 203 (B.L. I east unit). Its top was encircled by two layers of large stones, suggesting that it was primarily intended for use as a well. (It is true that a hard clay surface was reached in pit 195 in 1976, but it is probable that this surface resulted from weathering effects between the 1974 and 1976 seasons and that it did not represent the original bottom of the pit. The fact that pit 195 contained relatively little trash also suggests that it may have been intended originally as a well rather than as a place of refuse disposal.)

Subsidence of the fill above the pit caused pit 195 to be visible during the excavation of stratum 1 as a circular interruption in the underlying pebble layer, stratum 2. The "missing" pebbles were present below, however, sloping downward in a circular depression. It seems clear (given the presence of the stone edging directly on the floor of B.L. I) that the pit was dug from stratum 4, the fill within it settled over many years, the pebbles of stratum 2 were pulled downwards by this action, and the illusion of a pit in stratum 1 was thereby created.

Pit 195 (c. 1.05 m in diameter) disturbed the fill and floor of courtyard 30 of B.L. II and the fill and floor of room 219 of B.L. III. It is tempting to speculate that well 195 may have originally been dug from courtyard 30 of B.L. II, for pits 195 and 199 seem to occupy un-

usually symmetrical positions within that courtyard. Against this interpretation, however, is the apparent break in utilization of this area indicated by stratum 6 deposits.

Pit 199
(Plate 9a)

This pit originated from stratum 4, being cut from the floor of room 181 (B.L. I south unit). The feature was neatly circular, about 90 cm in diameter, and like pit 195, might have been originally intended for use as a well. The feature when discovered was covered with a series of large, long stones and large body sherds which lay on a circle of smaller stones around the top of the pit. These smaller stones and the top of the pit were exactly at the floor level in room 181. Covering of the feature with large stones suggests that the well was abandoned during the occupation of the building and covered for safety reasons.

Pit 199 differed from pit 195 in that it appeared to have been used intentionally as a place of substantial refuse collection at one point in its history. It contained some sherds, a lot of animal bone, and an unusual number of artifacts.

Pit 199 disturbed a portion of the fill and floor of courtyard 30 of B.L. II and part of the fill and floor of room 284 of B.L. III (west wing). As noted in the discussion of pit 195, it is tempting to speculate that well 199 may have originally been dug from courtyard 30.

PLASTERED PITS

Pit 38
(Plate 9b)

This pit originated in stratum 7, in an alcove of the north unit of B.L. II. This alcove was formed by walls

TABLE 14

OTHER PITS

Feature Number	Location	Stratum of origin	Horizontal dimensions	Depth	Comments
14	southeast V168	1	2 x 0.6 m	down to upper stratum 6	Interrupted pebble layer and destroyed part of wall 2 (B.L. I); contained very little bone or sherds
53	room 36, B.L. II north	7 (floor)	small	shallow	Lay west of hearth 29 and may have been associated with use of that hearth as it contained numerous small bones and fire-cracked rocks
60	southeast V166	3	110 x 45 cm	shallow	Sealed over by pebble layer stratum 2, generally filled with fine loose soil
74[a]	room 75(?), B.L. II north	7 (12 cm above floor)	15 cm diameter	shallow	Associated with a "white surface" in the fill; contained some charcoal
101	room 87, B.L. I	4	58 cm diameter	21 cm deep	See discussion of room 87 in architecture of B.L. I
190	W168	0 (present surface)	1 m diameter	very shallow	Result of digging up roots?
191	W168	1	50 cm diameter	10 cm deep	Contained carbonized material, fragments of burnt clay and brick, bone and sherds
194	W168	1	40 cm diameter	shallow	Similar to pit 191 in content
197	southern U168	0/1	1 x 1.5 m	shallow	
198	U168	1	80 cm diameter	shallow	
220	U168	9	75 cm diameter	84 cm deep	Intrusive through fill and floor of room 284, B.L. III. Some bone at top of pit, but lower fill practically sterile, extremely dark and very soft.
269	U168	1	1 m diameter	disturbs all three B.L.s	*Overlapped* east end of burial pit 196, disturbed foot and lower leg bones of Sassanian burial.
345	south V166	9	irregular edges but less than 75 cm in diameter	25 cm. deep (?)	Disturbed wall 294 of B.L. III and fill of alley 307; contained soft fill with many roots and much animal bone, including a small horn core. Some red earth and many small charcoal flecks at top; lower pit fill generally grey.

[a] Pit 74 placed in room 75 by a plan but said to be in room 69 in the text of the notes.

21, 35, and 40 to the east, south and north respectively. It opened from room 36 and lay immediately south of hearth 29. The 60 cm wide pit was mud plastered and a large storage vessel was set inside it.

Pit 130

(Plate 4a)

This stratum 7 pit originated from area 386 of the southwest unit of B.L. II. The 50 x 100 cm feature was mud-plaster lined and thus may have been primarily used for storage. It was approximately 70 cm in depth.

Pit 277

This feature originated from a point immediately underneath platform 263 of B.L. IIIA in V168. The irregular top outline of the pit's ashy matrix was clearly visible when the platform was removed. It appeared to be surrounded by a circle of loosely spaced stones and to be mud plastered. This feature was not excavated.

TRASH PITS

Pit 132

This pit originated from stratum 8b within room 102 of the B.L. II southwest unit. It lay against the east face of wall 105 and against the south balk of U166, and was at least 80 x 55 cm in area. It was associated with the lower of two floors in room 102. The fill of this feature contained seal impressions.

Pit 163

This pit originated from B.L. IIIA stratum 10 in the southwestern portion of V164 and extended into the south balk of that square; part of the balk was removed to excavate the pit completely. The feature was irregular in shape, approximately 2 m long, with a maximum width of 75 cm, and at least 30 cm deep. It contained numerous sherds, seal impressions, and three Proto-Elamite tablet fragments.

Pit 165

This pit originated from B.L. IIIB stratum 12 in the southwest part of V164, north of wall 166. It was 1 x 1.25 m in extent, and at least 50 cm deep. It contained large amounts of burned bone, sherds, some fire-cracked rock, and many seal impressions.

Pit 285

This was a 92 cm deep pit, at least 120 cm in diameter, which originated in B.L. IIIA deposition in area 308 (southeast corner of U166). The feature appeared to extend into both the east and south balks. The top of the pit was sealed over by bricks of the B.L. II courtyard 30 floor. Feature 285 contained ash and very soft soil, generally reddish brown in color. Fifteen stones of about 20 cm in diameter were included in the fill. The density of sherds was high. There was very little bone in the upper portion of the pit, but bone be-

came plentiful in the lower fill. The function of this pit seemed clearly that of refuse disposal.

Pit 299

This 24 cm deep pit originated in B.L. IIIA stratum 10 of T168, and disturbed part of wall 319 of the B.L. IIIB south unit. The feature was probably roughly circular (about 40 x 50 cm) but an intrusive rodent burrow created the illusion of an extension of this pit toward the south. The top of the pit contained sealing clay, the middle fill was dark brown and very soft, and a bulla was found near the bottom.

Pit 348

This feature was found in V168 east of platform 263, but was not excavated. It is not clear from the notes to which stratum the pit belonged. Visible at the top of pit 348 was soft fill, a large sherd, two cobbles and several vertebrae, suggesting it was a mixed trash pit.

BURIAL PITS (also see Burials)

Pit 196

This pit (1 x 2.15 m in area, 1.65 m deep) originated in stratum 1 of U168, and disturbed the architecture of all three building levels. In B.L. I it made unclear the relationship of area 87 and room 181; in B.L. II it disturbed the fill and floor of a portion of courtyard 30; and in B.L. III it destroyed most of the south wall of room 258 with its associated hearth and bin features (273/281). At the bottom of pit 196 lay burial 283, of Sassanian date (Balcer 1978).

Pit 257

This pit (62 x 55 cm in area, 56 cm deep) originated from B.L. IIIA stratum 10 in the southeast quadrant of V168; it also ran on into the east balk of that square. Burial 274 was found in this feature.

OTHER PITS

See Table 14.

Drainage Features

(Figure 18)

Only two features from TUV can be assigned to this category. Feature 261 was a small drainage channel, and feature 333 a stone-filled pit. In addition to these immoveable features, a number of ceramic drain pipe segments were found; the distribution of these artifacts is reviewed in a later chapter.

Drain 261

The sides of this 30 cm wide channel were lined with stones and an interior facing of large flat sherds stand-

ing on edge; the channel bottom was not lined. The drain ran east-west; it cut through wall 262 of the B.L. IIIB north unit, but its further course to the east was destroyed by hearth 266. To the west, the level at which the drain lay was not excavated. Thus this feature was traced only for c. 1.3 m and the direction of flow within the drain could not be determined. It was also not clear whether the drain was built into wall 262 when the wall was constructed (stratum 13c) or added subsequently in connection with the B.L. IIIA remodelling of that zone.

Drainage Pit 333
(Plate 10a)

This unusual feature originated from the southwestern quadrant of V168 in stratum 9; it was just below but definitely sealed over by an unbroken floor in room 27 of the B.L. II north unit.

Pit 333 was approximately 150 cm in diameter. Viewed in plan when initially discovered, the feature consisted of areas of medium-sized stones in both the southern and northeastern segments of the circle, with sherds covering the entire mid-portion. When feature 333 was sectioned, this topmost middle zone was seen to consist of two layers of sherds, lying flat with relatively large spaces between the individual sherds (unlike the "jig-saw puzzle" closeness of the sherds in the plastered sherd concentrations discussed above). Directly below the sherds was a thin layer of soft fill; under that the entire pit was filled with cobbles, loosely packed with open spaces remaining between them into which no dirt had penetrated. Intermixed with these rocks were a number of chunks of earth burned hard and red. Some of the rocks shattered as they were removed; many were fire-cracked.

Below the initial cobble fill, a curving packed-mud partition divided pit 333 into two compartments. The northern compartment was smaller and shallower (about 40 cm deep) than the southern (70 cm deep), but both were filled with loosely packed cobbles. Some of the interstices between the larger cobbles were filled with smaller stones, and in the case of the southern compartment, with large gravel and small pebbles. In this southern compartment, nine layers of cobbles were visible in the cross-section.

The total number of stones removed from this feature, exclusive of the small pebbles, was 3,117. This elaborate arrangement of stones is reminiscent of a sump pit, but there is no evidence as to what it was draining or why two compartments were needed.

Possible Foundation Trench
(Figure 18; Plate 10b)

Feature 76 is the only example of a possible foundation trench found at TUV. This 15 m long channel was intrusive into the architecture of B.L. II in V166 and U166. In this 80 cm wide ditch there were some pebbles and a number of quite large rocks resting on the pebbles. There was no water-worn pottery (except for one sherd) and no water-laid sediment, so it does not seem probable that this was a drainage channel.

Rather, feature 76 may have been a foundation trench which originally contained numerous stones for a wall footing, but which had been robbed-out, leaving some isolated rocks behind. Due to erosion in this sector of the mound, there was no evidence to indicate from which level feature 76 was dug. It was obviously more recent than stratum 6, but as there was no overlying architecture preserved in this area, feature 76 could only be assigned to stratum 1; it was thus not necessarily Banesh in date.

Bins
(Figure 18)

A bin is an unburned compartmented space that is demarcated by low curbings from the main floor space of a room. In another sense, the lower surfaces in the raised-box hearth complexes might be considered bins, and there was also a bin associated with cobble hearth 137. Table 15 summarizes the four large or discrete bins found at TUV. All were in rather fragmentary condition.

Miscellaneous Unburned Cobble Areas
(Figure 18)

The builders of the TUV architecture and features utilized cobbles and smaller pebbles by the thousands. Some cobble features have been discussed above (e.g., cobble hearths; drainage pit 333). The remaining miscellaneous cobble features are discussed in this section.

TABLE 15

STORAGE BINS

Feature Number	Location	Stratum	Dimensions	Comments
28	alcove 25, B.L. II north	8c	43 x 43 cm	Projects north from south wall, with north end open. Sides formed by 11 cm high mud brick dividers.
42	room 43, B.L. II north	8c	35 x 40 cm	South end of room; north end open.
131	room 103, B.L. II southwest	8c	45 x 125 cm	An unusual large "triangular" or semi-circular bin; north end of room; sides formed by mud bricks; interior plastered; cf. discussion of unburned cobble area 353.
281	room 258, B.L. III west	13c	Not estimable	Near hearth 273 at the south end of room; largely destroyed by pit 196; found in association with a number of large tile fragments.

Cobble Feature 77

This feature was found in B.L. II stratum 8c in V166. It consisted of rounded stones about 9 cm in average diameter, lying on a hard, unpitted, good surface that sloped sharply downward toward the west. This surface had an unclear relationship to a platform in the western part of V166. The pebbles covered a zone 4.25 m long by 1.3-1.6 m wide, with a few additional cobbles lying to the north.

Cobble Feature 150

This was an isolated 1.5 x 1 m patch of cobbles (each c. 15 cm wide) in V164. It may represent a patch of stratum 2 that had been isolated by erosion.

Cobble Feature 252

When excavated, the stones of feature 252 appeared to be in stratum 10 fill in the southern end of room 250 and to continue into the south balk of U168, well above the level of the B.L. III floor. The cobbles were surrounded only by dirt and covered an irregularly shaped area of 85 by 50 cm. The fill in room 250 had similar stones scattered lightly throughout; feature 252 was just an area of much higher density of cobbles.

It would now seem, however, that these densely clustered cobbles were probably part of the fill of a pit undetected during excavation of room 250. Re-examination of the south balk section of U168 after a heavy rain suggested that there had been an intrusive pit in this area. It would appear that pit 197 (originating in stratum 1) may have been much deeper than was originally perceived. If pit 197 did in fact penetrate into the fill of B.L. III, it must also have disturbed the fill and floor of courtyard 30 of B.L. II and gone unrecognized there as well.

Cobble Feature 276

This feature was a scatter of 56 pebbles and cobbles (diameters ranging from 5 to 12 cm) in association with a heavy bone concentration in the northeastern part of room 258 (B.L. III). The scatter had an irregular configuration covering about 52 cm from west to east, and ran into the north balk of U168. The feature was found in stratum 10 fill just above the floor of the room. None of the rocks exhibited any sign of use as a pounding implement.

Cobble Feature 288

This was an area of cobbles and pebbles occurring on both sides of the U168/U166 balk. In U168 the feature projected 20 cm east of the balk and had a length of 1.2 m from north to south. In U166, the feature ran 1.3 m from north to south (and extended into the south balk). It measured 1.15 m wide along the south balk. It was partially cut through by pit 285.

The stones in this feature ranged from about 5 to 10 cm in diameter at the east end of the feature, up to an average of 30 cm in diameter at the west end. No sherds or bone were found in association; nor was there any sign of burning. In the U168 balk it could be seen that at least in places the feature was 14 cm thick with two layers of cobbles; however, most of the feature consisted of just one layer of stones. This feature is most plausibly interpreted as being a late B.L. IIIA phenomenon.

Cobble Feature 327

This feature was an irregularly shaped concentration (covering 2 m x 50 cm) of 48 stones in the northwest corner and about midway along the north wall of room 320 (B.L. IIIB south unit, stratum 12). Only a small amount of fill separated the stones from the room floor. Near the eastern end of the cluster the stones overlay a burned patch, casual hearth 328. Most of the stones in feature 327 were 10-12 cm x 7-12 cm, but there was one considerably larger rock (30 x 15 cm) and a handful of smaller ones.

Cobble Feature 353
(Plate 11a)

This feature lay just south of bin 131 in room 103 (B.L. II southwest unit). The stones in this feature were described in the field notes as 60-70 cm in diameter, but restudy of all the plans suggests that they were actually normal cobbles in size (10-20 cm). The stones extended in a carpetlike layer all the way across the 1.5 m width of the room from wall 105 to wall 106, and ran about 1.2 m south of the bin, thus filling nearly the entire room. It is possible that room 103 was in actuality a giant hearth, but against that interpretation is the fact that no signs of burning were noted.

Exterior Trash Dumps

(Figure 18)

There were three major trash dumps in exterior zones at TUV. These features contained very high concentrations of sherds, bone, ash, and so forth, and were given feature status in the field recording system. (Trash that accumulated in *interior* contexts was not given feature status but referenced through an appropriate deposit code [see chapter 2]. Trash was also discarded in some pits, discussed above. Spatial distribution of major trash loci at TUV is reviewed in the discussion of site structure in chapter 7.)

Trash Dump 241

This was an extensive trash deposit of B.L. IIIA stratum 10 found in northeast V168, covering about 2.5 x 4.25 m. It consisted of cobbles, sherds, bones, charcoal flecks, and generally soft, dark soil. This deposit was much shallower on its western margin than on the east, in general varying between 12 and 25 cm in thickness. On the south edge of this deposit the trash sloped up and in places ran up against the edge of platform 263. It is conceivable that this trash was deliberately deposited there to fill in an existing depression in ground level and to provide relatively even ground for the building of B.L. II.

Trash Dump 279

This layer of trashy deposit was thinner than dump 241, but also came from B.L. IIIA stratum 10 in V168. It consisted of stones, bones, and large sherds, as well as ash. The trash occurred beneath brick packing to the north and west of platform 263, covering about 2 x 2 m.

Trash Dump 301

This trash deposit occurred in stratum 10 in southern area 308 (B.L. IIIA). It was an intensive concentration of sherds, black ashy material, bones, and stones lying along the south balk of U166. The feature was relatively broad horizontally (at least 3 m and it continued into the western unexcavated zone) but its depth was a maximum of 40 cm at the west and a minimum of 8 cm at the east. The dump extended at most 1.5 m north of the balk.

Stratigraphic analysis leads to the conclusion that a trash deposit found in northeastern T166 during the 1974 season was most probably a continuation of trash dump 301. The T166 trash was found in a small test below the floor of B.L. II.

Burials

(Figure 18)

Very few burials were found at TUV; of these, five can be dated to the Banesh phase. The sixth (and last) of the burials can be dated to the Sassanian phase (Balcer 1978) and is not described here.

Of the five Banesh burials, three were of infants (burials 226, 278, and 336), one of a child (221) and one of an adult (274).

Infant Burial 226

This fragmentary infant burial in a poorly preserved ceramic vessel was found in the southeast quadrant of V168. Due to the extremely poor state of preservation of this burial, little can be said about it. Presumably this feature was analogous to the better preserved infant burial, 278.

Infant Burial 278

This burial was a stratum 9 phenomenon in U168; it disturbed trashy fill and a part of the floor of room 219 (B.L. III). The infant was found within a 26.5 x 30 cm Banesh pot placed on its side within the trash and slightly imbedded into the floor in the northwest corner of the room.

Infant Burial 336

This burial lay within stratum 10 in the southwest quadrant of V168. The skeleton was found as a tightly flexed bundle of bones, lying on its left side. The skull was at the west, facing north. It appeared that the child had been wrapped in a loosely woven cloth shroud or mat, as an excellent white fiber impression (mf 6105) showing the pattern of the weave was found in association with the skeletal remains. Evidently the infant had simply been placed in the fill accumulating in the north area of B.L. IIIA. No pottery container was used, and no indication of a pit could be discerned around the bones. The soil directly overlying the bones was hard and sticky, not soft and loose. Preservation of the skeleton was poor; many bones crumbled away when touched. Loose deciduous teeth were found. In the case of the molars, only crowns were present. General size of the long bones suggested that this may have been a child under one year in age.

Child Burial 221

This burial consisted of the skeleton of a child, aged 2-4, found lying on its side in a tightly flexed position. This burial can be ascribed to stratum 9; it was sealed over by an undisturbed portion of the floor of B.L. II courtyard 30 and lay within the uppermost fill of room 284 of the B.L. III west wing. The outlines of a burial pit could not be traced. This burial was found only 20 cm from a medium-sized jar (mf 1930) with painted bands on its shoulder, but it could not be determined if the jar was deposited as a grave gift or if the close association of the two was accidental.

Adult Burial 274

(Figure 19; Plate 12a-b)

This burial was from the southeast quadrant of V168 (stratum 10), and extended slightly into the east balk of that square. Of the burials found at TUV, feature 274 provided the most details about Banesh phase burial customs.

This feature consisted of a single individual lying on its left side, in a flexed position with its head oriented slightly north of west. A clear burial pit (257) which was filled with loosely packed, soft, reddish earth, intermixed with occasional bits of harder material could be delineated. Some charcoal was collected from around the skeleton.

The general state of preservation of the bone was poor. However, as in the case of infant burial 336, fabric impressions, presumably from a shroud, were recovered. The burial 274 impressions (mf 3896) came from the skull and left tibia, and also from earth to the left of the face. An area of 20 x 10 cm was found behind mf 5078 (see below) with additional white impressions of cloth or matting.

Burial 274 also included grave goods—a stone vessel and a ceramic vessel. A flaring-sided white limestone bowl with a beveled (re-cut) rim (mf 5078: Plate 27a) was found lying south of and directly behind the pelvis. A lens of charcoal and ash was found associated with this stone bowl in a position suggesting it may have originally been inside the container. The other artifact in the burial pit was a medium-sized, painted, completely intact ceramic vessel (mf 5055: Plate 19c), found above the leg bones. This vessel falls within the restricted ledge-rim group of Banesh grit ware described in chapter 4.

Miscellaneous Features

(Figure 18)

This category groups all other immoveable features discovered at TUV.

Feature 78

This feature was briefly described in the notes as a "platform." It was only one brick high and came from stratum 7 of V166, adjacent to the south balk and bordering foundation trench 76 on the west. This feature was not included on the plan of B.L. II, and the notes did not discuss the relationship of the feature to the walls of that area.

Feature 153/155

This was a 1.4 m long linear alignment of 8 cut stone bricks in the center of V164, stratum 1. Three bricks were 5 x 7 x 4 cm, five bricks were 15 x 15 x 7 cm.

Feature 156

This stratum 1 feature was found in west-central V164. It consisted of 13 large stones, up to 40 cm in length. Most of these ran in a line from south to north, but at the north a few extended eastward in a rough alignment with feature 153/155 (but 1.3 m west of it). Some cobbles (of stratum 2?) were found to the west of feature 156. This feature may be a fragmentary wall foundation (cf. features 210, 332).

Feature 210

This was a roughly linear alignment of 6 large stones (30-40 cm long) in the southeast section of U168, set within the pebbles of stratum 2. It may represent the footing for a mud-brick wall which had totally eroded away (cf. features 156, 332).

Feature 236

This was a feature of stratum 9 in the southeast quadrant of V168. It was an oval arrangement (about 90 x 65 cm) of very small holes (c. 2.5 cm in diameter) filled with very soft soil. The workmen advanced the idea that these were root holes, but the positioning of the holes in an oval was so peculiar as to cast some doubt on that explanation. It was true that the holes had no consistent depth or orientation and some seemed to curve at peculiar angles. However, it is possible that they were miniature "post-holes" left behind in the spot where perhaps a skin had been stretched on a stick frame to dry, or a small wind-break erected.

Feature 300

This feature lay within upper stratum 10 fill in room 306 (B.L. III west unit). It was a flattened, sloping lens of white clayey soil about 50 cm wide at its base. Its appearance suggested the spilling of a bucket of thickened lime plaster in this area. Mf 6028 was a sample of this material.

Feature 321

This feature was found in stratum 10 fill of southern alley 307 (B.L. III) near the point at which the alley opens into exterior zone 308. The feature was a concentration of burned, black, organic material in varying shades of darkness. The maximum width of the feature was 70 cm; thickness was irregular but maximum depth was 8 cm.

Feature 332

This was a 1.5 m long linear alignment of 6 medium-large stones (up to 20 x 30 cm) found in the southwest quadrant of V168. It was probably a foundation for wall 24 of the B.L. II north unit (stratum 8c) (cf. features 156, 210).

Feature 334

This stratum 1 feature was intrusive into stratum 9 of southeastern V166. It was an alignment of five parallel, elongated holes, all containing soil mixed with a whitish substance. According to the staff zoologist, these were merely animal burrows, despite the odd arrangement. Indeed, when one hole was then traced beyond the limits of the excavation, it did behave as one would expect a burrow to do, taking a sudden dramatic dip downward.

Chapter Conclusion

This concludes the descriptive catalog of the architecture and features excavated in the TUV operation. Further interpretation of these elements can be found in chapter 7. At this time it is necessary to continue the basic description of the archaeological record at TUV. Description of the finds begins with a discussion of the ceramic corpus.

IV

The TUV Ceramic Assemblage

This chapter presents the typological description and illustrative documentation for the TUV ceramic assemblage. Review of the spatial distribution patterns of ceramic types within each individual level is reserved for later chapters.

Development of a Banesh Typology

The original ceramic chronology for the Kur River Basin rested on the surveys and soundings of Vanden Berghe (1959). Vanden Berghe, however, found no ceramic material indicative of the Banesh phase. This assemblage was first defined by Sumner (1972a); he described the new ceramic phase on the basis of surface collections made during his survey of the Kur River Basin, begun in 1967. Banesh ware was found at 26 of Sumner's sites, but most of these sites yielded only 3-4 diagnostic pieces. From this small collection, Sumner was able to tentatively describe four "subwares" of Banesh (Sumner 1972a:42).

More detailed typological analysis of the Banesh assemblage has since been undertaken on excavated material from Malyan ABC (Sumner 1974, 1976; Keirns n.d.), Malyan TUV (Nicholas 1980a), and Tal-e Kureh (Alden n.d.).

In 1976 a resurvey of Banesh phase sites in the Kur River Basin was conducted by Alden. His survey collections span a much greater time range than do the excavated Banesh assemblages. Alden's typology (1979) delineates stylistic and formal attributes in Banesh ceramics which can be used to subdivide a long range of time (c. 800 years) into smaller chronological divisions.

The largest and most diverse corpus of Banesh ceramics at Malyan is from the TUV operation. The present author began analysis of the TUV ceramics in 1975; at that time a large proportion of the sherds from the 1974 excavation season, as well as the sherds from Test Trench F excavated in 1971, were studied at The University Museum in Philadelphia. The 1976 excavation essentially doubled the size of the ceramic sample, and increased the known range of diversity within the Banesh assemblage at TUV. These additional sherds, as well as 1974 season sherds not shipped to the United States, were studied at Malyan during the 1976 and 1978 field seasons.

Principles Underlying the TUV Ceramic Assemblage Typology

It is generally accepted among archaeologists today that there is no such thing as just one typology for a set of material. Different typologies can be constructed from the same data base if different questions are asked of the evidence.

In the case of the TUV ceramic assemblage, two kinds of questions were being asked of the material. The primary goal was measurement of functional variation within a broadly contemporaneous ceramic assemblage.[1] The internal temporal relationships among the ceramics constituting the data base were derived from stratigraphic analysis; relative contemporaneity was not an issue which the typology itself had to address. As a subsidiary goal, however, the typology was intended to facilitate comparison of TUV ceramics with other published collections of ceramics from the ancient Near East, so that ceramic evidence could be used to place TUV within the general relative chronology of Greater Mesopotamia.

What, then, is the nature of the data base of which these questions are being asked? The majority of the TUV evidence is in the form of sherds rather than complete vessels: about 20,688 coded sherds, and 28 registered intact or nearly complete vessels. During the 1974 and 1976 field seasons, all diagnostic sherds (rims, bases, handles, spouts, decorated sherds, and other sherds yielding significant information about vessel shape) were saved for further study and became the basis of the TUV typology. (In 1976, nondiagnostic body sherds were counted and weighed before they were discarded. These additional data have been used in the study of fragmentation signatures for various deposits.)

The ceramic assemblage at TUV can be divided into two major ware families through the criterion of temper. Temper is defined as any non-clay matter found in such quantity in a sherd body that it can be assumed to have been deliberately added to the paste (Sumner 1972a:34). (Isolated bits of non-clay matter are considered to be inclusions.) The Malyan project designates any vegetal temper as *straw/chaff*, and any mineral temper as *grit*. Chaff-tempered ware by count comprises about 62% of the TUV Banesh assemblage, and grit-tempered ware by count comprises about 38%. Two subwares of chaff ware and three subwares of grit ware are defined later in this chapter.

Table 16 summarizes morphological variation within the assemblage. Despite the fact that it constitutes over three-fifths of the ceramic corpus from TUV, chaff-tempered ware occurs in only seven forms; the complete profiles of most of these forms are well-documented from the sherds. The quantitatively less common grit-tempered ware occurs in a much greater variety of shapes. Knowledge of *whole* vessel shapes within grit ware, however, is poor. The overwhelming majority of the evidence for vessels in this ware occurs in the form of relatively small sherds.

In the absence of a large number of complete vessel profiles for grit ware, rim sherds were chiefly utilized in the initial organization of the TUV typology. Unlike the base and body sherds in this corpus, the rim sherds convey consistent information on critical attributes connected to functional variation. Within the

TABLE 16
MORPHOLOGICAL VARIATION WITHIN THE TUV CERAMIC CORPUS

CHAFF-TEMPERED WARE

Low trays
Drain spout segments
Bevelled-rim bowls
Goblets with necked bases
Cups (flaring-sided)
Straight-sided goblets
Crucible/furnace fragments

GRIT-TEMPERED WARE

Restricted
  Inward orientation of upper body
    Hole-mouth group
  Necked forms
    Everted group
    Folded group
    Ledge group
    Expanded group
    Vertical rounded group
Unrestricted
  Complete profiles
    Cups
      Flaring-sided
      Vertical-walled
    Burnished plates
    Trays
      High trays
      Grills
    Bowls
      Direct rims
        Rounded lip
        Square lip
        Truncated lip
      Ledge rims
      Exteriorly expanded rims
      Bilaterally expanded rims

TUV assemblage, for example, variation in base diameter is not nearly so large as variation in rim diameter, and is consequently a much poorer indicator of general vessel size. Variations in the shape of the base are minimal and can not be used to determine general vessel form. In addition, decoration almost never occurs on the lower bodies of Banesh ceramics. The difficulties in using base and body sherds to measure functional variation are therefore obvious.

Fortunately, unless it is a very small fragment, each rim sherd *can* be used to determine general vessel form (restricted versus unrestricted) and general vessel size (as measured through rim diameter). In the TUV assemblage, decoration tends to be confined to the rim and upper body of vessels. Rim sherds thus also allow us to check on the presence or absence of non-utilitarian elaboration of the vessel surface.

All grit-tempered rims have thus been coded as representing either a restricted vessel, an unrestricted vessel, or an indeterminate form (if not enough of the sherd was present to permit assessment of general vessel shape). Restricted and unrestricted vessels were defined following Shepard (1971:228-230):

> The restricted orifice is generally defined as having a diameter less than the maximum vessel diameter; the unrestricted, as having the maximum vessel diameter.... Spreading to vertical walls mark the unrestricted vessel; converging walls, the restricted.

In addition to determining the general shape of each vessel, it is important to have a sense of the general size of the container if one is concerned with functional variation within an assemblage. To take this variable into account, the restricted and unrestricted vessel categories each have been further broken down into four arbitrary size classes. These categories are intended to reflect the general suitability of the vessels for different kinds of functions. If a vessel opening is too narrow for an adult hand to pass through it easily, such a container is presumably intended for easily poured substances. A medium rim diameter suggests either pouring or scooping out of the contents by hand. For large diameter vessels, effective pouring would have been very difficult, and scooping out by hand or with a ladle would be indicated. Furthermore, the larger the rim diameter of the vessel, the more unwieldy the container would generally have been. Small and medium vessels would probably have been readily transportable. Large and extra-large containers are more likely to have been utilized as stationary objects.

The sizes for restricted vessels are:

1) small, having a diameter of less than 7 cm; an adult hand will not fit easily through an opening of this size;
2) medium, having a diameter of at least 7 cm but less than 14 cm, through which one adult hand normally will fit;
3) large, having a diameter of at least 14 cm but less than 21 cm, through which two hands should fit easily;
4) extra-large, having a diameter of at least 21 cm.

Some restricted vessels can logically be expected to have very narrow orifices (e.g. bottles). Unrestricted vessels, however, in practice can not occur with such extremely small rim diameters (except on special *miniature* forms). Therefore the assumption was made that unrestricted vessels were likely to have a rim diameter

size-range curve skewed slightly to the right of that of the restricted forms (toward greater diameter size). Thus the unrestricted size categories used here are:

1) small, having a diameter less than 14 cm;
2) medium, having a diameter of at least 14 but less than 21 cm;
3) large, having a diameter of at least 21 cm but less than 30 cm;
4) extra-large, at least 30 cm in diameter.

It is recognized that these size divisions were imposed by the analyst and do not necessarily correspond to the mental templates of sizes carried by the Banesh potters. Nonetheless, the size categories do adequately indicate different orders of magnitude for the vessels being studied, and are of considerable utility in functional analysis.

Within each form/size group, further breakdown of the sherds was made on the basis of variation in surface treatment and decoration of the vessels. In the typology presented below, the following definitions are used (Sumner 1972a:34).

surface treatment

1) rough: the surface of a vessel that is extremely pitted or uneven
2) matte: a vessel surface that is unmodified but not extremely rough
3) smoothed: a vessel surface that has been evenly made smooth to the touch, but has not been burnished or polished
4) burnished: a vessel surface that has been rubbed until it shines, but which still shows the marks of the rubbing instrument (if no marks remain, the vessel is described as polished)
5) slipped: a vessel surface on a broad section of which any apparent thin coating has been applied; no assumption is implied by this term about the manner in which the application was done

decorative treatment

1) monochrome painted: a vessel which has a distinct design or small surface area(s) covered in one color
2) bichrome painted: a vessel which has a distinct design or small surface area(s) covered in two colors

3) relief: patterned raised areas of clay serving as decoration, such as ridges or ropes
4) impressed: pattern impressions on the surface of a vessel

In summary, typological description of the TUV ceramics has been arranged using the following criteria. Initial breakdown is made on the basis of ware. The next division is made on the basis of shape. When possible (as it is for the chaff ware and for some of the grit ware material), this division is based on exact whole vessel shape. For the majority of the grit-ware rim sherds, however, categorization is first into restricted/unrestricted forms, and then into a series of types based on upper body and rim shape. (Details of the exact lower body shapes of these vessels are not firmly known.) Each shape group is then further described in terms of the size categories, surface treatment, and decoration occurring within the type. Finally, non-rim sherds such as bases, handles, spouts, and decorated body sherds are described in terms of size and surface treatment; placement of these latter kinds of sherds into general vessel shape categories is usually not possible.

Description of the TUV Ceramics

Chaff-Tempered Ware

Vessels in Banesh chaff-tempered ware are vegetable tempered, rather crudely shaped, and low fired; sherds frequently have black cores. The exterior surfaces of vessels made in this ware are consistently fired in the light orange to light brown color range (Munsell 5/6 5-7.5 YR). Two subwares can be identified: standard and densely tempered.

While chaff-tempered ware constitutes (by count) over three-fifths of the TUV ceramic corpus, only seven forms occur in this ware family. Six of these were made in the standard subware. Some of these forms were most probably "mass-produced," in particular the mold-made bevelled-rim bowls and the wheel-turned goblets with necked bases. Handmade low trays also occur in great quantity. Much less frequent in occurrence are wheelmade flaring-sided cups, handmade drain spout segments, and goblets with straight-sided bases. The one form made in the densely tempered subware is a type of furnace lining used in copper-base metallurgy.

Each of the seven chaff-ware forms will now be described in detail.

LOW TRAYS
(Plates 13a-j, 14c-d)

The Banesh phase low tray is handmade in a general shape varying from roughly circular through oval in plan. These trays appear to have been formed by pressing out a wad of clay on an earthen surface, resulting in the characteristically rough undersurface of the base. The sides of the tray were evidently pulled up from the margins of the flattened clay wad and given a slight everted flare. The interiors of the trays and the exterior side walls are smoothed.

DRAIN SPOUT SEGMENTS
(Plate 27 l-m)

Drain spouts are shallow ceramic troughs with straight vertical sides and flat bases, presumably designed to carry away excess rainwater. Five examples in the TUV corpus were complete enough to have been registered as finds (mf 1313, 3964, 5400, 6247, 6272). On the basis of these complete examples, such troughs can be described as narrow (about 9-14 cm in width) with two straight, parallel sides and open ends. Some of the complete examples widen slightly at one end of the trough. Two examples (mf 1313 and 5400) have a hole in the base of the trough near one end. It is possible that such spouts were secured to a wall or roof by placing a peg through this hole.

Drain spout sherds occur in both chaff-tempered and grit-tempered ware, but the chaff-tempered variant is much more common. These drain spouts were made in the same basic way as low trays. A wad of clay was pressed out on an earthen surface, resulting in the characteristic rough undersurface of the base of these drain spouts. The sides of the drains were pulled up from the edges of the clay block, but with the walls of the trough at right angles to the base rather than in the trays' characteristic slight everted flare. The interiors of the spouts and the exterior side walls are smoothed.

BEVELLED-RIM BOWLS
(Plate 13k-l)

The bevelled-rim bowl is, of course, a well known ceramic form in ancient Near Eastern archaeology. Like bevelled-rim bowls elsewhere, the TUV vessels appear to have been made using prepared holes in the ground as molds (Johnson 1973:131); the exterior side walls and the undersurfaces of the bases are rough, and the interiors of the bases frequently show a thumb im-

TABLE 17

TEMPORAL VARIATION IN SELECTED CHAFF-WARE FORMS AT TUV[1]

B.L.	Stratum	Total Chaff Sherds	Goblet Sherds	Tray Sherds	BRB Sherds
I	4	82	35 (43%)	37 (45%)	10 (12%)
II	7 & 8b	543	163 (30%)	303 (56%)	77 (14%)
IIIA	9 & 10	3490	667 (19%)	1491 (43%)	1332 (38%)
IIIB	12 & 13b	855	115 (13%)	391 (46%)	349 (41%)

[1]This table is based on diagnostic rim sherds from non-tertiary lots. All percentages have been calculated to the nearest whole number. Note the apparent temporal break in chaff ware patterns between B.L. IIIA-B and B.L. II-I. While the proportion of trays is relatively constant throughout all these levels, the proportions of goblets and bevelled-rim bowls shift dramatically between the earlier and later levels. It is unclear to what extent this pattern may be skewed by the small sample size in levels II-I.

pression where the clay was pressed down into the mold. The interiors of the vessels were smoothed, and the exterior rims finished off by smoothing the upper exterior edge in such a way as to create the diagnostic bevel. As the walls of the bevelled-rim bowls are relatively thin, this form does not exhibit the black core so common in the low trays and goblets at TUV. Rather, the walls are completely oxidized or have only a slight grey tinge in their centers, even under presumed low-firing conditions.

Except for two fairly complete specimens (mf 1724 and mf 1725), the TUV examples of bevelled-rim bowls are sherds, not whole vessels. As it has not been possible to obtain a series of volume measurements on these containers, we do not know whether these bowls were made in standard sizes.[2]

GOBLETS WITH NECKED BASES
(Plate 13m-bb)

These vessels are wheelmade, with string-cut bases ranging between 4.5 and 8.25 cm in diameter. The bases are not completely solid pedestals; hollow center spaces penetrate down from the bodies of the vessels to varying depths into the bases. The upper portions of the bases are "necked" (i.e., distinctly narrower than the foot). The middle and upper bodies of the vessels are generally rather asymmetrical in appearance, with the upper walls thinning significantly to end in one of a small variety of simple and pinched rims.

GOBLETS WITH STRAIGHT-SIDED BASES
(Plate 22a-c)

This vessel type is rare at TUV; no complete profiles exist in the assemblage. The sides of these vessels do not turn inwards to create a "neck," but rise more or less vertically from the base. It is probable that the upper portions of these vessels ended in simple or pinched rims such as those known to occur on the goblets with necked bases.

FLARING-SIDED CUPS
(Plate 15j, l, m)

These wheelmade vessels have string-cut, roughly circular disc bases ranging between 3 and 5 cm in diameter. From the base, thin sides flare strongly outward and upward, tapering to very thin (2-3 mm) direct rounded rims. The thinness of the walls suggests that these would not have been very sturdy vessels. This form is rare in chaff-tempered ware, but more common in grit-tempered ware (see below).

FURNACE LININGS
(Plate 25a)

These fragmentary containers are made in a very flaky straw-tempered fabric; the density of the vegetable matter incorporated into the paste is noticeably higher than in the standard chaff-tempered subware used for the six form categories just summarized. The sherds of densely tempered chaff ware are

2. Nissen (1970:137) has suggested that bevelled-rim bowls were used as ration containers. If bevelled-rim bowls functioned in that way, it is logical to expect that they would have been made in standard sizes.

Beale (1978) measured the volumes of two assemblages of bevelled-rim bowls (one from Khuzistan and one from Tepe Yahya) and found that there were no standard volumes for bevelled-rim bowls in either case.

identified as furnace linings on the basis of the copper slags adhering to their interior surfaces. For further evidence of copper-base metallurgy at TUV, see chapter 5, functional class 2.

Grit-Tempered Ware

Banesh grit-tempered ware is a more diverse ware family than is Banesh chaff-tempered ware. The characterization of subwares given here is based on macroscopic examination (for technical analysis of Banesh ceramics see Blackman 1981). There are three immediately recognizable subwares. The first two of these are much less common than the third.

1) Shiny white crystalline temper consistently occurs in restricted vessels with everted rims, fired in the grey-brown range. A hole-mouth vessel (mf 3834, Plate 15b) in this subware is also documented at TUV. This subware appears to continue into the Kaftari ceramic assemblage (c. 2000 B.C.) at Malyan.

2) Specular-hematite temper consistently occurs in unrestricted plates with rounded direct rims, red to brown-grey in color.

3) Standard grit temper characterizes most of the grit ware corpus and is found in many different forms. Sherds in this subware are generally very coarsely tempered, with varying combinations of white, black, and reddish grit particles, occasionally accompanied by a low incidence of straw temper as well.

To some extent it is possible to generalize about the "typical" *lower body* form of vessels made in the standard grit-temper subware. Such a vessel would have a flat base from which the lower vessel sides flare out. (Ring bases are found within the assemblage but are rare.) The sides of the typical form would continue upward to a distinct carination; globular vessels with gently rounded sides do occur in the assemblage, but frequent distinct carinations distinguish the Banesh from other phase assemblages in the Kur River Basin.

It is not possible, however, to characterize even on so gross a level the "typical" *upper body* form for the standard grit-temper subware vessels. It is precisely in this upper body zone that the great formal diversity of the Banesh grit-ware family lies.

The entire Banesh grit-tempered ware family constitutes less than two-fifths of the total ceramic assemblage recovered from the TUV operation. Only a small number of complete form profiles in this ware were recovered. The general arrangement of the following descriptions is of necessity largely by sherd groups (Table 16). Registered vessels will be listed with the rim groups into which they fall. An idea of the variation within each morphological rim-group is shown on the accompanying plates and tables. Following the rim-groups, bases and other diagnostic sherds will be described.

RESTRICTED, UN-NECKED VESSELS

Hole-Mouth Rim-Group
(Plate 15a-b, d-e, g; Table 18)
   Definition: Rims which are inwardly rather than outwardly or vertically oriented, and which arise directly from the wall of the vessel without the existence of a distinguishable neck.
   Registered Vessels: mf 1457, 3834.

RESTRICTED, NECKED VESSELS

Simple Vertical Rim-Group
(Plate 16a-b; Table 18)
   Definition: Unexpanded rims with rounded lips, oriented at 90° to the plane of the ground.
   Registered Vessels: None.
Simple Everted Rim-Group (Plates 16c-m, 17a-o, 18a; Table 18)
   Definition: Unexpanded rims which bend or flare outwards (generally at an angle of 45°) from the shoulder of the vessel.
   Registered Vessels: mf 1256, 1449, 1927, 1930.
Expanded Rim-Group
(Plate 18b-e; Table 18)
   Definition: Everted rims convexly thickened on one or both sides.
   Registered Vessels: mf 1189.
Ledge Rim-Group
(Plates 14a-b, 19a-t; Table 18)
   Definition: Thin, flattened everted rims, bent at right angles to the vessel wall.
   Registered Vessels: mf 1453, 1458, 1926, 1928, 5055.
Folded Everted Rim-Group
(Plate 18f-l; Table 18)
   Definition: Everted rims which have been bent down to an angle beyond 90° from the vessel wall and pushed back towards the neck of the vessel.
   Registered Vessels: None.

UNRESTRICTED, FLARING-SIDED CUPS
(Plates 15k, n-p, 22 e, f)

This shape is well-documented by complete profiles (mf 1450, 1451, 1723, and 1727) and also consistently

TABLE 18
GRIT WARE RESTRICTED FORMS[a]

Rim-group	Number of sherds	Subwares	Surface treatments	Size ranges[b]	Relief decoration	Painted decoration	Carinations[c]	Globular bodies[c]
Hole-mouth	19	Standard; grey-brown with crystalline temper	Plain oxidized; red, grey, orange, creamy-brown slips	S, M,* L, XL	Raised bumps; stepped shoulders	None	D	?
Simple vertical	6	Standard	Plain oxidized; red slipped; incised horizontal band; burnished dark brown	M, XL	None	None	?	D
Everted, short-necked	81	Standard; grey-brown with crystalline temper	Plain oxidized; plain and burnished reduced; burnished oxidized; red, grey, dark brown, creamy-brown slips	S, M, L,* XL	None	Monochrome black, maroon	D	D
Everted, long-necked	28	Standard	Plain oxidized; burnished grey-brown; burnished oxidized; red, grey, creamy-brown slips	S, M,* L	None	Monochrome maroon	D	D
Ex-panded	28	Standard	Plain oxidized; incised horizontal band; creamy-brown, red, grey, black slips	M, L, XL*	None	None on sherds (maroon paint over white slip on mf 1189)	D	D
Ledge, short-necked	28	Standard	Plain oxidized; grey-black, red, orange, creamy-brown slips	M,* L, XL*	None	Monochrome maroon; bichrome black and white on creamy-brown slips	D	D
Ledge, long-necked	33	Standard	Plain oxidized; plain reduced; red, grey-black, orange, creamy-brown slips	S, M,* L	None	Monochrome maroon	?	?
Folded	16	Standard	Plain oxidized; burnished orange; red, orange, grey-black, creamy-brown slips	M, L, XL*	None	Black paint over red slip	?	?

[a] Based on 1976 typological study sample.

[b] S = small, M = medium, L = large, XL = extra-large.

[c] Most rim sherds in the TUV corpus do not have enough of the vessel body attached to establish whether the vessel was globular or carinated. D means the feature is documented for a particular rim group.

* Indicates the most common size category.

recognizable from less complete sherds. These vessels are wheelmade, with string-cut, roughly circular disc bases ranging between 3 and 5 cm in diameter. From the base, thin sides flare strongly outward and upward, tapering to very thin (2-3 mm) direct rounded rims.

The thinness of the walls suggests that these would not have been very sturdy vessels. Generally the sherds from these cups are fired in the orange range, but some grey examples occur. The paste generally has a distinct grey core; tempering was done with a mixture of grit, lime,

TABLE 19

GRIT WARE UNRESTRICTED BOWL FORMS[a]

Rim-group	Number of sherds	Subwares	Surface treatments	Size ranges	Observed types of decoration
Direct rounded, carinated side	21	Standard	Plain oxidized; red, orange, grey-black, creamy-brown slips	Small,* medium, large, extra-large*	Monochrome black paint on plain oxidized; Monochrome black paint on creamy-brown slip; Monochrome black paint on red slip; Incised bands, lozenge
Direct rounded, gently curving side	8	Standard	Plain oxidized; orange, grey-black and burnished creamy-brown slips	Medium, large, extra-large*	None
Direct rounded, flaring side	5	Standard	Plain oxidized; red, grey-black, creamy-brown slips	Medium, large, extra-large	Monochrome black paint on red slip
Direct rounded, side indeterminate	8	Standard	Plain oxidized, red, grey-black, creamy-brown slips	Small, medium, large, extra-large*	Polychrome (yellow, white, maroon) slanting bars; Incised lines; Relief ridge
Direct square, carinated (c), gently curving (g), indeterminate sides (i)	18	Standard	Plain oxidized (i); burnished orange (i); red (g, c, i), grey-black (c, i), orange (g, i) slips	Small, medium,* large, extra-large	Monochrome maroon stripe on red slip (c)
Direct truncated, inward flaring side (f), indeterminate side (i); carinated side on mf 1721	12	Standard	Plain oxidized (f, i); red (f, i) grey-black (f, i) slips	Medium,* large, extra-large	None
Ledge, carinated (c), gently curving (g), indeterminate (i) sides	8	Standard	Plain oxidized (c, i); Red (i, g), orange (i), grey-black (g, i) slips (one g example slipped red on exterior, grey-black on interior)	Medium, extra-large*	Incised horizontal band (g); Monochrome maroon stripe (c)
Exteriorally expanded, carinated side	16	Standard	Plain oxidized; red, orange, grey-black, creamy-brown slips; 1 example black slipped exterior, red slipped interior; 2 examples red slipped exterior, black slipped interior	Small, medium, large*	Bichrome white and black bands on red-slipped rim; Monochrome maroon stripe (on plain oxidized)
Exteriorally expanded, gently curving side	16	Standard	Plain oxidized; red, brown, grey-black slips	Small, medium, large, extra-large*	Monochrome grey-black stripes on red slip; Incised horizontal band on red slip
Exteriorally expanded, flaring (f), vertical (v), sinuous (s) sides	10	Standard	Plain oxidized (f); red (f), grey-black (f, v, s), creamy-brown (f) slips (one f example creamy-brown slipped on exterior, black slipped on interior)	Small, medium, large, extra-large	Monochrome maroon stripe on creamy-brown slip (f)

TABLE 19—*Continued*

Rim-group	Number of sherds	Subwares	Surface treatments	Size ranges	Observed types of decoration
Exteriorly expanded, indeterminate side	39	Standard	Plain oxidized; red, grey-black, orange slips	Small, medium, large,* extra-large	Incised horizontal band
Bilaterally expanded, inward flaring (f) gently curving (g) indeterminate (i) sides	8	Standard	Red (i, f), orange (g), grey-black (f, i) slips	Medium, large,* extra-large	None

^a Based on 1976 typological study sample.
* Indicates most common size category.

and chaff. (Rare examples of this vessel shape also occur in chaff ware: see above.) Generally both the exterior and the interior surfaces of the flaring-sided cups are smoothed, but occasionally rough surfaces occur.

UNRESTRICTED, VERTICAL-SIDED CUPS
(Plate 15h-i)

This shape is well-documented by complete profiles (mf 1455, 1461) and also consistently recognizable from less complete sherds. These small vessels (c. 7 cm high) are much less common than flaring-sided cups. The form of these vessels is that of a direct rounded rim on nearly vertical sides, with a very low and gentle carination above a more rounded base. The general color of the fabric is light red to reddish yellow; standard grit temper is used. Cups of this type generally seem to have been painted on the exterior with vertical maroon stripes over a white slip. (Sometimes yellow paint was also used to border the maroon stripes.)

UNRESTRICTED PLATES
(Plate 15c)

This shape is well-documented by complete profiles (including registered vessel mf 1719 and a number of unregistered sherds). These plates have a direct rounded rim on sides flaring smoothly from a flat base. These plates are low (about 7 cm in height), oval rather than round in plan (at least in some instances), and fall into the category of extra-large rim diameters. Plates range in color from red to brown-grey, but all sherds are consistently burnished and tempered with glittery specular hematite.

UNRESTRICTED HIGH TRAYS
(Plate 15q)

All the known sherds of this type seem to have come from the same (unregistered) vessel. The surface of the tray is heavily altered. The tray is handmade with a thick base and thick walls, and generally very awkward looking. The walls rise more or less vertically from the edge of the base and end in a direct rounded rim.

UNRESTRICTED GRILLS
(Plate 15f)

This form is known only from one essentially complete vessel (mf 1310), which is grit and straw-tempered, 39 cm in diameter, and 5 cm tall. It is essentially a high tray (see above) with a series of circular holes punched through its flat base. The largest hole is in the center, and numerous smaller holes radiate outward from that.

UNRESTRICTED BOWLS

Direct Rounded Rim-Group
(Plates 20c-g, j-l; Table 19)
  Definition: These vessels have no distinct rim, other than the rounded lip itself.
  Registered Vessels: None.
Direct Square Rim-Group
(Plate 20a; Table 19)
  Definition: Similar to direct rounded but with a "squared-off" lip.
  Registered Vessels: mf 1729.
Direct Truncated Rim-Group
(Plate 20b; Table 19)
  Definition: Similar to direct rounded but with a pointed lip.
  Registered Vessels: mf 1721.

TABLE 20

TEMPORAL VARIATION IN SELECTED GRIT-WARE FORMS AT TUV[1]

B.L.	Stratum	Total painted sherds	Mono-chrome sherds	Bichrome sherds	Total rim sherds[2]	Exteriorally expanded rims	Hole-mouth	Everted rims	Folded rims	Ledge rims
I	4	39	34	5	85	13	1	56	10	5
			87%	13%		15%	1%	66%	12%	6%
II	7&8b	134	96	38	273	35	6	131	46	55
			72%	28%		13%	2%	48%	17%	20%
IIIA	9&10	137	103	34	129	35	8	40	18	28
			75%	25%		27%	6%	31%	14%	22%
IIIB	12&13b	35	24	11	57	6	4	28	2	17
			69%	31%		11%	7%	49%	3%	30%

[1] This table is based on diagnostic sherds from non-tertiary lots. All percentages have been calculated to the nearest whole number.

[2] This total is for only those rim types entered on this table.

Ledge Rim-Group
(Plate 20h, i, m, n; Table 19)
   Definition: Thin, flattened everted rims, bent at right angles to the vessel wall.
   Registered Vessels: mf 1459.
Exteriorally Expanded Rim-Group
(Plate 21a-i, m; Table 19)
   Definition: Rims convexly thickened on the exterior.
   Registered Vessels: None.
Bilaterally Expanded Rim-Group
(Plate 21j-l; Table 19)
   Definition: Rims convexly thickened on both sides.

   Registered Vessels: mf 1452.

BASE SHERDS
(Plate 22)

The small amount of variation in grit-tempered bases reduces the usefulness of base form in identification of functional vessel types. The special bases of cups, plates, and trays have been described above. Most of the other grit-tempered bases in the TUV assemblage are flat bases. A few ring bases also occur.

VESSEL SPOUTS
(Plates 15a, 19s, 23c)

Both trough spouts and tubular spouts occur but in very small quantity. Both types were clearly made independently of the vessel, and then attached to the vessel wall.

HANDLES
(Plate 23f, p)

While handles are not common in the assemblage, there are four distinct varieties documented: *a* strap handle—a relatively wide and flat handle that is oriented vertically on a vessel wall; *b* loop handle—a relatively narrow handle, rounded in cross-section, oriented vertically; *c* crescent handle—a horizontally oriented handle set just below the rim of a vessel, with a curved or crescentlike lower edge; *d* square handle— similar to type *c* but with a lower edge which is more sharply square.

LUGS
(Plates 17b, f, 23k-l, n)

All the lugs from TUV are pierced; this suggests that they may have been means by which lids or covers could be fastened onto vessels. Five types of lugs occur: both *a* large vertical nose lugs (7.5-8 cm) and *b* small vertical nose lugs (3-5 cm) are generally found as detached pieces, but they are known to occur on vessels with raised ridges running along at the level of the lug tops. Painted decoration also occurs on some of these vessels. Both *c* large bent nose lugs (7.5-8 cm) and *d* small bent nose lugs (3-5 cm) are similar to regular nose lugs but have a curved or bent lower portion. Horizontal pierced lugs *e*, set high on the shoulder of a vessel, occur but are very rare in the assemblage.

PERFORATED SHERDS

(not illustrated)

Several body sherds in the assemblage have a number of small, purposefully made round holes punched completely through the sherd walls. Such sherds appear to have been parts of sievelike vessels.

RELIEF-DECORATED SHERDS

(Plate 23a-b, g-h, j, m, o)

The following distinct types of raised-relief decoration occur in the TUV assemblage: *a* bumpy ware—body sherds with even, smooth bump(s); *b* "knobby" ware—body sherds studded with irregular bumps; *c* "rope" decoration; *d* "string" decoration, with less of a squashed appearance than *c*; *e* horizontal ridging; *f* vertical ridging or spines; *g* stepping-down effect in shoulder.

INCISED AND IMPRESSED SHERDS

(Plate 23d-e, i, l)

The following distinct types of incised and impressed decoration occur in the TUV assemblage: *a* incised horizontal lines; *b* incised vertical lines; *c* string impressions; *d* incised slanting lines; *e* incised lozenge design; *f* finger nail impressions; *g* punctate (circular) depressions.

PAINTED SHERDS

(Plate 24)

In painted decoration the basic colors employed are maroon, white, and grey-black. Designs occur in both monochrome and bichrome. Sometimes a bichrome effect is achieved by using one color of paint over a slip; at other times two colors of paint overlie a slip in a third color. The most common monochrome motif (in all colors) is one or more horizontal stripe(s), generally on the shoulder of the vessel or near a carination. Two stripes bordering a meander is also very common, but occurs only in maroon. Bichrome designs include such motifs as chevrons and checkerboards. There is no painting of animals or people on the TUV pottery.

Chapter Conclusion

Table 20 summarizes the temporal distribution of selected grit-tempered sherd types at TUV. This completes the typological description of the TUV ceramic assemblage. The next chapter continues with a morphological description of the non-ceramic finds.

V

Registered Items

Morphological description of site content has been shown above to be a necessary prelude to analytical characterization of the internal structure and function of a settlement. The current chapter completes this basic description of site content for the TUV operation by discussing the registered finds. This chapter is not intended to be a catalog or complete register of the TUV finds,[1] but rather a paradigmatic discussion of those general classes of functionally similar artifacts which are documented in the archaeological record of TUV. Each such class is defined and briefly described. The assignment of bulk finds (sherds and bones) to appropriate classes is also included in this discussion.

The focus throughout this chapter is on the finds as "utilized items," emphasizing the tasks for which items were probably employed. Considerations of shape, material, and condition are paramount at this level of descriptive analysis. The full range of registered material from TUV is described here in the text and via the figures. Some of this material was found in tertiary deposition, however, and must be excluded from later analyses of site structure and function. In order to establish which material was not in tertiary context but rather in primary, secondary, or secondarily admixed deposition, this chapter also briefly reviews the depositional placement of each class of items. Detailed analysis of activity patterning is reserved for chapter 6.

The Functional Class Model

The basic typological description of the registered finds from TUV is organized directly around the concept of function, rather than around the basic substances (e.g., bone, ceramic, stone) of which finds are composed. This arrangement facilitates the discussion to follow in subsequent chapters. Organization by raw material industries alone does not produce a sufficiently comprehensive paradigm for functional analysis. Small round balls, tablets, figurines, and grills, for example, can all be made of the same basic raw material, clay, yet their intended functions (the purposes for which they are being manufactured) are dramatically different.

Furthermore, when describing artifacts and other finds, it is in fact rather natural to attempt to infer the presumed functions of those items. Archaeologists can assign functions to many artifacts through a process of analogical reasoning coupled with experimental investigations when necessary. The functions of some artifacts, of course, may not be clear from study of the objects alone. In such cases, study of associated contextual material may lead to insights about object function.

Most of the registered finds from TUV are of sorts already well-known to Near Eastern archaeologists. It therefore does not seem appropriate to present elaborate justifications of the presumed functions for each object. Finds were assigned functions consonant with their shape, material, and condition when viewed against current knowledge of the ancient Near East. No claim is made that the "true" functions of all of these finds have been correctly recognized.

Finds were next sorted into appropriately designated *functional classes*, a general concept derived from South's (1977a) analysis of historic period American sites. Specific functional classes appropriate for TUV were created after initial study of the register. Items that had related functions were placed within the same class, even if made of different raw materials. As an ex-

1. A complete listing of the mf numbers for all items assigned to each functional class is found in the appendix. This listing is intended to serve as a bridge between the present paradigmatic treatment of finds and the original item-by-item register. The complete register of TUV finds is available in the archives of The University Museum.

TABLE 21
SUMMARY OF FUNCTIONAL CLASSES

Production/Processing	Storage	Consumption/Use	Control
1. Manufacture of chipped stone tools	10. General Storage	11. Basketry/matting	21. Information processing
2. Copper-base metallurgy		12. Special containers	
3. Manufacture of stone beads		13. Cutting tools	
4. Shell industry		14. Miscellaneous stone tools	
5. Preparation of plasters/ pigments		15. Piercing/boring tools	
6. Cloth industry		16. Personal ornaments	
7. Food preparation		17. Items of architectural use	
8. Pottery production		18. Food consumption	
9. Miscellaneous raw materials		19. Carpentry	
		20. Decorative items	

ample, small balls made of stone and of clay were grouped together; both varieties were probably used as counters or tokens.

The functional classes used in the TUV analysis are summarized on Table 21[2]. This Table and Figure 20 taken together illustrate the manner in which these classes can be integrated to model the "life-cycle" of individual utilized items. Procurement, production, storage, use (consumption), control, recycling, discard, and export phases are all represented in the model.

Procurement

In general, little trace of activities related to resource procurement was uncovered by the TUV operation. The only artifacts which may reflect direct procurement activity are chipped stone blades exhibiting sickle gloss (see class 13). The general absence of farming, mining, or hunting equipment at TUV implies that most elements of the archaeological record probably made their initial entry into the TUV system through an exchange network, rather than through direct procurement activities on the part of those individuals who inhabited the excavated buildings.

Production and Processing

Of the 21 functional classes based on the Banesh finds from TUV, nine classes contain items related to basic processing of materials which had entered the TUV system. These activities included the manufacture of various craft items and the preparation of basic food resources.

---

2. There are 25 non-Banesh finds (appendix p. 137) which have not been assigned to functional classes. Furthermore, there are 124 other items in the register which are not classifiable in the functional class system (see appendix p. 136-137). Many of these finds are in actuality technical samples (e.g., mineral samples, pollen samples) but others are finds exhibiting traces of human workmanship (Plate 27 k) or even portions of finished artifacts for which the function can not be plausibly inferred (Plates 26 a, h; 27 i; 37 c-e).

TABLE 22

DEPOSITIONAL PLACEMENT OF FINDS IN PRODUCTION/PROCESSING CLASSES

Functional class	Deposit type[a]	Above B.L. I[b]	B.L. I	B.L. II	B.L. IIIA	B.L. IIIB	Below B.L. III	Row totals
1. Manufacture of chipped stone tools	Primary/ secondary	9 (2m)	8	10 (4m)	11	45	0	83 (6m)
(N = 270)	Secondary admixture	0	0	11	6	0	0	17
	Tertiary	91	6	36	28	2	1	164
2. Copper-base metallurgy	Primary/ secondary	1	1	5 (3m)	26	3	1	37 (3m)
(N = 225)	Secondary admixture	0	1	13	22	5	0	41
	Tertiary	25	2	37	69	10	1	144
3. Manufacture of stone beads	Primary/ secondary	1	0	0	2	4	0	7
(N = 25)	Secondary admixture	0	0	0	2	0	0	2
	Tertiary	4	0	3	9	0	0	16
4. Shell industry	Primary/ secondary	1 (1m)	5	3 (2m)	7	3	0	19 (3m)
(N = 104)	Secondary admixture	0	1	5	8	0	1	15
	Tertiary	13	1	21	27	5	0	67
5. Preparation of plasters/ pigments	Primary/ secondary	2 (2m)	1	2	10	4	0	19 (2m)
(N = 60)	Secondary admixture	0	0	1	6	0	1	8
	Tertiary	3	0	6	19	3	0	31
6. Cloth industry	Primary/ secondary	0	0	1	1	0	0	2
(N = 8)	Secondary admixture	0	0	0	0	0	0	0
	Tertiary	2	0	1	2	1	0	6
7. Food production[c] —general	Primary/ secondary	0 (1m)	4	7	5	1	0	17 (1m)
(N = 41)	Secondary admixture	0	0	9	2	1	0	12
	Tertiary	2	0	6	2	1	0	11
—charcoals	Primary/ secondary	4 (3m)	11	18 (2m)	41 (1m)	8	1	83 (6m)
(N = 173)	Secondary admixture	0	0	4	14	1	0	19
	Tertiary	3	0	18	31	13	0	65

TABLE 22—*Continued*

Functional class	Deposit type[a]	Above B.L. I[b]	B.L. I	B.L. II	B.L. IIIA	B.L. IIIB	Below B.L. III	Row totals
8. Pottery production	Primary/ secondary	1	0	0	0	1	0	2
(N = 13)	Secondary admixture	0	0	2	0	0	1	3
	Tertiary	1	0	2	4	0	1	8
9. Miscellaneous raw materials	Primary/ secondary	1 (1m)	0	0	2	1	0	4 (1m)
(N = 21)	Secondary admixture	0	0	0	0	0	0	0
	Tertiary	4	0	4	6	2	0	16

[a]Finds coming from lots which were in part primary or secondary, but mixed with another deposit type during excavation are listed in ( ) with the symbol m. See chapter 1.

[b]Strata 0-2 are here considered above B.L. I, 3-4 are B.L. I, 5-8c are B.L. II, 8d-10 are B.L. IIIA, 11-13c are B.L. IIIB, and 13d-14 are below B.L. III.

[c]Registered items only. High concentrations of bulk finds of this class are shown on figure 25.

Functional Class 1: Manufacture of Chipped Stone Tools
(Table 22; Figure 21; Plate 28; Appendix p. 133)

SHAPE, CONDITION, AND MATERIAL

This class contains all the evidence from TUV which suggests manufacturing of chipped stone tools: appropriate raw material, cores, debitage, and larger waste flakes. Finished tools are not included in this class.

RAW MATERIALS

Unworked cryptocrystalline quartz (flint, chert, jasper, prase, and quartzite) occurred in small quantities at TUV (13 registered samples).

CORES

A core is a nodule of raw material from which one or more flakes have been deliberately removed. Seventeen examples of cryptocrystalline quartz cores were found at TUV.

3. Criteria for units to be screened are discussed above in chapter 1.

DEBITAGE AND LARGER UNRETOUCHED FLAKES

Debitage is here used to mean small waste chips from the production or maintenance of chipped stone tools. At TUV 113 examples were registered. Many such chips are so tiny as to be missed during excavation unless fine screening is carried out. Because not every lot at TUV could be screened,[3] examples of debitage were almost certainly missed. Larger unretouched flakes are less likely to have been missed in hand-picked lots, and 125 examples were registered in this category. Some of these larger flakes possibly might have been utilized for cutting. It is hoped that a specialized micro-wear study will eventually clarify this possibility.

DEPOSITIONAL PLACEMENT

Table 22 and Figure 21 indicate that a modest amount of flint knapping occurred in each building level, as demonstrated by finds in primary/secondary and secondarily admixed deposits. (Of the 270 finds in functional class 1, 39% came from non-tertiary contexts.) In B.L. I, a small cluster of a core, debitage, and a larger waste flake were found in pit 199. Evidence from B.L. II was scattered, but predominantly from the north unit and adjacent exterior zone. The evidence from B.L. IIIA was also scattered, but the major cluster was found in a secondary deposit in room 250.

Probably the best evidence for a discrete moment of flint-knapping activity at TUV came from B.L. IIIB, on the lower floor of room 215. A secondary deposit there produced two cores and a large collection of debitage (as well as some finished tools assigned to other classes). This collection of debris was sealed over by the upper floor of that room.

Functional Class 2: Copper-Base Metallurgy
(Table 22; Figure 22; Plates 25a-d, l, n, 29a-c; Appendix pp. 133-134)

SHAPE, CONDITION, AND MATERIAL

This class groups the abundant evidence at TUV for copper-base metallurgy; production debris (comprising slag and fragments of associated ceramic furnace linings), pieces of metallic ores, mold fragments, small prills of copper metal, and debris which may represent "intermediate" stages in artifact production (e.g., sheet stock, bar stock).

Although individually massive pieces of ore or slag were not found, this class, comprised of 225 individual finds, is one of the largest functional classes of material from TUV.

In the present report a general characterization of this class is presented. Preliminary analyses conducted by affiliates of the Museum Applied Science Center for Archaeology (MASCA) of The University Museum have shown that arsenic-rich copper ores were generally utilized at TUV; there is also a reasonable content of magnesium in the analyzed slags. At this point, no trace of tin has been discovered in the TUV evidence (Milton n.d.). In the light of Muhly's review of copper-base metallurgy in the Near East, which found (1976:88) no tin-bronze prior to the third millennium B.C., it would be extremely unlikely for Banesh material from TUV to contain tin.

The preliminary categorization of finds in this class has been prepared with the assistance of Vincent Pigott of MASCA, who is continuing analysis of the metallurgical debris and preparing a detailed technical report.

ORES

A small number of pebble-sized bits of possible copper ores (malachite and azurite) was found at TUV. These small fragments may be remnants of larger ore chunks used in the production of copper at the site. It is also possible that such ores were intended for use in the production of blue and green pigments (cf. Hodges 1970:55).

SLAGS AND SMALL FRAGMENTS OF COPPER

The TUV register contains 153 listings of small pieces of slag and/or copper, generally ranging from 1-19 gm in weight. Slag is the waste product which results from the smelting of copper ores. Small bits of copper can result from a variety of processes. In the smelting process, small blebs of copper known as prills form and may subsequently weather out of the slag. Small fragments of copper may also result from spillage during the casting process.

FURNACE LININGS

There are 39 registered pieces (some very small) of very flaky, densely chaff-tempered ceramic, bearing copper slag on their interior surfaces. Judging by the larger examples, these appear to be remnants of furnace linings rather than crucibles (e.g., mf 3977, Plate 25a). Two furnace linings had charcoal adhering to their exterior surfaces.

MOLDS

Molds are artifacts with depressions which can be filled with molten metal in order to cast implements or ingots. Four possible mold fragments of very densely straw-tempered, low-fired ceramic were found at TUV (Plate 25b-d). Two (mf 3827 and 3838) were somewhat oval in shape, one (mf 3905) triangular, and the last (mf 3831) troughlike in shape. These appear most likely to have been ingot (rather than implement) molds.

BAR STOCK

At TUV were found four copper pieces which were bar-shaped, i.e., relatively long but thin and rectangular or square in section. One example (mf 6938) had pinched ends, two (mf 1488, 1490) had one "chisel-like" end each, and the fourth (mf 5434) a thinned end, triangular in section. The intent behind these modifications is unclear. These finds may represent intermediate stages in the production of implements such as nails, needles, or pins.

SHEET STOCK

Sixteen small fragments of copper sheet were found at TUV. Although one of these (mf 3811) does look as if it formed a section of a tube, it is possible that the other sheet fragments represent debris from an intermediate stage in the manufacture of objects rather than broken remnants of finished artifacts.

FINDS NOT READILY CLASSIFIED

From TUV there are two registered pieces of odd looking metal which appear to have been purposefully shaped (possibly ingots?). Mf 3877 weighed 218 gm, was 14 x 2.8 x 1.7 cm, had rounded ends, one flat side and one convex side. Mf 3953 weighed 165 gm, was 9.2 cm long and 4.0 cm wide; this bar was rounded on one end and broken on the other; one surface was flattish and the other convex. The corrosion of both bars was reminiscent in general appearance of that of iron, but each bar was only slightly magnetic. The apparent iron content of these two artifacts might have resulted from (1) use of copper ore containing abundant iron, or (2) the addition of iron oxide to a smelting furnace to serve as a flux facilitating the slagging off of impurities.

LEAD FINDS

In addition to copper-related debris, a few worked and unworked lead fragments were found at TUV (see the discussion of functional class 12 below). Preliminary examination of these finds by MASCA suggests that lead smelting also may have taken place at this locality.

DEPOSITIONAL PLACEMENT

Of the 225 finds assigned to class 2, 36% came from primary/secondary or secondarily admixed deposits (see Table 22 and Figure 22). Only two such finds came from B.L. I. Metallurgical evidence from B.L. II was scattered, but with a notably higher incidence in the northeast area (V168).

Noticeably more debris of class 2 occurred in B.L. IIIA than in the higher levels. It would seem likely that in B.L. IIIA copper-base metallurgy was a relatively important activity. Class 2 remains were found widely throughout B.L. IIIA, but B.L. IIIB had only a few scattered occurrences. It might be speculated that one of the reasons for the remodelling of the north unit in B.L. IIIA was to pursue metallurgical activities in that vicinity.

Functional Class 3: Manufacture of Stone Beads

(Table 22; Figure 23; Appendix p. 134)

SHAPE, CONDITION, AND MATERIAL

Finished stone beads (see class 16) of lapis, quartz, turquoise, carnelian, zeolite, chlorite, chalcedony, calcite, limestone, and unidentified stones were collected at TUV. In class 3 are placed those finds suggestive of actual manufacture of such stone beads. One type of bead seems to have been definitely manufactured at TUV. In the course of conducting analyses of TUV mineral samples, J. Blackman of the Smithsonian Institution (personal communication) discovered both raw material and partially drilled tiny beads of zeolite. Although such partially worked beads were not found in other stones, finds of suitable raw material for beads were made of lapis(?), turquoise, quartz (rock crystal), and carnelian.

DEPOSITIONAL PLACEMENT

Of the 25 finds assigned to class 3, 36% were from primary/secondary or secondarily admixed deposits (see Table 22 and Figure 23). Zeolite, lapis, carnelian and quartz were the only materials coming from such deposits. The single find of unworked carnelian was from enigmatic stratum 2. All the other finds in nontertiary context were associated with B.L. IIIA and B. Especially noteworthy is the small cluster of material on the lower floor of room 215, including unworked zeolite, quartz, and probable lapis, plus a partially drilled zeolite bead broken during manufacture.

Functional Class 4: Shell Industry

(Table 22; Figure 23; Plate 30a-c, e; Appendix p. 134)

SHAPE, CONDITION, AND MATERIAL

This class contains finds which might relate to the activity of working shell. The largest category of evidence within this class consists of unworked raw material (88 finds), possibly originally intended for the manufacture of shell inlay or beads.

The varieties of unworked shell represented are: marine cone, olive and dentalium shells from the Persian Gulf, spiral shells representing both fresh water and land snails, and bivalve shells of as yet undetermined origin. (Comparative marine material was collected by William Sumner on Persian Gulf beaches and is in his possession at Ohio State University.)

In addition to these finds, there are 15 finds of partially worked shells, including cut or partially shaped chips of "mother of pearl" (the shiny interior surface of bivalve shells) probably intended for use as inlay.

Completed beads of shell are not included within this class, but in class 16, personal ornaments.

DEPOSITIONAL PLACEMENT

Of the 104 finds assigned to this class, 36% were found in primary/secondary or secondarily admixed deposits. Table 22 and Figure 23 show that elements of this class occurred in all building levels, but in a rather haphazard fashion. In B.L. I there was a cluster of three unworked shells in pit 199, and one isolated shell in room 88. The largest cluster in B.L. II was the three finds (including one worked piece) in room 43. In B.L. IIIA evidence was again scattered; adjacent rooms 247-250 appear to have had the biggest concentration of finds of this class. Finally, very little shell came from B.L. IIIB; the only finds were in pit 165.

Functional Class 5: Preparation of Plasters/Pigments

(Table 22; Figure 24; Appendix p. 134)

SHAPE, CONDITION, AND MATERIAL

FINDS RELATED TO LIME PLASTER PREPARATION

It was noted in chapter 3 that lime plaster was present on some walls and floors at TUV. Lime plaster is produced through heating calcium carbonate ($CaCO_3$) to drive off carbon dioxide (CO_2), leaving CaO or quicklime. When water is then added to this substance, quick reaction with evolution of heat occurs, resulting in slaked lime [$Ca(OH)_2$]. This material, when dried and powdered, can be stored. When later mixed with water, the slaked lime solution can be applied to walls and will quickly harden into lime plaster. Over the passage of time, as a result of exposure to carbon dioxide in the air, calcium carbonate crystals will grow in this plaster, giving further inner strength to the material. Eventually, slaked lime will thus chemically change back to $CaCO_3$. Accordingly it is not always possible to distinguish between a natural lump of unprocessed raw material[4] and an unutilized lump of prepared plaster (discarded after mixing) that has undergone such a chemical transformation

through time (Blackman 1982, and personal communication).

The TUV register lists 24 lumps of chalky limestone which may be either raw material or prepared (but unused) lime plaster.

FINDS POSSIBLY RELATED TO PIGMENT PRODUCTION

Twenty pieces of hematite and 16 pieces of limonite, minerals which could have served as raw materials for the production of red and yellow pigments, were found at TUV. As stated in chapter 3, traces of red- and black-painted plasters were found at TUV; yellow-painted plaster was not found there but is known from ABC. Black pigment would be made from organic carbon, readily available at TUV in the form of charcoal (see class 7).

DEPOSITIONAL PLACEMENT

Of the 60 finds assigned to class 5, 48% were from primary/secondary or secondarily admixed deposits

---

4. There are chalk deposits near Malyan, in the vicinity of Tang-i Tur, where chalky limestone occurs naturally in a pebblelike form

(personal communication J. Blackman).

(see Table 22 and Figure 24). The majority of these finds came from B.L. IIIA. The greater frequency of these raw materials in that level may be correlated with the more elaborate uses of plain and painted plasters in B.L. III than in the other levels at TUV (see chapter 3).

Functional Class 6: Cloth Industry
(Table 22; Figure 24; Plates 25m, 26f-g, 30h; Appendix p. 134)

SHAPE, CONDITION, AND MATERIAL

This category groups artifacts related to the manufacture of thread, the weaving of fabric, and the sewing together of finished pieces of cloth. These artifacts are spindle whorls, perforated sherds, and a needle.

Finished fabric logically does not belong in this class, but in any case, fabric is generally perishable and does not normally remain for the excavator of a Near Eastern mound to discover. Only two finds at TUV might represent traces of cloth, but they might equally well represent matting. These finds (mf 6105 and 3896) are whitish impressions associated respectively with Banesh burials 336 and 274 (cf. class 11).

SPINDLE WHORLS
(Plate 26f-g)

Spindle whorls, small perforated objects of clay or stone, are used in the process of making thread on a spindle as a flywheel to maintain the momentum of the spin (Childe 1954:194). Use of such whorls is well-known ethnographically (for an Iranian example, see Watson 1979:174-178).

Only three spindle whorls were found at TUV, one of soft greenish stone and two of clay.

PERFORATED SHERDS
(Plate 30h)

At TUV there were found four examples of sherds (both chaff and grit ware) which had been shaped into discs and had holes deliberately punched through their centers. Such sherds may have been a variant form of a spindle whorl made through the recycling of broken ceramics. It would seem likely, however, that such perforated sherds did not work so well as did the true spindle whorl; otherwise the inexhaustible supply of broken sherds that would have been available as raw material would have made the manufacture of whorls from "scratch" relatively uneconomical. Alternatively, perforated sherds may have been used as loom-weights. Pottery pierced with holes and tied to bundles of warp threads is known to have been used on warp-weighted looms in Iceland (Crowfoot 1954:427-8).

NEEDLE
(Plate 25m)

At TUV only a single eyed needle was found. This copper artifact (mf 3813) was complete, 8.3 cm long, 0.4 cm wide, had an oval eye-hole, and was presumably intended to be used in sewing.

DEPOSITIONAL PLACEMENT

Of the eight finds assigned to class 6, only two (25%) were found in non-tertiary deposition (Table 22, Figure 24). A spindle whorl was found in a secondary deposit in B.L. II's north unit, while a perforated sherd disc came from trashpile 301 of B.L. IIIA. (The sole needle in the TUV corpus was found in tertiary deposition in stratum 9.)

Functional Class 7: Food Preparation
(Table 22; Figure 25; Plates 6a, 14a-b, 15c-d, f, q, 16b, 17b-e, g-i, 18a-c, f, 19c, g-t, 20e-f, j-k, 21f-g, i-m, 27j, 31a-d, 32a; Appendix pp. 134-135)

SHAPE, CONDITION, AND MATERIAL

Included in this class are those finds which seem directly related to the preparation and cooking of food: faunal and botanical remains, artifacts of the grinding and pounding complexes, charcoal and ash residue, and various pottery forms.

FAUNAL AND BOTANICAL REMAINS

The methods employed in collecting faunal and botanical remains have been discussed in chapter 1. Animal bones were common finds at TUV, but despite an extensive sampling program, very little preserved botanical material was discovered. Miller (1980, 1982) reviews the limited botanical evidence; detailed study of the faunal material is ongoing (Zeder 1980, 1984, 1985).

GRINDING COMPLEX: QUERNS AND HANDSTONES

Thirteen querns and ten handstones were found in the TUV operation (Plate 6a, 31a-b). A quern is a rock slab upon which some substance was ground. Through grinding action, flat grinding slabs over time become "basined" and eventually troughed (Kraybill 1977:493). A handstone is a pecked stone tool of a size suitable to be held in one or both hands, and which is likely to have been used as a grinding agent on such a quern. Such handstones probably started out rounded and developed a flat lower surface with time, as a result of the grinding action (Hodges 1970:41).

The querns and handstones found at TUV were made of jasper sandstone, jasper conglomerate, diorite, hematitic sandstone, and limestone.

Ethnographic data on functions of grinding stones have been reviewed by Kraybill (1977); Sumner (1967) provides a general discussion of grinding activity in the ancient Near East. It is theoretically possible that some of the slabs and handstones from TUV might have been used for the pulverizing of pigments, but none of our examples had any visible traces of pigment on the grinding surfaces. (Had microscopic examination of the grinding surfaces been available, it is possible that such traces might have been found.) In the absence of macroscopic pigment traces, these artifacts have been taken as indicative of food preparation activity (such as the grinding of grain), except for those grinding stones which had been recycled. One quern (mf 6275) had been reused as a door socket (functional class 17), and another quern fragment (mf 3706) had been incorporated into the internal structure of hearth 227 of B.L. III.

POUNDING COMPLEX: MORTARS AND PESTLES

Pounding is a percussion technique used to crush fruits and vegetables, and to hull and pulverize seeds and nuts. It is useful in mechanically reducing seeds to a porridgelike texture as well (Kraybill 1977:492-493). Mortars and pestles could also be used in the preparation of pigments and cosmetics, but the TUV finds did not exhibit stains indicative of this.

There was just one mortar from TUV, mf 6274 (Plate 27j, 31d), which was set into a mud-plastered depression in alcove 26 of B.L. II. There were three possible pestle fragments, and also three pecked stone balls of 5.5, 4.5, and 5.5 cms in diameter, which may have been percussion tools although they are not pestle-shaped.

CHARCOAL AND ASH RESIDUE

This evidence has been placed in class 7, but with some hesitation, for this material may have resulted from any of several activities. Clearly bits of charcoal and concentrations of ash might be residue from cooking fires, but it is equally likely that any particular piece of material may have been part of a fire used for heating or lighting purposes. The distribution of hearths discussed in chapter 3 can also be taken as a tentative indication of the location of cooking fires. Finer discrimination of cooking versus general heating/lighting fires is attempted below, in the discussion of site structure in chapter 7.

POTTERY FORMS

Using general analogical reasoning, we would expect that food preparation vessels would be large enough to hold servings for several people, but not so huge as to be unwieldy. Therefore all medium restricted vessels, large unrestricted vessels, and burnished plates have been tentatively assigned to class 7. (For typological description of size and form categories, see chapter 4.)

DEPOSITIONAL PLACEMENT

REGISTERED FINDS

Of the 173 finds of charcoal made at TUV, 63% were found in non-tertiary deposition, while 70.7% of the other registered finds from class 7 came from primary/secondary or secondarily admixed contexts (see Table 22 and Figure 25). The limited material from B.L. I was scattered, with most of the registered finds coming from pits or wells. While there is some scattering in B.L. II, there was a concentration of material of this class in the north unit. Rooms 43, 36, 32, 26, and 25 were particularly rich in such debris. (This is not surprising as these rooms were the locus of an extensive set of hearths, ovens and storage bins, as noted in chapter 3.) B.L. IIIA was much more rich in charcoals than B.L. II, but less rich in other registered finds of this class. This leads to the suspicion that much of the B.L. IIIA charcoal may have originated from fires not used primarily for food preparation. These charcoals were distributed widely throughout the level with no particular clustering apparent. Finally, only a few random finds of this class were recovered from B.L. IIIB.

BULK FINDS

(High Concentrations Plotted on Figure 25)

Animal bone was recovered from non-tertiary contexts in all four building levels. B.L. I produced 5,363 gm, B.L. II, 12,081 gm, B.L. IIIA 15,818 gm and B.L. IIIB 4,662 gm. In B.L. I, 71% of the recovered bone came from well 199; the remainder came from five scattered loci. In B.L. II, small room 32 in the north unit produced the largest single quantity of bone in that level (2,276 gm or about 19% of the level's yield). Area 39 and room 157 each had over a kilogram of bone remains. The remaining bone was found widely spread over the building level.

B.L. IIIA had seven loci having over a kilogram of bone debris each. The largest concentration was found in trashpile 301, which had nearly 23% of the faunal remains discovered in that level. Pit 163, alley 307, pit 285, room 284, room 258, and trashpile 241 were the other high concentrations. The remainder of the bone was found widely scattered over the level. Bone was also widespread in the non-tertiary deposits of B.L. IIIB; the largest concentration was in pit 165, containing almost 62% of the faunal remains from that level.

Of the ceramic bulk finds, diagnostic rim sherds of medium restricted vessels, large bowls, and burnished plates were assigned to class 7. Sherds of these kinds were not plentiful in B.L. I; no non-tertiary loci in that level had ten or more sherds of this class. B.L. II had more evidence of this class. Room 102, courtyard 30, area 39, and room 36 each had at least 10 sherds, and lesser quantities occurred in a number of other loci. B.L. IIIA also had scattered sherds of this class; concentrations of at least 10 sherds were found in two loci, trashpile 301 and room 250. Finally, B.L. IIIB also produced a few sherds of class 7 with a concentration of such sherds in pit 165.

Functional Class 8: Pottery Production(?)

(Table 22; Figure 24; Plate 30i; Appendix p. 135)

SHAPE, CONDITION, AND MATERIAL

Certain artifacts (unperforated sherd discs, ceramic slag, and possible kiln wasters) which may reflect the production of ceramics have been grouped together in class 8. There were nine unperforated sherd discs; these may have served as smoothers or burnishers in the manufacture of pottery, but this is only a suggestion. Also found were three pieces of possible kiln wasters (sherds warped in some way in the firing) and a piece of ceramic slag.[5]

DEPOSITIONAL PLACEMENT

Of the 13 finds assigned to class 8, 39% were found in non-tertiary contexts (Table 22, Figure 24). The only such finds in secure Banesh context were three unperforated sherd discs—one from B.L. IIIB and two from B.L. II. When this highly limited distribution is combined with the lack of kilns among the TUV features, and with the observation that no ceramic slag or wasters were recovered in the 5% surface pickup of the remainder of the TUV mound by Alden (1979), it seems that there is very little evidence to suggest that TUV was ever a major pottery production locus.

Functional Class 9: Miscellaneous Raw Materials

(Table 22; Figure 24; Appendix p. 135)

SHAPE, CONDITION, AND MATERIAL

The final class among those assigned to the production and processing group is a miscellaneous one, composed of unworked finds of agate, carbonate rock, travertine, calcite, limestone, specular hematite, and bitumen. Such substances were presumably procured for some purpose, but there are no indications remaining as to what this purpose may have been.

DEPOSITIONAL PLACEMENT

Of the 21 finds assigned to this class, only 24% were found in non-tertiary context (Table 22 and Figure 24). No such finds came from B.L. I or B.L. II. Some specular hematite and travertine were found in B.L. IIIA trash deposits, while a piece of carbonate rock was recovered in secondary context in B.L. IIIB.

5. The category "pebble-polisher" used by Nicholas (1980a:444-445) has been eliminated here. Upon reconsideration of the finds originally placed in this category, those finds appear to be too small to have been usable as burnishers.

Storage

While some items may be used or consumed immediately following the production/processing phase of their life-cycles, many items will be stored for a period of time, that is, held aside in appropriate rooms or containers until they are actually needed. Of the 21 functional classes defined for TUV, one class was created to group items used in the act of storing goods. (Storage as used here implies relatively long-term containment of materials. Containers which may have held substances for short periods of time are discussed under "Consumption and Use.")

Functional Class 10: General Storage

(Table 23; Figure 26; Plates 15e, 16c-m, 17f, j-o, 18e, g-l, 19d-f, 20g, l, n, 21h, 24s, 35a-f; Appendix p. 135)

SHAPE, CONDITION, AND MATERIAL

This class contains those finds which are most clearly related to storage activities: large pottery vessels, unsealed jar stoppers, unimpressed sealings, and seal impressions. Seal impressions are also indicative of class 21, information processing.

LARGE POTTERY FORMS

Pottery vessels of sizes too large to be easily picked up and moved about were most probably storage vessels. Large and extra-large restricted vessels, plus extra-large unrestricted vessels, have been assigned to class 10 for this reason. (Typological descriptions of these vessels are found in chapter 4.) It is possible that vessels of smaller size may also have been used for storage purposes, but it has not been possible to distinguish such containers from those used in daily activities.

UNSEALED JAR STOPPERS, OTHER UNIMPRESSED SEALINGS, AND SEAL IMPRESSIONS

The word "sealing" as used by the Malyan Project refers to any clay used to secure vessels, baskets, doors, etc. Such sealings may or may not have been *impressed* with a seal. There is an extensive literature on the functions of seals and sealings in the ancient Near East (see for example Gibson and Biggs 1977). In the present volume, this category of evidence is treated only in general terms. An ongoing specialized study (Pittman 1980) treats in detail both the stylistic attributes and the practical functions of the Banesh sealings from TUV (and ABC as well).

At TUV, unimpressed jar stoppers, other unimpressed sealings, and both cylinder and stamp seal impressions occur. The impressions include both naturalistic (representational) and geometric (abstract) designs. Utilizing the general comments in the Malyan

TABLE 23

DEPOSITIONAL PLACEMENT OF FINDS IN THE STORAGE CLASS

Functional class	Deposit type[a]	Above B.L. I[b]	B.L. I	B.L. II	B.L. IIIA	B.L. IIIB	Below B.L. III	Row totals
10. General storage[c]	Primary/ secondary	0	0	20	57 (1 m)	135	0	212 (1 m)
(N = 304)	Secondary admixture	0	0	2	37	0	0	39
	Tertiary	25	0	16	10	1	0	52

[a] Finds coming from lots which were in part primary or secondary, but mixed with another deposit type during excavation are listed in ( ) with the symbol m. See chapter 1.

[b] Strata 0-2 are here considered above B.L. I, 3-4 are B.L. I, 5-8c are B.L. II, 8d-10 are B.L. IIIA, 11-13c are B.L. IIIB, and 13d-14 are below B.L. III.

[c] Registered finds only. High concentrations of bulk items of this class are given in figure 26. Note that seal impressions are counted both here and in class 21.

Project register, it is possible to conclude that most of the seal impressions from TUV are on vessel sealings, which frequently also bear impressions of string, heavy cord, and/or leather. Tag sealings also occur (cf. Sumner 1976:108-09), but are not numerous.

DEPOSITIONAL PLACEMENT

REGISTERED FINDS

Of the 304 registered finds assigned to class 10, 83% were found in non-tertiary context (Table 23 and Figure 26). No such finds were recovered from B.L. I. All finds of this class from B.L. II were associated with room 102 of the southwest unit: 15 seal impressions and five unimpressed sealings from pit 132 on the lower floor and two additional seal impressions from a secondarily admixed deposit on the upper floor of the room.

The great majority of the sealings (impressed and unimpressed) at TUV were associated with B.L. III. Ten examples were recovered from pit 163 and 53 from room 164 in B.L. IIIA. Room 284 was also an important locus for sealings, and there were a few scattered additional finds. All the 135 finds of this class in B.L. IIIB came from pit 165.

It appears from the register that the impressions from the extreme western locus in B.L. IIIA and B (pits 163, 165, room 164) differed from those found elsewhere in B.L. III. Both stamp and cylinder seal impressions were found in the western group. The stamp seal designs were diverse, including animal, human, floral, and geometric motifs. Most of the cylinder seal impressions were geometric, with a "triangles and ladders" motif being particularly common.

On the other hand, each impressed sealing from room 284 appears to represent a different design, both naturalistic and geometric. In addition to vessel sealings, two tag sealings were found in this latter area, as well as a sealing which may have been on a box. Six unimpressed jar stoppers were also recovered from room 284.

It is thus possible that large sets of similar stored items may have been opened near the western locus, while more diverse stored goods were opened near the room 284 site.

BULK FINDS

(High Concentrations Plotted on Figure 26)

Rim sherds of large and extra-large restricted vessels and of extra-large unrestricted vessels have been assigned to class 10. Some sherds of this class were found scattered in non-tertiary deposition in every building level. Concentrations of at least 10 such sherds came from room 102, courtyard 30, room 36, and area 39 in B.L. II, trashpile 301, room 284, and room 250 in B.L. IIIA, and pit 165 in B.L. IIIB. There were no such concentrations in B.L. I.

Consumption and Use

Ten functional classes have been defined to group artifacts used (or consumed) in activities other than manufacturing, food preparation, storage, or control. It is difficult to define this group of classes except by specifying what it does not contain, for consumption and use are ambiguous terms. (Ores are "consumed" in the smelting of copper, needles are "used" in the sewing of cloth, large jars are "used" to store water or grain....) The intent of the model here is to distinguish between items primarily related to production, holding, and information processing from those "used" in other ways. In an important way, many of these classes can be conceptualized as the products of classes 1 through 9. For example, class 13, cutting tools, involves the use of chipped stone blades which may have been among the tools manufactured at TUV as shown by class 1 debris. Similarly, class 16, personal ornaments, contains shell and stone beads which may have been manufactured at TUV (class 4 and class 3 debris), as well as copper pins which might be related to the copper-base metallurgy shown by class 2 debris to have been important at the site. Class 18 (food consumption) represents the logical completion of the food preparation activities documented in class 7. Figure 20 indicates in schematic form such connections between production and consumption activities at TUV. (Of course, it must be remembered that these are general connections; it is not possible to say for any one item in particular that it was *definitely* made at TUV and not imported from elsewhere.)

Functional Class 11: Basketry/Matting

(Table 24; Figure 27; Plate 12b; Appendix p. 135)

SHAPE, CONDITION, AND MATERIAL

Basketry and matting have been grouped together because both types of items represent utilitarian artifacts "used" to "contain" other items in ways that most likely differed from general storage. Unfortunately, these items are highly perishable, and evidence for this class at TUV is almost nonexistent.

BITUMEN-LINED BASKETS?

There are three finds of small, thin bitumen fragments with matlike impressions of reeds on one side and a smooth surface on the other. These may be remnants of bitumen-lined baskets intended for short-term storage of liquids. Baskets are also known to have been used in ancient Mesopotamia to shape or mold liquid bitumen mastic into cakes of standard volume (Forbes 1954:254).

MAT IMPRESSIONS?

As noted in the discussion of class 6, two whitish impressions were found associated with Banesh burials at TUV. Mf 6105 was found with burial 336, mf 3896 with burial 274 (Plate 12b). It is not possible to tell whether these are impressions of mats or of loosely woven cloth. The impressions would appear to represent the shrouds or mats which contained the individuals being buried.

DEPOSITIONAL PLACEMENT

Only five finds have been assigned to this class. All of these came from primary/secondary or secondarily admixed deposits, but only four were from secure Banesh context (B.L. IIIA). These finds were two remnants of bitumen-lined baskets (from room 258 and room 250) plus the two cloth/mat impressions from burials 336 and 274.

Functional Class 12: Special Containers

(Table 24; Figure 27; Plates 13a-bb, 14c-d, 19a, 22a-c, 27a-f, h, 29d, 33a-c; Appendix p. 135)

SHAPE, CONDITION, AND MATERIAL

This class groups vessels of three kinds: (1) those made of substances more "exotic" than ceramic, (2) miniature ceramic forms, and (3) certain mass-produced ceramic vessels, the function of which constitutes an interpretative problem in the general archaeology of this era in the ancient Near East.

STONE VESSELS

Fifty-five fragments of such vessels, including sherds of flat bases and of plain rounded rims, were registered at TUV: 23 of travertine, 19 of limestone, 9 of calcite, 1 of green marble, and 3 of unidentified stone.

A complete limestone vessel (mf 5078) was found accompanying adult burial 274. This vessel had a flat base (9.2 cm in diameter), extremely flaring sides, and a rough rim, apparently cut down from a rim originally more carefully finished (Plate 27a).

METAL VESSELS

No finds were made of copper/bronze vessels at TUV, but one unusual find[6] was made of a lead bowl (mf 3878a, Plate 27h) in good Banesh context. Two lead discs were found inside this bowl (Plates 27k, 29d). As mentioned in the discussion of class 2, a number of worked and unworked lead fragments were also discovered at TUV.

PLASTER VESSELS

Two sherds of a plaster vessel(s) were found in the same tertiary deposit at TUV. One was a simple everted rim sherd and the other a body sherd with three deeply incised parallel horizontal bands.

MASS-PRODUCED CERAMICS

Bevelled-rim bowls and necked goblets (described in chapter 4) were present in large quantity at TUV. The function of these forms in the ancient Near East is still

---

6. Lead metallurgy appears to have been a relatively late development in the ancient Near East, perhaps because this metal entirely lacked the physical properties needed for the production of weapons and tools (Forbes 1964:197). Cf. Hodges (1970:146): "lead as a metal had

been known from perhaps 3000 B.C., for it is comparatively easy to smelt, but little use had been found for it because it was far too soft for making tools and too unattractive for making personal ornaments."

TABLE 24
DEPOSITIONAL PLACEMENT OF FINDS IN CONSUMPTION/USE CLASSES

Functional class	Deposit type[a]	Above B.L. I[b]	B.L. I	B.L. II	B.L. IIIA	B.L. IIIB	Below B.L. III	Row totals
11. Basketry/ matting	Primary/ secondary	1m	0	0	4	0	0	4 (1m)
(N = 5)	Secondary admixture	0	0	0	0	0	0	0
	Tertiary	0	0	0	0	0	0	0
12. Special containers: stone vessel sherds	Primary/ secondary	3	0	0	4[c]	0	0	7
(N = 58)	Secondary admixture	0	0	5	3	0	0	8
	Tertiary	17	5	14	5	2	0	43
other registered special containers[d] (N = 6)	Primary/ secondary	0	0	0	2	1	0	3
	Secondary admixture	0	0	1	1	0	0	2
	Tertiary	0	0	1	0	0	0	1
13. Cutting tools	Primary/ secondary	9	2	0	4	11	0	26
(N = 116)	Secondary admixture	0	1	3	5	0	1	10
	Tertiary	42	3	19	14	2	0	80
14. Miscellaneous chipped stone tools	Primary/ secondary	1	1	0	4	10	0	16
(N = 83)	Secondary admixture	0	0	6	1	1	0	8
	Tertiary	22	4	9	21	3	0	59
15. Piercing/ boring tools	Primary/ secondary	0	0	0	0	0	0	0
(N = 3)	Secondary admixture	0	0	0	1	0	0	1
	Tertiary	0	0	1	1	0	0	2
16. Personal ornaments	Primary/ secondary	0	4	2	1	1	0	8
(N = 41)	Secondary admixture	0	0	3	1	0	0	4
	Tertiary	5	4	11	9	0	0	29
17. Items of architectural use[e]	Primary/ secondary	2	1	0	2	0	0	5
(N = 22)	Secondary admixture	0	0	0	3	1	0	4
	Tertiary	3	1	3	5	1	0	13
18. Food consumption[f]	Primary/ secondary	0	1	1	0	2	0	4
(N = 12)	Secondary admixture	0	0	1	1	0	0	2
	Tertiary	1	0	5	0	0	0	6

TABLE 24—*Continued*

Functional class	Deposit type[a]	Above B.L. I[b]	B.L.I	B.L. II	B.L. IIIA	B.L. IIIB	Below B.L. III	Row totals
19. Carpentry	Primary/ secondary	0	0	0	1	0	0	1
(N = 1)	Secondary admixture	0	0	0	0	0	0	0
	Tertiary	0	0	0	0	0	0	0
20. Decorative items[g]	Primary/ secondary	0	3	0	2	0	0	5
(N = 17)	Secondary admixture	0	0	1	1	0	0	2
	Tertiary	1	0	6	3	0	0	10

[a] Finds coming from lots which were in part primary or secondary, but mixed with another deposit type during excavation are listed in ( ) with the symbol m. See chapter 1.

[b] Strata 0-2 are here considered above B.L. I, 3-4 are B.L. I, 5-8c are B.L. II, 8d-10 are B.L. IIIA, 11-13c are B.L. IIIB, and 13d-14 are below B.L. III.

[c] One of these, mf 5078, is a complete vessel.

[d] High concentrations of bulk items of this class are shown on figure 27.

[e] Registered items only, including samples of plasters. Distribution of unregistered items of this class is shown on figure 30.

[f] Registered items only. There are no high concentrations of bulk items for this class.

[g] Registered items only. High concentrations of bulk items of this class are shown on figure 31.

enigmatic (but see chapter 8). Low trays have also been placed in class 12, for sherds of this form were also very common at TUV.

MINIATURE CERAMIC VESSEL

Mf 1458 has been assigned to the class of special containers because it is unique in the TUV corpus; it is a restricted vessel only 7.7 cm tall (Plate 19 a).

DEPOSITIONAL PLACEMENT

REGISTERED FINDS

Of the 58 registered finds of stone vessel parts, 26% were found in non-tertiary context (Table 24, Figure 27). B.L. I and B.L. IIIB had no such finds, while B.L. II had five; three of those came from the north unit and adjacent area 39. B.L. IIIA had six finds of stone vessel sherds, primarily from the west unit and adjacent exterior zone. Whole vessel mf 5078 was found in burial 274. Evidently only in this special ritual context was an intact stone vessel discarded purposefully by the ancient inhabitants of TUV. Stone containers were probably too valuable to be carelessly thrown away. In fact, the burial vessel shows signs of having undergone a rough repair on its rim, which may have increased the life-span of this vessel.

The B.L. II finds were of travertine, calcite, and limestone; the B.L. IIIA sherds of green marble and limestone.

Five of the six registered vessels made of materials other than stone in this class came from non-tertiary context. Once again, no finds came from B.L. I. Miniature vessel mf 1458 came from room 32 of the B.L. II north unit. Low tray mf 5084, bevelled-rim bowl mf 1725, and the lead bowl (mf 3878) came from B.L. IIIA, while bevelled-rim bowl mf 1724 came from B.L. IIIB.

BULK FINDS

(High Concentrations Plotted on Figure 27)

Diagnostic rim sherds of bevelled-rim bowls, goblets, and low trays were assigned to class 12 (Plates 13a-bb, 22a, g, i). Compared to the other levels, the number of such sherds in non-tertiary deposition in B.L. I was very low. Sherds of bevelled-rim bowls were the least numerous in that level. Room 88 had small concentrations of over 10 rim sherds each of low trays and goblets.

In B.L. II, sherds of this class were generally widely scattered, but bevelled-rim bowl sherds were both less scattered and less numerous than the other forms. Bevelled-rim bowl sherds were most plentiful in rooms 102 and 174. Low trays were most plentiful in room 174, with other noteworthy concentrations in room

102, courtyard 30, area 39, area 43, and area 379. Goblet sherds were most plentiful in room 102, northern courtyard 30, and area 379.

In B.L. IIIA, goblet sherds were the least numerous of the three forms included in this class. All three forms were very numerous in absolute terms, however. All three forms were widely spread throughout the main structure and adjacent exterior areas, but bevelled-rim bowls were almost absent from the far western area of the operation.

Trash pile 301 contained the largest concentration of these forms in B.L. IIIA, with 756 rim sherds of bevelled-rim bowls, 883 rim sherds of low trays, and 291 rim sherds of goblets. The second largest con-

centration was in room 284 with 195 rim sherds of bevelled-rim bowls, 143 rim sherds of low trays, and 42 rim sherds of goblets. Pit 285 had 111 rim sherds of bevelled-rim bowls, 198 rim sherds of low trays, and 57 rim sherds of goblets. Room 306 had 99 rim sherds of bevelled-rim bowls, 82 of low trays, and 73 of goblets. Lesser concentrations were scattered throughout the level.

In B.L. IIIB, the three forms were all widely represented in non-tertiary deposition, but goblets were considerably less numerous. Room 306 had the largest concentration, with 187 bevelled-rim bowl rim sherds, 220 low tray rim sherds, and 20 goblet rim sherds.

Functional Class 13: Cutting Tools
(Table 24; Figure 28; Plate 26j-n; Appendix p. 135)

SHAPE, CONDITION, AND MATERIAL

From Banesh context at TUV only chipped stone blades and blade segments can be firmly assigned to this class. No metal knives were found in Banesh levels.

In lithic descriptions, the term blade is generally applied to parallel-sided flakes at least twice as long as they are wide. Freshly manufactured blades normally have exceedingly sharp edges and make ideal cutting implements.

Even macroscopic examination of the TUV blade assemblage revealed the presence of sickle gloss on some of the artifacts. One example exhibited bitumen remnants, which would have served to haft the tool in a sickle handle. It is hoped that the chipped stone tool assemblage from TUV will undergo further specialized study, including edge-wear analysis. Such analysis hopefully will discriminate among possible uses for the blades and blade segments, such as use in sickles, use in butchering meat, etc.

All but two of the 116 blades and blade segments from TUV are of cryptocrystalline quartz (jasper, flint,

chert, and prase). One example is of an unidentified stone, and one of limestone.

It is of course also possible that some of the "large waste flakes" documented in class 1 might have been used for cutting. The projected edge-wear study should detect the use of such items for cutting or other purposes if they were indeed utilized.

DEPOSITIONAL PLACEMENT

Of the 116 finds assigned to class 13, 31% were found in non-tertiary contexts (Table 24, Figure 28). A small number of such finds occurred in each building level. The largest cluster came from room 215 in B.L. IIIB. As noted in the discussion of class 1, a cluster of chipping debris was also found in this locus. This raises the possibility that the blade segments found in room 215 may have been discarded without ever being used.

There is a tendency for blade segments to be relatively more important in B.L. III, while unsegmented blades predominate in B.L. II and B.L. I.

Functional Class 14: Miscellaneous Chipped Stone Tools
(Table 24; Figure 28; Plate 26i; Appendix pp. 135-136)

SHAPE, CONDITION, AND MATERIAL

As a miscellaneous class, this is one of the least satisfying artifact groups in the model. The category is defined more on a negative criterion than on positive grounds. Class 14 holds those chipped stone tools

which are not macroscopically interpretable as having a primary cutting function. These tools have been categorized by gross shape and overall character into such types as "scrapers," "notched tools," "geometric microliths," etc. The functions of these tools would also be clarified by the projected edge-wear study.

DEPOSITIONAL PLACEMENT

Of the 83 finds assigned to class 14, 29% were found in non-tertiary deposition (Table 24, Figure 28). One geometric microlith was found in secondary context in B.L. I. All the finds in B.L. II were in secondarily admixed deposits; these tools include an apparent scraper, two possible drills, and three notched tools. An apparent scraper, drill(?), microblade segment, and geometric microlith were found in secondary context in B.L. IIIA; a notched tool in secondarily admixed deposition.

The largest cluster of finds in this class came from B.L. IIIB, in secondary context in room 215. Four geometric microliths, three notched tools, and three retouched flakes were recovered there from the same deposit which produced clusters of class 1 and class 13 debris. One additional notched tool was recovered from secondarily admixed context elsewhere in the level.

Functional Class 15: Piercing/Boring Tools
(Table 24; Figure 28; Appendix p. 136)

SHAPE, CONDITION, AND MATERIAL

This small group of artifacts holds tools which were probably used in boring or piercing actions (such as might occur in leather working, for example). These artifacts include a worked bone awl and two fragmentary pieces of bone which may have been used for piercing.

If the edge-wear study becomes possible, some of the stone tools in class 14 may prove to have been used for drilling, a type of boring action.

DEPOSITIONAL PLACEMENT

Only one of the three finds assigned to class 15 was found in non-tertiary context. Bone awl mf 7972 came from a secondarily admixed deposit in area 372 of B.L. IIIA.

Functional Class 16: Personal Ornaments
(Table 24; Figure 29; Plates 25e-k, o, 26o-x, 30d, f-g; Appendix p. 136)

SHAPE, CONDITION, AND MATERIAL

This class groups those artifacts which are presumed to have been worn about the person or attached to one's garments, i.e., beads, pins, and a ring. No other kinds of Banesh ornaments were recovered (see the appendix for non-Banesh finds of jewelry).

No constellations of many beads representing necklace chains were found at TUV. The scattered beads found represented a considerable variety of raw materials: shell, calcite, chalcedony, limestone, rock crystal, lapis, carnelian, chlorite, zeolite, unidentified stone, frit, and bone.

The TUV pins are nine copper artifacts which look as if they might have been used to hold together the edges of a garment or as decoration. Most of these were "straight pins" with bulbous or rectangular heads and shafts which tapered slightly toward the lower ends;

two pins ended in hooks, however, and one was curved (but had its head missing).

Finally, the one Banesh ring at TUV was of copper, 3.2 x 3.0 x 0.3 cm and thus too big to have been a finger-ring. It is unclear whether this was actually an ornament.

DEPOSITIONAL PLACEMENT

Of the 41 finds assigned to class 16, 29% were found in non-tertiary context. Scattered, rare finds occurred in each building level (Table 24, Figure 29). B.L. I had four stone beads, B.L. II had two stone beads, one frit bead, one shell bead, and a copper pin. B.L. IIIA had a copper pin and a stone bead, and B.L. IIIB a copper ring.

Functional Class 17: Items of Architectural Use

(Table 24; Figure 30; Plate 27g, l-m, 32b-c; Appendix p. 136)

SHAPE, CONDITION, AND MATERIAL

The items in this class all appear to have had primary functions directly related to the construction and use of walls, rooms, and doorways. These elements are: door sockets, drains, wall cones, tiles, and fired bricks. (The basic building materials of mud brick and plaster are discussed in chapter 3.)

DOOR SOCKETS

The four TUV door sockets are relatively heavy objects, each of which has in its upper surface a rather narrow, rounded depression with circular wear marks. Presumably a door pole was once set in this depression; the pole would have rotated in the socket when the door was opened or closed.

All of the TUV examples of door sockets were made by *recycling* items originally used in other ways. Two (mf 1742, 1743) were made from broken fragments of fired bricks, one (mf 1312) from a heavy, grit-tempered pot sherd (Plate 27g), and one (mf 6275) from a sandstone grinding stone. (Mf 6275 is distinctly an example of a reused grinding stone, not a mortar. The door socket is in a different face of the artifact than that which was the grinding surface.)

DRAIN SPOUTS
(Plate 27l-m, 32b-c)

A typological description of this ceramic form has been given in chapter 4.

WALL CONES

The TUV excavations found six ceramic (i.e., baked, tempered clay) cone-shaped objects plus one cylindrical fragment of Banesh straw-tempered ware which might have been part of such a cone. No stone wall cones were found. (Mf 6972 is a fragmentary limestone cylinder with a diameter of 3.3 cm. It exhibits no tapering, however, and is slightly flattened. This find has been considered a possible pestle and placed in functional class 7.)

Clay and stone cones are a well-known decorative device used in mosaic patterns on the facades of important Mesopotamian buildings in major centers during the Uruk and Jemdet Nasr phases. Frequently, colored pigments were applied to the heads of such cones. There are also rare finds of cone mosaic in the Early Dynastic period: at Uruk (Frankfort and Davies 1971:77) and at Al'Ubaid (Mallowan 1965:38).

Wall cones are generally taken as indicative of a "public" or administrative function for the buildings so adorned. Johnson (1973:104, 105, 123) reviewed the distribution of wall cones, finding that both around Warka in southern Iraq and around Susa and Chogha Mish in Khuzistan wall cones have also been found on smaller sites. Johnson predicted that such sites might have served as small centers administering local exchange. While Johnson did demonstrate a significant correlation between the presence of wall cones and the distribution of locally traded vessels with wide strap handles, no study has yet proved that such wall cones occurred *only* on administrative structures.

None of the TUV cones were found *in situ* in a wall, and all were isolated finds. If these cones were originally part of a mosaic, they must have derived from buildings lying beyond the excavated zone. Otherwise, one could not account for the paucity of cones at TUV; to create a mosaic, hundreds of cones would have been used, yet baked clay cones would not be destroyed by normal weathering. Perhaps cones occasionally had other, as yet unrecognized, functions.

TILES

Tiles are rectangular or square ceramic slabs, often having one or more bevelled edges. There were 16 mostly fragmentary examples found at TUV; only one of these was registered (mf 3830). An intact example measures 28.3 x 15.2 x 3.6 cm. Most of the tiles, however, are thinner than this, with thicknesses ranging from 2.1 to 3.0 cm. No tiles were found in primary context, and the exact manner of their use at TUV is unknown. It would seem plausible that they served as decorative and/or protective architectural elements on the roof. Two specimens provide clues to the possible method of attachment: mf 3830 had a 4.3 cm wide strip of bitumen along one edge of the tile. An unregistered tile from area 308 of B.L. IIIA had two holes (each with a diameter of c. 2.2 cm) through the tile.

FIRED BRICKS

The virtue of rain resistance of fired brick over sun-dried mud brick is obvious. In ancient Mesopotamia, important buildings were sometimes given outer facades of such fired brick for protective purposes.

Fired bricks were very rare at TUV; most of the 17 examples were fragmentary. These bricks occurred in at least three distinctly different sizes. One type appeared to be rectangular, with a width of about 7 cm. The total length of these could not be determined; the largest fragment had a length of 9.4 cm. Thickness of this type averaged about 3.2 cm. The second type of fired brick was square: dimensions were slightly variable (suggesting these bricks were not moldmade), but the average size was about 14 x 14 x 3 cm. It is possible that these first two categories of fired bricks might represent approximationsto "half" and "whole" bricks, respectively.

The third size of fired brick was observed in only one specimen, the only fired brick found in its primary context. This 41 x 22.75 x 10.75 cm brick was built into mud brick wall 246 of B.L. III, adjacent to doorway 317.

DEPOSITIONAL PLACEMENT

REGISTERED FINDS

Of the 22 registered finds assigned to class 17, 41% were found in non-tertiary context (Table 24, Figure 30). In well 195 of B.L. I was found a wall cone. There were no registered finds in B.L. II, but B.L. IIIA yielded a drain spout in secondary deposition and a door soc-

ket and wall cone in secondary admixture. (The other specimens from B.L. IIIA were registered samples of plasters.) B.L. IIIB had a tile in secondarily admixed deposition.

Although it would be very interesting to know with which kind of rooms door sockets were used, it is not possible to answer this question, for none of the TUV examples were in primary context. Also, there were obviously far more doorways at TUV than there were door sockets recovered by our excavation. Most door sockets may have been carefully saved for re-use when rooms were abandoned. Alternatively, many doorways may have been left open, had doors hung on wooden or leather hinges, or been closed by material curtains.

BULK FINDS

Figure 30 shows the distribution of unregistered drain spout sherds in non-tertiary deposition. Scattered examples of such sherds were found in every building level.

Functional Class 18: Food Consumption

(Table 24; Figure 31; Plates 15a-b, g-p, 17a, 18d, 19b, 20a-e, h, i, 21a-e, 22e, f, 24j; Appendix p. 136)

SHAPE, CONDITION, AND MATERIAL

General analogical reasoning leads to the expectation that vessels used in food consumption activity would generally be of smaller sizes than those used in food preparation. Therefore small restricted vessels, small and medium bowls, flaring-sided cups, and vertical-sided cups have been tentatively assigned to this class. The typological descriptions of these forms can be found in chapter 4.

DEPOSITIONAL PLACEMENT

REGISTERED FINDS

Of the 12 registered finds assigned to this class, 50% were in non-tertiary deposition. A small restricted ves-

sel was found in well 199 in B.L. I. Two flaring cups were recovered from B.L. II, a medium vessel (with a slightly inverted rim) from B.L. IIIA, and a flaring cup and small bowl from B.L. IIIB's pit 165.

BULK FINDS

Rim sherds of cups, small and medium bowls, and small restricted vessels were assigned to class 18. Some scattered sherds of these types were found in non-tertiary deposition in each building level, but no level had any concentrations of at least 10 sherds.

Functional Class 19: Carpentry

(Table 24; Figure 30; Plate 26b; Appendix p. 136)

SHAPE, CONDITION, AND MATERIAL

Carpentry (in the sense of general woodworking and utilization) must have been practiced at TUV. For ex-

ample, wooden beams would have been employed in the roofing of the structures found there. Only one tool, however, can at present be assigned to this class.

East (cf. Schmandt-Besserat 1979), except that the TUV examples did not enclose sets of geometric objects. Rather, a thin outer clay shell was molded around a second solid large clay ball that was the sole interior content of each bulla. (One of the TUV bullae was sawn in half, and others were fragmentary enough to allow the interior construction to be seen.)

Both stamp and cylinder seal impressions occurred on the TUV bullae. Eight sealed bullae were found, plus three large, unsealed clay balls which may have been interior cores of bullae.

SMALL GEOMETRICS
(Plates 26c-e, 35g-h)

In this kind of artifact, the objects themselves have become the symbols which convey information. Schmandt-Besserat (1977) reviewed the widespread occurrence of small geometric objects in the Near East between the ninth and the second millennia B.C. She concluded that such objects were part of a complex informational token system originally used long before the development of writing and perhaps linearly related to the origins of pictographic writing systems.

It would not seem possible, however, to say that *all* small geometric objects were necessarily counters. Some may have been gaming pieces, for example.

Small geometrics were rare at TUV. There were two small clay balls, three squat clay cones, two clay cylindrical rods, eight small stone balls (generally polished) and two small asymmetrical stone balls. (Only balls with a diameter 3.0 cm or less have been classified as small geometrics.) These finds are examples of Schmandt-Besserat's (1977) classes of spheres, cones, and cylindrical rods. No examples of her disc class have been found at TUV.

POTTER'S MARKS
(Plates 23i, 34a-d)

A potter's mark is a symbol impressed on a pottery vessel by the maker of the pot to indicate authorship of

Recy

It should be noted here that many items used at TUV were recycled when they had finished their original function. Some grinding stones and heavy pot sherds were made into door sockets, while some smaller sherds were made into sherd discs. Numerous sherds were in-

Mf 5067, a very fine polished adze, was made of a basic igneous rock (possibly basalt).

DEPOSITIONAL PLACEMENT

The adze was found in secondary context in room 250 of B.L. IIIA.

Functional Class 20: Decorative Items
(Table 24; Figure 31; Plates 14a-b, 15h-i, 16f, m, 17a, d, f, 18b-c, 19c, g, t, 20h, j, n, 21b, d, 23a, b, e, g, h, j, l, m, o, 24a-t, 34e; Appendix p. 136)

SHAPE, CONDITION, AND MATERIAL

This class groups items bearing nonutilitarian decoration. The "use" reflected in this class is a symbolic/social function. The items included here are wall painting fragments (described in chapter 3), painted pottery (chapter 4), and relief pottery (chapter 4). No examples of objects assignable to class 20 *alone* have been recognized at TUV (i.e., no figurines, sculpture, etc). Thus this is a class of items which cross-cuts many of the classes of items previously described.

DEPOSITIONAL PLACEMENT

REGISTERED FINDS

Of the 17 registered finds assigned to class 20, 41% were found in non-tertiary context (Table 24, Figure 31). Examples from B.L. I include two painted vessels from well 199 and one from a secondary deposit in room 10. In B.L. II, an elaborately painted vessel was recovered from secondarily admixed context in courtyard 30. B.L. IIIA yielded a registered relief sherd from pit 163, a simply painted vessel (with stripes) from burial 274, and another striped vessel from secondary admixture in room 284. B.L. IIIB had no such finds.

BULK FINDS

(High Concentrations Plotted on Figure 31)

Both monochrome and bichrome painted sherds were found in every building level. Concentrations of at least 10 painted sherds came from room 102, courtyard 30, room 36, and area 379 of B.L. II, pit 285, area 366, rooms 306, 284, and 250 of B.L. IIIA, and room 306 of B.L. IIIB. There were no such concentrations in B.L. I.

TABLE 25

DEPOSITIONAL PLACEMENT OF FINDS IN THE CONTROL CLASS

Functional class	Deposit type[a]	Above B.L. I[b]	B.L. I	B.L. II	B.L. IIIA	B.L. IIIB	Below B.L. III	Row totals
21. Information processing[c] (N Œ 278)	Primary/ secondary	1	0	15	27 (1 m)	121	0	164 (1 m)
	Secondary admixture	0	0	5	56	1	0	62
	Tertiary	22	0	14	14	1	0	51

[a] Finds coming from lots which were in part primary or secondary, but mixed with another deposit type during excavation are listed in ( ) with the symbol m. See chapter 1.

[b] Strata 0-2 are here considered above B.L. I, 3-4 are B.L. I, 5-8c are B.L. II, 8d-10 are B.L. IIIA, 11-13c are B.L. IIIB, and 13d-14 are below B.L. III.

[c] Note that seal impressions are counted both here and in class 10.

All of the procurement, production, and con
tion activities discussed above, as well as ot
tivities which have left no identifiable traces
archaeological record, would have been undertal
cause of *control decisions* made on the part
human beings living at TUV. There are no at

Functional Clas

(Table 25; Figure 32; Plates 11b, 2

SHAPE, CONDITION, AND MATER.

This class groups artifacts which appear to
specific information through visual symbols: sea
impressions, Proto-Elamite tablets, bullae,
geometric objects, and sherds bearing potter's m:
Many of the artifacts within this class are ge:
interpreted by Near Eastern archaeologists a
nected to administrative accounting activity.
devices such as the geometric counters and p
marks may have been part of a more generalized
of information dissemination. Flannery (1972), '
(1977), and Johnson (1978) have discussed the :
tance of information processing to the developr
complex society.

SEALS

The basic functions of seals in the ancient Ne
are well-known (see for example Gibson and
1977). Here it is appropriate to stress the fact t
design on a seal is intended to convey inform
This point has been made by Johnson (1973:99):

The simple use of seals implies not specializ
ministrative organization, but rather the trans
certain types of information. The developme
complex administrative organization in the
text of an economic system in which seals wer
viously in use could be expected to result
proliferation of sealing agencies. A marke
crease in seal design complexity could be exp
with this development.

No stamp seals have been found at TUV, but f
amples of cylinder seals were found (Plate 37a-b

SEAL IMPRESSIONS
(Plate 35a-f)

The distribution of stamp and cylinder seal i
sions on "sealings" has been summarized dur

TABLE 27—*Continued*

Functional class	Number of secondary find-spots	Ubiquity index A[a]	Number of secondary plus secondarily admixed find-spots	Ubiquity index B[b]
10 bulk sherds	3	0.50	4	0.36
11	0	0.00	0	0.00
12 registered items	1	0.17	1	0.09
12 bulk sherds	5	0.83	9	0.82
13	2	0.33	2	0.18
14	1	0.17	2	0.18
15	0	0.00	0	0.00
16	1	0.17	1	0.09
17 registered items	0	0.00	1	0.09
17 bulk sherds	0	0.00	1	0.09
18 registered items	1	0.17	1	0.09
18 bulk sherds	2	0.33	3	0.27
19	0	0.00	0	0.00
20	3	0.50	5	0.45
21	1	0.17	2	0.18

[a] Ratio of the number of secondary find-spots for a given artifact class (in each building level) over the total number of secondary deposits in that level.

[b] Ratio of the number of secondary and secondarily admixed find-spots for a given artifact class (in each building level) over the total number of secondary and secondarily admixed deposits in that level.

[c] N = the total number of deposits of this category in a level.

[d] Includes two primary loci (burials).

made in studying ubiquity signatures. This assumption rests on a goal-oriented, effort-minimization model of human actions (Zipf 1949). It is assumed that people, when given a choice of several refuse dumping zones, will choose the one reached with the least expenditure of energy, i.e., that closest to their work place. The goal of and constraints upon this minimization strategy (Christenson 1982) can be specified as follows. The desired goal is the saving of time and human energy. The constraints on this strategy are imposed by cultural standards of cleanliness and land ownership. Given the existence of several culturally legitimate dumping sites, the corollary of this model follows. If the practice of a given activity was widespread in systemic context at a site, traces of that activity will also be relatively widespread in archaeological context. It must be remembered, however, that curation rates also affect the incidence of finds of each class in archaeological context.

Taphonomic and ethnoarchaeological observations suggest special caution is necessary in ubiquity and other analyses of faunal remains (Binford 1981b; Kent 1981). Kent (1984:183) concludes from a study of Navajo, Spanish-American, and Euroamerican homes "that, unless a very specific pattern emerges from analysis,... the spatial positioning of bones should in most cases be attributed to dog and/or other scavenger behavior rather than to human behavior." Kramer (1982:44, 48) found the same situation in an Iranian village. The ubiquity of faunal remains in the archaeological record may thus appear very high as a result of non-human activities!

At TUV, the ubiquity of each class (or subclass) of material has been measured as a ratio of the number of secondary *find-spots* per building level over the number of secondary *deposits* found in that level. A completely ubiquitous class would be one found in every secondary deposit, yielding an index of 1.00. Decreasing ubiquity is shown by a drop in this index.

Table 27 summarizes the observed ubiquity for each functional class at TUV. Ubiquity index A is calculated in the manner described above. Ubiquity index B reflects the addition of secondarily admixed deposits to the sample. Discussion of the implications of this table is combined with information on concentration and structural position at the end of this chapter.

Concentration

Concentration is a measure of the *rate* at which activities produced trash. Rate is affected by two factors. The first factor is the amount of debris generated in an individual unit of activity. The second factor is the frequency or periodicity with which that unit of activity is repeated.

Rate of trash production has a relatively direct relationship to the number of items discarded in trash deposits. By examining the quantity of debris of each functional class over the full range of non-tertiary deposits with such debris in a building level, one can begin to assess the consistency of the trash-production rate. To the extent that this measure compares item concentration in a deposit with item quantity in other deposits *of the same class of items*, this measure is relatively free from the effect of curation.

Table 28 summarizes the observed concentration signatures for each functional class at TUV. The implications of this table are discussed at the close of this chapter.

Structural Position

Structural position measures patterned regularities in the spatial placement of trash deposits. Such regularities include association with particular feature types, interior or exterior location, central or peripheral location, and general accessibility of the loci. Structural position should not be confused with site structure. The latter type of analysis focuses on the "particular" aspects of spatial patterning rather than on repeated regularities (see chapter 7).

For some functional classes, association of trash debris with the vicinity of specific feature types is a logical prediction, following an effort-minimizing assumption. Such associations have been indicated on Table 26. It is much harder to offer any predictions on the other types of possible regularities in spatial placement of trash deposits. A generalized prediction would be that people would tend to keep actively occupied rooms clean, so that exterior and peripheral locations for trash would be favored (Schiffer 1972:161- 162; De-Boer and Lathrap 1979:127-133). Another generalized prediction would be that material deposited in exterior trash dumps would be subjected to some possible random scattering by the actions of people and/or dogs (Kent 1981, 1984); material in interior contexts would seem less likely to be thus scattered, but would most probably date only to the end of occupation of the structure.

In addition to examining the spatial distribution of each functional class in interior and exterior contexts, distribution in the somewhat differently defined central and peripheral contexts was considered. The main structure in each building level (as defined in chapter 3) was considered to be central; exterior zones, outbuildings, and/or parts of adjacent structures were considered to be peripheral.

An attempt was also made to quantify the general accessibility of each trash locus. Negative accessibility was defined as characterizing rooms that had only one doorway; that is, such rooms were dead ends. Neutral accessibility was defined as typical of rooms with two doorways, or of areas from which movement could be made in two directions. Positive accessibility was defined as typical of rooms with three doorways, or of apparently wide open areas from which movement could be made in more than two directions. Areas of positive accessibility are hubs which do not strictly channel movement. One could predict that such trash as was deposited indoors would generally occur in areas of negative accessibility. Outdoors, either negatively or positively accessible zones would seem suitable for trash, but one would expect areas of neutral accessibility (which channel movement) to be relatively trash-free.

Accessibility of trash loci in B.L. IIIB-A was characterized in this fashion. It was generally not possible to characterize the loci of B.L. II-I in this way, for in those upper levels most doorways were not identified (due to poor wall preservation combined with the Banesh tendency to use doorsills, as explained in chapter 2).

The results of the search for patterned regularities in general accessibility, feature association, and other characteristics of location are summarized in the next section.

TABLE 28

OBSERVED CONCENTRATION OF FUNCTIONAL CLASS DEBRIS

Functional class[a]	*Number of secondary loci with:*				*Number of secondary and secondarily admixed loci with:*			
	low concentrations[b]	mod. concentrations[c]	high concentrations[d]	Rate of trash production	low concentrations[b]	mod. concentrations[c]	high concentrations[d]	Revised rate of trash production
BUILDING LEVEL I								
1	0	0	1	High, irregular	0	0	1	No change
2	1	0	0	Low, irregular	2	0	0	No change
4	0	1	0	Moderate, irregular	1	1	0	Variable
5	1	0	0	Low, irregular	1	0	0	No change
7 registered items	4	0	1	Variable, tending to low and regular	4	0	1	No change
7 bulk bone	2	1	1	Variable	2	3	1	No change
7 bulk sherds	2	1	0	Variable	3	1	0	No change
10 bulk sherds	1	2	0	Variable	1	4	0	No change
12 bulk sherds	3	0	0	Low, moderately regular	4	1	0	Variable, tending to low and regular
13	2	0	0	Low, irregular	3	0	0	Low, moderately regular
14	1	0	0	Low, irregular	1	0	0	No change
16	2	0	0	Low, irregular	2	0	0	No change
17 registered items	1	0	0	Low, irregular	1	0	0	No change
17 bulk sherds	2	0	0	Low, irregular	2	0	0	No change
18 registered items	1	0	0	Low, irregular	1	0	0	No change
18 bulk sherds	2	0	0	Low, irregular	2	0	0	No change
20[e]	1	3	0	Variable	2	3	0	No change
BUILDING LEVEL II								
1	2	3	0	Variable	6	5	0	No change
2	2	2	0	Variable	7	3	0	Variable, tending to low and regular
4	4	0	0	Low, irregular	6	1	0	Variable, tending to low and regular
5	2	0	0	Low, irregular	3	0	0	No change
6	1	0	0	Low, irregular	1	0	0	No change
7 registered items	8	3	0	Variable, tending to low and regular	8	3	2	More variable
7 bulk bone	6	5	1	Variable	8	14	3	No change
7 bulk sherds	4	1	0	Variable	6	4	5	More variable but frequent

TABLE 28—*Continued*

	Number of secondary loci with:				Number of secondary and secondarily admixed loci with:			
Functional class[a]	low concentrations[b]	mod. concentrations[c]	high concentrations[d]	Rate of trash production	low concentrations[b]	mod. concentrations[c]	high concentrations[d]	Revised rate of trash production
8	0	0	0	Absent	2	0	0	Low, irregular
10 registered items	0	0	1	High, irregular	1	0	1	Variable, irregular
10 bulk sherds	5	2	1	Variable	9	2	4	Variable but frequent
12 registered items	0	0	0	Absent	5	0	0	Low, irregular
12 bulk sherds	7	2	0	Variable, tending to low and regular	14	7	1	Variable but frequent
13	0	0	0	Absent	2	0	0	Low, irregular
14	0	0	0	Absent	5	0	0	Low, irregular
16	2	0	0	Low, irregular	5	0	0	No change
17 bulk sherds	1	0	0	Low, irregular	5	0	0	No change
18 registered items	1	0	0	Low, irregular	2	0	0	No change
18 bulk sherds	2	0	0	Low, irregular	6	0	0	No change
20[e]	4	4	0	Variable	7	5	4	More variable
21	0	0	1	High, irregular	3	0	1	Variable
BUILDING LEVEL IIIA								
1	2	1	0	Variable	7	1	0	Variable, tending toward low and regular
2	4	2	0	Variable	13	3	0	Variable but more frequent
3	1	0	0	Low, irregular	3	0	0	No change
4	5	0	0	Low, irregular	10	0	0	Low but more regular
5	3	1	0	Variable, tending to low and irregular	7	1	0	Variable, but tending to low and regular
6	1	0	0	Low, irregular	1	0	0	No change
7 registered items	7	1	1	Variable, tending to low and regular	16	1	1	No change
7 bulk bone	1	4	5	Variable, tending toward high	2	6	7	No change
7 bulk sherds	4	1	2	Variable	10	1	2	Variable, but tending toward low, regular
9	1	0	0	Low, irregular	1	0	0	No change

TABLE 28—*Continued*

Functional class[a]	Number of secondary loci with:				Number of secondary and secondarily admixed loci with:			
	low concen- trations[b]	mod. concen- trations[c]	high concen- trations[d]	Rate of trash production	low concen- trations[b]	mod. concen- trations[c]	high concen- trations[d]	Revised rate of trash production
10 registered items	3	0	1	Variable, sporadic	6	0	3	No change
10 bulk sherds	4	0	3	Variable	9	1	4	No change
11	4[f]	0	0	Low, irregular	4[f]	0	0	No change
12 registered items	4	0	0	Low, irregular	6	0	0	No change
12 bulk sherds	3	3	3	Variable	5	8	5	No change
13	3	0	0	Low, irregular	5	0	0	No change
14	4	0	0	Low, irregular	5	0	0	No change
15	0	0	0	Absent	1	0	0	Low, irregular
16	1	0	0	Low, irregular	2	0	0	No change
17 registered items	2	0	0	Low, irregular	5	0	0	No change
17 bulk sherds	2	0	0	Low, irregular	1	1	0	Variable
18 registered items	0	0	0	Absent	1	0	0	Low, irregular
18 bulk sherds	5	2	0	Variable, tending to low and irregular	8	3	0	No change
19	1	0	0	Low, irregular	1	0	0	No change
20[e]	4	3	3	Variable	10	3	5	No change
21	4	0	1	Variable	7	2	2	More variable
BUILDING LEVEL IIIB								
1	0	1	1	Variable	0	1	1	No change
2	2	0	0	Low, irregular	6	0	0	Low, more regular
3	1	0	0	Low, irregular	1	0	0	No change
4	1	0	0	Low, irregular	1	0	0	No change
5	2	0	0	Low, irregular	2	0	0	No change
7 registered items	6	0	0	Low, regular	7	0	0	No change
7 bulk bone	0	3	1	Variable	2	4	1	More variable
7 bulk sherds	1	0	1	Variable, irregular	3	0	1	No change
8	1	0	0	Low, irregular	1	0	0	No change
9	1	0	0	Low, irregular	1	0	0	No change
10 registered items	0	0	1	High, irregular	0	0	1	High, irregular
10 bulk sherds	2	0	1	Variable	3	0	1	No change
12 registered items	1	0	0	Low, irregular	1	0	0	No change
12 bulk sherds	1	1	3	Variable	4	2	3	No change
13	1	0	1	Variable	1	0	1	No change
14	0	0	1	High, irregular	1	0	1	Variable

TABLE 28—*Continued*

Functional class[a]	Number of secondary loci with:				Number of secondary and secondarily admixed loci with:			
	low concentrations[b]	mod. concentrations[c]	high concentrations[d]	Rate of trash production	low concentrations[b]	mod. concentrations[c]	high concentrations[d]	Revised rate of trash production
16	1	0	0	Low, irregular	1	0	0	No change
17 registered items	0	0	0	Absent	1	0	0	Low, irregular
17 bulk sherds	0	0	0	Absent	1	0	0	Low, irregular
18 registered items	1	0	0	Low, irregular	1	0	0	No change
18 bulk sherds	2	0	0	Low, irregular	3	0	0	No change
20[e]	0	2	1	Variable	2	2	1	More variable
21	0	0	1	High, irregular	1	0	1	Variable, infrequent

[a] Functional classes not represented in a building level's deposits are omitted from this table.

[b] Low concentrations = 1 or 2 finds, 1-99 gm of bone, 1-4 grit ware and drain spout sherds, 1-25 chaff ware sherds.

[c] Moderate concentrations = 3-5 registered finds, 100-999 gm of bone, 5-9 grit ware and drain spout sherds, 26-99 chaff ware sherds.

[d] High concentrations = more than 5 registered finds, at least 1000 gm of bone, at least 10 grit ware and drain spout sherds, at least 100 chaff ware sherds.

[e] Painted and registered relief sherds are combined in one row.

[f] Includes two primary loci (burials).

Implications of Observed Characteristics

CLASS-BY-CLASS REVIEW

Ubiquity, concentration, and structural position can now be reviewed for each functional class, and the observed characteristics compared to the predictions of expected signatures on Table 26. The production/processing classes are considered first.

Class 1 groups debris from the manufacture of chipped stone tools. Observed ubiquity was lower than expected. Combined with the variable concentration pattern, this suggests that flint-knapping was only a sporadic activity in the area of the TUV operation. No regularities in structural position were found.

Class 2 groups debris related to copper-base metallurgy. While low to moderate in ubiquity in B.L. I-II, ubiquity was higher than predicted in B.L. IIIA and B. The large clusters of by-products and waste materials which had been predicted failed to materialize, however; concentrations of class 2 debris were in the low to moderate range. Some preference for discarding trash of this type in exterior or peripheral areas removed from the living quarters was indicated in B.L. IIIA, but no special installations could be clearly demonstrated as associated with this activity. (Platform 263 remains a possibility as many finds of this class came from the areas surrounding it. Alternatively, the actual smelting could have been done in an area lying beyond the bounds of our excavation.) In any case, only a relatively modest amount of copper-base metallurgy is indicated for the immediate vicinity of the TUV operation. This suggests that the practice of metallurgy there was a "cottage industry."

In general, the observed behavior of class 3 debris (manufacture of stone beads) fits the expectations in Table 26. Absent from B.L. I-II, class 3 debris was low in ubiquity in B.L. IIIA-B. Low concentrations occurred, and no spatial regularities were indicated. Manufacture of stone beads seems likely to have been a specialized, but infrequently carried out, task.

Class 4 groups debris related to possible shell-working. In general, the ubiquity of this class was low to moderate, but higher than class 3 as had been predicted. (Working shell seems in the abstract like a less difficult task than making stone beads, and therefore likely to be less specialized.) Concentrations of class 4 items tended to be small, and no spatial regularities were noted. This pattern is suggestive of a relatively unspecialized craft practiced with modest frequency in the area of the TUV operation.

Class 5 contains materials related to the production of plasters and pigments. Ubiquity was low in B.L. I-II, but moderate in B.L. III. This change in ubiquity would appear to correlate with the greater incidence of plastered and painted walls in B.L. III (see chapter 3). Concentrations tended to be low throughout. Finds of this class were much more frequent in interior rather than exterior contexts.

Class 6 groups items suggestive of a cloth industry. Absent in B.L. I and B.L. IIIB, this class had very low ubiquity in the other levels. Concentration was also consistently low, and no spatial regularities were noted. While it is clear that very little trash of this class was produced at TUV, it is more difficult to infer the actual incidence of cloth-related industry, because of the high curation rate to be expected for looms, needles, etc.

Class 7 is a diverse class grouping items possibly related to food production activity. It was expected that ubiquity of this class would be low as it represents an activity specialized by its needs for hearth or oven installations. It was also predicted that concentrations of garbage (animal remains) would be relatively high, and concentrations of other items in this class relatively low.

The spatial distribution of animal bone is discussed first. Ubiquity values for faunal remains were among the highest of any class of items at TUV, exactly the opposite of our theoretical expectation. Concentrations were markedly variable, and no *overall* spatial regularities were discernible. This pattern is suggestive of the scattering of faunal remains by dogs, an ethnoarchaeologically common event discussed above. In the light of this possibility, it would seem more appropriate to focus on the high and apparently unscattered concentrations of bone material. The great majority of such concentrations were in exterior and peripheral loci, removed from actual kitchen areas. In B.L. II, however, there was a large concentration of faunal remains in and adjacent to the kitchen zone. Large concentrations also occurred in a few interior loci in B.L. I and B.L. IIIA (see chapter 7 for detailed interpretation of specific structural units).

The ubiquity of registered items and bulk sherds in class 7 was in general moderately high. This also appeared to contradict our theoretical expectation of low

ubiquity for this class. Many of the registered finds, however, are pieces of charcoal, and it is certainly possible (probable?) that much of this charcoal came from fires other than ones used in cooking. The ubiquity of class 7 is perhaps better represented by that of the bulk sherds, which was moderate. Concentrations and spatial placement were irregular.

Class 8 groups finds which might be indicative of pottery production. It was noted in chapter 5 that such finds are very rare at TUV. The class occurred with very low ubiquity, low concentration, and no spatial regularities in B.L. II and in B.L. IIIB. Given the lack of large clusters of debris and the lack of any kilns in the excavated zone, it must be concluded that pottery making was not likely to have been conducted in the actual area of our operation.

The last of the production/processing classes (class 9) groups miscellaneous raw materials. Because this class was a miscellaneous one, no attempt was made to predict its ubiquity, concentration, and structural position characteristics on Table 26. In fact, items of this class occurred only in B.L. IIIA-B, at low ubiquity and low concentration levels. This class thus does not suggest the presence of any other significant trash-producing crafts at TUV.

Class 10 represents items used in general storage activity. Observed patterning of this class essentially meets the theoretical expectations outlined in Table 26. The ubiquity of storage jar sherds was moderate in all four levels. Registered items of this class were absent in B.L. I, but in the levels where such items (e.g., sealings) occurred, ubiquity was less than that of the storage jars (as predicted). Concentrations were variable; some were very high. No regularities in structural position were noted. This ubiquity and concentration pattern would seem to indicate that storage was one of the fundamental activities at TUV.

The first consumption/use class, class 11, groups items of basketry and matting. These elements are so perishable that few traces of this class remained at TUV; those discovered all came from B.L. IIIA. Both the low ubiquity and low concentration values for this class probably stem from this fragility factor. Thus it is not possible to estimate what the actual use rate of such items may have been.

Class 12 is a diverse class of special containers. The registered stone, metal, and plaster items in this class were predicted to be low in ubiquity as such relatively exotic materials were likely to be used for special purposes. It was predicted that while such exotic vessels might occasionally be found intact in a primary deposit such as a burial, generally such vessels would not be discarded until they were broken. Thus clusters of joinable vessel sherds would be expected in the trash. Half of these expectations were met. Ubiquity of registered items was low, and the only intact stone vessel turned up in a primary deposit (burial). On the other hand, the intact lead bowl turned up discarded in a trash deposit, and clusters of joinable vessel sherds did not occur. Stone vessel sherds were found mostly as scattered finds. This might suggest scattering of already discarded trash by people or dogs, but for the fact that such finds were far from ubiquitous. It would seem that when a stone vessel was broken, some of its sherds ended up in trash within the TUV operation, but the remainder ended up in deposits elsewhere. Clearly some mechanism was influencing the process of discard which we have not yet explicitly considered. Most probably even at the end of occupation of each building level, a proportion of the trash was carried away and dumped elsewhere. The class 12 evidence clearly cautions us that the trash *deposited* at TUV may not be a representative sample of the trash *produced* there.

Bevelled-rim bowls, necked goblets, and low trays are also assigned to class 12. It was predicted on Table 26 that these apparently mass-produced forms should have a correspondingly high ubiquity and variable concentration. These expectations were met. Sherds of these forms had moderate to high ubiquity in all building levels. While concentration tended toward low/moderate in B.L. I-II, this measure tended to moderate/high in B.L. IIIA-B. Due to the high ubiquity, no overall regularities in structural positioning occurred. Use of bevelled-rim bowls, goblets, and low trays was clearly another fundamental activity at TUV, especially in B.L. IIIA-B.

Class 13 groups cutting tools. High ubiquity and variable concentration were the expected patterns for this class. The class in fact had a relatively low ubiquity, with somewhat variable concentration. This pattern suggests that activities involving cutting tools were relatively infrequent in the zone of the TUV operation, and that the use of such tools may in fact have been restricted to special tasks.

Class 14 groups chipped stone tools with uses other than simple cutting. Because this class was a miscellaneous one, no attempt was made to predict its ubiquity, concentration, and structural position characteristics on Table 26. Ubiquity ranged from low to moderate, while concentration levels were generally low. This depositional pattern suggests the occasional practice of one or more activities involving the use of such tools. (Microwear studies may eventually allow determination of the specific nature of these activities.) While more finds of this class were found in interior rather than exterior contexts, this apparent regularity in structural position may be a result of the increased incidence of screening in interior contexts at TUV, as many of the finds in this class are very small.

Class 15 groups piercing and boring tools. Finds of this class were present only in B.L. IIIA, with low ubiquity and low concentration. There is thus no indication that piercing or boring actions were an important activity at TUV.

Class 16, personal ornaments, was predicted to have a distributional pattern of high ubiquity but very low concentration. (While ornaments might become broken or lost almost anywhere, the rate of loss/discard would generally be one at a time.) The observed ubiquity and concentration levels were both low, but no general regularities in structural position were discernible. Since the ubiquity of such finds was much lower than expected, but find spots were still scattered, it would seem likely that a low absolute frequency of ornament breakage/loss events produced this pattern. Because ornaments are likely to be highly curated, it is probable that the wearing of personal ornaments was in fact a common occurrence at TUV.

Class 17 groups items used in conjunction with architecture. The distributional pattern of this class was predicted to be one of high ubiquity and relatively low concentration. In actuality, ubiquity was low to moderate, concentration low, and there were no regularities in structural position. This pattern seems to have been produced by a relatively low "decay" rate of architecture during the actual occupation of each structure, coupled with a high curation rate of things like door sockets.

Class 18 groups evidence of vessels used in food consumption. (Organic garbage remaining after consumption of food was analytically indistinguishable from garbage produced during food preparation and is not included in this class; see class 7.) The distributional pattern for class 18 was predicted to be one of moderate ubiquity with variable clusters of sherds and/or vessels. Observed ubiquity was quite variable, ranging from low in B.L. II to high in B.L. IIIA. Concentrations tended toward low throughout. No regularities in structural position were observed. The distribution pattern reflects the occurrence of food consumption activity in each building level, but does not allow any localization of this activity.

Class 19, carpentry, only contains one item, an adze. Presumably this incidence was so low because tools of this type were highly curated. Also, as the great majority of trash recovered from each level presumably dates to the end of occupation rather than the beginning, it is likely that carpentry was not an on-going craft at TUV, but rather one employed only at the moments when each building level was being constructed or remodelled.

Class 20, the last consumption/use class, contains decorated items. The depositional pattern was predicted to be one of high ubiquity and variable concentration. These expectations were essentially met; ubiquity varied from moderately high to very high, and concentrations were variable. Use of nonutilitarian decoration was evidently an important component of life at TUV.

Finally class 21 groups items used in information processing and is thus reflective of control or decision-making. Because formal administration was likely to be a highly specialized task at this time period, it was predicted that finds of this class should exhibit low ubiquity. Concentration was predicted to be variable. Absent in B.L. I, this class had an observed ubiquity that was low in B.L. II and IIIB and moderate in B.L. IIIA. Concentration was variable, including some very high concentrations in B.L. IIIA and B. The highest concentrations of items of this class were found in trash pits, but class 21 debris also occurred in a variety of other contexts. This depositional pattern suggests that formal control activity was an important function in B.L. III, one of lesser importance in B.L. II, and absent in B.L. I.

GENERAL DISCUSSION

What has the above class-by-class review revealed about the usefulness of ubiquity, concentration, and structural position measures?

At this point, the extent to which these three measures are interrelated should be clear. If the frequency or periodicity of a type of activity is low, this affects not only the concentration level of individual deposits but also overall ubiquity. Similarly, if traces of an activity are found to be relatively regular in structural positioning, the ubiquity of that class is lowered as a result. Of these two effects, the former was far more significant a factor at TUV. Very few classes had any

repeated regularities in structural positioning as part of their depositional pattern.

With respect to ubiquity, most of the functional classes scored in the low or low-moderate range. Three classes had some exceptionally high values for this measure: the faunal remains of class 7, the mass-produced ceramics of class 12, and the decorated items of class 20. It has been argued above that the unusually dispersed distribution pattern of the faunal remains may reflect scattering by dogs. The high ubiquity of class 20 probably results from the fact that it cross-cuts *several* other classes; sherds of food preparation vessels, food consumption vessels, and storage vessels can all be decorated in addition to serving their primary utilitarian functions. The high ubiquity of the class 12 ceramics is certainly correlated to the sheer volume of sherds of this class (especially in B.L. III).

Simple ubiquity alone, then, is not very useful as a signature to distinguish consistently one kind of activity from another, since most of the functional classes fall in the same range of ubiquity values. Also, it is clear that ubiquity values for any given activity can vary from building level to building level. Where ubiquity *is* useful, however, is in assessing the relative importance of each activity (as a trash-producer) for each level.

The concentration variable can then be used to refine this assessment, as has been done in the class-by-class discussion. Furthermore, when varying rates of curation are taken into account, these ubiquity/concentration patterns provide clues to the *scale* at which each activity was conducted (see Figures 33 through 36 and discussion in chapter 8).

Chapter Conclusion

In sum, it would appear that, in the absence of primary deposits, types of activities are *not* characterized by uniquely distinctive signatures in their depositional patterns. Production classes, for example, can not be recognized as having a signature different from those of use, storage, or control classes. It would appear that at TUV, each activity class had a pattern whose position in the spectrum of all possible configurations was determined not by its type but by several other factors. Most important were (1) the amount of trash produced per unit of activity and (2) the periodicity or frequency with which units of activity were repeated. Possible effects of specialization on ubiquity were obscured by the very low incidence of trash in some classes. In general, however, the extent to

which activities were specialized (either in requiring specific knowledge or the use of specific features) appeared to have a relatively muted effect on depositional configurations, possibly due to the limited area sampled in the TUV operation. Each building level essentially uncovered only one structural complex and its periphery. Specialization might be more readily visible in its effects on ubiquity at a scale of inter-building variation in depositional patterns, which is presently impossible to investigate at TUV. Alternatively, specialization can be approached via the analytical hierarchy's next level, that of the institution (chapters 7 and 8).

To fully understand activities, it is necessary both to study the utilized items employed in or resulting from each activity and to examine the depositional characteristics of functional classes. Examining ubiquity, concentration, and structural position can lead to an assessment of the nature of each activity. Insofar as was possible on this basis, the incidence and degree of specialization involved in each activity have been discussed in this chapter. Discussion can now move on to examine composite patterns formed by associations among all the functional classes, the architecture, and features. Such complex associations reflect the institutional level of the functional hierarchy, and are the subject of the next two chapters.

VII

Site Structure

This chapter discusses site structure, composite spatial patterning in the archaeological record, which most likely has been shaped by institutional coordination of activities. Site structure can be modelled for each building level by examination of complex associational patterns among moveable and immoveable elements of site content.

There were very few primary deposits at TUV. Site structure analysis must thus rest on a combination of inferences to be drawn from the architecture, features, and existing trash deposits. Such inferences are built upon the functional classes and activity signature patterns reviewed in earlier chapters.

For each building level the following points are discussed below: (a) the general character of depositional processes in the level, with an overview of refuse disposal patterns (identification of favored trash dumping zones); (b) possible clues to the spatial localization of activities, both from the architecture/features and from the trash distribution patterns.

Trash (as used here) is by definition material which has been discarded and removed from its primary use location. In order to conduct a site structural analysis using this kind of evidence, a major assumption must be made. This assumption was explained in the analysis of activity patterning in chapter 6, but is reiterated here as it is also central to the conclusions of this chapter. If a building level or division thereof had several secondary loci, it is assumed that the occupants probably most often threw away their refuse in the trash dumping zone *closest* to the area in which the trash had actually been produced. Thus, trash in secondary deposits found within a particular architectural unit would be more likely to have been produced in that unit than in another. An analysis of site structure founded on such an assumption could be described as a goal-oriented, effort-minimization model (Zipf 1949), the goal being the saving of time and human energy, and the constraints on the strategy the cultural concepts of cleanliness and land-ownership.

It is important to recognize that trash-producing functions do not necessarily represent the *only* functions of a zone. At the present level of analytical methodology in archaeology, it is very difficult to compensate for the different trash-producing rates and curation rates characteristic of different activities. An attempt has been made to identify such differences in the analysis of activity patterning in the preceding chapter. Discussion of site structure employs those insights and uses the same criteria listed on Table 28 to define low, medium, and high concentrations of debris. These criteria are weighted so as to reflect (in a very general sense) differing curation/breakage rates for various broad categories of material. (As a reminder, a trash deposit is considered to have a high concentration of a functional class if it contains more than 5 registered items of that class, at least 10 grit-tempered sherds assignable to that class, or at least 100 chaff-tempered sherds assignable to that class. In the case of bone, at least 1000 gm are required to warrant the designation of being a high concentration.)

In chapter 8 an attempt is made to suggest some of the more complicated effects which different trash-producing rates and curation rates may have had on the archaeological record and thus on our evolving model of site structure and function.

Building Level III

General Depositional Character

As noted in chapter 3, preservation of this level was excellent. About 247 m^2 of this level were exposed. The general plan of the architecture was slightly less rectilinear than that of Levels I and II; that is, some of the B.L. III rooms did not have parallel sides. A number of immoveable features were preserved, though the great range of features characteristic of B.L. II was not found. From the architecture and features alone, satisfactory functional characterization of this level does not seem to be possible.

Site structure analysis of B.L. III is complicated by the major remodelling activity which occurred in certain sectors of the level. For the initial phase, B.L. IIIB, we have knowledge of the architectural framework as it then appeared, but have non-tertiary *deposits* only in areas which were abandoned early, refloored, or remodelled (with the new construction or new floors sealing in earlier IIIB trash). Deposits overlying new construction or new flooring plus those found in unremodelled sections of the level have been assigned to IIIA, on the assumption that trash is likely to reflect the last phase of use of any space in which it is found.

Expressed as a percentage of excavated lots, the depositional character of B.L. III (strata 9-13c, phases A and B combined) is primary 1%, secondary 27%, secondary admixture 12%, and tertiary 60%. For the purposes of examination of site structure, only primary, secondary, and secondarily admixed deposits are considered. The following unit divisions are used:

east unit: as defined in chapter 3
south unit: as defined in chapter 3
west unit: as defined in chapter 3

north unit: as defined in chapter 3
peripheral area: trash pile 301, area 308, alley 307, feature 315, area 318
area 338
V164 group: pit 163, pit 165, room 164, area 171

Figure 37 illustrates the spatial distribution of primary, secondary, and secondarily admixed deposits in B.L. IIIB-A. From the pattern of secondary deposits it can be seen that refuse disposal was a very dispersed phenomenon in B.L. III. Surprisingly, many of the trash deposits from this level were in interior rather than exterior or peripheral areas. This appears to contradict the general theoretical expectation (discussed in chapter 6) that trash should tend to accumulate in exterior and peripheral areas while interior zones are kept relatively clean. In terms of the sheer quantity of trash, however, the amount found in exterior and peripheral loci is roughly 2.5 times the amount found in interior contexts. The interior trash deposits are found in rooms of quite varied accessibility, and no tendency for more trash to accumulate in "dead end" rooms is discernible. All of this suggests that the trash in interior contexts dates from the final days of use of the structure, while the trash in exterior contexts probably accumulated over a longer period.

Review by Spatial Loci

B.L. IIIB

SOUTH UNIT

In B.L. IIIB the south unit consisted of room 320 plus areas 325 and 326. The only preserved features in this zone were casual hearth 328 and cobble feature 327 in room 320, neither of which immediately imply a particular functional characterization of the zone. No high trash concentrations were deposited here. In secondarily admixed deposits were found slight traces of class 2, copper-base metallurgy (3 registered finds), class 7, food preparation (a few sherds and bones), class 12 (a few sherds of bevelled-rim bowls, low trays, and goblets), class 14 (1 registered chipped stone tool), and class 17 (1 drain-spout sherd). No suggestion as to the primary trash-producing function of the south unit is warranted on this evidence.

EAST UNIT

The east unit as a whole contained few features, but rooms 215 and 225 appeared to be "special" rooms of some kind, with walls decorated with white- and black-painted plaster, and hearths in the middle of their east walls. Hearth 227 in room 225 was especially elaborate, with its top drainage groove and cup arrangement (see chapter 3 and Plate 7a). Room 219 may have had white plastered walls and floors, and room 242 white plastered walls. This was the only unit in B.L. IIIB with traces of such elaborate plastering.

The east unit was not remodelled in B.L. IIIA. The only deposits which can be considered IIIB in origin, therefore, are in rooms 215-219, which were closed off from use in IIIA by the blocking of doorway 224.

A large secondary deposit was found on the lower of two floors in room 215. This trash included a large amount of flint-knapping (class 1) debris (2 cores and 38 pieces of debitage). Accompanying these remains was a high concentration of finished stone tools, including 10 cutting tools (class 13) and 10 miscellaneous tools (class 14). Traces of another craft, stone bead manufacture, were also found in this trash deposit; the 4 finds representing class 3 included a zeolite bead broken during manufacture. There was also a high concentration of sherds of mass-produced ceramics from class 12 (special containers). Small amounts of items from several other classes were also represented in this trash deposit in room 215. There were 2 finds—charcoal and a pestle—from class 7 (food preparation); no bulk sherds of that class were found. A piece of carbonate rock was assigned to class 9, as a possible raw material. Finally, 7 painted sherds were assigned to class 20, decorative items. All of the material described above was sealed over by the upper floor of room 215.

The upper floor of room 215 did not itself have a trash deposit on it, but adjacent room 219 had both secondary and secondarily admixed deposits. There were traces of class 2, copper-base metallurgy (2 finds), class 5, preparation of plasters and pigments (2 finds), class 7, food preparation (3 pieces of charcoal and some animal bones), class 10, storage (1 sherd), class 12 (2 sherds of bevelled-rim bowls and 1 of a goblet), and class 20 (2 painted sherds). A Proto-Elamite tablet (class 21) was found in doorway 216.

The primary trash-producing functions of the east unit in B.L. IIIB would thus seem to have been the use of bevelled-rim bowls, low trays, and goblets, followed by the manufacture and use of chipped stone tools. Noteworthy for their virtual absence are two classes which normally generated large amounts of debris at TUV (see chapter 6): food preparation and storage. A wide range of other classes are represented, but by a very low incidence of debris. When this distribution profile is viewed in conjunction with the "special" character of the architecture in this room-block, it would appear that we are not looking at an area utilized for mundane activities (like storage) or messy activities (like cooking) but at a "fancy" area kept relatively clean and neat (the trash in room 215 was plastered over; the trash in room 219 probably was thrown there just prior to the blocking off of that room). This suggests that the area may have been general living/entertainment quarters of some type.

NORTH UNIT

The architectural framework of this B.L. IIIB unit was partially destroyed by extensive IIIA remodelling in the southern part of V168, while IIIB remains were not reached by excavation in the western and northern sectors of that square. It is known, however, that there were at least two rooms in the original north unit, rooms 265 and 234. The latter may have been white-plastered, but had no features preserved. Casual hearth 267 was found in room 265, and sherd-lined drainage channel 261 was constructed through the west wall of that room. There were no high concentrations of trash in either room. The only registered finds came from class 7 (a quern and a piece of charcoal) and class 17 (a tile). There was a moderate concentration of class 12 low tray sherds (in room 265) accompanied by a low incidence of bevelled-rim bowl sherds, goblet sherds, and class 20 painted sherds. Bone lots were not analyzed

from this zone, but there is no mention in the field notes of large quantities of bone debris here. On the basis of the evidence just described, it does not appear possible to infer the primary function of this zone.

WEST UNIT

This unit was generally lacking in features "built-into" the architectural framework. The only exception was room 258, which evidently once had a hearth and bin complex (273/281) along its southern wall. (These features, the south wall, and any indication of the manner of connection between room 258 and the remainder of the west unit were all destroyed by Sassanian burial pit 196.)

B.L. IIIB deposits existed only in room 309 and room 306. Room 306 had a very high concentration of class 12 ceramics, consisting of many low tray and bevelled-rim bowl sherds, together with much fewer goblet sherds. Small quantities of sherds of these forms also appeared in room 309. Although the total quantity of grit-ware sherds in both room 306 and 309 was comparatively small, 17 painted sherds (class 20) did occur in room 306, as well as low concentrations of class 10 (storage) and class 18 (food consumption) sherds. Moderate concentrations of bones and 2 charcoal pieces of class 7 also occurred in these rooms.

The major trash-producing function of this zone thus seems to have been the use of special containers, particularly the low tray and the bevelled-rim bowl.

PERIPHERAL AREA

The peripheral zone represents exterior areas lying west and south of the B.L. IIIB structure just discussed. The only phenomenon in these areas which can be firmly assigned on stratigraphic grounds to B.L. IIIB is feature 315, a large, free-standing, circular, possibly domed structure (described in chapter 3; Plate 3b). The function of this feature could not be positively determined from the immoveable evidence alone, but the cementlike floor and traces of burning suggest it may have been a granary or large oven. Unfortunately, there were no high concentrations of trash in this feature. A small amount of mixed trash (comprised of low concentrations of bone, sherds of classes 7, 10, 12, and 18, and one registered find of class 2, copper-base metallurgy) was found there, but the nature of the trash sheds no further light on the possible function of feature 315.

AREA 338

This area was only partially excavated, and it is not known how large a room this space represents, or even whether it is necessarily an inside space at all. No IIIB deposits were found in this zone.

V164 GROUP

In the 1974 season, excavation in southwestern V164 reached what would appear to be B.L. III strata. Room 164 may be part of a second major B.L. III structure, the east wall of which was partially exposed as the western boundary of alley 307.

Room 164 was bordered by two trash pits. The earlier, pit 165, lay to the north of the room and can be regarded as IIIB in origin. This pit contained a very large collection of trash. It had high concentrations of faunal remains (class 7), class 12 ceramics (a registered bevelled-rim bowl profile and 26 rim sherds of bevelled-rim bowls, 57 rim sherds of goblets, and 66 rim sherds of low trays), diagnostic class 10 sherds (storage), diagnostic class 7 sherds (food preparation), unimpressed sealings (15 examples, class 10), and impressed sealings (129 examples, classes 10 and 21). Class 21, information processing, was also represented by a small geometric. Moderate quantities of registered items represent class 1, chipped stone tool manufacture (5 finds), class 4, shell-working (3 finds), and sherds of classes 18 (food consumption) and 20 (decorated items). A flaring-sided cup assignable to class 18 was also found. Low concentrations were found of class 2, copper-base metallurgy (2 finds), class 5, preparation of plasters and pigments (2 finds of hematite), charcoal from class 7 (2 pieces), class 8, pottery-making (?) (an unperforated sherd disc), class 13, cutting tools (1 find), and class 16, personal ornaments (a large ring). The dominant components in the trash suggest that this pit may have been near primary centers of storage, control, meat processing, and special container-use activity.

PHASE IIIB SUMMARY

Attempts to delineate site structure for the earlier phase of B.L. III have been handicapped by the relative paucity of non-tertiary deposits that can be assigned through stratigraphic analysis to this phase. Of the seven zones defined from study of the architectural framework of B.L. IIIB, no estimates of primary function can be hazarded for three of these. Of the remaining four a strong case can be made that the V164 group was near a locus of storage, control, meat processing, and special container-use activity. The west unit would appear to have been another area where special containers were utilized in large numbers. The east unit appears to have been a relatively "fancy" area with elaborately plastered rooms and unusual hearths. Judging from the debris found in the "annex" (rooms 215, 219) the activities of special container use, flint knapping, and manufacture of zeolite beads probably took place somewhere in this unit. Finally, peripheral feature 315 may have been a large granary or oven.

B.L. IIIA

PERIPHERAL ZONE

The south room-block (rooms 320, 325 and 326) as well as adjacent feature 315 were all levelled and the entire area became part of the exterior peripheral zone in B.L. IIIA, along with area 308 and alley 307. During this phase, no deposits with high concentrations of trash were laid down in the eastern part of this zone. A small trash pit (feature 299) was dug there, however; it contained a moderate amount of animal bone and moderate concentrations of class 10, storage (3 seal impressions) and class 21 (the seal impressions and a bulla). Low concentrations were found of class 7, food preparation (2 pieces of charcoal and 2 rim sherds), class 12, special containers (a small amount of rim sherds of bevelled-rim bowls, goblets, and low trays), and classes 18 (food consumption) and 20 (decorated items) (a few diagnostic sherds of each).

To the west of trash pit 299 was constructed plastered sherd concentration 302, which may have been a hearth or a small storage platform. Unfortunately there were no non-tertiary deposits associated with this feature.

Still farther to the west, there was an enormous trash deposit (feature 301) in the peripheral zone; it is not known whether this dump *began* to accumulate in B.L. IIIB, but certainly the uppermost layers were IIIA in origin, and the contents of the dump appeared uniform throughout. This trash pile had very large quantities of class 7 faunal remains and class 12 mass-produced ceramics (756 rim sherds of bevelled-rim bowls, 883 of low trays, and 291 of goblets). There were high concentrations of class 7 sherds (food preparation vessels), class 10 sherds (storage vessels), and class 20 (decorated sherds). Lesser concentrations were found of class 2, copper-base metallurgy (4 finds), class 4, shell-working (1 find), class 6, cloth industry (1 find—a perforated sherd disc), class 7, food preparation (2 pieces of charcoal and a quern), miscellaneous class 14 (a scraper?), class 18, food consumption (6 sherds), and class 21 (a Proto-Elamite tablet).

Northeast of dump 301 was trash pit 285, assigned to stratum 9 because it appears to be slightly higher stratigraphically than trash pile 301; it is therefore slightly younger but still relevant to an understanding of B.L. IIIA. In this pit were found high concentrations of animal bone and class 12 ceramics (111 rim sherds of bevelled-rim bowls, 57 of goblets, and 198 of low trays). There were relatively high concentrations of sherds of class 10 (storage vessels) and class 20 (decorated vessels), and a moderate concentration of sherds of class 18 (food consumption vessels). Also found were items of class 1, manufacture of chipped stone tools (3 finds), class 2, copper-base metallurgy (4 finds), class 4, shell-working (1 find), class 7 (a piece of charcoal and a few sherds of food preparation vessels), class 10, storage (a seal impression), miscellaneous stone tool class 14 (a microblade segment), and class 21, information processing (a seal impression and a potter's marked sherd).

North of trash pile 301 and west of pit 285, area 308 had a moderate concentration of class 12 ceramics (9 rim sherds of bevelled-rim bowls together with 9 of low trays and 5 of goblets). Also found were low concentrations of class 4, shell-working (1 find), class 7 (sherds of food preparation vessels), class 10 (sherds of storage vessels), and class 20 (decorated sherds).

Blind alley 307, which led away from area 308, had a high concentration of bone debris (class 7) and a moderate amount of sherds of class 12 ceramics (bevelled-rim bowls, low trays, and goblets). Also found in the alley were low concentrations of class 1, manufacture of chipped stone tools (1 find), class 7, food preparation (3 pieces of charcoal), class 10, storage (1 seal impression), class 20 (4 decorated sherds), and class 21 (a seal impression and a possible bulla "interior"). This alley also contained feature 321 (black, burned organic material) and cobble hearth 305. The latter two features suggest that one of the functions of the blind alley may have been trash burning.

In general, the evidence from the peripheral trash deposits suggests that this zone was receiving large quantities of trash from areas of meat processing and special container-use activity. While some of this trash may have been produced in areas beyond the bounds of our excavation, it is very possible that much of it was generated in the west unit of the excavated structure (see below).

WEST UNIT

The architectural framework of this unit was not remodelled in B.L. IIIA, but left in its original format. While only room 258 had "built-in" features (hearth/bin complex 273/281), IIIA strata contained a number of other sorts of features. Casual hearth 314 and spilled lime plasterlike feature 300 were found in room 306, while room 284 contained gravel hearths 290 and 292, and room 258 contained casual hearth 331 and cobble feature 276. Non-tertiary deposits were laid down in every room of the western unit; moreover, each of the three main rooms (306, 284, and 258) contained a high trash concentration.

Rooms 306 and 284 had large amounts of class 12 ceramics. Sherds of bevelled-rim bowls predominated in these deposits (91 rim sherds in room 306, 195 in room 284) followed by sherds of low trays (82 rim sherds in room 306 [including an essentially complete tray smashed directly on the floor of the room], 143 in room 284) and goblets (83 rim sherds in room 306, 42 in room 284). Both rooms had high concentrations of class 20 (painted sherds) as well. Room 284 also had high concentrations of bone debris (class 7), class 10, storage (22 registered items and 16 sherds), and class 21, information processing (25 finds, including 8 Proto-Elamite tablets and fragments, 14 seal impressions, 2 small geometrics and a possible bulla "interior"). Room 258, the third main room, had high concentrations of bone remains (class 7, food preparation) and of class 2, copper-base metallurgy (6 finds).

These rooms also had lesser concentrations of other sorts of trash. In room 306 were found items of class 2, copper-base metallurgy (2 finds), class 3, manufacture of stone beads (1 find), class 5, preparation of pigments and plasters (a piece of chalky limestone), class 7, food preparation (5 pieces of charcoal and 2 diagnostic sherds, also a moderate amount of animal bone), class 10, storage (6 diagnostic sherds), class 12, special containers (3 sherds of stone vessels), class 13, cutting tools (4 finds), class 17, architecturally related items (a registered drain spout and 8 additional drain sherds), class 18, food consumption (4 diagnostic sherds), and class 21, information processing (2 small geometrics).

In room 284, the lesser concentrations were of class 2, copper-base metallurgy (1 find), class 5, preparation of plasters and pigments (2 pieces of chalky limestone and 1 piece of limonite), class 7, food preparation (a medium restricted vessel and a piece of charcoal together with 2 diagnostic sherds), class 12, special containers (a complete teardrop shaped low tray), and class 18, food consumption (7 diagnostic sherds).

In room 258, the lesser concentrations were of class 1, manufacture of chipped stone tools (2 finds), class 4, shell-working (2 finds), class 5, preparation of plasters and pigments (3 finds), class 7, food preparation (3 pieces of charcoal and 2 diagnostic sherds), class 10, storage (2 diagnostic sherds), class 11 (1 fragment of a bitumen-lined basket), class 12, special containers (1 stone vessel sherd and a few sherds of mass-produced ceramics), miscellaneous stone tool class 14 (a notched flake), class 18, food consumption (1 diagnostic sherd), and class 20 (2 painted sherds).

Smaller room 309 (which may have served as an entry hall into the west unit from area 308) had a high concentration of class 21 debris (information processing). These finds included a small "archive" of 5 bullae piled in a heap; 2 additional bullae, 2 seal impressions, and a small geometric object were found nearby. Room 309 also had moderate concentrations of class 12 mass-produced ceramics, including 3 essentially complete low trays, and low concentrations of class 2, copper-base metallurgy (1 find), class 7, food preparation (2 charcoal pieces), class 10, storage (2 finds), and class 20 (1 painted sherd).

In corridor 313, which apparently connected rooms 309 and 284, were found low concentrations of class 1, manufacture of chipped stone tools (1 find), class 4, shell-working (1 find), and class 7, food preparation (a piece of charcoal and a quern).

In summary, the rooms of the west unit had very extensive trash deposits within them. Just as in the peripheral zone (which borders this unit), very large amounts of bevelled-rim bowls, goblets, trays, and faunal remains were recovered. This similarity suggests that the west unit may have been the locus generating much of the trash dumped in the peripheral area. The trash found *within* the unit presumably dates to the very end of the occupation there. Examination of the trash distribution pattern suggests that most of the west unit (rooms 306, 309, 313, 284) may have been characterized by mass-produced ceramic use activity. This activity appears to have been carried out concurrently with information processing activity. The importance of administrative control activity is reflected by the bulla "archive" in room 309 and the extensive class 21 debris in room 284, including many seal impressions and Proto-Elamite tablets and fragments. Room 284 also may have shared in another activity, that of meat processing, together with room 258 to the north. In the light of the very extensive faunal debris of class 7 in those two rooms, the traces of hearth/bin complex 273/281 in room 258 take on new significance. Although an intrusive Sassanian burial pit demolished most of that feature, enough remains to establish its original presence at the south end of room 258. Might not that room have been a kitchen? (The trash found here is very different from that in the rest of the unit, having almost no mass-produced ceramics and no class 21 debris).

Finally, the relatively high concentration of class 2, copper-base metallurgy, in room 258 may indicate that this room had a connection to the remodelled north unit, where metallurgy may have been localized (see below).

NORTH UNIT

The original north unit of B.L. IIIB was thoroughly destroyed and remodelled, and this zone became an exterior area in B.L. IIIA, with platform 263 in its center. Built into the platform was sunken oven 223, a possible clue to the function of the platform. Ash had accumulated in this oven from at least three or four separate instances of use, and perhaps from many more (see chapter 3). The platform obviously served as some kind of a pyrotechnic installation.

Trash dump 241 accumulated against the north face of platform 263. This trash dump had the only high concentration of trash debris in the north sector. The contents of this dump might provide some further clues to the nature of the activities once carried out on and around platform 263. The dump had a high con-

centration of faunal remains (class 7) and a moderately high concentration (for registered items) of debris of class 2, copper-base metallurgy (7 finds including sheet metal, a mold fragment, furnace lining, and slag).

Trash pile 241 also had lesser concentrations of class 1, manufacture of chipped stone tools (2 finds), class 3, manufacture of stone beads (2 finds), class 4, shell-working (1 find), class 5, preparation of plasters and pigments (1 find), class 7, food preparation (4 pieces of charcoal and 2 diagnostic sherds), class 10, storage (1 find and 1 diagnostic sherd), class 12, special containers (1 stone vessel sherd and a moderate amount of mass-produced ceramics), class 13, cutting tools (1 find), class 14, miscellaneous chipped stone tools (1 find), class 17, architecturally related items (1 find), and class 20 (6 decorated sherds).

Elsewhere in the northern zone, there were a number of trash deposits with relatively low concentrations of debris (see Figure 37). The contents of these deposits are summarized collectively here. Particularly widespread were finds of class 2, copper-base metallurgy (8 finds, including a piece of slag from oven 223). Also present were finds of class 1, manufacture of chipped stone tools (1 find), class 3, manufacture of stone beads (1 find), class 4, shell industry (1 find), class 5, preparation of plasters and pigments (2 finds), class 7, food preparation (1 diagnostic sherd and a moderate amount of faunal remains), class 10, storage (4 diagnostic sherds), class 11 (2 possible finds of matting in burials 336 and 274), class 12, special containers (a complete stone vessel in burial 274 and moderate amounts of mass-produced ceramics), class 13, cutting tools (2 finds), class 15, piercing and boring tools (an awl), class 17, architecturally related items (2 finds, including a wall cone), class 18, food consumption (4 diagnostic sherds), and class 20 (13 painted sherds).

Very widespread in the northern zone were finds of charcoal (17 finds). Many of these finds were associated with the three casual hearths and one ash pit also found in this northern sector. The juxtaposition of these scattered hearths and the platform oven installation in association with the widely scattered metallurgical debris leads one to wonder whether some of those hearth features were not in some fashion connected with the metallurgical industry. The high concentration of bone debris from dump 241 would suggest, however, that at least meat processing aspects of food preparation activity were being conducted nearby as well.

Another function of the area south and southwest of platform 263 was use as a burial ground. Adult burial 274 and infant burial 336 were interred here before the end of B.L. IIIA. Immediately following the abandonment of B.L. IIIA and just prior to the construction of

B.L. II, additional burials were interred here (infant burial 226) and further south (infant burial 278 and child burial 221).

One additional feature was found in the northern area, again dated to the very close of B.L. IIIA occupation. That feature is drainage pit 333; the reason for this sump pit being situated in the northern zone is unclear.

AREA 338

Area 338 lay west of the northern zone just described. It was only partially excavated and it is not clear whether it was an interior or an exterior space. No features were discovered, but a deposit of mixed trash was present. In this trash were a high concentration of class 21, information processing (7 finds, including 5 Proto-Elamite tablets and fragments) and lesser concentrations of class 2, copper-base metallurgy (4 finds), class 4, shell-working (2 finds), class 5, preparation of plasters and pigments (1 piece of hematite), class 7, food preparation (2 pieces of charcoal and 1 diagnostic sherd), class 10, storage (2 seal impressions and 3 diagnostic sherds), class 12, special containers (a moderate amount of diagnostic sherds of mass-produced ceramics), class 16, personal ornaments (1 stone bead), and class 20 (2 painted sherds). This diverse trash profile does not suggest any dominant trash-producing function for the zone near area 338.

V164 GROUP

In B.L. IIIA, trash deposits were laid down both in room 164 and in pit 163 to the east. Both loci had high concentrations of class 10, storage (10 finds and 3 diagnostic sherds in room 164, 53 finds and 2 diagnostic sherds in pit 163) and class 21, information processing (20 finds in pit 163 including 3 Proto-Elamite tablets and fragments, and 9 finds in room 164). Pit 163 also had a high concentration of animal bone (class 7).

In room 164, there were lesser concentrations of class 1, manufacture of chipped stone tools (1 find), class 2, copper-base metallurgy (1 find), class 7, food preparation (a moderate amount of bone), class 12, special containers (some sherds of goblets and low trays), class 13, cutting tools (1 find), and class 20, decorated items (4 sherds).

In pit 163 there were lesser concentrations of class 7, food preparation (2 pieces of charcoal and 3 diagnostic sherds), class 12, special containers (a registered nearly intact bevelled-rim bowl and a few sherds of each mass-produced ceramic form), class 18, food consumption (1 diagnostic sherd), and class 20 (7 decorated sherds).

From this trash profile, it would seem that the area near room 164 and pit 163 had several important trash-generating activities conducted there. These activities were the processing of stored items, information processing, and meat processing.

EAST UNIT

During B.L. IIIA, the east unit was smaller than during IIIB. For unknown reasons, doorway 224 was blocked, creating a niche opening off room 225, and apparently preventing any access to rooms 219 and 215.

The unusually "fancy" architecture in the east unit was described in the discussion of B.L. IIIB. No remodelling other than of hearth 227 (see chapter 3) and the blocking of doorway 224 was done in this unit.

Unlike the west unit (which had extensive interior trash deposits), in the east unit the central room (225) was kept very clean right up to abandonment of the level, when it was carefully filled with packing bricks. Rooms 242 and 247 also appear to have been kept clear of any significant trash accumulation. A few sherds and bones were found in these rooms, also a cone shell (class 4) in room 247 and a piece of charcoal (class 7) in room 225.

Room 250 did have an extensive trash deposit, however. This room also contained a casual hearth (254) in its northwest corner. Present in the trash were high concentrations of class 1, manufacture of chipped stone tools (7 finds), class 7, food preparation (1 quern, 2 handstones, and 6 pieces of charcoal, also 11 diagnostic sherds and a moderate amount of bone debris), class 10 (10 diagnostic sherds of storage vessels), and class 20 (14 decorated sherds). There were also lesser concentrations of class 2, copper-base metallurgy (4 finds), class 4, shell-working (3 finds), class 5, preparation of plasters and pigments (2 pieces of limonite and 3 pieces of hematite), miscellaneous raw-material class 9 (a piece of specular hematite), class 11 (a remnant of bitumen-lined basket), class 12, special containers (a lead bowl and a few sherds of each mass-produced ceramic form), class 13, cutting tools (1 find), miscellaneous chipped stone tool class 14 (1 find), class 16, personal ornaments (a copper pin), class 17, architecturally related items (a door socket), class 19, carpentry (an adze), and class 21, information processing (a small geometric).

From this evidence, what conclusions can be drawn about the basic function of the east unit? Such trash as was found there was very diverse. No activities truly seem to stand out as dominant trash-producers in the same manner that they did elsewhere in B.L. IIIA. This lack of specificity in activities represented in the trash along with the relative elaborateness of the architecture may imply that the east unit was a general living/working area.

Room 225, in addition to being elaborately plastered and painted, had a special hearth (feature 227) and was given unusual treatment by being neatly filled up with packing bricks at the end of occupation. The room certainly warrants designation as the "best" room in the B.L. III complex. The room's special treatment when B.L. III was levelled might be a sign that, when in use, that room had been employed for purposes other than purely secular, utilitarian ones. Might it have been the symbolic center for the institution which utilized the complex?

PHASE IIIA SUMMARY

Analysis of site structure for B.L. IIIA has been somewhat more successful than the analysis of the earlier phase, because more widespread trash deposits were available for study. Only for zone 338 could some general conclusions not be drawn.

The V164 group contained trash suggestive of storage, information processing, and meat processing activities nearby. The peripheral zone received very large quantities of trash from areas of meat processing and special container use. Much of the trash deposited in the peripheral zone may have been produced in the west unit, judging by the kinds of debris deposited in that unit at the close of occupation there. Most of the west unit was characterized by a mix of mass-produced ceramic use and information processing activity, while room 258 may have been a kitchen where meat processing occurred. To the north, the area around platform 263 may have been the locus of small-scale copper-base metallurgy; south of the platform a number of burials were interred during and at the close of B.L. IIIA. Finally, the east unit was a relatively fancy zone containing the "best" room in the excavated complex. This room was given the special treatment of being filled with packing bricks when the structure was levelled. Thus room 225 may have been the symbolic center for the institution utilizing this complex.

Building Level II

General Depositional Character

B.L. II was the most extensively recovered (455 m^2) building level at TUV, and preservation of this level was very good. The architectural plan consisted of rooms of many different shapes and sizes, but all regularly laid out with parallel sides and right-angled corners. Due to the excellent preservation of this level, many of the doorways were detectable, and many built-in features such as hearths and bins were preserved.

Expressed as a percentage of excavated lots, the depositional character of B.L. II (strata 6-8c) is primary less than 1%, secondary 14%, secondary admixture 14%, and tertiary 72%. For examination of site structure, only primary, secondary, and secondarily admixed deposits are employed. The spatial distribution of these deposits is shown on Figure 37. The following unit divisions are used in this chapter:

southwest unit: as defined in chapter 3
north unit: as in chapter 3 but without areas 47 and 39
east unit: as defined in chapter 3, but without area 183; courtyard 30 is an integral part of the east unit but represents an exterior rather than an interior space
western peripheral zone: round structure and adjacent exterior zones 162, 379
northern peripheral zone: areas 47 and 39
eastern peripheral zone: area 183

The three peripheral zones lacked preserved immoveable features. Of the three room-blocks in the main structure, the north unit was the richest in features and the east unit the poorest.

Just as in B.L. III, many of the trash deposits in this level were found in interior contexts. In B.L. II, however, a much higher proportion (roughly 50%) of the total amount of trash recovered was in interior deposition. This trash was not uniformly scattered throughout the rooms of the structure; rather, each unit appeared to contain a favored trash dumping zone (see below).

Review By Spatial Loci

EAST UNIT

The east unit combined a very large unroofed courtyard (30) with several presumably roofed rooms to its south. The only two features were casual hearth 272 in courtyard 30 and plastered sherd concentration 182 in room 188. The architectural plan and features of the east unit were not very suggestive of any particular functions for the zone. Courtyard 30 lacked any signs of such features as animal pens or outdoor ovens, which one might expect to find in household courtyards. It is possible, however, that wells 199 and 195 of B.L. I may have *originally* been dug from this level, as their positions seem curiously regular with respect to courtyard 30. If this supposition is correct, the courtyard may have been the source of water for the B.L. II complex.

Courtyard 30 contained surprisingly little trash for its great area. It contained a relatively high concentration of class 7 (food preparation) sherds, accompanied by other class 7 material: a moderate amount of animal bone, a registered medium restricted vessel, and a piece of charcoal. There were also relatively high concentrations of sherds of class 10, storage, and class 20, decorated items. There were moderate amounts of class 12 goblet and low tray sherds, but bevelled-rim bowl sherds were present only in low quantity. The courtyard also contained low concentrations of class 1, manufacture of chipped stone tools (1 find), class 2, copper-base metallurgy (2 finds), class 14, miscellaneous chipped stone tools (a notched blade), class 16, personal ornaments (a shell bead), class 17, architecturally related items (3 drain-spout sherds), and class 18, food consumption (a flaring-sided cup and 1 diagnostic sherd).

In addition to the diagnostic sherds tabulated above, a number of large body sherds suggestive of storage jars were found in the central and northern part of the courtyard, increasing the likelihood that courtyard 30 was a zone where storage vessels were kept. No traces of jar stoppers or sealings were found there, suggesting that these storage vessels were both in daily use and had not been shipped in from elsewhere. If wells 199 and 195 *were* originally dug from B.L. II, at least some of these vessels may have been water jars.

Room 175 had only low concentrations of class 1, manufacture of chipped stone tools (1 find), class 7, food preparation (faunal remains) and class 12, special containers (a few rim sherds of goblets and low trays).

Room 174, on the other hand, had a moderate concentration of class 12 mass-produced ceramics (7 goblet rims, 68 tray rims, and 22 bevelled-rim bowl rims), accompanied by a moderate amount of faunal material (class 7). There were also 2 diagnostic sherds of class 7 and 1 find of class 2, copper-base metallurgy.

In sum, categorization of the possible functions of the east unit must remain tentative. Courtyard 30 appears to have been the site of a number of (unsealed) storage vessels and may have contained the water source for the B.L. II structure. The unit evidently also saw a moderate amount of mass-produced ceramic use, possibly localized in or near room 174.

EASTERN PERIPHERAL ZONE

Area 183, lying just to the east of the last discussed room-block, is believed to have been an exterior zone because of the rock buttressing piled up against the face of wall 179 in this area. This is the only one of the three peripheral zones defined for B.L. II *not* to have a high trash concentration of some kind. With no preserved features and only a small amount of trash, including a moderate amount of animal bone, 1 stone vessel sherd of class 12, and a few sherds of classes 7 (food preparation), 12 (goblets and low trays), and 20 (decorated sherds), there are no real clues to the function of this zone. It may have been primarily a street, but if so it was kept unusually clean.

SOUTHWEST UNIT

Room 102, the largest room in the southwest unit, appears to have been the favored trash dumping spot in that unit. This room contained a high concentration of class 7 (food preparation) diagnostic sherds, accompanied by 2 querns, a piece of charcoal, and a moderate amount of bone. There was also a high concentration of class 10 (storage) sherds, accompanied by 2 seal impressions. (Fifteen additional seal impressions, 5 unimpressed sealings, and 2 diagnostic class 10 sherds came from pit 132, dug from the lower of two floors in room 102.) Room 102 also had a high concentration of painted sherds of class 20 and a moderate concentration of mass-produced ceramic sherds (class 12).

Also found in room 102 were lesser concentrations of class 1, manufacture of chipped stone tools (1 find), class 2, copper-base metallurgy (1 find), class 5, preparation of plasters and pigments (1 find), class 14, miscellaneous chipped stone tools (2 finds of notched flakes), class 17, architecturally related items (1 drain-spout sherd), class 18, food consumption (1 flaring-sided cup and 3 diagnostic sherds), and class 21, information processing (2 seal impressions).

Pit 132 produced (in addition to the class 10 debris cited above) material of class 2, copper-base metallurgy (3 finds), class 4, shell-working (1 find), class 7, food preparation (a moderate amount of bone), class 12, mass-produced ceramics (a few sherds of goblets and low trays), and class 21, information processing (15 seal impressions).

In addition to the material described above for room 102 and its associated pit, many *large* body sherds were found in the room 102 trash deposits. These sherds suggest the presence of vessels too big to have been used for anything other than storage. When these large body sherds are combined with the diagnostic sherds and sealings discussed above, it would seem likely that room 102 (or its adjacent rooms in the southwest unit) were used for storage activity. The presence of sealings in the trash suggests either long-term storage or the opening and disbursing of goods transported in from elsewhere, quite different types of activity than that indicated for the east unit.

Although relatively little trash was found elsewhere in the southwest unit, the architectural framework is also suggestive of a basic storage function for this room-block. This unit had a distinctive alignment of small compartmented spaces which may have been storage areas (areas 127, 128, 129, 138, 139), as well as a plastered pit (130), which may once have stored grain. Room 103 contained a bin (feature 131) and a carpet of cobbles (feature 353). As no signs of burning were associated with these cobbles, feature 353 may have served as a "dry" platform on which perishable items could be stored to raise them above the damp ground. Only one hearth, feature 137, was associated with the southwest unit, and it was quite simple.

Three trash deposits were found in the southwest unit in addition to those in room 102. Small compartment 128 had a moderate amount of bone (class 7) and a single diagnostic goblet sherd of class 12 (special containers). The plastered pit, which had become a trash pit by the end of occupation of B.L. II, had finds of class 1, manufacture of chipped stone tools (3 finds), class 2, copper-base metallurgy (1 find), class 5, preparation of plasters and pigments (1 find), class 7, food preparation (a moderate amount of animal bone, 2 diagnostic sherds, 2 pieces of charcoal, and a pestle), class 10, storage (1 diagnostic sherd), class 12, special containers (a few sherds of low trays and goblets), and class 20 (9 decorated sherds).

Room 141 contained material of class 4, shell-working (1 find), class 7, food preparation (a trace of bone and 1 diagnostic sherd), class 10, storage (6 diagnostic sherds), class 12, special containers (a few sherds of low trays), and class 20 (7 decorated sherds).

It should also be noted here that room 141 when excavated in 1974 evidently contained a pottery cluster sufficiently striking to be designated as feature 142. This complex was reported as being not directly on the floor, but rather associated in the fill with several mud bricks which might have been props for the pottery. Unfortunately this pottery complex does not appear in any record photograph, and by the time the present author became associated with the TUV work, the sherds constituting this feature had disappeared. (Only low counts of chaff- and grit-ware sherds turned up in the analysis of the regular lot bags from this room.) Consequently, it is not possible to say what kinds of vessels composed this feature, and whether or not this deposit would further strengthen the inference of storage activity in this room-block.

Nevertheless the review of the southwest unit just completed suggests that, although a diverse range of trash was represented in small quantity, the major function of this room-block was that of storage activity. This inference is supported by the character of the architecture and features, and by the extensive class 10 trash component in room 102.

NORTH UNIT

To clarify discussion, the north unit is divided below into sector A, comprised of rooms 31, 69, 71, 75, 109, 115, 362, 363, and 364, and sector B, rooms 25, 26, 27, 32, 36, 43, and 45. Sector A lies south and west of sector B, and is characterized by a far lower incidence of associated features. Sector A is discussed first.

In sector A, the only built-in features were raised-box hearths. Hearth 344 opened into room 115 and double hearth 68 opened into rooms 69 and 363. In general, the rooms of sector A were relatively free of trash. Only rooms 69, 71, and 109 had non-tertiary deposits.

In room 69 were found items of class 1, manufacture of chipped stone tools (1 find), class 6, cloth industry (a spindle whorl), class 7, food preparation (a moderate amount of faunal remains plus a handstone and 2 pieces of charcoal), class 10, storage (1 diagnostic sherd), class 12, special containers (a few sherds of mass-produced ceramics), and class 20 (1 painted sherd).

Room 71 produced material of class 7, food preparation (a low concentration of bone), class 10, storage (2 diagnostic sherds), class 16, personal ornaments (a copper pin), class 20 (2 painted sherds), and class 21, information processing (2 Proto-Elamite tablets).

Room 109 produced finds of class 1, manufacture of chipped stone tools (2 finds), class 4, shell-working (1 find), class 7, food preparation (a small amount of bone), and class 13, cutting tools (1 find).

The small number of features and the relative cleanliness of sector A are reminiscent to some degree of the pattern seen in the east unit of B.L. III. Room 69 may be analogous to room 225 of B.L. III, in that it is central, relatively spacious, and contains a hearth. As far as could be determined from excavation, however, room 69 was not painted; nor was it ever filled with packing bricks. Despite this difference in pattern, it would seem likely that B.L. II sector A was also a general living/entertainment zone.

Sector B of the north unit (Plates 5, 6a) differed sharply from sector A both in the number of its associated features and in the quantity and character of its trash. Doorways were not discernible in sector B. As explained in chapter 3, many of the "rooms" and "alcoves" of this sector may actually have been segments of one larger room, demarcated by low and rather flimsy dividers of mud brick.

Room 36 was exceptionally rich in features. In its southwest corner was feature 38, a large vessel set into a plastered pit in the floor. In the northeast corner was cobble hearth 29, and just west of that feature, pit 53, containing numerous small bones and fire-cracked rocks. The northwest corner of the room had domed oven 54 built on the floor. Casual hearth 55 lay in the southwestern part of the room.

In addition to these constructional features, several large (class 10) storage jars were found crushed on the floor of the room. Although these jars (except for 14 diagnostic sherds) could not be located by the present author during study of the 1974 ceramics, record photographs confirmed the existence of at least the lower portions of these vessels, lying between domed oven 54 and cobble hearth 29 along the northern wall of room 36. The appearance of the sherd clusters in the photographs suggests that these were the remnants of containers broken *in situ* in primary use positions.

Room 36 also contained a high concentration of class 7, food preparation (9 diagnostic sherds, 9 pieces of charcoal, a quern, 2 handstones, and 765 gm of bone). Lesser trash concentrations included class 1, manufacture of chipped stone tools (1 find), class 2, copper-base metallurgy (1 find), class 12, special containers (1 stone vessel sherd and a few sherds of mass-produced ceramic forms), class 16, personal ornaments (a frit bead), class 18, food consumption (2 diagnostic cup sherds), and class 20 (18 decorated sherds).

The features and trash found in room 36 combine to indicate very strongly that this room functioned as a kitchen.

South of room 36 lay small room 32. Feature 33, a very massive cobble hearth installation, filled an entire alcove on the east side of room 32. Room 32 had the single largest concentration of faunal remains in B.L. II: 2,276 gm, about 19% of the level's total bone. Also present in room 32 were debris of class 1, manufacture of chipped stone tools (3 finds), class 2, copper-base metallurgy (1 find), class 7, food preparation (charcoal, a large pecked stone ball and 7 diagnostic sherds), class 8, pottery-making(?) (an unperforated sherd disc), class 10, storage (3 diagnostic sherds), class 12, special containers (a stone vessel sherd, miniature vessel mf 1458, and a few sherds of mass-produced ceramics), class 18, food consumption (2 diagnostic sherds) and class 20 (3 painted sherds).

South of room 32 lay room 27, which had two small alcoves on its east side. Room 27 contained hearth 51, alcove 25 contained storage bin 28, and alcove 26 contained hearth 52. Mortar mf 6274 was found set into a plastered depression in the floor of alcove 26, about 50-75 cm east of this hearth. This mortar was thus in primary context.

Room 27 had only a small amount of trash, consisting of 61 gm of bone (class 7) and 3 diagnostic sherds of class 12 mass-produced ceramics. Alcove 25 had a relatively high concentration of debris of class 1, manufacture of chipped stone tools (5 finds),[1] as well as lesser concentrations of class 4, shell-working (1 find), class 7, food preparation (a moderate amount of bone, a handstone, and a piece of charcoal), class 12, special containers (a few sherds of mass-produced ceramics), class 17, architecturally related items (a drain-spout sherd), class 18, food consumption (1 diagnostic sherd), and class 20 (1 painted sherd). Alcove 26 yielded only a piece of charcoal (class 7) from its hearth.

West of rooms 36 and 32, and north of room 27, lay room 43. Storage bin 42 was constructed in its southwest corner. The field notes for room 43 describe sherds from at least two storage vessels as present on the floor of the room. These containers may have been crushed in primary use locations. One of these vessels was drawn during the 1974 field season (Plate 17f). The field notes also report a number of grinding stones on the floor of room 43. (These, however, were never turned in to the registrar for coding.) A field photograph (Plate 6a) shows what appear to be four possible grinding stones or fragments thereof lying on the floor in the middle of the room. These artifacts look like querns (lower grinding stones) rather than upper handstones. (These four finds have been added to the register *ex post facto* on the grounds of the above cited evidence.)

Trash found in room 43 contained items of class 1, manufacture of chipped stone tools (1 find), class 4, shell-working (3 finds), class 7, food preparation (a small amount of bone, 2 pieces of charcoal, 4 diagnostic sherds), class 10, storage (1 diagnostic sherd), class 12, special containers (1 diagnostic bevelled-rim bowl sherd), class 14, miscellaneous chipped stone tools (1 find), and class 20 (4 decorated sherds).

Room 45 lay west of room 43. Room 45 contained raised-box hearth 48 at its south end and one of the record photographs reveals what appears to be sherds of a large storage vessel lying at the north end of this room. Like the vessels from rooms 36 and 43, this jar may have been smashed in place in its primary use location.

A small amount of trash was found in room 45, consisting of material from class 2, copper-base metallurgy (2 finds) and class 7, food preparation (a moderate amount of bone and a piece of charcoal).

In summary, sector B of the north unit appears to have been a complex kitchen area, with multiple hearths, ovens, bins, grinding stones, and storage vessels. These jars may well have held kitchen supplies such as water, grain, or wine. In the trash from this zone there are no seal impressions or jar stoppers to in-

_____

1. Finds of class 1 in alcove 25 might total more than 5. The field notes alluded to "a considerable number of flint chips" recovered there during screening; it does not appear that all of these were registered.

dicate that these large containers were ever sealed; they appear more probably to have been left open (or covered with something easily removable) and therefore to have been holding materials in frequent use.

The trash from sector B is exceptionally rich in class 7 (food preparation) debris, reinforcing the interpretation of this zone as a kitchen. Judging by the large amounts of faunal remains, meat processing was an important aspect of the food preparation activity.

NORTHERN PERIPHERAL ZONE

In this chapter areas 47 and 39 have been designated as peripheral because their relationship to the north unit of B.L. II is not clear. On the one hand, wall 264 between these areas and rooms 36, 43, and 45 of the north unit is quite thin; but on the other hand, wall 264 is one of those key walls initially laid out in the construction of the main B.L. II structure (bonded with walls 20 and 21; see chapter 3). This may mean that the builders of this structure did not view areas 47 and 39 as integrally related to the functioning of the north unit.

The entire surface of area 47 was covered with a layer of cobbles, implying that it may have been a crudely paved courtyard. Area 39 may have been an unpaved exterior zone. Although the final plan shows no doorway connecting 47 and 39, the field notes mention that such a doorway (with a high doorsill) may have existed.

Area 47 contained low or moderate concentrations of trash of each of the following classes: class 2, copper-base metallurgy (4 finds), class 7, food preparation (a low amount of bone plus 5 diagnostic sherds), class 8, pottery-making(?) (an unperforated sherd disc), class 10, storage (4 diagnostic sherds), class 12, special containers (low amounts of each mass-produced ceramic form), class 17, architecturally related items (1 drain spout sherd), and class 20 (9 decorated sherds).

Area 39 had a high concentration (1786 gm) of faunal remains of class 7. Accompanying these bones were other finds assigned to class 7 (a relatively high concentration of diagnostic sherds and 2 pieces of charcoal) plus relatively high concentrations of class 2, copper-base metallurgy (5 finds) and class 10, storage (12 diagnostic sherds). Also found were lesser concentrations of class 1, manufacture of chipped stone tools (4 finds), class 4, shell-working (2 finds), class 5, manufacture of plasters/pigments (1 find), class 12, special containers (a stone vessel fragment and low quantities of each mass-produced ceramic form), class 14, miscellaneous chipped stone tools (1 find), class 18, food consumption (3 diagnostic sherds), and class 20 (9 decorated sherds).

It is very possible that the high concentration of bone debris found in area 39 was derived from the kitchen area (sector B) of the north unit. It will be interesting to have the final results of the faunal analysis by Zeder currently in progress. This analysis will provide answers to such questions as whether the bone debris in area 39 is similar to that in room 32 of the north unit, or whether these assemblages have different characters representing different stages in the meat processing sequence.

WESTERN PERIPHERAL ZONE

In the northwestern portion of the TUV operation was a free-standing round structure containing three partitioned rooms (157, 158, 159). An exterior surface outside this feature was traceable to its south (area 162). An erosion gully destroyed both the easternmost portion of the wall of the structure itself and the exterior surface immediately to its east. Somewhat closer to the main structure, however, there were undisturbed deposits of B.L. II, designated as area 379. No features were discovered in any portion of the western periphery.

Room 157, the central room in the round structure, contained a high concentration of faunal remains (class 7), accompanied by 2 diagnostic sherds of food preparation vessels. Also found were items of class 10, storage (2 diagnostic sherds), class 12, special containers (a stone vessel fragment and a few sherds of low trays and goblets), class 14, miscellaneous chipped stone tools (1 find), class 16, personal ornaments (a stone bead), and class 21, information processing (a small geometric).

In the northern room of the round building were found a moderate concentration of bone (class 7) accompanied by 5 diagnostic sherds of food preparation vessels. Also found were a few sherds of low trays and goblets (class 12) and 1 sherd of class 20 (decorated items).

Area 162 produced only 109 gm of bone (class 7) and a few sherds of class 12 mass-produced ceramics (low trays and goblets).

Area 379 had relatively high concentrations of class 7 (food preparation) sherds and of decorated sherds (class 20). Also found were lesser concentrations of class 4, shell-working (1 find), class 7, food preparation (a moderate amount of bone), class 10, storage (4 diagnostic sherds), class 12 (low amounts of each mass-produced ceramic form), class 13, cutting tools (2 finds), class 16, personal ornaments (1 stone bead), and class 17, architecturally related items (1 drain-spout sherd).

In general, the character of the trash was quite mixed in the western peripheral zone. There were no clear associational patterns suggestive of a distinct primary function for the round structure.

BUILDING LEVEL II SUMMARY

Analysis of site structure for B.L. II has illuminated the spatial organization of activities inside the main structure, but has been less helpful for the peripheral zones, where trash profiles were generally diverse. The lack of clear associational patterning in the periphery probably is related to our general expectation (see chapter 6) that trash of all sorts tends to be relegated to the periphery of an occupied zone, and that such trash is subject to scattering by people and animals.

The main B.L. II structure appears to have had at least 4 main activity zones. The east unit was the scene of short-term storage activity in the courtyard, which may also have been the water source for the structure. The east unit apparently was also the site of mass-produced ceramic use. The southwest unit's architecture, features and trash form an associational pattern indicative of relatively long-term storage, and perhaps of the receipt and disbursal of goods shipped in from elsewhere.

Sector A of the north unit appears to have been a general living/entertainment quarter, while sector B of the north unit was a large and elaborate kitchen zone.

Building Level I

General Depositional Character

B.L. I was the most enigmatic of the three building levels excavated at TUV. Only c. 200 m² of this level escaped total destruction by erosion. The extant architectural plan of this level was neatly rectilinear, suggesting careful planning had gone into its construction. Two wells (199, 195) and one pit (101) originated from this level; no other features were present. This lack could be related to the functional character of the structure when in use or simply caused by the poor preservation, for walls were standing only 1-2 courses high.

Expressed as a percentage of lots excavated, the depositional character of B.L. I was primary 0%, secondary 35%, secondary admixture 8%, and tertiary 57%. Only primary, secondary, and secondarily admixed deposits are used in the analysis of site structure. These deposits' locations are shown on Figure 37. For purposes of the present discussion, the level can be said to have three divisions: the main structure to the south, alley 16, and a small portion of a second structure to the northeast.

Review by Spatial Loci

THE MAIN STRUCTURE

The architectural framework provides relatively few clues to the function of this building. Part of the main structure (rooms 9, 10, 11, 12, 65) did have a floor plan reminiscent of that of a storage magazine.

Wells 199 and 195 were both located in the main structure, but in separate rooms (courtyards?). Presumably both were originally used as water sources. Well 199 may have been abandoned as a well prior to well 195, for the former was capped with large stones (Plate 9a) and contained considerably more trash debris than the latter.

Well 199 was the only locus in B.L. I to have any high concentrations of material. Those high concentrations were of class 1, manufacture of chipped stone tools (8 finds), class 4, shell-working (5 finds), and class 7, food preparation (3,809 gm of bone, 2 registered vessels, 3 diagnostic sherds, and 7 pieces of charcoal). Also found were lesser concentrations of class 2, copper-base metallurgy (1 find), class 5, preparation of plasters and pigments (1 find), class 10, storage (9 diagnostic sherds), class 12, special containers (a few sherds of each mass-produced ceramic form), class 13, cutting tools (1 find), class 14, miscellaneous chipped stone tools (a geometric microlith), class 16, personal ornaments (2 stone beads), class 17, architecturally related items (4 drain-spout sherds), class 18, food consumption (a small restricted vessel), and class 20, decorated items (8 sherds).

Well 195 yielded material of class 7, food preparation (519 gm of animal bone, a piece of charcoal and 5 diagnostic sherds), class 12, special containers (a few sherds of low trays and goblets), class 13, cutting tools (1 find), class 16, personal ornaments (2 stone beads), class 17, architecturally related items (a wall cone), class 18, food consumption (1 diagnostic sherd), and class 20 (8 decorated sherds).

Trash was found in a number of other loci in the main structure, but in very low quantity. Room 10 contained only a medium restricted vessel (class 7) and a drain-spout sherd (class 17). Pit 101 contained material of class 7, food preparation (2 pieces of charcoal and a trace of bone). Room or corridor 87 (see chapter 3) had items of class 7, food preparation (a moderate amount of bone), class 10, storage (7 diagnostic sherds), class 12, special containers (a few sherds each of goblets, low trays, and bevelled-rim bowls), class 13, cutting tools (1 find), and class 20 (2 painted sherds). Finally, room 88 contained finds of class 2, copper-base metallurgy (1 find), class 4, shell-working (1 find), class 7, food preparation (a moderate amount of bone and 3 diagnostic sherds), class 10, storage (6 diagnostic sherds), and class 12, special containers (5 bevelled-rim bowl rims, 16 low tray rims, and 21 goblet rims).

The trash from the main structure thus was very diverse. Unfortunately its spatial distribution does not allow reconstruction of the spatial organization of activities in this structure. For example, there was relatively little in the trash to confirm the inference that part of the building was a storage zone. No seal impressions or unimpressed jar sealings were recovered. A relatively small number of sherds of large storage vessels was found, suggesting that such storage as took place in the structure was limited in scale and only short term, as stoppers and sealings were evidently not required.

The class of activity represented by the greatest quantity of debris was food preparation activity, specifically meat processing. (In total, 5,325 gm of bone were recovered from the main structure.) The kitchen area, however, could not be identified. It may have been in an area of the building destroyed by erosion.

ALLEY 16

This alleyway ran between the main structure and structure 2. Within the bounds of our excavation, there were no doorways visible from the alley into either structure. The source of the trash in the alley is unknown. This trash consisted of material of class 7, food preparation (a smashed grill and a piece of charcoal), class 10, storage (3 diagnostic sherds), and class 20 (1 painted sherd). This alley was relatively clean of debris in non-tertiary deposition.

STRUCTURE 2

Structure 2 was represented only by the corners of two rooms within the bounds of our excavation. Neither room contained any features. The more westerly room had a small amount of trash consisting of class 7, food preparation (a low concentration of bone and 1 diagnostic sherd), class 10, storage (6 diagnostic sherds), class 12, special containers (a few sherds of the mass-produced ceramic forms), class 18, food consumption (1 diagnostic sherd), and class 20 (9 decorated sherds). This trash does not allow differentiation of the function of structure 2 from that of the main structure.

BUILDING LEVEL I SUMMARY

Analysis of site structure for B.L. I has been hampered by the severe erosion which this level suffered and by the relatively low—but diverse—incidence of trash. Unlike the other levels discussed previously, the spatial organization of activities of B.L. I can not be inferred.

Chapter Conclusion

This chapter has searched for composite spatial patterning in the archaeological record of each building level at TUV. Discovery of such patterning can lead to an understanding of site structure or the spatial organization of activities. It is likely that particular spatial configurations of activity-related architecture, features, and trash reflect the coordination of activities by various institutions.

Analysis of site structure was quite informative for B.L. III and B.L. II, but unsatisfactory for B.L. I, where poor preservation coupled with a relatively low incidence of trash hindered analysis. For B.L. III, more insight was gained for IIIA than for IIIB, as the IIIA phase had more widely dispersed trash deposits.

Although the architectural plans of B.L. IIIA and B.L. II were completely different, these two levels proved to share some interesting structural characteristics, visible even through the palimpsest of diverse trash deposits characteristic of these structures. Firstly, each level consisted of a complex multi-room structure and surrounding peripheral areas. Secondly, in each of these levels certain key activities were evidently largely segregated in space, while other activities were practiced more ubiquitously. Storage, kitchen, mass-produced ceramic use, and living/entertainment quarters were identifiable in the main structures of both B.L. IIIA and B.L. II (see Figure 38). In addition, B.L. IIIA had a distinct cemetery zone on its northern periphery, and possibly a metallurgical zone north of that. Both levels, then, were clearly organized around a segmented or compartmented concept of space. Furthermore, the number of rooms devoted to each basic function and the large quantities of certain kinds of trash suggest that both buildings were organized under the control of institutions more complex than that of the domestic family.

Further investigation into the characteristics of these institutions can be done via a study of functional profiles for each building level. The next chapter addresses this question of overall level function at TUV and how functions changed through time.

VIII

Site Function

The analysis of site structure in the last chapter resulted in a partial reconstruction of the spatial organization of activities at TUV. This reconstruction was necessarily incomplete. Study of trash deposits could only suggest, not firmly establish, localization of activities, for in sedentary cultures most trash is discarded away from its location of use (Murray 1980). There were other difficulties involved in the analysis of trash desposits. First, large trash deposits did not occur in every sector of the site. Second, certain functional classes of debris were never found in great quantity but rather as relatively minor amounts of debris, scattered widely over a level. Third, some of the trash in our excavation may have been generated by activity conducted in zones lying *beyond* the operation's boundaries in unexcavated rooms and areas. Despite these problems, use of previously effort-minimizing assumptions allowed some inferences on likely activity loci to be drawn from study of the trash distribution patterns. Localization of some activities could be substantiated by characteristics of the architecture and features, but many activities did not have distinct material correlates.

Despite these difficulties, it has been shown that at least B.L. III and B.L. II had certain key activities spatially organized in a compartmented way. The scale of these activities was such as to indicate the controlling influence of a supra-familial institution.

This chapter attempts to further illuminate the as yet shadowy institution which operated at TUV. Focus is now on "site function" (South 1979), the overall role of each building level in the greater cultural system of which it was a part. These roles can be assessed via the study of the functional profile of each level.

A *functional profile* is a summary of the various activities documented for a level, with a weighted assessment of the relative importance of each activity in systemic context. Construction of functional profiles is based on the assumption that the presence of trash of a given functional class indicates that that activity must have existed *somewhere* in the level, even if somewhat beyond the bounds of our excavation. That function can thus be considered documented for the building

level *viewed as a whole*. This assumption allows a listing of such documented functional classes to be compiled for each level (see Tables 29-32).

Functional size (Johnson 1977), the total number of different activities or functions indicated for a level, can in turn be derived easily from the functional profile. The number shown at the bottom of each table represents the *minimum* possible functional size for that level. Unexcavated areas of the mound may have varied significantly in function from the contemporaneous structures exposed by the TUV operation. This does not invalidate the attempt to reconstruct minimal functional size for each excavated level, however. The likelihood that some of the trash discovered in the excavated zone was produced in areas lying beyond the bounds of our excavation actually works in favor of an improved understanding of site function by increasing the representativeness of our sample of each level's trash-producing activities.

B.L. IIIB has a minimal functional size of 17, B.L. IIIA 20, B.L. II 16, and B.L. I 13. Before discussing the details of each functional profile, it is useful to consider whether minimal functional size is only an artifact of the total volume of deposit excavated within each building level (Nicholas 1980b). Despite the small volume of material removed from B.L. I (only 30 m^3), its functional size is quite close to that of B.L. II (with 182 m^3 of deposits excavated). B.L. III (as a whole) is intermediate between B.L. I and B.L. II both in area and in volume of matrix removed, yet phase IIIA (estimated at 95 m^3) has the highest documented functional size of the three main levels. Only about 15 m^3 of deposits can be considered phase IIIB, yet even this small volume yields a minimal functional size of 17 for that phase. It can be concluded that minimal functional size is a good general indicator of the relative complexity of activities once undertaken in or near the structures found in the TUV operation, and is *not* directly correlated with the total volume of deposits excavated in each level.

In preparing the functional profiles for TUV, an attempt has been made to weigh the significance of each activity in systemic context; that is, to estimate the relative incidence of units of different activities when the cultural system was in operation.[1] This is quite a different thing from the simple comparison of numbers of trash items in each functional class. To convert raw numbers of finds in archaeological context to an estimate of activity incidence in systemic context, a number of factors must be taken into account. The first factor is the condition of each find: is it an intact (or nearly intact) object or by-product, or is it broken? Bulk sherds and bones clearly need to be handled in a different manner from essentially intact finds. The following correction factors have been devised and applied in drawing up the functional profiles on Tables 29-32:

—Rim sherds are converted to rough whole vessel equivalents by dividing by 7. This number was chosen by examination of a number of TUV sherds to estimate the ratio of sherd size to complete rim circumference.

—Stone vessel fragments (rims, bodies, and bases) are converted to rough whole vessel equivalents by dividing by 15. This estimate is based on a hypothetical reconstruction of stone vessels from existing fragments.

—Bone mass is converted into units of 250 gm each, an arbitrary figure chosen only to represent the order of magnitude.

Secondly, the relative degree of curation (see chapter 6 and Figures 33-36) must be taken into account. Three degrees of curation are distinguished here: highly curated objects, curated but fairly breakable objects, and uncurated material. The following additional correction factors were designed to make allowances for these distinctions:

—Uncurated material is counted only once in the tabulation.

—Curated but fairly breakable objects are multiplied by a factor of 10, to indicate their extended use-life.

—Highly curated objects are multiplied by a factor of 25, to indicate their even more extended use-life.

No claim can be made that these correction factors for curated objects are "true" ones; obviously some curated objects may have been used only 5 times, while others were used in 100 or more activity units. Nonetheless, the basic difference in scale between non-curated, curated but breakable, and highly curated items is shown by application of those correction factors.

The degree of curation characteristic of each functional class of finds is in most cases obvious (cf. Figures 33-36). All by-products or waste-products of manufacturing classes are considered to be non-curated, for example, as are sealings and jar stoppers (which were of necessity discarded when storage vessels were opened). Implements used in production/processing or other activity (such as a quern used in food preparation) are

generally considered to be highly curated. For ceramic vessels, grit-ware containers are considered to be highly curated, but the less durable chaff-tempered forms (bevelled-rim bowls, goblets, and low trays) are considered curated but readily breakable. Chipped stone tools are also considered curated but fragile.

B.L. IIIB

In B.L. IIIB (Table 29), the major activity indicated by the weighted functional profile is mass-produced ceramic use; over 50% of the estimated activity units for that level involve the use of low trays, bevelled-rim bowls or goblets. (Goblet use was by far the least important of these three actions.) The next most important activities are storage (9.35%), information processing (7.2%) and food preparation (6.77%). Together, mass-produced ceramic use, storage, information processing, and food preparation comprise 75% of the estimated activity units for this level. A wide range of other activities, including several crafts, make up the other 25% of the activity units.

This profile certainly does not resemble one of ordinary domestic activity. It is true that the people using the IIIB structure were being fed there (and possibly housed there as well in the east, north, or south units), but most of the effort being invested in activities seems to have been of a very specialized nature. The presence of a notable component of information processing activity is especially significant, as the items suggesting this activity are ones reflecting *formalized* decisions. The institution using this structure was an administered one. Account tablets were written, sealed goods were opened and disbursed, and large numbers of bevelled-rim bowls and low trays, plus lesser numbers of goblets, were utilized. Various crafts such as the manufacture of chipped stone tools also were practiced there at less frequent intervals.

B.L. IIIA

Because far more trash was recovered from the last phase of B.L. III, the functional profile for IIIA (Table 30) should give us an even more accurate impression of the functional role of this complex.

Over 60% of the estimated activity units in B.L. IIIA are attributable to the use of mass-produced ceramics. Just as in the IIIB phase, goblets were less frequently used than bevelled-rim bowls or low trays. The next most significant activity is information processing (11.39%). In B.L. IIIA, these two activities thus comprise about 73% of the total estimated activity units, fol-

---

1. In the preliminary report on TUV (Nicholas 1980a), functional profiles were based only on registered finds and curation rates were not taken into account. The weighted functional profiles presented here are believed to be significantly more accurate in their portrayal of TUV site function.

TABLE 29

WEIGHTED FUNCTIONAL PROFILE FOR B.L. IIIB[a]

	Functional class	Raw number of finds	Correction factor[b]	Weighted number of activity units	Percentage of total weighted activity units in level IIIB
1.	Manufacture of chipped stone tools	45	x 1	45	1.90
2.	Copper-base metallurgy	8	x 1	8	0.34
3.	Manufacture of stone beads	4	x 1	4	0.17
4.	Shell-working industry	3	x 1	3	0.13
5.	Preparation of plasters and pigments	4	x 1	4	0.17
6.	Cloth industry	0	x 25	0	0.00
7.	Food preparation				
	—general registered items	2	x 25	50	2.12
	—charcoals	9	x 1	9	0.38
	—animal bone	4,662 gm	÷ 250	19	0.80
	—bulk sherds	23	÷ 7, x 25	82	3.47
8.	Pottery-making(?)	1	x 10	10	0.42
9.	Miscellaneous raw materials	1	x 1	1	0.04
10.	Storage				
	—sealings and stoppers	135	x 1	135	5.29
	—bulk sherds (diagnostic rims only)	27	÷ 7, x 25	96	4.06
11.	Basketry and matting	0	x 25	0	0.00
12.	Special containers				
	—whole vessels	1	x 25	25	1.06
	—stone vessel fragments	0	÷ 15, x 25	0	0.00
	—bevelled-rim bowl sherds (rims only)	349	÷ 7, x 10	499	21.11
	—goblet sherds (rims only)	115	÷ 7, x 10	164	6.94
	—low tray sherds (rims only)	391	÷ 7, x 10	559	23.65
13.	Cutting tools	11	x 10	110	4.65
14.	Miscellaneous chipped stone tools	11	x 10	110	4.65
15.	Piercing and boring tools	0	x 25	0	0.00
16.	Personal ornaments	1	x 25	25	1.06
17.	Architecturally related items				
	—registered	1	x 25	25	1.06
	—sherds (diagnostic rims only)	1	÷ 7, x 25	4	0.17
18.	Food consumption				
	—registered vessels	2	x 25	50	2.12
	—sherds (diagnostic rims only)	7	÷ 7, x 25	25	1.06
19.	Carpentry	0	x 25	0	0.00
20.	Decorated items				
	—vessels	0	x 25	0	0.00
	—sherds	37	÷ 7, x 25	132	5.58

TABLE 29—*Continued*

Functional class	Raw number of finds	Correction factor[b]	Weighted number of activity units	Percentage of total weighted activity units in level IIIB
21. Information processing				
—seal impressions	120	x 1	120	5.08
—durable items	2	x 25	50	2.12
Functional size = 17		TOTALS	2,364	100%

[a] Based on material in primary, secondary, and secondarily admixed deposits.

[b] Correction factors are intended to represent differing rates of curation and durability of items (see the text). Briefly, a noncurated item is equal to 1 weighted item. A curated but readily breakable item is corrected by a factor of 10. Curated but durable items are corrected by a factor of 25. Rim sherds are first divided by 7 to convert sherd totals to approximate whole vessel equivalents, and then multiplied by the appropriate durability factor. (Grit-tempered ware is considered durable; chaff-tempered ware, readily breakable.) Stone vessel fragments (consisting of rims, bases, and body parts) are first divided by 15 to convert to approximate whole vessel equivalents and then multiplied by 25 to indicate their durability. Finally, total bone mass has been divided into units of 250 gm each.

lowed by use of decorated items (6.26%), food preparation (5.65%), and storage (4.43%). The remainder of the functional profile is comprised of a wide range of other activities.

The impression of a complex devoted to something other than domestic activity is even stronger in phase IIIA than in IIIB. Most of the human effort expended in this level seems to have been spent on mass-produced ceramic use and administration. As in IIIB, sealed goods were opened and disbursed in this area, and food prepared for the people who worked in the complex. While relatively little energy was expended on craft activity, this level produced notable traces of copper-base

metallurgy, suggesting that at infrequent intervals a specialized smelting operation may have been conducted under the aegis of this administration.

B.L. II

The functional profile of B.L. II (Table 31) differs in a number of ways from that of B.L. III. The most significant activity is food preparation (26.53% of the estimated activity units), closely followed by mass-produced ceramic use (25.07%). Of the mass-produced forms, low trays were used most frequently and bevelled-rim bowls least frequently. Storage is the

TABLE 30

WEIGHTED FUNCTIONAL PROFILE FOR B.L. IIIA[a]

Functional class	Raw number of finds	Correction factor[b]	Weighted number of activity units	Percentage of total weighted activity units in level IIIA
1. Manufacture of chipped stone tools	17	x 1	17	0.21
2. Copper-base metallurgy	48	x 1	48	0.59
3. Manufacture of stone beads	4	x 1	4	0.05
4. Shell-working industry	15	x 1	15	0.19
5. Preparation of plasters and pigments	16	x 1	16	0.20
6. Cloth industry	1	x 25	25	0.31

TABLE 30—*Continued*

Functional class	Raw number of finds	Correction factor[b]	Weighted number of activity units	Percentage of total weighted activity units in level IIIA
7. Food preparation				
—general registered items	7	x 25	175	2.16
—charcoals	56	x 1	56	0.69
—animal bone	15,818 gm	÷ 250	63	0.78
—bulk sherds	46	÷ 7, x 25	164	2.02
8. Pottery-making(?)	0	x 10	0	0.00
9. Miscellaneous raw materials	2	x 1	2	0.02
10. Storage				
—sealings and stoppers	95	x 1	95	1.17
—bulk sherds (diagnostic rims only)	74	÷ 7, x 25	264	3.26
11. Basketry and matting	4	x 25	100	1.23
12. Special containers				
—whole vessels	4	x 25	100	1.23
—stone vessel fragments	6	÷ 15, x 25	10	0.12
—bevelled-rim bowl sherds (rims only)	1,322	÷ 7, x 10	1889	23.30
—goblet sherds (rims only)	667	÷ 7, x 10	953	11.75
—low tray sherds (rims only)	1,491	÷ 7, x 10	2130	26.27
13. Cutting tools	9	x 10	90	1.11
14. Miscellaneous chipped stone tools	5	x 10	50	0.62
15. Piercing and boring tools	1	x 25	25	0.31
16. Personal ornaments	2	x 25	50	0.62
17. Architecturally related items				
—registered	5	x 25	125	1.54
—sherds (diagnostic rims only)	9	÷ 7, x 25	32	0.39
18. Food consumption				
—registered vessels	1	x 25	25	0.31
—sherds (diagnostic rims only)	36	÷ 7, x 25	129	1.59
19. Carpentry	1	x 25	25	0.31
20. Decorated items				
—vessels	2	x 25	50	0.62
—sherds	128	÷ 7, x 25	457	5.64
21. Information processing				
—seal impressions	49	x 1	49	0.60
—durable items	35	x 25	875	10.79
Functional size = 20		TOTALS	8,108	100%

[a] Based on material in primary, secondary, and secondarily admixed deposits.

[b] For explanation of correction factors, see Table 29, note b, and further discussion in the text.

TABLE 31

WEIGHTED FUNCTIONAL PROFILE FOR B.L. II[a]

	Functional class	Raw number of finds	Correction factor[b]	Weighted number of activity units	Percentage of total weighted activity units in level II
1.	Manufacture of chipped stone tools	25	x 1	25	0.81
2.	Copper-base metallurgy	21	x 1	21	0.68
3.	Manufacture of stone beads	0	x 1	0	0.00
4.	Shell-working industry	10	x 1	10	0.32
5.	Preparation of plasters and pigments	3	x 1	3	0.10
6.	Cloth industry	1	x 25	25	0.81
7.	Food preparation				
	—general registered items	16	x 25	400	12.9
	—charcoals	24	x 1	24	0.78
	—animal bone	12,081 gm	÷ 250	48	1.55
	—bulk sherds	98	÷ 7, x 25	350	11.30
8.	Pottery-making(?)	2	x 10	20	0.65
9.	Miscellaneous raw materials	0	x 1	0	0.00
10.	Storage				
	—sealings and stoppers	22	x 1	22	0.71
	—bulk sherds (diagnostic rims only)	127	÷ 7, x 25	454	14.66
11.	Basketry and matting	0	x 25	0	0.00
12.	Special containers				
	—whole vessels	1	x 25	25	0.81
	—stone vessel fragments	5	÷ 15, x 25	8	0.26
	—bevelled-rim bowl sherds (rims only)	77	÷ 7, x 10	110	3.55
	—goblet sherds (rims only)	163	÷ 7, x 10	233	7.53
	—low tray sherds (rims only)	303	÷ 7, x 10	433	13.99
13.	Cutting tools	3	x 10	30	0.97
14.	Miscellaneous chipped stone tools	6	x 10	60	1.94
15.	Piercing and boring tools	0	x 25	0	0.00
16.	Personal ornaments	5	x 25	125	4.04
17.	Architecturally related items				
	—registered	0	x 25	0	0.00
	—sherds (diagnostic rims only)	6	÷ 7, x 25	21	0.68
18.	Food consumption				
	—registered vessels	2	x 25	50	1.61
	—sherds (diagnostic rims only)	12	÷ 7, x 25	43	1.39
19.	Carpentry	0	x 25	0	0.00

TABLE 31—*Continued*

	Functional class	Raw number of finds	Correction factor[b]	Weighted number of activity units	Percentage of total weighted activity units in level II
20.	Decorated items				
	—vessels	1	x 25	25	0.81
	—sherds	123	÷ 7, x 25	439	14.18
21.	Information processing				
	—seal impressions	17	x 1	17	0.55
	—durable items	3	x 25	75	2.42
	Functional size = 16		TOTALS	3,096	100%

[a] Based on material in primary, secondary, and secondarily admixed deposits.

[b] For explanation of correction factors, see Table 29, note b, and further discussion in the text.

third most important activity, with 15.37% of the estimated activity units. Information processing is present, but comprises only 2.97% of the total estimated activity. More important than information processing is the use of decorated items (14.99%) and the use of personal ornaments (4.04%). A range of other activities, including several crafts, comprises the remaining 11% of the estimated activity units.

Despite differences from the profile of B.L. III, B.L. II's profile is not particularly reminiscent of a domestic one. While the administrative element is less pronounced, it is still visible, as are the storage and mass-produced ceramic components. Food preparation has increased in significance in this level, an observation which parallels the much more elaborate kitchen installation found in B.L. II than in B.L. III.

The preliminary results of the faunal analysis are very interesting in the light of this increased emphasis on food preparation in level II's functional profile. Zeder found that meat processing in B.L. II was more "formalized" than in B.L. III (1980:4):

When limb bones are subdivided into meat bearing and non-meat bearing categories, we see a 10% increase in meat to non-meat bearing elements in the building level II over the building level III assemblage...

Thus while butchery of whole animals seems to have occurred in all levels, there is a greater likelihood of the distribution of selected parts as well to the residents of later occupations [B.L. II and B.L. I] at TUV.

In short, the occupants of B.L. II may have "had less direct contact with actual production of these [animal] resources" than had the residents of B.L. III, who received meat "on the hoof" (Zeder 1980:4). This would seem to indicate that segmentation of activities in the

cultural system of which TUV was a part may even have increased in complexity between B.L. III and B.L. II.

B.L. I

The functional profile of B.L. I (Table 32) is different from those of B.L. III and B.L. II both because of its smaller overall functional size and because information processing in particular has completely vanished from the profile. Such activities as are indicated are still diverse, however. One of the most important activities is food preparation (21.64% of the estimated activity units.) This discovery is especially striking because of the inability of site structural analysis to locate a kitchen in this level. Equally important is decorated-item use (21.63%). The next most significant activity is mass-produced ceramic use (14.34%); low trays and goblets were each utilized 3.5 times more frequently than were bevelled-rim bowls. Storage activity represents 13.72% of the estimated total, while use of personal ornaments accounts for 12.36%. The remaining 16% is composed of a number of activities, including various crafts.

Some caution needs to be employed in interpreting this profile as it is based on a much smaller amount of trash than were the functional profiles for the other levels. Except for the disappearance of information processing activity, the B.L. I profile is rather reminiscent of that of B.L. II. The characteristics of the faunal assemblage (Zeder 1980) are also reminiscent of the "formalized" pattern seen in B.L. II. Given the very poor preservation of B.L. I, it is impossible to know whether the absence of a formal administrative presence in this level was real or a result of erosional processes.

SITE FUNCTION IN DIACHRONIC PERSPECTIVE

The TUV operation excavated only a small portion of the TUV mound, and interpretations of "site function" must be understood to refer only to the building complexes lying within the bounds of our excavation, not to the mound as a whole.

While there is no perfectly satisfactory way to estimate the relative importance of different activities in the functioning of these buildings, weighted functional profiles provide us with a reasonable approximation of the basic activity trends in each level.

Throughout the time period encompassed by B.L. IIIB to B.L. I, the area of the TUV operation was occupied by multi-roomed structures under the control of supra-familial (non-domestic) institutions. An administrative presence was especially marked in B.L. III and visible in B.L. II to a lesser degree. It is not known if the absence of this administrative presence from B.L. I is real or due to erosional processes.

Who were these administrators, and what activities were they controlling? In each level a diverse set of production, storage, and consumption activities took place. While interesting traces of crafts appear in each level, it is clear that TUV's primary role was not as a workshop quarter. Manufacturing waste-products and by-products were found only in relatively small numbers. When the incidence of these materials is compared to that of curated items, the energy expended on craft activity is seen to have been *relatively* small. This does not mean that the nature of the crafts practiced there is unimportant, however. The most securely documented crafts (viewed in a broad sense) include those related to the construction and maintenance of the buildings (i.e., class 5, preparation of plasters and pigments), to the production of simple chipped stone tools (class 1) and to the production of personal ornaments (classes 3, manufacture of stone beads, and 4, shell-working). Another well-documented craft, copper-base metallurgy (class 2), would appear to have required the most specialized knowledge. This craft might also have been used to produce personal ornaments, since a number of copper pins (class 16) are known from the site. It can not be proven, of course, that those pins were manufactured at TUV, and other types of copper objects might have been produced at TUV as well. Despite this qualification, the overall impression of the nature of craft activity at TUV is one of a combination of simple maintenance crafts combined with a number of luxury-oriented crafts which produced personal ornaments.

If crafts, then, took up relatively little of the energy expended at TUV, what *were* the major activities? In the earliest excavated building complex, B.L. IIIB-A, the major activity was the use of mass-produced ceramics, especially low trays and bevelled-rim bowls. Storage (including that of sealed goods) and food processing were lesser but still basic activities. As noted above, information processing was also a very important activity.

Site structural analysis has suggested that these key activities were not carried out uniformly throughout the building complex, but rather that to a large extent (though not exclusively) they were spatially restricted (see chapter 7). Information processing probably was centered in much the same area of the west unit as were the use of bevelled-rim bowls, low trays, and goblets. The kitchen appears to have been in another portion of the west unit, while the most messy craft, copper-base metallurgy, was centered either in an exterior zone to the north or beyond the bounds of our excavation. The east unit does not appear to have been a major focus of any of the key activities designated above, although at times the less messy crafts of stone tool production, stone bead manufacture, and shell-working may have been practiced there, and some mass-produced ceramic use is documented for the "annex" in B.L. IIIB. Despite the absence of key activities from this zone, the east unit was probably (in a cognitive sense) the most important wing of the complex. This unit was the most elaborately constructed room-block in B.L. III, and room 225 (with its painted walls, unusual hearth, and special treatment upon abandonment) was the center of the unit. The east unit was probably the living/entertainment quarter for the individuals who controlled the use of this building complex. Once again, then, the question arises of the identities of these individuals and of the institution they represent. It seems likely that this institution was a relatively elite one, since it participated fully in the cultural system's information processing network.

Relatively little is known about institutions in Protohistoric Iran. It is unlikely that the boundaries between political, religious, and commercial institutions would have been drawn along the same lines as they are today. In the ancient Near East in general, the sacred and the secular were often intertwined in complex ways, as were official and private economic ventures.

The institution utilizing the B.L. III complex at TUV is therefore not easily understood. Speculating on the internal evidence from the site, it would seem that the *main* purpose of the institution was not strictly a commercial one, although a certain amount of trading was carried out with other communities in the Kur River Basin (see chapter 9). This suggests that the B.L. III complex was unlikely to have been occupied by merchants. It has been shown above that craft activity was a relatively minor function of the complex, so it is unlikely to have been occupied solely by artisans. Instead we have an administrative presence which sug-

TABLE 32

WEIGHTED FUNCTIONAL PROFILE FOR B.L. I[a]

	Functional class	Raw number of finds	Correction factor[b]	Weighted number of activity units	Percentage of total weighted activity units in level I
1.	Manufacture of chipped stone tools	8	x 1	8	0.99
2.	Copper-base metallurgy	2	x 1	2	0.25
3.	Manufacture of stone beads	0	x 1	0	0.00
4.	Shell-working industry	6	x 1	6	0.74
5.	Preparation of plasters and pigments	1	x 1	1	0.12
6.	Cloth industry	0	x 25	0	0.00
7.	Food preparation				
	—general registered items	4	x 25	100	12.36
	—charcoals	11	x 1	11	1.36
	—animal bone	5,363 gm	÷ 250	21	2.60
	—bulk sherds (diagnostic rims only)	12	÷ 7, x 25	43	5.32
8.	Pottery-making(?)	0	x 10	0	0.00
9.	Miscellaneous raw materials	0	x 1	0	0.00
10.	Storage				
	—sealings and stoppers	0	x 1	0	0.00
	—bulk sherds (diagnostic rims only)	31	÷ 7, x 25	111	13.72
11.	Basketry and matting	0	x 25	0	0.00
12.	Special containers				
	—whole vessels	0	x 25	0	0.00
	—stone vessel fragments	0	÷ 15, x 25	0	0.00
	—bevelled-rim bowl sherds (rims only)	10	÷ 7, x 10	14	1.73
	—goblet sherds (rims only)	35	÷ 7, x 10	50	6.18
	—low tray sherds (rims only)	37	÷ 7, x 10	52	6.43
13.	Cutting tools	3	x 10	30	3.71
14.	Miscellaneous chipped stone tools	1	x 10	10	1.24
15.	Piercing and boring tools	0	x 25	0	0.00
16.	Personal ornaments	4	x 25	100	12.36
17.	Architecturally related items				
	—registered	1	x 25	25	3.09
	—sherds (diagnostic rims only)	5	÷ 7, x 25	18	2.22
18.	Food consumption				
	—registered vessels	1	x 25	25	3.09
	—sherds (diagnostic rims only)	2	÷ 7, x 25	7	0.87
19.	Carpentry	0	x 25	0	0.00
20.	Decorated items				
	—vessels	3	x 25	75	9.27
	—sherds	28	÷ 7, x 25	100	12.36

TABLE 32—*Continued*

	Functional class	Raw number of finds	Correction factor[b]	Weighted number of activity units	Percentage of total weighted activity units in level I
21.	Information processing				
	—seal impressions	0	x 1	0	0.00
	—durable items	0	x 25	0	0.00
	Functional size = 13		TOTALS	809	100%

[a] Based on material in primary, secondary, and secondarily admixed deposits.

[b] For explanation of correction factors, see Table 29, note b, and further discussion in the text.

gests the possibility of a connection to local government; furthermore we have room 225, which was decorated elaborately and given special treatment upon abandonment, suggesting sacred overtones to this basically secular institution. These administrators devoted much of their energy (at any rate within the immediate vicinity of this building complex) to an activity employing large numbers of bevelled-rim bowls and low trays, along with a smaller number of goblets.

The nature of this institution might be clear at this point if it were not for the fact that these mass-produced ceramic forms constitute some of the most enigmatic artifacts in ancient Near Eastern archaeology. While there has been relatively little discussion of trays and goblets in the literature, a number of scholars have offered interpretations of bevelled-rim bowl function. No general agreement has yet been reached, but three basic sorts of theories have been widely discussed. First, it has been suggested that bevelled-rim bowls were used for *utilitarian purposes* (Delougaz 1952:127-128). Second, it has been suggested they were *ration bowls* (Nissen 1970:137). Third, it has been suggested they were *votive, offering*, or *presentation bowls* (most recently Beale 1978).

Of these three types of hypotheses, that of simple utilitarian purposes does not seem to fit the TUV data. In B.L. III, where massive amounts of bevelled-rim bowl sherds were recovered, this trash was probably generated in the sector of the complex characterized by information processing (administrative) debris. The incidence of bevelled-rim bowls (along with that of trays and goblets) was *very markedly less* in other areas of the complex, including the likely kitchen zones, yet we would expect simple utilitarian bowls to be either more randomly distributed or to show a marked association with food preparation areas, and this is not the case at TUV.

This leaves us with the ration bowl and votive bowl hypotheses. If bevelled-rim bowls served to hold rations for workers, it is logical to expect that the bowls would have been made in standard sizes. Beale (1978) cast doubt on the ration bowl hypothesis by measuring the volumes of two assemblages of bevelled-rim bowls and establishing that there were no standard volumes in either corpus. At TUV, bevelled-rim bowls were found not as whole vessels, but as sherds, making it impossible to obtain a set of volume measurements for these containers. On logical grounds, however, the ration bowl hypothesis would not appear to fit the TUV situation. Ration bowls would be expected to be disbursed to the homes of the workers, and to end up in trash there, not at the administrative center. At TUV, we admittedly do not have any excavated examples of possible workers' residences. It does seem unusual, though, that so many ration bowls would have been broken and discarded at the administrative center which would normally be presumed to be the agency *disbursing* the rations.

This leaves us with the votive, offering, or presentation bowl theory. At TUV, there were possible sacred overtones to the institution utilizing B.L. III, but this sacred element was focused on the east unit of the complex, while the massive amounts of bevelled-rim bowls appear more likely to have been associated with the west unit. The juxtaposition of large amounts of bevelled-rim bowls with the presence of predominantly secular administrators raises the possibility that those vessels were being *brought* to the administrators' building, but as tax-containing bowls rather than votive bowls (Nicholas 1987).

The main structure in B.L. III would thus be interpreted as a governmental post on the TUV mound. The residents of the TUV community can be viewed as bringing taxes to the administrators in bevelled-rim bowls, trays, and goblets. The administrators received these goods and discarded the vessels once their contents had been accounted for and consumed. It is possible that animals may also have been brought to the complex as part of tax payments.

This interpretation is admittedly speculative and needs further testing. It is a view compatible both with Beale's presentation bowl theory and with the internal evidence at TUV B.L. III, however. In the Protohistoric Near East, some regions were characterized by administrations that were more sacredly oriented than others. In areas such as Mesopotamia proper, "gifts" brought to temple administrators might properly be called votive gifts. At TUV, the governing institution appears to have been more secular (though with a few sacred overtones). The bowls and other containers brought to this building complex would thus be more properly regarded as tax bowls.

What happened to this institution as time passed at TUV? We do not know why B.L. III was torn down and B.L. II constructed immediately thereafter on a totally different ground plan. The main structure in this new level has a much more "planned" look to it than did the main building in the earlier level. Although it is difficult to assess the extent to which the apparent differences between the levels are due to accidents of discovery, it is possible that B.L. II represents an *expansion* of the governmental center. B.L. II appears to have a much more elaborate set of kitchens than did B.L. III, implying that more people needed to be fed. Food preparation activity occupies a correspondingly greater part of the functional profile of B.L. II.

Although traces of it are less numerous in B.L. II, an administrative presence is still visible, but now without any recognizable sacred overtones. The administrators appear to have received taxes in trays, goblets, and bevelled-rim bowls, to have managed a substantial storage wing, and to have participated in the local Kur River Basin exchange network.

Note that in B.L. II, while trays, goblets, and bevelled-rim bowls again constitute a functionally related complex of vessel forms, goblets are now more numerous than bevelled-rim bowls. This pattern also holds true for B.L. I (cf. Table 17). This tendency for bevelled-rim bowls to be gradually replaced by another kind of coarse ware, open vessel is reflected in data from other sites in the ancient Near East. In the Susa Acropole I sounding, for example, bevelled-rim bowls are very common in Susa 17, but in Susa 16 appear only as isolated sherds; in Susa 16, however, goblets appear and continue to exist throughout Susa 16-14B long after the bevelled-rim bowl sherds have totally disappeared from the sequence (LeBrun 1971:192). The general tendency for bevelled-rim bowls in Mesopotamia proper to vanish from the record while the solid-footed goblet appears and flourishes is also a similar phenomenon (Adams and Nissen 1972:99-100).

It is not clear exactly how much time elapsed between B.L. II and B.L. I (see chapter 3). As has been said before, B.L. I is more difficult to interpret because it was nearly totally destroyed by erosion. While no direct traces of information processing were found, the rest of the B.L. I functional profile is quite reminiscent of B.L. II's profile, and B.L. I is also a very well-planned structure. These similarities to B.L. II suggest that the administrative function may have persisted in location at this end of the TUV mound into B.L. I.

Chapter Conclusion

In this chapter, a weighted functional profile has been presented for each building level. These profiles convert the raw number of finds recovered in archaeological context into an estimate of the relative importance of various activities in systemic context. The activity pattern revealed by the functional profiles has illuminated the hitherto shadowy nature of the institution using the southern end of the TUV mound. At present, the best interpretation of that institution is as follows. It was primarily a secular governmental institution which appears to have received taxes from local residents and to have participated in local Kur River Basin exchange. Within each building complex food was prepared for consumption by the administrative workers, and occasionally basic maintenance crafts and the production of various luxury items (personal ornaments) were carried out. The most sophisticated of those crafts was copper-base metallurgy. Most of these activities tended to be spatially organized in a compartmented way.

The earliest level, B.L. III, revealed traces of sacred overtones to this institution, as reflected in the special character of room 225 in the east wing. The sacred aspect of this area may also have inspired the burial of five individuals in adjacent zones just before and during the abandonment of the complex. These sacred overtones are not visible in later levels at TUV, but the basic functional profile persists through B.L. II and B.L. I, suggesting that throughout the time span represented by our excavations, governmental administration was the primary function of the southern end of the TUV mound.

IX

Conclusion

TUV In Its Broader Cultural Setting

The preceding analysis has focused on a small outlying mound of Tal-e Malyan, a large urban site in the Kur River Basin of highland Iran. The TUV operation, excavated on the southern end of the small outlying mound, uncovered portions of three building levels dated to the Banesh phase of the late fourth millennium B.C. The fourth millennium had seen great increase in the complexity of society in the ancient Near East: the rise of the state (Wright and Johnson 1975), the development of urbanism (Redman 1978) and the beginnings of civilizations such as that termed Proto-Elamite in Iran (Lamberg-Karlovsky 1978; Alden 1982a; Sumner 1986). In presenting this analysis of the TUV operation, two major goals have been held in mind. It is hoped this report (1) adds substantive knowledge to our data base for the Kur River Basin of Fars Province, Iran, and for sites characterized by possession of Proto-Elamite tablets, and (2) contributes to the analytical methodology by which the complexity of ancient urban systems can be investigated.

The major focus of discussion throughout this volume has been reconstruction of the internal functioning of the TUV buildings. Before turning to consideration of the broader cultural setting in which those buildings operated, it is appropriate to briefly review the major points made during this analysis.

Any functional analysis must rest on a secure understanding of the general depositional processes which created the archaeological site being studied. Material in tertiary deposition must be recognized and excluded from the analysis, for such material can not be established as contemporaneous in use with the occupation of the level in which it was found. In the TUV study, density signatures were used to check deposit classifications originally made on visual and tactile criteria.

The next step in analysis was morphological description of the architecture, features, and finds from TUV. In describing the find corpus, the concept of utilized item was employed. This concept allows a material find which had more than one function to be

counted in analysis as two or more utilized items. Thus impressed sealings, for example, were discussed twice, once as items used in storing or packaging goods, and again as items used to convey information.

The basic typological description of these utilized items was organized directly around the concept of function. Finds were grouped into functional classes, and the functional classes in turn integrated to form a model of the "life-cycle" of a prototypical utilized item in systemic context, consisting of procurement, production, storage, use, control, and recycling phases. The manner by which items left systemic context and entered the archaeological record at TUV was also discussed.

The next stage in the TUV analysis was the discussion of activity patterning. An activity is defined as any set of related actions undertaken with a specific aim in mind. Activity patterning was sought by examination of the ubiquity, concentration, and structural position characteristic of each functional class of finds. Different types of activities (such as production activities, storage activities, etc.) were not found to be characterized by uniquely distinctive depositional patterns. The pattern of each activity was determined not by its type but by several other factors. Most important were (1) the amount of trash produced per unit of activity and (2) the periodicity or frequency with which units of activity were repeated.

Site structure (composite associational patterns among different activity classes, features, and the architectural framework) was next studied, as an initial approach to the characterization of the institution utilizing the TUV buildings. Using a goal-oriented, effort-minimizing model of trash disposal behavior, it was possible to learn a great deal about the spatial organization of activities in B.L. III and B.L. II. (In B.L. I, poor preservation coupled with a relatively low incidence of trash hindered this analysis.) Both B.L. III and B.L. II proved to be clearly organized around a segmented or compartmented concept of space, and to be organized at an institutional scale more complex than that of the domestic family.

The nature of this institution was further illuminated by the study of weighted functional profiles for each building level. These profiles represent an attempt to convert the raw number of finds recovered in archaeological context into an estimate of the relative importance of activities in systemic context, by compensating for find condition (whole or broken) and differing curation rates. While there is no perfectly satisfactory way to accomplish this conversion, the weighted functional profiles did provide a reasonable indication of the basic activity trends in each level. Throughout the time span represented by our excavations, this area of the TUV mound appears to have been the site of a largely secular administrative institution, which may have collected taxes in bevelled-rim bowls, low trays, and goblets. The institution was involved in storage activity, in local Kur River Basin exchange, in (rather infrequent) craft production, particularly of personal ornaments, and in "in-house" food preparation to feed its workers.

The last two levels of the functional hierarchy of analytic units (set forth in chapter 1) have not yet been discussed. These levels are the community and the general cultural system.

One of the questions of greatest interest at these higher levels of analysis concerns the relationship between the TUV mound and the main city at Malyan. Was TUV a largely self-sufficient community that lay by chance close to Malyan but which bore no closer (functional) relationship to it than did other, more distant, Banesh sites in the Kur Valley? Or did TUV have a special subordinate relationship to Malyan which made it in effect a "suburb" of that city?

Physically, there is no question that TUV meets all the denotative criteria of a suburb. It is both smaller than Malyan (3 hectares compared to an estimated 47 hectares for Malyan in the Banesh phase) and very close to Malyan, although not connected to the main mound by a zone of continuous occupation. No other Banesh site lies within 10 km of Malyan (Alden 1979:69).

A suburb, however, must also be tied to its dominant community in a functionally dependent way. Unfortunately, the TUV excavations were limited to only a small sector of the TUV mound. The functional character of the major part of the TUV community thus remains unknown. Perhaps someday it will be possible to return to the site, sample other parts of it, and reconstruct its internal community organization. For the moment, however, resolution of the Malyan-TUV relationship must rest on comparison of the relatively small TUV operation with the ABC operation on the main mound.

The character of the ABC operation (Sumner 1974, 1976, n.d.a) can be briefly described as follows. Four Banesh building levels were discovered, designated B.L. V, B.L. IV, B.L. III, and B.L. II (from the earliest to the latest occupation). Each of the first three building levels was razed, and the next building level then constructed. Both these levels and level II (which was not razed but simply abandoned) were very clean and contained little trash.

In general, architecture at ABC was larger scale and more carefully planned than that at TUV. The character of the associated finds was such as to suggest elite utilization of these structures. B.L. V may represent a high status residential area while B.L. IV "is interpreted as representing public space, commercial-scale craft production and associated record keeping" (Sumner n.d.a:3). The craft referred to is the production of personal ornaments (beads), particularly of shell. The next higher level, B.L. III, was the most elaborate Banesh structure discovered. Many rooms in this large complex had walls painted in multi-colored step, swirl, and rosette patterns (Janet Nickerson 1977). ABC B.L. III "is interpreted as a public building, possibly religious in character, or as a high status residence" (Sumner n.d.a:3). Finally B.L. II contained many extraordinarily large storage jars, shell raw-material, and hundreds of pieces of (stored) shell inlay bits. B.L. II "is interpreted as a warehouse for both bulk items, such as oil or grain, and both imported and local raw materials used in craft production or trade" (Sumner n.d.a:3). Sealings and Proto-Elamite tablets were found in every Banesh level at ABC except B.L. V.

How do the TUV structures compare to this evidence from ABC? If the ABC buildings can be collectively labelled as high status structures, the TUV buildings would seem to fall just one or two steps down the status hierarchy. The TUV buildings were less elaborate architecturally and (except for room 225 of B.L. III) not treated carefully after abandonment. Far more trash was found in and around the TUV buildings than at ABC, suggesting that there was no ritual necessity to clean up the TUV buildings before abandonment, whereas there was at ABC.

Although the TUV buildings are not as high status as those at ABC, the two sets of structures share some important similarities. These similarities are an emphasis on craft production of personal ornaments and participation in a formalized information-processing network. TUV (apparently) differs from ABC in having a wider range of crafts, in having greater amounts of mass-produced ceramic use, and in having "in-house" kitchens where food was prepared for the users of the buildings. (Bear in mind, however, that most of the trash presumably generated at ABC was never discovered.)

This comparison between TUV and ABC suggests a *hypothetical* scenario of their relationship. The ABC structures probably were among the most prestigious buildings in the Banesh city. If Malyan was the seat of the paramount tribal Khan in the Kur River Basin and neighboring sectors of the Zagros, as Sumner has recently suggested (1986), the ABC structures were probably in the area of the city where the Khan and his close associates lived.

The TUV mound may originally have been a fairly independent farming/herding village. By the time of the earliest excavated structure (B.L. III), however, this village had been brought firmly under the control of the Malyan Khan. The structures excavated in the TUV operation would appear to represent the residence of a subordinate member of the Khan's administration (who may or may not have once been a petty tribal leader himself). This individual and his staff administered the TUV community from the southern end of the TUV mound (where, incidentally, a good view could be had of the city lying a short distance to the southwest). In the process of administration, Proto-Elamite tablets and sealings were employed, and, it has been suggested in chapter 8, taxes collected. By B.L. I times or shortly thereafter (Sumner 1986:206), the TUV mound's close relationship to the main city was made even more explicit with the construction of the massive city wall. This wall encompassed not only the main city but also TUV within its bounds.

Even though TUV may have had a special relationship with respect to Malyan, it also was part of the general regional economic network in the Kur River Basin. Alden (1979) has reconstructed this economic network on the basis of survey data; it is clear that the TUV mound received goods shipped from other sites in the valley. For example, low trays found on the surface of the TUV mound appear to have been manufactured at site 7G16 (Alden 1979:107), and stone vessels to have come from site 8G38 (1979:110-111).

Neither in the TUV operation nor in Alden's stratified 5% surface pickup of the unexcavated portion of the TUV mound were there any indications that pottery was ever produced in quantity at TUV. Therefore, it must be concluded that not only low trays but also many other pottery forms discovered at TUV were imported to the site from other communities. In fact, the only elements of TUV site content for which we have some evidence of production at TUV itself are the architecture and features, plasters, pigments, chipped stone tools, stone beads, shell items, and copper items. The latter three crafts may all have primarily produced personal ornaments. The amount of debris resulting from these activities does not suggest large-scale production in the area of our excavations, but it is possible that ornaments such as copper pins may have oc-

casionally been traded to Malyan itself or the other communities in the urban system.

Finally, the nature of the broader Proto-Elamite cultural system is also somewhat illuminated by the TUV results, especially when the TUV analysis is viewed in conjunction with the ABC excavation (Sumner 1974, 1976, n.d.a) and survey evidence (Alden 1979; Sumner 1972a, n.d.b). Elsewhere on the Iranian Plateau, late fourth millennium occupations with Proto-Elamite tablets at Godin, Yahya, and Sialk seem to represent the arrival of small groups of outsiders who utilized the tablets and other Mesopotamian-related artifacts such as the bevelled-rim bowl in special architectural complexes situated on the tops of those three mounds (cf. Lamberg-Karlovsky 1978). At TUV and ABC, Proto-Elamite tablets are also used in administrative contexts, but the authors of these tablets are best interpreted not as outsiders but rather as the *local* inhabitants of the Kur River Basin.

The TUV operation has thus uncovered a portion of a community which was closely tied to the urban center of Malyan and to a substantial network of local Kur River Basin exchange. There is little to suggest that TUV itself was directly involved in *long-distance* trade (Nicholas 1983c). For example, TUV sealings tested by neutron activation analysis had elemental compositions characteristic of the *local* Kur River Basin clays (Blackman 1980). By sharing in the information processing sub-system characterized by Proto-Elamite tablets and sealings, however, the TUV community *indirectly* participated in a broad communicative network which reached west into the lowlands of Khuzistan and east to Shahr-i Sokhta. As part of the Malyan urban system, the TUV community was located in the heartland of highland Proto-Elamite civilization.

The analysis of the TUV operation at Tal-e Malyan, Iran, has been conducted in the belief that if archaeologists are to reach better understandings of such issues as the rise of complex society and the meaning of the Proto-Elamite cultural system, it is necessary to painstakingly investigate the structural organization of function within ancient communities of different sizes and at different stages in the development of social complexity. Despite the numerous difficulties inherent in such analyses, it is necessary to persist if answers to these questions are to be obtained, for there are no cultures directly comparable to those early societies available to be observed by ethnoarchaeologists today (cf. Wobst 1978). In conclusion, then, the TUV work (a case study of a small suburban community in the late 4th millennium B.C.) is offered as one building-block towards such an improved understanding of cultural processes in the ancient Near East.

Appendix

Assignment of Registered Finds to Functional Classes

Except for bulk finds of sherds and animal bones, all artifacts and samples removed from the TUV operation were registered, i.e., described and assigned an *mf* number. One master registration sequence was used for all material from Malyan. The TUV finds thus do not occur in a discrete or continuous sequence of numbers.

The entire Malyan register has been entered into a computer data bank. There are 1515 registered entries for TUV material. A number of these entries refer to more than one item. Multiple items are indicated by the addition of lower-case letters to the mf number.

This appendix documents the assignment of TUV finds to the functional classes used in this volume. It is intended to serve as a guide whereby an interested researcher can connect the discussion in this volume to the original data base. The complete register of TUV finds is available in the archives of The University Museum.

CLASS 1

MANUFACTURE OF CHIPPED STONE TOOLS
TOTAL ENTRIES = 270

Raw Materials: 3513, 3590, 3592, 3615, 5053, 5395, 6047, 6233, 6291, 6313c, 6316, 6338, 6975, 6979.

Cores: 3509(?), 3516, 3715, 3718, 3984, 5181(?), 6217-6219a, 6290, 6303, 6317, 6331, 6332a, 6343(?), 7091, 10312.

Debitage: 1060a, 1063a-b, 1064, 1071a, 1074b, 1239b-c, 3504, 3686, 3690, 3820a, 3840, 3844, 5049, 5154, 5314, 5366, 5367a-b, 5371, 6100, 6223, 6224, 6226 (38 pieces), 6287a-b, 6294, 6298a-c, 6300a, 6308, 6310, 6328a, 6329a, 6335a, 6340a-e, 6346a-c, 6350a-b, 6357a-d, 6358c, 6363a-c, 6367a-d, 6380, 6387a-c, 6388a-b, 7049, 7050, 7052, 7053, 7055, 7069, 7084, 7088, 7095, 8571, 8572.

Larger Waste Flakes: 1060b, 1062b, 1071c, 1073b, 1076, 3502, 3514, 3518-3519, 3521, 3528-3529, 3530, 3531, 3709-3711, 3713a-b, 3714, 3819, 3843, 3848, 3958, 3976, 3980, 5152, 5206, 5359, 5363, 5365, 5373, 6296,

6304, 6311, 6312, 6313ab, 6314, 6315, 6318, 6321a-b, 6322, 6324a-b, 6325-6327, 6328b, 6329b, 6330, 6332c, 6333, 6334, 6335b, 6336, 6337, 6341a-b, 6342, 6344, 6347a-b, 6349, 6350c, 6351a-b, 6352a-b, 6353, 6355, 6358a-b, 6359a-b, 6360, 6361, 6362a-c, 6364-6366, 6390, 6391, 6955, 6960, 6962, 6964, 6978, 6981, 6985, 7044, 7046-7048, 7051, 7054, 7057, 7058, 7060-7065, 7067, 7074-7079, 7081, 7083, 7135, 7248, 11241, 11251a-b, 11252-11256.

CLASS 2

COPPER-BASE METALLURGY
TOTAL ENTRIES = 225

Slags and Bits of Metal *Coded as Slag by Registrar:* 1144, 1146, 1153, 1480, 1482, 1483, 1485, 3532-3535, 3537-3539, 3563-3566, 3568, 3570-3572, 3575-3577, 3606-3609, 3680-3683, 3719, 3729, 3806, 3807, 3810, 3812, 3849-3854, 3857, 3863, 3895, 3908, 3950, 3952, 3954, 3966, 3971, 3972, 5039, 5040, 5043, 5045, 5087, 5097, 5144, 5148, 5220, 5231, 5311, 5313, 5384, 5386, 5388, 5438, 5439, 5977, 6036, 6037, 6084, 6086, 6094, 6096, 6933, 6943, 6947, 7102, 7105, 7112-7116, 7133, 10304, 10309, 11244.

Coded as Metal Blobs by Registrar: 1141, 1489, 3540, 3541, 3569, 3580, 3582, 3584, 3678, 3679, 3684, 3808, 3809, 3858, 3967, 3973, 5001, 5042, 5044, 5066, 5143, 5146, 5161, 5163-5165, 5209, 5227, 5302, 5304, 5312, 5318-5320, 5378, 5387, 5389, 5437, 5440, 6035, 6042, 6043, 6097, 6929, 6934, 6936, 7109, 7117-7126, 11243, 11245.

Iron-Rich Copper Slags?: 3610, 7106, 7107.

"Furnace Linings": 1152, 1479, 1484, 3536, 3558-3560, 3562, 3573, 3859, 3901-3903, 3951, 3965, 3968, 3969, 3975, 3977, 5038, 5046, 5147, 5149, 5208, 5303, 5309, 5379, 5385, 6044, 6085, 6087, 6095, 6930, 6935, 6944, 6946, 6948, 6951, 7244(?).

Sheet Metal: 3561, 3574, 3578, 3581, 3611, 3613, 3811, 3970, 5041, 5145, 5441, 6932, 6945, 7097, 7099, 10247.

Bar Metal: 1488, 1490, 5434, 6938.
Molds for Metal Casting(?): 3827, 3831, 3838, 3905.
"Ingots": 3877, 3953.
Raw Materials (Ores): *malachite* 5222; *azurite* 7127(?), 7246, 9803; *azurite with malachite* 5192.

CLASS 3

STONE BEAD MANUFACTURE
TOTAL ENTRIES = 25
Definite Finds of Zeolite: 5071, 5073-5075, 5077, 5297.
Possible Zeolites (not examined by geologist): 5076, 6228, 6230, 7245, 11228.
Zeolite Bead Broken during Manufacture: 6229.
Other Possible Raw Materials for Beads: *lapis?* 6252; *turquoise?* 5069; *definite turquoise:* 5064; *(rock crystal) quartz* 5061, 5085, 5223, 5321, 6231, 6967, 7128-7130; *carnelian* 6974.

CLASS 4

SHELL INDUSTRY
TOTAL ENTRIES = 104
Inlay, Loose: 3604.
Possible Raw Materials:
Unidentified Shells 1257, 1258, 3702, 3869, 3870, 5317, 5422, 5443, 6397, 6399, 6869, 6877.
Bivalve / Mother of Pearl 1097, 1104, 1105, 3549, 3550, 3603, 3605, 3695, 3699, 3814-3816, 3988, 3989, 3991, 5052, 5150, 5151, 5162, 5177, 5178, 5204, 5221, 5294, 5381-5383, 5442, 5444, 6045, 6090-6092, 6396, 6398, 6862-6864, 6867, 6870, 6871, 6874, 6876, 6878, 6883, 6884, 6888, 6890, 7134, 7973.
Dentalium 3701, 3703, 6880, 6886, 6889, 7098a-c.
Cowrie 3555a-b.
Cone 3556, 3696, 3697, 3700, 3728, 3871, 3990, 5051, 5088-5090, 5380, 6882.
Olive 6088, 6089, 6885.
Shell Bits Coded by Registrar as Showing Evidence of Human Workmanship 1091, 1099, 1100, 3551, 3554, 3698, 6865, 6866, 6868, 6872, 6873, 6875, 6887, 6891, 6963.

CLASS 5

PREPARATION OF PLASTERS / PIGMENTS
TOTAL ENTRIES = 60

Marly Limestones/Prepared Lime Plaster: 3594, 3595, 3672-3674, 3822, 3824, 3860, 3861, 3864, 3866,

3906, 3962, 5166, 5167, 5446, 5450, 6026, 6028, 6029, 6892, 6893, 6971, 6977.
Limonite/Yellow Pigment: 3543, 3664, 3671, 3705, 3823, 3865, 5070, 5086, 6076, 6078, 6079, 6896, 6952, 7131, 7132, 7243.
Earthy and Compact Hematite/Red Pigment: 3542, 3544, 3593, 3665-3670, 3704, 3862, 3992, 5156, 6077, 6080, 6897-6900, 6927.

CLASS 6

CLOTH INDUSTRY
TOTAL ENTRIES = 8
Perforated Sherd Discs: 1174, 5179, 5449, 9464.
Spindle Whorls: 1522, 3597, 6950.
Needle: 3813.

CLASS 7

FOOD PREPARATION
TOTAL ENTRIES = 214
Burnished Plates: 1719.
Grill: 1310
Large Bowls: 1452.
Grinding Complex:
Possible Handstones 2636, 2637, 3706, 3721, 3722, 5974, 5975, 5982, 6039(?), 6237.
Possible Querns 2632, 3720, 3723, 3724, 3833, 5157, 5210, 10297, 10301, 10305-10308.
Pounding Complex:
Pestles 5390, 6227, 6972.
Mortar 6274.
Pounding Tools(?) 6940-6942.
Medium Restricted Vessels: 1189, 1449, 1453, 1926-1928, 1930, 3834, 5055.
Smaller Charcoal: 3899, 3904, 4000, 4004-4006, 4012, 4017, 4018, 4023, 4027-4029, 4033, 4039-4041, 4044, 4046, 4050, 4051, 4054, 4057, 4062, 4063, 4069, 4070, 4111, 4113, 4114, 4120, 4121, 4127, 4133-4135, 4140, 4143, 4147-4150, 4154, 4157-4159, 4202-4205, 4210, 4213-4216, 4218, 4219, 4249, 4250, 4292, 5095, 5155, 5158, 5183, 5191, 5398, 5399, 5451, 5454-5456, 6084, 6053, 6054, 6058, 6060, 6065-6069, 6082, 6083, 6206, 6208-6210, 6212, 6214-6216, 6273, 7176, 7484, 10275-10279, 10299, 11242.
Larger Charcoal: 3898, 3960, 4071, 4073, 4074, 4078-4081, 4239, 5141, 5159, 5323, 6207, 6211, 6213.

Carbonized Botanical Material: 3837, 3872-3874, 3897, 7335-7345, 7357, 7359-7361, 7370-7372, 7374-7391, 7393, 7394, 7396, 7397, 7411, 7424, 7426, 7427, 7452, 7455-7457, 7473, 7475, 9931.

CLASS 8

POTTERY MAKING
TOTAL ENTRIES = 13
Unperforated Sherd Discs: 1201, 1517, 1518, 1520, 5180, 5973, 6051, 6052, 6061.
Ceramic Slag: 7976.
Kiln Wasters: 5300, 5301, 5445(?).

CLASS 9

RAW MATERIALS/BY-PRODUCTS OF
UNDETERMINED INDUSTRIAL RELATION
TOTAL ENTRIES = 21
Agate (chipped stone? beads?): 3717, 5092, 5377.
Carbonate rock: 6225.
Travertine: 5063, 6235.
Calcite: 3712, 7094, 7247.
Limestone: 1050, 3508, 5299, 5370, 6234, 6965.
Specular Hematite (temper for burnished plates?): 3616, 3618, 3867, 6928, 6966.
Bitumen Patty: 6395.

CLASS 10

GENERAL STORAGE
TOTAL ENTRIES = 304
Sealings Without Impressions: 1785a, 1793a-f, 1803, 1825a-b, 1826a, 1879a-c, 1881a-b, 1883, 1884a, 1885a, 1886a, 1887a-c, 1935a-d, 1937a-d, 1938a-c, 1939a-c, 1940a-c, 1941a-e, 1942a-b, 1943a-c, 1945a-d, 1946a-d, 1947a-c, 1952a, 1953a, 1954a-f, 3828, 3836, 5392, 5969, 6107, 6191, 6202, 6204, 6241.
Jar Stoppers Without Impressions: 5999a-f.
Seal Impressions: 1785b, 1786a-b, 1787-1792, 1794-1802, 1804a-j, 1805-1817b, 1818-1824, 1825c-s, 1826b-n, 1878, 1879d-j, 1880, 1881c-h, 1882, 1884b-g, 1885b-g, 1886b-l, 1887d-n, 1936, 1937e, 1938d, 1942c-d, 1943d-f, 1944a-p, 1945e-l, 1947d-e, 1948, 1950, 1951a-b, 1952b, 1953b, 1955a-c, 1957-1965b, 1966, 5986-5988, 5990, 5992-5996, 5995a-c, 5997, 5998, 6059, 6181-6185, 6189, 6190, 6192-6197, 6199, 6201a-f, 6238-6240.

CLASS 11

BASKETRY/MATTING
TOTAL ENTRIES = 5
Bitumen With Reed Impressions—*Possible Basket Linings:* 5393-5394, 6070.
  Cloth/Fine Mat Impressions: 3896, 6105.

CLASS 12

SPECIAL CONTAINERS
TOTAL ENTRIES = 64
Stone Vessels:
  Whole 5078.
  Sherds 1027, 1120, 1121, 1123-1125, 1129, 1432-1435, 1437, 1438, 1440, 1442, 1443, 1445, 3591, 3829, 5048, 5058, 5062, 5202, 5205, 5230, 5295, 5322, 5976, 6031, 6034, 6104, 6248-6251, 6909-6912, 6914-6926, 7092, 7110, 11222.
  Possible Fragments of Such Vessels 3821, 7111.
Low Trays: 5084.
Bevelled-rim Bowls: 1724, 1725.
Lead Bowl: 3878a.
Fragments of a Plaster Vessel: 6894.
Miniature Ceramic Vessel: 1458.

CLASS 13

CUTTING TOOLS
TOTAL ENTRIES = 116
Blades and Blade Segments: 1062a, 1067, 1068, 1212, 1228, 1234, 3501, 3503, 3507, 3520, 3526, 3586-3589, 3614, 3687, 3689, 3691, 3846, 3847, 3907, 3978, 3985, 3986, 5091, 5093, 5232, 5233, 5305, 5360, 5361, 5364, 5368, 5372, 5436, 6033, 6098, 6101, 6102, 6109, 6219b, 6220-6222, 6280-6284, 6286, 6288, 6292, 6293, 6299, 6302, 6305, 6348a-b, 6354, 6356b, 6358d, 6362d, 6368-6370, 6372, 6373, 6375-6378, 6381-6384, 6386, 6389, 6392, 6986-6994, 6996-6999, 7039-7041, 7043, 7045, 7059, 7066, 7073, 7080, 7082, 7085, 7086, 7089, 7090, 10313, 10317, 10322-10325, 10327, 10328, 11250.

CLASS 14

MISCELLANEOUS CHIPPED STONE TOOLS
TOTAL ENTRIES = 83
Diverse Flaked Tools: 1063c, 1071b, 1073a, 1074a, 1239a, 3505, 3506, 3510-3512, 3515, 3517, 3522-3525, 3527, 3688, 3692, 3817, 3818, 3820b, 3835, 3841, 3842, 3845, 3959, 3979, 3981-3983, 5047, 5050, 5153, 5315,

5316, 5369, 5374, 5376, 5435, 6032, 6041, 6099, 6285, 6289, 6295, 6297, 6300b, 6301, 6306, 6307, 6309, 6319, 6320, 6323, 6332b, 6339, 6345, 6356a, 6358e, 6371, 6374a-b, 6379, 6385, 6995, 7042, 7056, 7068, 7070-7072, 7087, 10310, 10311, 10314-10316, 10318-10321, 10326.

Vertical Cups: 1455, 1461.
Small Bowls: 1459, 1721, 1729.
Small Restricted Vessels: 1256, 1457.
Medium Restricted Vessel With Slightly Inverted Rim: 3834.

CLASS 15

PIERCING/BORING TOOLS
TOTAL ENTRIES = 3
  Awl: 7972.
  Bone Implements Possibly Used for Piercing: 7878, 7975.

CLASS 16

PERSONAL ORNAMENTS
TOTAL ENTRIES = 41
  Beads:
  Stone 1281, 1292, 1295-1297, 1299, 1309, 6093, 6901, 6903, 6907, 7100, 7140, 9801, 9802.
  Bone 3868, 5096.
  Frit 6906, 6908.
  Shell 1914, 3546a-c, 3547, 3548, 3552, 3553, 3557, 6030, 6879, 6905.
  Pins: 1487, 3583, 3585, 3676, 3677, 5060, 5160, 6931, 6937.
  Ring: 1920.

CLASS 17

ARCHITECTURAL USE
TOTAL ENTRIES = 22
  Door Sockets: 1312, 1742, 1743, 6275.
  Drain Spouts: 1313, 3964, 5400, 6247, 6272.
  Plasters: 3596, 3602, 3909, 3963, 5396.
  Wall Cones: 1172, 1548-1550, 3599, 3726; *cylindrical fragment* 6050.
  Tiles: 3830.

CLASS 18

FOOD CONSUMPTION
TOTAL ENTRIES = 12
  Flaring Cups: 1450, 1451, 1723, 1727.

CLASS 19

CARPENTRY
TOTAL ENTRIES = 1
  Adze: 5067.

CLASS 20

DECORATED ITEMS
TOTAL ENTRIES = 17
  Relief Sherds: 1738, 1931, 3600, 3957, 3993, 5054, 5190.
  Decorated Registered Vessels: 1189, 1256, 1453, 1455, 1459, 1461, 1926, 1928, 1930, 5055.

CLASS 21

INFORMATION PROCESSING
TOTAL ENTRIES = 278
  Cylinder Seals: 1290, 1902, 5056, 5057.
  Seal Impressions: Listed under class 10.
  Tablets: 1691, 1858-1862, 4426, 4435, 4469, 4474-4482.
  Bullae: 5452, 5453, 6046, 6176-6180.
  Interiors of Bullae: 5420, 5421, 6106.
  Small Geometric Objects:
  Asymmetrical Balls 1046, 3693.
  Stone Balls 5065, 5094, 5229, 6103, 6902, 6904, 6939, 6961.
  Clay Balls 3598, 6959.
  Squat Cones 1912, 3601, 5228.
  Cylindrical Rods 5182a-b.
  Potter's Marks: 6243-6246, 8685.

Banesh Finds Not Assigned to Functional Classes

TOTAL ENTRIES = 125
  Specimen, unknown substance: 6159

  Mineral Specimens (as yet unidentified): 3900, 5068, 5072, 5298, 6071, 6072, 6074, 6232, 6236, 6954, 6970, 6973, 7104.

Coprolites: 6957.

Fossils: 6881.

Identified Mineral Specimens: *barite* 6984; *siltstone* 5397; *igneous rock* 3707, 5448; *sandstone* 3716; *carbonaceous clay with white calcite bands* 6976; *bitumen* 6394.

Soil Samples: 6958, 5296.

Hearth Samples: 6158, 5447(?) (not ash but clay-pebble matrix).

Phytolith/Pollen: 4088, 4092-4097, 4104, 4162-4164, 4170, 4171, 4184-4191, 4225, 4226, 4234, 4280-4284, 4294, 4305, 4321, 7492-7498.

Miscellaneous Botanical Samples: 4316, 4325.

Sherds for Technical Analyses: 1735, 3500, 5457, 6049, 6075, 6968, 10300.

Other Finds: 1194, 1519, 1741, 3545, 3612, 3675, 3685, 3694, 3708, 3725, 3727, 3825, 3826, 3832, 3876, 3878b, 3955, 3974, 3987, 5207, 5375, 5391, 5972, 6024, 6025, 6027, 6038, 6040, 6081, 6895, 6949, 6953, 6956, 6969, 6980, 6982, 6983, 7103, 7108, 7136-7139, 7974, 10298, 10776, 11257.

Non-Banesh Finds from the TUV Operation

TOTAL ENTRIES = 25

Sassanian Silver Bowl: 5310.

Iron Bracelet: 1138.

Possibly Sassanian Copper/Bronze Hook: 3856.

Iron Hook: 1486.

Iron Hook, Sassanian: 5267.

Inscribed Brick (Middle Elamite): 1182.

Iron Ring: 3579.

Glass Fragments: 1291, 1314, 7093, 7096.

Iron Knob, Sassanian: 6175.

Ceramic Knob: 1734.

Iron Blob: 9704.

Sassanian Iron Knives: 5265, 5266, 5268, 6174.

Sassanian Coin: 5226.

Sassanian Belt Buckle (copper/bronze): 5000.

Preserved Cloth and Wood: 9705.

Wood from Hilt of 5265: 4194.

Copper/Bronze Slag: 3855.

Sheet Copper/Bronze: 3956.

Charcoal or carbonized material: 3875.

Bibliography

Adams, Robert McC.

1965 Land Behind Baghdad: A History of Settlement on the Diyala Plains. Chicago: University of Chicago Press.

Adams, Robert McC., and Hans J. Nissen

1972 The Uruk Countryside: The Natural Setting of Urban Societies. Chicago: University of Chicago Press.

Alden, John R.

1978 Excavations at Tal-i Malyan, Part I. A Sasanian Kiln. Iran 16:79-86.

1979 Regional Economic Organization in Banesh Period Iran. Ph.D. dissertation, University of Michigan.

1982a Trade and Politics in Proto-Elamite Iran. Current Anthropology 23:613-640.

1982b Marketplace Exchange as Indirect Distribution: An Iranian Example. In Contexts for Prehistoric Exchange. T. Earle and J. Ericson, eds. pp. 83-101. New York: Academic Press.

n.d. The Early Banesh Period in Iran: Results of a Test Excavation at Tal-i Kureh. Manuscript on file, Ohio State University.

Amiet, P.

1979 Archaeological Discontinuity and Ethnic Duality in Elam. Antiquity 53:195-204.

Amiet, Pierre, and Maurizio Tosi

1978 Phase 10 at Shahr-i Sokhta: Excavations in Square XDV and the Late 4th Millennium B.C. Assemblage of Sistan. East and West 28 (N.S.): 9-31.

Ashmore, Wendy

1981 Some Issues of Method and Theory in Lowland Maya Settlement Archaeology. In Lowland Maya Settlement Patterns. W. Ashmore, ed. pp. 37-69. Albuquerque: University of New Mexico Press.

Balcer, Jack Martin

1978 Excavations at Tal-i Malyan, Part 2. Parthian and Sasanian Coins and Burials (1976). Iran 16:86-92.

Beale, Thomas Wight

1973 Early Trade in Highland Iran: A View From a Source Area. World Archaeology 5(2):133-148.

1978 Bevelled Rim Bowls and Their Implications for Change and Economic Organization in the Later Fourth Millennium B.C. Journal of Near Eastern Studies 37:289-313.

Binford, Lewis R.

1976 Forty-Seven Trips: A Case Study in the Character of Some Formation Processes of the Archaeological Record. In Contributions to Anthropology: The Interior Peoples of Northern Alaska. Edwin S. Hall, Jr., ed. pp. 299-351. National Museum of Man, Mercury Series. Archaeological Survey of Canada, Paper 49. Ottawa: National Museums of Canada.

1980 Organization and Formation Processes: Looking at Curated Technologies. Journal of Anthropological Research 35: 255-273.

1981a Behavioral Archaeology and the "Pompeii Premise." Journal of Anthropological Research 37:195-208.

1981b Bones: Ancient Men and Modern Myths. New York: Academic Press.

Biscione, Raffaele, Sandro Salvatori, and Maurizio Tosi

1977 Shahr-i Sokhta: L'abitato Protostorico e la Sequenza Cronologica. In La Citta Bruciata del Deserto Salato (The Burnt City in the Salt Desert). G. Tucci, ed. pp. 77-102 with Eng. translation pp. 103-112. Venice: Erizzo Editrice.

Blackman, M. James

1980 Long Range and Local Exchange Patterns in Southern Iran. Paper delivered at the annual meetings of the Society for American Archaeology, Philadelphia.

1981 The Mineralogical and Chemical Analysis of Banesh Period Ceramics from Tal-e Malyan, Iran. In Scientific Studies in Ancient Ceramics. M.J. Hughes, ed. pp. 7-20. British Museum Occasional Papers 19.

1982 The Manufacture and Use of Burned Lime Plaster at Proto-Elamite Anshan (Iran). In Early Pyrotechnology: The Evolution of Fire Using Industries. T. Wertime and S. Wertime, eds. pp. 107-116. Washington: Smithsonian Institution.

Bovington, C., A. Mahdavi, and R. Masoumi.

1973 Tehran University Nuclear Centre Radiocarbon Date List II. Radiocarbon 15(3): 595-598.

Braidwood, Robert J.

1974 The Iraq Jarmo Project. *In* Archaeological Researches in Retrospect. Gordon R. Willey, ed. pp. 61-83. Cambridge, Massachusetts: Winthrop Publishers.

Brice, William C.

1962 Studies in the Structure of Some Ancient Scripts, I. The Writing System of the Proto-Elamite Account Tablets of Susa. Bulletin of the John Rylands Library 45:15-39. Manchester.

Caldwell, Joseph R.

1968 Pottery and Cultural History on the Iranian Plateau. Journal of Near Eastern Studies 27: 178-183.

Carter, Elizabeth

1974 Susa: The Ville Royale. Iran 12:218-220.

1975 Excavations at Tappeh Malyan, 1974: The Middle Elamite Building. *In* Proceedings of the IIIrd Annual Symposium on Archaeological Research in Iran. F. Bagherzadeh, ed. pp. 163-170. Tehran: Iranian Centre for Archaeological Research.

1978 Suse "Ville Royale." Paléorient 4:197-211.

1981 Excavations in Ville Royale I at Susa: The Third Millennium B.C. Occupation. Cahiers de la Délégation Archéologique Française en Iran 10.

Carter, Elizabeth, and Matthew Stolper

1976 Middle Elamite Malyan. Expedition 18(2): 33-42.

Childe, V. Gordon

1954 Rotary Motion. *In* A History of Technology, Vol. 1. From Early Times to Fall of Ancient Empires. Charles Singer, E.J. Holmyard, and A.R. Hall, eds. pp. 187-215. Oxford: Clarendon Press.

Christenson, Andrew L.

1982 Maximizing Clarity in Economic Terminology. American Antiquity 47:419-426.

Clarke, David L.

1968 Analytical Archaeology. London: Methuen.

Crawford, Harriet E.W.

1977 The Architecture of Iraq in the Third Millennium B.C. Copenhagen: Akademisk Forlag.

Crowfoot, Grace M.

1954 Textiles, Basketry, and Mats. *In* A History of Technology, Vol. 1. From Early Times to Fall of Ancient Empires. Charles Singer, E.J. Holmyard, and A.R. Hall, eds. pp. 413-447. Oxford: Clarendon Press.

DeBoer, Warren R., and Donald W. Lathrap

1979 The Making and Breaking of Shipibo-Conibo Ceramics. *In* Ethnoarchaeology: Implications of Ethnography for Archaeology. Carol Kramer, ed. pp. 102-138. New York: Columbia University Press.

Delougaz, P.P.

1952 Pottery from the Diyala Region. O.I.P. LXIII. Chicago: University of Chicago Press.

Delougaz, P.P., and H.J. Kantor

1972 New Evidence for the Prehistoric and Protoliterate Culture Development of Khuzestan. *In* The Memorial Volume of the Vth International Congress of Iranian Art and Archaeology, Vol. 1. A. Tajvidi and M.Y. Kiani, eds. pp. 14-33. Tehran: Special Publication of the Ministry of Culture and Arts.

1975 The 1973-74 Excavations at Čoqa Miš. *In* Proceedings of the IIIrd Annual Symposium on Archaeological Research in Iran. F. Bagherzadeh, ed. pp. 93-102. Tehran: Iranian Centre for Archaeological Research.

Dunnell, Robert C.

1978a Archaeological Potential of Anthropological and Scientific Models of Function. *In* Archaeological Essays in Honor of Irving B. Rouse. R.C. Dunnell and E.S. Hall, Jr., eds. pp. 41-73. The Hague: Mouton.

1978b Style and Function: A Fundamental Dichotomy. American Antiquity 43:192-202.

Dyson, Robert H., Jr.

1966 Excavations on the Acropolis at Susa and Problems of Susa A, B, and C. Ph.D. dissertation, Harvard University.

1983 The Genesis of the Hasanlu Project. *Introduction to* Mary M. Voigt. Hajji Firuz Tepe, Iran: The Neolithic Settlement pp. xxv-xxviii. University Museum Monograph 50. Hasanlu Excavation Reports, vol. 1.

Fishman, B. and B. Lawn

1978 University of Pennsylvania Radiocarbon Dates XX. Radiocarbon 20 (2): 210-233.

Flannery, Kent V.

1972 The Cultural Evolution of Civilizations. Annual Review of Ecology and Systematics 3: 399-425.

Forbes, R.J.

1954 Chemical, Culinary, and Cosmetic Arts. *In* A History of Technology, Vol. 1. From Early Times to Fall of Ancient Empires. Charles Singer, E.J. Holmyard, and A.R. Hall, eds. pp. 238-298. Oxford: Clarendon Press.

1964 Studies in Ancient Technology. Vol. 9. Leiden: E.J. Brill (2nd ed.).

Frankfort, Henri, and Leri Davies

1971 The Last Predynastic Period in Babylonia. *In* Early History of The Middle East. I.E.S. Edwards et al., eds. pp. 71-92. The Cambridge Ancient History, Vol. 1, Pt. 2. Cambridge: Cambridge University Press (3rd ed.).

Ghirshman, Roman

1938 Fouilles de Sialk, près de Kashan 1933, 1934, 1937, Vol. 1. Paris: Librairie Orientaliste Paul Geuthner.

Gibson, McGuire, and Robert D. Biggs, eds.

1977 Seals and Sealing in the Ancient Near East. Vol. 6. Bibliotheca Mesopotamica. Malibu: Undena Publications.

Hansman, John

1972 Elamites, Achaemenians and Anshan. Iran 10: 101-124.

Hodder, Ian

1978 Simple Correlations between Material Culture and Society: A Review. *In* The Spatial Organization of Culture. Ian Hodder, ed. pp. 3-24. Pittsburgh: University of Pittsburgh Press.

Hodges, Henry

1970 Technology in the Ancient World. New York: Alfred A. Knopf.

Hoffman, Michael A.

1974 The Social Context of Trash Disposal in an Early Dynastic Egyptian Town. American Antiquity 39: 35-50.

Johnson, Gregory A.

1973 Local Exchange and Early State Development in Southwestern Iran. Museum of Anthropology, University of Michigan, Anthropological Papers 51. Ann Arbor.

1977 Aspects of Regional Analysis in Archaeology. Annual Review of Anthropology 6:479-508. Palo Alto, California.

1978 Information Sources and the Development of Decision-making Organizations. *In* Social Archaeology. C.L. Redman et al., eds. pp. 87-112. New York: Academic Press.

Kantor, Helene J.

1973 Excavations at Chogha Mish. The Oriental Institute of the University of Chicago Report 1972/1973. pp. 10-17.

1974 Excavations at Chogha Mish. The Oriental Institute of the University of Chicago Report 1973/1974. pp. 20-28.

1975 Excavations at Chogha Mish. The Oriental Institute of the University of Chicago Report 1974/1975. pp. 17-26.

1979 Chogha Mish and Chogha Bomut. The Oriental Institute Annual Report 1978/1979. pp. 33-39.

Keirns, Aaron J.

n.d. Banesh Sherd Typology. Manuscript on file, Ohio State University.

Kent, Susan

1981 The Dog: An Archaeologist's Best Friend or Worst Enemy—the Spatial Distribution of Faunal Remains. Journal of Field Archaeology 8:367-72.

1984 Analyzing Activity Areas: An Ethnoarchaeological Study of the Use of Space. Albuquerque: University of New Mexico Press.

Kramer, Carol

1982 Village Ethnoarchaeology: Rural Iran in Archaeological Perspective. New York: Academic Press.

Kraybill, Nancy

1977 Pre-Agricultural Tools for the Preparation of Foods in the Old World. *In* Origins of Agriculture.

Charles A. Reed, ed. pp. 485-521. The Hague: Mouton.

Lamberg-Karlovsky, C.C.

1971 The Proto-Elamite Settlement at Tepe Yahya. Iran 9:87-96.

1972 Tepe Yahya 1971: Mesopotamia and the Indo-Iranian Borderlands. Iran 10:89-100.

1976 Tepe Yahya Project. Iran 14:172.

1977 Foreign Relations in the Third Millennium at Tepe Yahya. *In* Le Plateau Iranien et l'Asie Centrale des Origines à la Conquête Islamique pp. 33-43. Centre National de la Recherche Scientifique (Paris), Colloques Internationaux No. 567.

1978 The Proto-Elamites on the Iranian Plateau. Antiquity 52:114-120.

Lamberg-Karlovsky, C.C., and Maurizio Tosi

1973 Shahr-i Sokhta and Tepe Yahya: Tracks on the Earliest History of the Iranian Plateau. East and West 23:21-57.

Lambert, Maurice

1972 Hutéludush—Inshushnak et le pays d'Anzan. Revue d'Assyriologie. 66:61-76.

Le Breton, L.

1957 The Early Periods at Susa, Mesopotamian Relations. Iraq 19:79-124.

Le Brun, Alain

1971 Recherches Stratigraphiques à l'Acropole de Suse (1969-1971). Cahiers de la Délégation Archéologique Française en Iran 1:163-216.

1978 Suse, Chantier "Acropole 1." Paléorient 4:177-192.

Mallowan, M.E.L.

1965 Early Mesopotamia and Iran. New York: McGraw-Hill.

MDP

Mémoires de la Délégation en Perse. Paris. (Also see later publications, under slightly varying titles, of the French Archaeological Mission to Iran).

Miller, Naomi F.

1980 Paleoethnobotanical Studies at Malyan: The Use of Wood as Fuel. Paper delivered at the annual meeting of the Society for American Archaeology, Philadelphia.

1982 Economy and Environment of Malyan, a Third Millennium B.C. Urban Center in Southern Iran. Ph.D. dissertation, University of Michigan.

Milton, Charles, Edward J. Dwornik, and Vincent Pigott

n.d. Preliminary Report on the Analyses of Prehistoric Copper Scoriae from late 4th Millennium B.C. Tal-e Malyan (TUV), Iran. Manuscript on file at MASCA, The University Museum.

Muhly, J.D.

1976 Supplement to Copper and Tin. The Distribution of Mineral Resources and the Nature of the Metal Trade in the Bronze Age. Transactions of the

Connecticut Academy of Arts and Sciences 46:77-136. Hamden, Connecticut: Archon Books.

Murray, Priscilla

1980 Discard Location: The Ethnographic Data. American Antiquity 45:490-502

Nicholas, Ilene M.

1980a A Spatial/Functional Analysis of Late Fourth Millennium Occupation at the TUV Mound, Tal-e Malyan, Iran. Ph.D. dissertation, University of Pennsylvania.

1980b Spatial/Functional Analysis of the Banesh Occupation at Malyan: The TUV Operation. Paper delivered at the annual meeting of the Society for American Archaeology, Philadelphia.

1981 Investigating an Ancient Suburb: Excavations at the TUV Mound, Tal-e Malyan, Iran. Expedition 23(3):39-47.

1983a Form, Function and Archaeological Inference in the Study of Ancient Near Eastern Urban Systems. Paper delivered at the annual meeting of the American Oriental Society, Baltimore.

1983b Function versus Process: The Archaeologist's Dilemma. Paper delivered at the annual meeting of the American Anthropological Association, Chicago.

1983c Comment on Alden's "Trade and Politics in Proto-Elamite Iran." Current Anthropology 24:531.

1987 The Function of Bevelled-Rim Bowls: A Case Study. Paléorient XIII (2): 61-72

Nickerson, Janet

1977 Malyan Wall Paintings. Expedition 19(3):2-6.

Nickerson, John

1983 Intrasite Variability during the Kaftari Period at Tal-e Malyan (Anshan), Iran. Ph.D. dissertation, Ohio State University.

Nissen, Hans J.

1970 Grabung in den Quadraten K/L XII in Uruk-Warka. Baghdader Mitteilungen 5:137.

Pittman, Holly

1980 Glyptic Arts of the Banesh Period: Work in Progress. Paper delivered at the annual meeting of the Society for American Archaeology, Philadelphia.

Potts, Daniel T.

1975 The Late 4th Millennium Universe of a Highland Community in Iran: Problems of Proto-Elam and Jamdat Nasr Mesopotamia. Unpublished B.A. thesis, Department of Anthropology, Harvard University.

1977 Tepe Yahya and the End of the 4th Millennium on the Iranian Plateau. In Le Plateau Iranien et l'Asie Centrale des Origines à la Conquête Islamique. pp. 23-31.Centre National de la Recherche Scientifique (Paris), Colloques Internationaux No. 567.

Redman, Charles L.

1978 The Rise of Civilization: From Early Farmers to Urban Society in the Ancient Near East. San Francisco: W.H. Freeman & Co.

Reiner, Erica

1972 Tall-i Malyan—Inscribed Material. Iran 10:177.

1973 The Location of Ansan. Revue d'Assyriologie 67 (1):57-62.

1974 Tall-i Malyan, Epigraphic Finds, 1971-72. Iran 12:176.

Sackett, James R.

1977 The Meaning of Style in Archaeology: A General Model. American Antiquity 42:369-380

1982 Approaches to Style in Lithic Archaeology. Journal of Anthropological Archaeology 1:59-112.

Scheil, V.

1905 Mémoires de la Délégation en Perse, VI. Textes Élamites-Semitiques (3e Series). Paris.

Schiffer, Michael B.

1972 Archaeological Context and Systemic Context. American Antiquity 37:156-165.

1976 Behavioral Archaeology. New York: Academic Press.

1983 Toward the Identification of Formation Processes. American Antiquity 48:675-706.

Schmandt-Besserat, Denise

1977 An Archaic Recording System and the Origin of Writing. Syro-Mesopotamian Studies 12:31-70.

1979 An Archaic Recording System in the Uruk-Jemdet Nasr Period. American Journal of Archaeology 83:19-48.

1981 From Tokens to Tablets: A Re-evaluation of the So-called "Numerical Tablets." Visible Language 15:321-344.

Shepard, Anna O.

1971 Ceramics for the Archaeologist. Carnegie Institution of Washington, Publication 609.

South, Stanley

1977a Method and Theory in Historical Archaeology. New York: Academic Press.

1977b Research Strategies in Historical Archaeology: The Scientific Paradigm. In Research Strategies in Historical Archaeology. Stanley South, ed. pp. 1-12. New York: Academic Press.

1978 Pattern Recognition in Historical Archaeology. American Antiquity 43:223-230.

1979 Historic Site Content, Structure and Function. American Antiquity 44:213-237.

Steve, M.-J., and H. Gasche

1971 L'Acropole de Suse. Mémoires de la Délégation Archéologique en Iran, Mission de Susiane, t. 46. Paris: Geuthner.

Stolper, Matthew

1985 Proto-Elamite Texts from Tall-i Malyan. Kadmos 24(1):1-12.

Sumner, William M.

1967   A Typology of Ancient Middle Eastern Saddle Querns. M.A. thesis, University of Pennsylvania.

1972a   Cultural Development in the Kur River Basin, Iran: An Archaeological Analysis of Settlement Patterns. Ph.D. dissertation, University of Pennsylvania.

1972b   Tall-i Malyan. Iran 10:176-177.

1973a   Excavations at Ancient Anshan. Archaeology 26: 304.

1973b   Malyan. Iran 11:199-200.

1973c   Tall-i Malyan and the Chronology of the Kur River Basin, Iran. American Journal of Archaeology 77: 288-290.

1974   Excavations at Tall-i Malyan, 1971-72. Iran 12: 155-180.

1975a   Excavations at Tal-e Malyan: A Summary of Three Seasons' Results. *In* Proceedings of the IIIrd Annual Symposium on Archaeological Research in Iran. F. Bagherzadeh, ed. pp. 157-162. Tehran: Iranian Centre for Archaeological Research.

1975b   How Should We Excavate Cities? Paper delivered at the annual meeting of the American Anthropological Association in San Francisco.

1976   Excavations at Tall-i Malyan (Anshan) 1974. Iran 14: 103-115.

1978   Revised Instructions for Site Supervisors, 1978 Season, Malyan Project. Manuscript on file at Ohio State University.

1980   The Malyan Project: Introduction. Paper delivered at the annual meeting of the Society for American Archaeology, Philadelphia.

1985   The Proto-Elamite City Wall at Tal-e Malyan. Iran 23:153-161.

1986   Proto-Elamite Civilization in Fars. *In* Ǧamdat Nasr: Period or Regional Style. U. Finkbeiner and W. Rölling, eds. pp. 199-211. Wiesbaden: Dr. Ludwig Reichert Verlag.

n.d.a   The Banesh Cultural Phase in the Kur River Basin, Iran: Chronology and Excavations at Tal-i Malyan. Background paper presented at the Tübingen Jemdet Nasr Colloquium.

n.d.b   Malyan Excavation Reports: Land Use and Settlement History of the Kur River Basin. In preparation.

Trigger, Bruce G.

1968   The Determinants of Settlement Patterns. *In* Settlement Archaeology. K.C. Chang, ed. pp. 53-78. Palo Alto, California: National Press Books.

1978   [1974] The Archaeology of Government. *Reprinted in* B.G. Trigger. Time and Traditions. pp. 153-166. New York: Columbia University Press. (Originally printed in World Archaeology 6:95-106.)

Vallat, F.

1971   Les Documents Epigraphiques de l'Acropole (1969-1971). Cahiers de la Délégation Archéologique Française en Iran 1:235-245. Paris: Paul Geuthner.

Vanden Berghe, L.

1959   L'archéologie de l'Iran Ancien. Leiden: E. J. Brill.

Voigt, Mary M.

1976   Hajji Firuz Tepe: An Economic Reconstruction of a Sixth Millennium Community in Western Iran. Ph.D. dissertation, University of Pennsylvania.

1983   Hajji Firuz Tepe, Iran: The Neolithic Settlement. Hasanlu Excavation Reports, vol. 1. Robert H. Dyson, Jr., gen. ed. University Museum Monograph 50.

Voigt, Mary M. and Robert H. Dyson, Jr.

n.d.   The Chronology of Iran, ca. 8000-2000 B.C. *In* Chronologies in Old World Archaeology. Robert Ehrich, ed. Chicago: University of Chicago Press.

Watson, Patty Jo

1979   Archaeological Ethnography in Western Iran. Viking Fund Publications in Anthropology 57. Tucson: University of Arizona Press.

Weiss, Harvey, and T. Cuyler Young, Jr.

1975   The Merchants of Susa. Godin V and Plateau-Lowland Relations in the Late Fourth Millennium B.C. Iran 13:1-17.

Wenke, Robert J.

1981   Explaining the Evolution of Cultural Complexity: A Review. *In* Advances in Archaeological Method and Theory, Vol. 4. Michael Schiffer, ed. pp. 79-128. New York: Academic Press.

Whitcomb, Donald Scott

1971   The Proto-Elamite Period at Tall-i Ghazir, Iran. M.A. thesis. University of Georgia.

Wobst, H. Martin

1978   The Archaeo-Ethnology of Hunter-Gatherers or the Tyranny of the Ethnographic Record in Archaeology. American Antiquity 43:303-309.

Wright, Henry T.

1969   The Administration of Rural Production in an Early Mesopotamian Town. Museum of Anthropology, University of Michigan, Anthropological Papers 38, Ann Arbor.

1972   A Consideration of Interregional Exchange in Greater Mesopotamia: 4000-3000 B.C. *In* Social Exchange and Interaction. E.N. Wilmsen, ed. pp. 95-105. Museum of Anthropology, University of Michigan, Anthropological Papers 46. Ann Arbor.

1977   Towards an Explanation of the Origin of the State. *In* Explanation of Prehistoric Change. J.N. Hill, ed. pp. 215-230. Albuquerque: University of New Mexico Press.

Wright, Henry T., ed.

1981   An Early Town on the Deh Luran Plain: Excavations at Tepe Farukhabad. Museum of Anthropology, University of Michigan, Memoir 13, Ann Arbor.

Wright, Henry T., and Gregory A. Johnson

1975   Population, Exchange and Early State Formation in South-Western Iran. American Anthropologist 77:267-289.

Wulff, Hans E.

1966   The Traditional Crafts of Persia. Cambridge, Massachusetts: The M.I.T. Press.

Young, T. Cuyler, Jr.

1969   Excavations at Godin Tepe: First Progress Report. Royal Ontario Museum, Art and Archaeology, Occasional Paper 17. Toronto: Royal Ontario Museum.

Zeder, M.A.

1980   Animal Resource Distribution and Early Urban Development in Southern Iran. Paper delivered at the annual meeting of the Society for American Archaeology, Philadelphia.

1984   Meat Distribution at the Highland Iranian Urban Center of Tal-e Malyan. *In* Animals and Archaeology: Vol. 3, Early Herders and Their Flocks. British Archaeological Reports. International Series 202. J. Clutton-Brock and C. Grigsam, eds. pp. 279-307.

1985   Urbanism and Animal Exploitation in Southwest Highland Iran, 3400-1500 B.C. Ph.D. dissertation, University of Michigan.

Zipf, G.K.

1949   Human Behavior and the Principle of Least Effort. Reading, Massachusetts: Addison-Wesley.

Index

(۱۱)

جنوبی تپه   TUV   (درمحلی که درضمن بخوبی شهردرفاصله نزدیکــــی مشاهده میگردد)اداره مینموده‌اند. درضمن اداره‌ء این اجتماع ازلوحه‌های گلی آغازایلامی واثرمهرها استفاده میگردیده‌وما لیا ت درکاسه‌های سفالی با لبه واریخته جمع آوری میگردیده‌است .دردوران همزمان با آثار طبقـه‌ء B.L.I   یا مدت کوتاهی پس ازآن ارتباط نزدیک تری بین تپه‌ء   TUV وشهراصلی با ساختمان حصارودیوارعظیمی مربوط به اواخردوره بانـــش بوجودآمده‌است .این دیوارعظیم نه فقط شهراصلی بکله منطقه تپــــه‌ء TUV   را نیزدربرمیگرفته‌است .

بالاخره با وجودیکه‌نمیتوان اظهارات زیادی راجع به تجــارت ودادوستدمستقیم تپه‌ء   TUV   بانواحی دوردست نمودولی مسلمــــا" این تپه دریک با فت ارتباطی این منطقه همکاری ومشارکت مینموده که آثارآن درلوحه‌های گلی آغازایلامی که درطرف مغرب تا دشت رسومــــی خوزستان ودرجهت مشرق تا شهرسوخته بدست آمده‌اند مشخص میگردد . تپــــه‌ء TUV   بعنوان قسمتی ازفضا ومنطقه شهرنشینی ملیان ودرقلب ومرکـــز ارتفاعات تمدن آغازایلامی قرارگرفته‌است .عملیات حفاری تپه   TUV وتحقیقات وبررسی آثاربدست آمده خشت دیگری درتکمیل بنای درک و ـ شناخت بهترسیرتکامل تمدنهای باستانی خاورنزدیک درا واخرهـــــزاره چهارم پیش ازمیلادمسیح عرضه میدارد .

عزت اله نگهبان

(۱۰)

صنایع عادی وهمچنین تزئینات مشخصی نیزتولیدمیگردیده است .مهمترین
فعالیت صنعتی استفاده ازمس بوده است .

درقدیمترین طبقه ساختمانی B.L.III آثاری که دلالت بروجود
عقایدمذهبی ومقدس دراین اجتماع باشددراطاق ۲۲۵ مشاهده گردید .
بعلت وجودهمین اهمیت مذهبی دراین محل پنج نفردراطراف آن قبل از
متروک شدن ویا درضمن متروک شدن این واحددفن گردیده اند این اهمیت
مذهبی درطبقات مذهبی درطبقات بعدیترانشه TUV مشاهدهنمیگردد
ولی انواع فعالیتهای اصلی درطبقات بعدی B.L.II و B.L.I
ادامه داردوبیانگراین مطلب است که درتمام طول مدت دورانهای
مربوط به طبقات حفاری کارهای دولتی وحکومتی وظیفهونوع فعالیت
اجتماع انتهای جنوبی تپه ترانشهٔ TUV بوده است .

درآخرین فصل کتاب ، تپیهٔ TUV دررابطه بابافت وسیع تر
فرهنگی موردمطالعه قرارگرفته است . تحقیقات ومقایساتی بین آثار
ترانشهٔ تپه TUV وآثارترانشهٔ ABC تپه بانش درتپه اصلی
ملیان انجام گردیده است .چنانچه اظها رشده است ساختمانهای ترانشه
ABC احتمالا"معتبرترین ومهمترین ساختمانها درشهربانش بوده واحتمالا"
محل مسکونی خان ایلات دره رودکررا معرفی مینماید . تپه TUV
دراصل احتمالا" یک دهکدهٔ مستقل کشاورزی ودامداری بوده است.
دردورانی که همزمان باآثارطبقه ساختمانی B.L.III میبا شدبنظر
میرسداین دهکده درتحت کنترل مستقیم فرمانروایی ملیان قرارگرفته
است . آثارساختمانی که درتپه TUV حفاری گردیدهنما یشگراین
مطلب است که این ساختمانها محل اقامت یکی ازاعضای زیردست خان و
حاکم منطقه بوده است .این فردوکارمندانش اجتماع TUV رااز قسمت

(۹)

این موضوع ازکثرت نوع بقایائی که درآنها باقیمانده بخوبی آشکار میشودونشان میدهدکه هردوساختمانها برای موردخاصی بغیرا ززندگانی معمولی موردا ستفاده قرارمیگرفته اند.

درفصل هشتم کتاب اطلاعات بیشتری درباره کیفیت ونوع فعالیتهای این اجتماع ونقش کلی هریک ازاین طبقات ساختمانی درفرهنگ وتمدن بزرگتری که قسمتی ازآنرا تشکیل میدادندعرضه گردیده است.

تنظیم جداول نمودارفعالیتها این تشخیصات را تسهیل مینماید.

یک نمودارفعالیت عبارت است از خلاصه فعالیتهای گوناگونی که برای یک طبقه ساختمانی مستندگردیده باشدبا تشخیص متینی ازاهمیت نسبی هریک ازفعالیتها درگردش آن اجتماع ،تنظیم وساخت جدول نمودارهای فعالیتی عموما " براساس این فرضیه است که وجودبقایای یک گروه از اشیاء دلیل برآنست که این نوع فعالیت درمحلی ازاین اجتماع درایـن طبقه حتی خارج ازحدودحفاری ما وجودداشته است . نحوه ووسعت اینگونه فعالیتها براساس نوع بقایا که تا چه اندازه سالم ویا شکسته هستندوهم چنین کثرت استعمال آنها درنظرگرفته میشود.

حاصل جمع ونتیجهٔ تحقیق نمودارفعالیت عملی نکات زیررا درباره وضع وکیفیت اجتماعی که ازساختمانهای مکشوفه درتراشهٔ TUV استفاده مینموده اندمعرفی مینماید. این اجتماع دارای یک حکومت عادی کـه بنظرمیرسدمالیات ازاهالی جمع آوری مینموده بودودردادوستدکلـی منطقه دره رودکرشرکت داشته است.

درهرواحدساختمانی غذا برای مصرف کارگران تهیه میگردیده وگاه هـی

---

(۸)

اساس اطلاعاتی است که در اثر بررسی گروههای اشیاء وطرز توزیع و تاثیر آنها بوده و قبلا" در فصول پنجم وششم این کتاب موردمطالعه قرار گرفته است.

در فصل هفتم کتاب برای هرطبقهٔ ساختمانی اولا" وضعیت عمومی نحوهٔ قرارگرفتن انبوه بقایای باستانی ومحل آنها وثانیا " امکان و احتمال بدست آورد اطلاعاتی از وضعیت نوع فعالیتها در هرمحل بررسی گردیده است .

بررسی ترکیب وساختمان محل درطبقات ساختمانی B.L.III وB.L.II بسیار آگاه کننده و آموزنده بودولی درطبقه ساختمانی B.L.I که بقایای بسیار محدود ودرعین حال مضطرب وبخوبی نگاهداری نشده بودرضایت بخش نبود .

اگرچه درطبقات ساختمانی B.L.IIIA و B.L.II نقشهٔ ساختمانی کاملا" با یکدیگر متفاوت بودولی درروضعیت وکیفیت ساختمان باهم درمواردی مشابه بودند. اولا" هرطبقه مرکب ازیک واحدساختمانی چندا طاقی وقسمتهای فرعی دراطراف آن بود. ثانیا " درهریک ازاین طبقات بعضی فعالیتهای مهم مخصوصی ظاهرا " درقسمتهای جداگانه ای انجام میگردید درصورتیکه فعالیتهای دیگردرتمام قسمتها انجام میگردیده است .محل نگاهداری اشیاء ،آشپزخانه ، استفاده از ظروف سفالی معمولی و زندگانی وپذیرائی درهردوطبقات B.L.III.A, B.L.II در قسمت اصلی ساختمانها وجودداررند. علاوه برآن درطبقه ساختمانی B.L.IIIA یک قبرستان درنواحی شمالی و احتمالا" یک کارگاه فلز کاری نیز درشمال آن وجودداشته است .درهردوطبقه ساختمانی وضعیت تمرکز فعالیتها درقسمتهای مختلف بخوبی آشکار بود . بعلاوه براین تعداد اطاقهائی برای هرفعالیت اصلی موردا ستفاده قرار میگرفته نبود و

(۷)

۱۰ـ ادوات مربوط به نگاهداری مواد ۱۱ـ صنایع حصیربافی ۱۲ـ محفظه های مخصوص ۱۳ـ ابزار بریدن ۱۴ـ ابزارهای مختلف ساخت ادوات سنگی ۱۵ـ مته ها وسوراخ کننده ها ۱۶ـ تزئینات شخصی ۱۷ـ ابزار ساختمانی ۱۸ـ وسائل مصرف غذا ۲۹ـ ابزار نجاری ۲۰ـ ادوات تزئینی و ۲۱ـ ادوات ـ اطلاعاتی ٠ گروههای ۱ تا ۹ را میتوان بعنوان گروه اشیاء تولیدی و گروه ۱۰ را گروه اشیاء نگاهداری وگروههای ۱۱ تا ۲۰ را گروه اشیاء مصرفی وگروه ۲۱ را میتوان بعنوان گروهی که معرف ونمایشگر فعالیتها ویا تصمیمات رسمی ساکنین این اجتماع TUV میباشد معرفی نمودکه این دسته شامل لوحه های گلی خطوط آغاز ایلامی ، اثر مهرها واشیاء گلی کوچک با شکال هندسی که وسیله شمارش ومبادلات بوده میباشد .

درفصل ششم این کتاب درباره فعالیتهای مختلف واحتمال وجود اثر وبقایای آنها درآثار باستانی با قیمانده از آنها در ترانشه TUV بررسی گردیده است .در این بررسی نحوه توزیع وتمرکز هریک از گروههای فوق درقسمتهای مختلف حفاری که نمایشگر نحوه استفاده از آن محل میباشد مورد مطالعه قرار گرفته است ٠طرز بافت هر گروه فقط بر اساس وجود وهویت آن نبوده بلکه اولا" بر مبنای مقدار ونسبت معمولی بقایا در هر وا حدو ثانیا " برپا ی یه تکرا رودفعات انجام فعالیت مبتنی میباشد .

درفصل هفتم کتاب ترکیب وساختمان این محل باستانی که مسلما" بر اساس نحوه فعالیتها ورابطه وهم آهنگی آنها بوجود آمده مورد بحث قرار گرفته است ٠بعلت اینکه آثار زیادی از بقایای باستانی از لایه های قدیمی واولیه درحفاری ترانشه TUV وجود ندارد بررسی نحوه ایجاد ترکیب وساختمان محل بهنا چار میبایست بر اساس نتیجه گیریهای ئی با شدکه از نحوه معماری ، مجموعه ادوات وانبوه سایر بقایای باستانی میتوان استنباط نمود. حاصل جمع این استنباط طها بر

(۶)

۱
گروه سفالها با خمیره مخلوط شنی که درحدود۳۸٪ درصدا این مجموعــــه را تشکیل میدهند.

ازنظرشکل فقط هفت نوع ظروف درمجموعهٔ سفالها با خمیرهٔ مخلـــوط گیاهی درترانشه TUV بدست آمده است . سه نوع ازآنها سفال معمولی ورایج این مجموعه بودوعبارتنداز: نوع کاسههای قالب زده با لبـــهٔ واریخته ، جامهای سفالی چرخ ساز پایه دار، وسینی های کم عمـــــق دست ساخته سفالی . انواع دیگری که بهوفور انواع فوق ساخته نشده انـد عبارتنداز: فنجانهای چرخ ساز با دیوارهای مایل بطرف خارج .قسمتها ئی از لولههای آبرو سفالی دست ساخته ، جامهای سفالی با کف مستقیم جانبی ویک نوع اشیاء سفالی که درساختمان کورههای مس بکاررفته است .

فقط تعداد کمی ظروف سفالی کا ملوسالم درمجموعه سفالهـــــــای خمیره مخلوط شنی ترانشه با نش بدست آمده است .بهمین علت طبقه بندی سفالهای دراین گروه براساس شکل لبهٔ ظروف درهریک ازسه گروه کـــــه عبارتنداز: ظروف بدون گردن ، ظروف با گردن ، وظروف بدون محدودیت ، انجام گردیده است .تکههای سفال مربوط به کف وبدنهٔ سفال با تزئینات نیزدراین قسمت شرح داده شده است .

درفصل پنجم این کتاب اشیاء وادوات بدست آمده درترانشـــــهٔ ۱
TUV شرح داده شده وطبقه بندی این اشیاء براساس نحوهٔ کاربــــرد آنها تنظیم گردیده است .دراین طبقه بندی جنس اشیاء رعایت نگردیــده وفقط براساس انواع کاربرد ۲ دسته بندی شدهاند . گروههای مختلـــف این مجموعه اشیاء عبارتنداز ۱ـ ادوات خرده سنگی ۲.ـ ادوات مســـــی ۳ـ مهرههای سنگی ۴ـ اشیاء صدفی ۵ـ اشیاء گچی ۶ـ صنایع پارچــه ۷ـ ادوات تهیه غذا ۸ـ صنایع سفالی ۹ـ موادخام مختلـــــــــف

1. Grit- Tempered
2. Function   3. Functional Classes

(۵)

مـرتفع ترین لایه ساختمانی TUV ، لایه B.L.I در اثر مـرور زمان سائیدگی وفرسایش داشته وفقط قسمتی از آن که درحدود۲۰۰ مترمربع مساحت داردباقیمانده است. آثار ساختمانی باقیمانده در اثر یک لایـه قلوه سنگ که آنرا فراپوشانیده تا اندازه‌ای محفوظ باقیمانده اسـت در اطراف ترانشه‌های محل کارما آثار دیوارهای مربوط به این لایه در اثـر فرسایش رفته از بین رفته است ،حتی درقسمتهای باقیمانده فقط ۱ تا ۲ردیـف از خشت دیوارها برجای مانده بود. آستانهٔ درها قابل تشخیص نبـــودو قسمتهای ساختمانی مرتفع ترمانندجاقها جاقها بکلی از بین رفته بودنـــد دوعددچاه شماره‌های ۱۹۵و۱۹۹ مربوط به این لایه میباشند.

قسمت دوم فصل سوم این کتاب اطلاعاتی درباره نحوهٔ دقیق ضمائـــم واشیاء مربوط به آثار معماری در اختیار قرار میدهد .قسمت اعظم ایـــن ضمائم شامل اجاقهای مرتفع جعبه‌ای شکل ، اجاقهای قلوه سنگـــی، انبوه خرده سفالها ،اجاقهای سنگ فرش ، اجاقهای ساده ، تنورهـــای گنبدی، تنورهای عمقی، گودالهای خاکستر، چاهها ، گودالهای انــدود شده ، گودالهای خاکروبه ، آبروها ، پی ریزی ، خمره‌ها ، سنگ فرش هـای سوخته ، محل خاکروبه ، قبوروسایر آثار متفرقه میباشد.

فصل چهارم این کتاب درباره انواع سفالهای ترانشـــه TUV وطبقه بندی وشرح ونمایش آنها میباشد ، قسمت اعظم مجموعهٔ سفالهـا از خرده سفال تشکیل گردیده است .درحدود۲۰٦۸۸ عددتکه سفال درمقابـل ۲۸ عددظرف کامل یا تقریبا " کامل بدست آمده است .این مجموعـــه سفالهای بدست آمده را میتوان بدوگروه کلی از نظر نوع وجنس سفـال طبقه بندی نمود. یکی گروه سفالها با خمیرهٔ مخلوط گیاهی که درحدود ٦۲% درصدکلیه سفالهای ترانشه TUV بانش شامل بودودیگـــری

---

1. Chaff – Tempered

(۴)

اصیل آن به علامت B.L.III.B وتعمیرات بعدی بعنوان B.L.IIIA
مشخص گردیده است. قسمتهائی از این بقایا تا ارتفاع لایه ساختمانی بعدی
یعنی B.L.II درهنگامیکه برای استقرار مجدد زمین تسطیح وقسمتهائی
با آثار مخروبه قدیمی پرگردیده ادامه دارند. پس از تسطیح زمین لایهٔ
بعدی با نقشه کاملا" متفاوت وگوشه اطاقها منطبق با جهات اصلی ساخته
شده است.

لایه ساختمانی B.L.II بزرگترین لایهٔ ساختمانی میباشـــد.
که درحفاری ترانشهٔ تپه TUV آشکار گردیده است ودرقسمت اصلـی
درحدود۴۱۵ مترمربع ودرقسمت دیگری درحدود۴۰ مترمربع وسعت دارد.
بقایای ساختمانی دراین لایه بخوبی با قیمانده وآثاری ماننداجاق ها و
غمره های نگاهداری مواد کشف گردیدند. ترانشهٔ شماره ۷۶ بطور موثـــر
تعدادی از اطاقهای قسمتهای شمالی وجنوب غربـی واحدهای ایـــن
لایه را مضطرب نموده بود. برخلاف وضع متروکه لایهٔ ساختمانی B.L.III
که اطاقها از بقایای خشتی پرشده بودهیچ یک از اطاقهای لایهٔ ساختمانـی
B.L.II پس از متروکه شدن با بقایای خشتی پرنشده بودند. بقایای
این لایه قبل از استقرار اجتماع بعدی یا درا ثرمرورزمان ویـــا
بوسیله ساکنان لایهٔ ساختمانی B.L.I از بین رفته بود. با وجودیکه
فاصله زمانی بین متروک شدن تپه دربین این لایه ها معلوم نیست ولـــی
آنچه مسلم است این تپه مدت زمان طویلتری بین لایه های دوم (B.L.II)
واول (.B.L.I) تا لایه های سوم (B.L.IIIA) ودوم (B.L.II)
متروک بوده است.

آثار ساختمانی لایه B.L.I با وجودیکه از نظر نقشه با لایه B.L.II
تفاوت کلی داردولی منطبق با جهات اصلی ساخته شده است.

(۳)

موردا ستفا ده ، فعا لیتها ، موسسا ت ، اجتما عا ت وفرهنگها متمرکزگردیـده است چندراه وطریقه کلی متدیک دربررسی عملی آثا ربا ستا نی حفـــا ری TUV درنظرگرفته شده است .اولین بررسی دربا ره طرزتشکیل وقـــرا ر گرفتن بقا یا ی با ستا نی ونحوه دقیق بوجودآمدن ا ین تپه TUV میبا شـد که درفصل دوم ا ین کتا ب موردبحث قرا رگرفته ا ست . پس ازبررســـــی لایه های با ستا نی وترتیب آنها درترا نشه TUV دراین فصل دوم کتــــا ب راجع به بقا یا ولایه های با ستا نی تپه ملیا ن ونحوه درجه بندی وتطبیـق آنها دررا بطه با لایه های ترا نشه تپه TUV برمبنا ی معیا رها ی نظـری وعمومی موا ردی اظها رگردیده ا ست .درا ین زمینه اظها رگردیده کــــه کا ربردآزما یش ها یتراکم جمعیت اطلاعا ت زیا دی دربا ره نحوه وطــــرز متشکل شدن تپه ولایه های با ستا نی آن درا ختیا رقرا رخوا هددا دکـــــهدر ا ین موردتشخیص دقیق قسمتهای حفا ری که یا فقط ازبتا یای دیوا رهـــا ی گلی فروریخته ویا ا زمخلوط خاکروبه وآثا رسا ختما نی بوجودآ مده ازیکدیگر بسیا رمهم میبا شد . آگا هی ا زا ین وضعیت واطلاعا ت بنوبه خودمیتوا نـــد درموردتشخیص نوع ا جتما عی که ا ین آثا ررا با قی گذا رده ودرفصل هـــا ی بعدی کتا ب سعی گردیده تعیین گرددرا هنما ی خوبی با شد .

درفصل سوم کتا ب آثا رمعما ری مکشوفه درترا نشه تپـــــه TUV موردمطا لعه قرا رگرفته ا ست . سه لایه سا ختما نی با نشکه ا زخشت خـا م سا خته شده بودندآشکا رگردیدند .

لابه سا ختما نی سوم وعمیقترین بهتر ا زدولایه با لاتربا قیما نده بود. قسمت ا صلی آشکا رشده ا ز ا ین لایه درحدود۲۲۵ مترمربع میبا شد. قسمتهای کوچک دیگری درحا شیه ترا نشه درحدود۲۲ مترمربع دیگر از ا ین لایـــه را آشکا رنمود. ا ین لایه سا ختما نی دا را ی دودوره میبا شدکه بقا یـــا ی

(۲)

متأسفانه بقایای طبقهٔ بانش درزیرآثار جدیدتری واقع گردیده‌اند .

خوشبختانه درمحوطهٔ مسطح شمالشرقی ملیان درنزدیکی حصارشهر تپهٔ کوچکی بمساحت ۳ جریب بفاصله ۳۰۰ مترجدا ازتپهٔ اصلی قرارگرفته بود .

دراین تپهٔ کوچک ترانشهٔ آزمایشی F درسال ۱۹۷۱ میلادی حفاری گردید . دراین ترانشه آثاری همزمان بادورهٔ بانش آشکار گردید . درسال ۱۹۷۴ عملیات حفاری وسیعتری دراین تپهٔ کوچک درمحوطهٔ جنوبی آن شروع گردیدکه بنام ترانشه‌ها یا عملیات TUV نامگذاری گردید . تصور میرفت که دراین حفاری آثاردیگری مربوط به دورهٔ بانش که دسترسی به بقایای آن درزیرطبقات عظیم آثارمعماری درتپهٔ اصلی در ترانشه‌های ABC بسیار مشکل بودآشکار گردد .

نگارندهٔ این کتاب پس ازفصل حفاری سال ۱۹۷۴ باهیأت حفاری ملیان شروع بهمکاری نمودودرادامهٔ کارخوددرسال ۱۹۷۶ ترانشهٔ TUV را حفاری وازآن پس درفصل حفاری سال ۱۹۷۸ سفالهای بدست آمده درترانشهٔ TUV را موردمطالعه وتحقیق قرارداد .

هدف کلی این کتاب اولاً بدست آوردن اطلاعات مستنددربارهٔ گذشتهٔ درهٔ رودکردرااستان فارس ونقاطی که درآنها آثارلوحه‌های مربوط به دوران آغازایلامی وجوددارد وثانیا " تحقیقاتی است که بتواندکمک به نحوهٔ ومتدبررسی بافت واصول قدیم شهرنشینی بطورکلی بنماید .

درفصل اول این کتاب اصول وپی بندیهای تئوری تجزیه آثار ترانشه TUV بررسی گردیده و بیانگراین نکته است که باستانشناسان لازم است توجه بیشتری نسبت به مفهوم عملکردبعنوان یک پل فرضی بین شکل ادوات وتطورتمدنی آنها بنمایند . عملیات TUV بیشتربرروی استعمال درجه بندی عملی۱ واحدهای تحلیلی مرکب ازاشیاء واقلام

---

1. Functional Hierarchy

تلخیص و ترجمه

عملیات حفاری ترانشه‌های TUV درتپه ملیان

انجام عملیات حفاری این ترانشه‌ها که دراین کتاب نتیجه آن شرح داده شده بدون کمک افراد زیادی غیر ممکن بود . آرزو دارم در اینجا مراتب قدردانی خود را نسبت به همکاران برنامهٔ حفاری ملیان بخصوص آقــــای ویلیام زامنر[1] مدیر حفاری و آقای رابرت دایسون[2] مسئول حفـــــاری در موزه دانشگاهی[3] ابراز دارم . همچنین تشکرات خاص خود را به اهالــــی دهکدهٔ ملیان در استان فارس ایران که درنهایت مهارت کمک به انجـــــام عملیات حفاری نمودند تقدیم دارم . درعملیات حفاری ترانشه‌های TUV آثاری از سه طبقه ساختمانی که متعلق به اواخر هزارهٔ چهارم پیــــش از میلاد مسیح بودند آشکار گردید . این ترانشه‌ها درتپه کوچکی درنزدیکی تپه ملیان (شهر قدیمی آنشان) که شهر بزرگی در درهٔ رودکور در ارتفاع عـــــات ایران در حدود ۴۶ کیلومتری شمال شیراز و با همین فاصله در مغرب تخـــت جمشید میباشد حفاری گردیدند . عملیات حفاری وبررسی ملیان به مسئولیت موزهٔ دانشگاهی دانشگاه پنسیلوانیا بین سالهای ۱۹۷۱ تا ۱۹۷۸ میـــلادی انجام گردیده است . در این عملیات بزودی آشکار گردید که قدیمتریـــــن بقایای باستانی درتپه ملیان درتپهٔ باستان درحدود اواخر هزارهٔ چهــــارم پیش از میلاد مسیح قرار گرفته است . در بیشتر قسمتهای این منطقـــــــه

---

1. William Sumner
2. Robert H. Dyson
3. University Museum

Figures

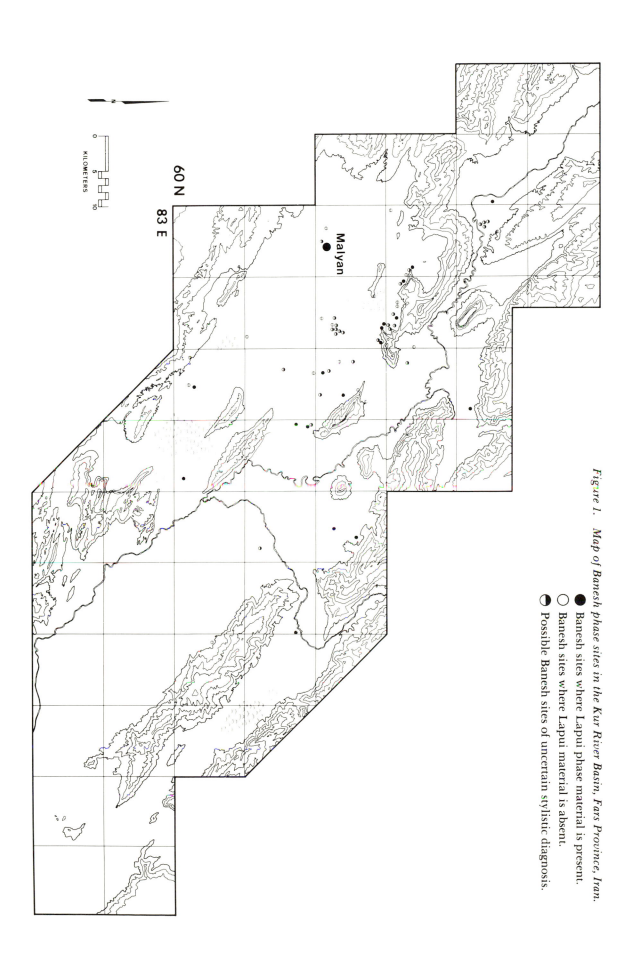

Figure 1. Map of Banesh phase sites in the Kur River Basin, Fars Province, Iran.

● Banesh sites where Lapui phase material is present.
○ Banesh sites where Lapui material is absent.
◐ Possible Banesh sites of uncertain stylistic diagnosis.

60 N

83 E

Malyan

0
5
10
KILOMETERS

N

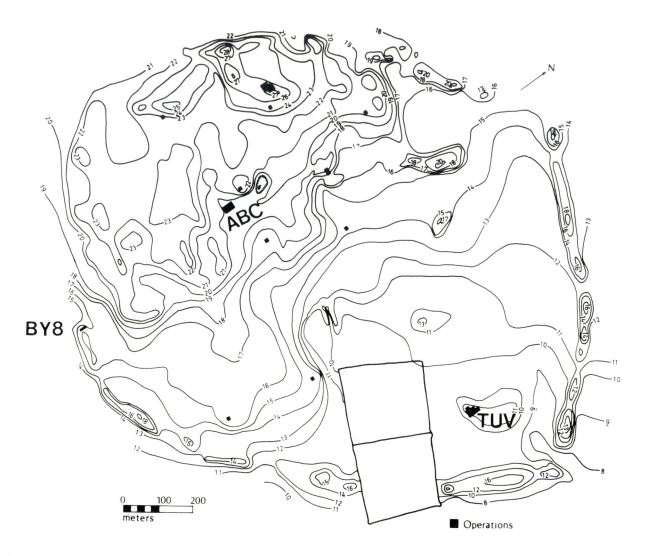

Figure 2. Map of Tal-e Malyan.
The ABC operation lies in the main mounded zone in the western sector of the site. The TUV operation lies on the southern end of the small mound in the northeastern sector. The mounded remains of the ancient enclosure wall, built in the late Banesh phase *after* the occupation of the area explored by the TUV operation, are clearly visible north and east of the TUV mound. Operation BY8 was established to investigate the city wall along the southern edge of Malyan and established the Banesh date for its construction (Sumner 1985). The two large empty squares south of the TUV mound indicate the area occupied by the modern village of Malyan and an adjacent garden zone.

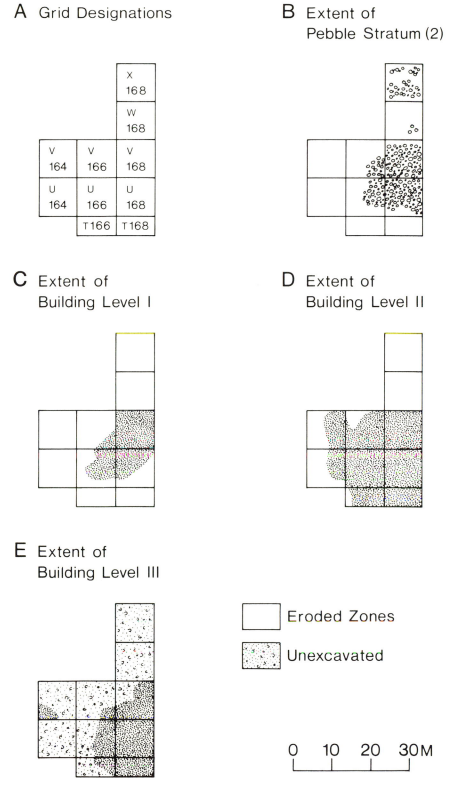

A Grid Designations

		X 168
		W 168
V 164	V 166	V 168
U 164	U 166	U 168
	T 166	T 168

B Extent of Pebble Stratum (2)

C Extent of Building Level I

D Extent of Building Level II

E Extent of Building Level III

☐ Eroded Zones

▨ Unexcavated

0   10   20   30 M

Figure 3.   Extent of major strata and building levels at the TUV operation.

A.   Grid designations for units opened during excavation of TUV.

B.   Extent of the pebble/cobble layer, stratum 2. Beyond the area indicated, this stratum was eroded away.

C.   Extent of B.L. I. Beyond the area indicated, this stratum was eroded away.

D.   Extent of B.L. II. This level was much more extensively preserved than B.L. I although it was removed by erosion in the areas left blank.

E.   Extent of *exposure* of B.L. III. Although not excavated over as wide an area as B.L. II, it is believed that preserved remains of this level may occupy the entire area of the TUV operation, with the possible exception of the W168 and X168 squares.

Figure 4. Schematic Summary of Master Stratigraphic Sequence, TUV Operation
This is a composite not-to-scale diagram intended to illustrate the general spatial relationships among the major TUV strata. The vertical dimension has been especially exaggerated to facilitate the clarity of presentation. This diagram is in no way to be regarded as an actual section from TUV. For actual representative sections, see figures 5 and 6.

Stratum Number	Brief description
0	present-day surface of mound
1	top erosion layer
2	pebble/cobble layer
3	material sealed over by stratum 2 but above defined architecture of stratum 4
4	deposit between walls of B.L. I
5	material actually comprising walls and floors of B.L. I
6a	material below bottom of B.L. I walls but above defined architecture of stratum 7
6b	surface above tops of B.L. II walls (only observed in V166)
7	deposit between walls of B.L. II
8a	in cases of B.L. II rooms with two floors, material actually comprising higher of two floors
8b	deposit between higher and lower of two floors in a B.L. II room
8c	walls and original floors of B.L. II
8d	deposit below last identifiable B.L. II floors but not yet below bottom of B.L. II walls
9	material below bottom of B.L. II walls but above defined architecture or features of B.L. IIIA
10	deposit above floors and surfaces in use during B.L. IIIA
11	material actually comprising features, walls, and floors built in B.L. IIIA
12	deposit below distinct B.L. IIIA phenomena but above latest floors of B.L. IIIB
13a	material comprising higher of two floors (if present) in B.L. IIIB room
13b	deposit between higher and lower of two floors in B.L. IIIB room
13c	walls and original floors of B.L. IIIB (many of which continued in use through B.L. IIIA)
13d	deposit below last identifiable B.L. III floors but not yet below bottom of B.L. III walls
14	material below bottom of B.L. IIIB walls

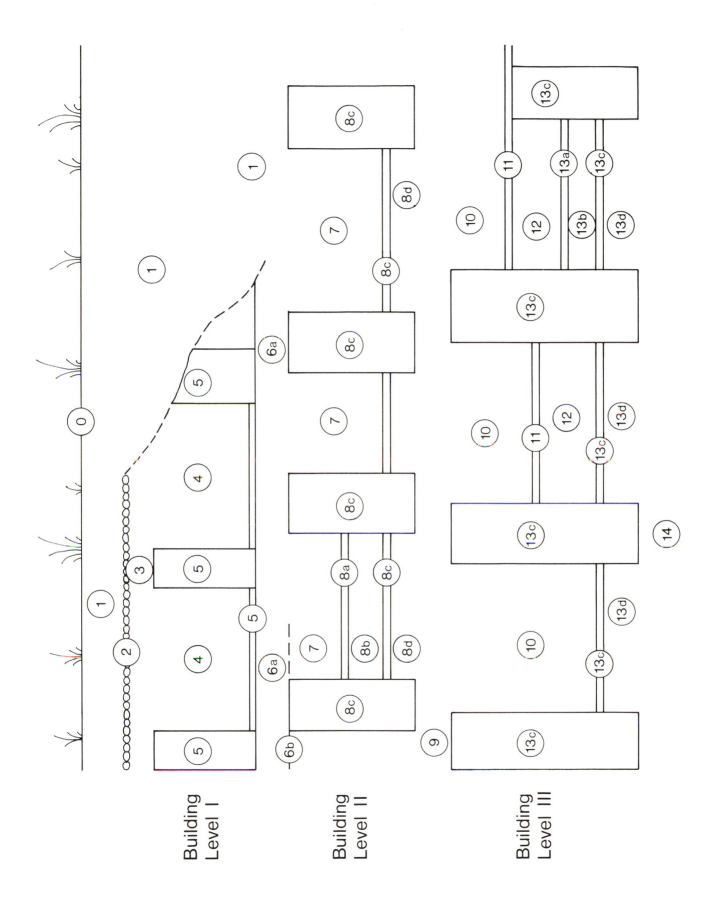

Building
Level I

Building
Level II

Building
Level III

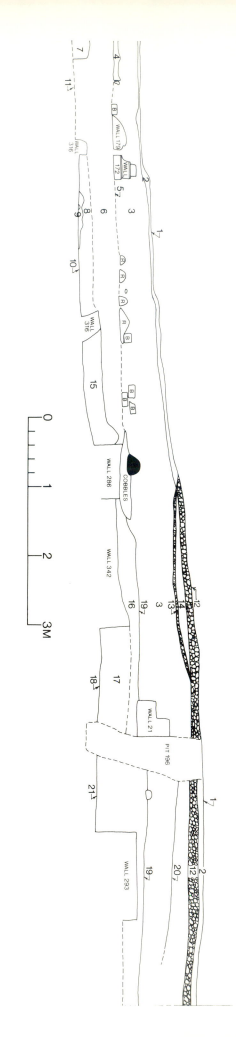

Figure 5. Representative north-south section at TUV; the west balk of T168–U168, drawn in the 1976 season. Walls 21, 172, and 179 are B.L. II walls; walls 286, 293, 342, and 316 are B.L. III walls. Reference numbers have been added to the section in a general south to north order. These reference numbers are not to be confused with the numbers used in the main stratigraphic sequence (Fig. 4). Rather, these numbers indicate microstratigraphic aspects of this particular section.

● = Isolated rocks
R = Rodent burrows
○ = Large sherds
B = mud brick fragment

1 present surface
2 top wash
3 bricky collapse
4 feature 182
5 B.L. II floor
6 loose bricky fill
7 compact bricky fill

8 reddish fill of feature 315
9 bricky fill
10 hard gravel floor
11 limit of excavation
12 stratum 2 pebbles
13 small lens of pebbles
14 loose fill, not bricky

15 very loose fill
16 B.L. III collapse
17 bricky fill
18 floor of room 284
19 B.L. II floor
20 B.L. I floor
21 floor of B.L. III room 258

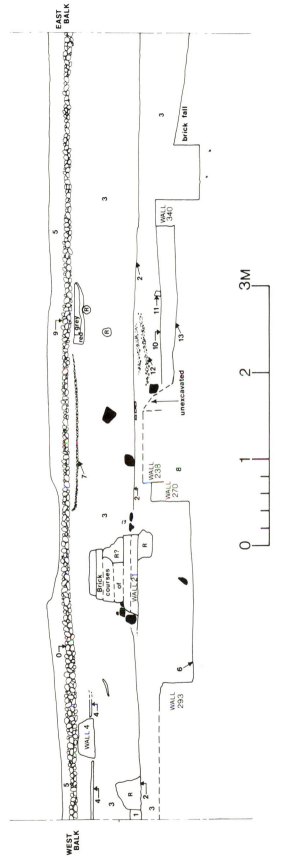

Figure 6. Representative east-west section at TUV: the north balk of U168, drawn in the 1976 season.

Wall 4 is a B.L. I wall; wall 21 is a B.L. II wall; the other walls are from B.L. III.
Solidly filled areas represent isolated rocks. Areas marked *R* indicate rodent burrows. Unfilled ovals represent large sherds. Reference numbers have been added to the section in a general west to east order. These reference numbers are not to be confused with the numbers used in the main stratigraphic sequence (Fig. 4). Rather, these numbers indicate particular microstratigraphic aspects of this particular section.

0   pebble/cobble layer of stratum 2 (individual cobbles schematically drawn).
1   part of an oven feature visible in U166(?).
2   B.L. II surface of packed earth.
3   bricky fill.
4   B.L. I floor.
5   stratum 1, top erosion layer
6   B.L. IIIB floor of area 258.
7   thin layer of small pebbles (average length 1-4 cm) quite distinct from main pebble/cobble stratum above.
8   corner where B.L. III walls 270 and 238 meet at balk.
9   from this point eastward typical size of stone in stratum 2 decreases from cobble-sized to pebble-sized.
10   intermediate surface in area 265.
11   burned brick chunk.
12   two B.L. IIIA lenses of sherds and rocks.
13   main B.L. IIIB surface in area 265.

Figure 7. Plan of most significant stratum 1 features.
a   feature 156, a possible fragmentary wall foundation of large stones, with some cobbles (of stratum 2?) to its west.
b   feature 153/155, an alignment of 5 large and 3 small cut stone bricks.
c   pit 196, which contained Sassanian burial 283.

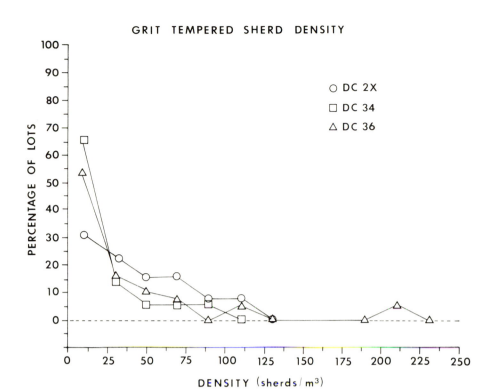

Figure 8.   Grit Tempered Sherd Density in unscreened lots.
The number of lots (n) in each category on this figure are: secondary (n=13), DC34 (n=35), and DC36 (n=37). There is one DC34 lot with a grit-ware density over 250/cubic meter and thus not shown on the figure; this represents the missing 2.86% of all lots coded 34. This is a minor anomaly.

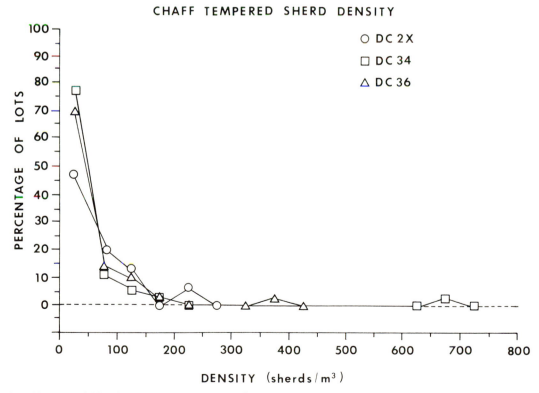

Figure 9.   Chaff Tempered Sherd Density in unscreened lots.
The total number of lots in each category shown on the figure is: secondary (n=15), DC34 (n=35), DC36 (n=37). There are two secondary (DC2x) lots with chaff-ware densities over 400/cubic meter and thus not shown on the figure; they represent the missing 13.33% of lots in this deposit category. These extreme values tend to confirm the difference between secondary and tertiary deposit signatures.

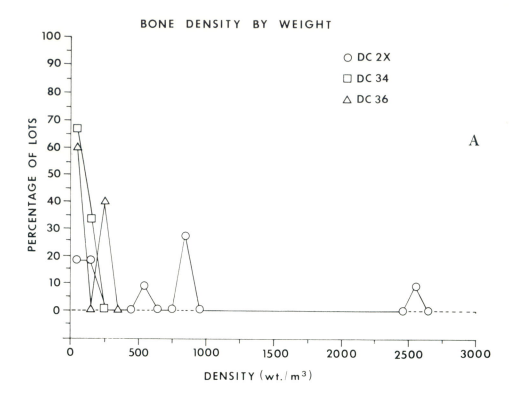

BONE DENSITY BY WEIGHT

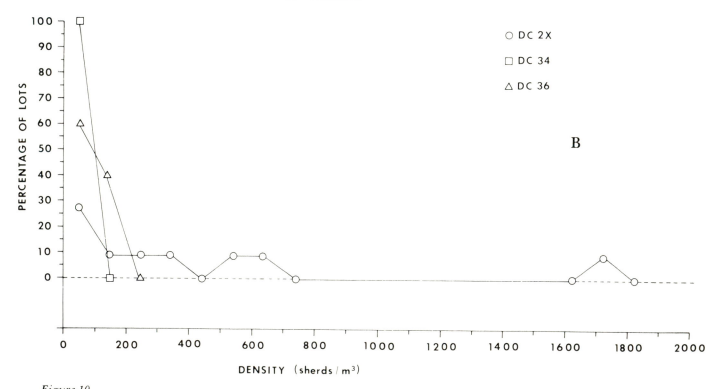

BONE DENSITY BY NUMBER

Figure 10.

A) Bone density by number in unscreened lots. The total number of lots in each category shown on this figure is: secondary (n=11), DC34 (n=3), and DC36 (n=5). There are 2 secondary (DC2x) lots with bone densities by number over 2000/cubic meter and thus not on the figure; they represent 18.18% of all lots in this deposit category.

B) Bone density by weight in unscreened lots. The total number of lots in each category is as in figure 10A. There are 3 secondary (DC2x) lots with bone densities by weight over 3000/cubic meter; they represent 27.27% of all lots in this deposit category. For both figure 10A and 10B, these unplotted extreme values tend to confirm the difference between secondary and tertiary deposit signatures.

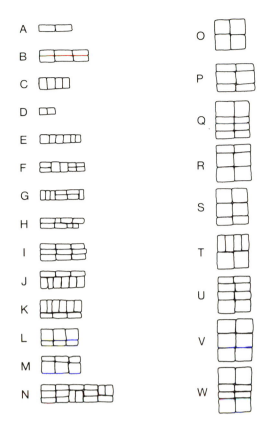

Figure 11. Brick-laying patterns found at TUV.

These diagrams illustrate the brick-laying pattern codes utilized on Tables 5, 7, and 9. On these tables, if the brick pattern in a wall is known to have alternated from course to course, codes are indicated thusly: B/C. If the pattern changed *within* a course, the designation is B + C. As used here, full brick = 36 x 36 x 8.5 cm; half brick = 18 x 36 x 8.5 cm or 20 x 40 x 8 cm; quarter brick = 20 x 20 x 8 cm. The patterns are:

A: row of half-brick stretchers
B: double row of half-brick stretchers
C: single row of half-brick headers
D: row of full bricks
E: half-brick headers mixed with fulls
F: double row of half-brick stretchers mixed with fulls
G: row of half-brick headers interspersed with double row of half-brick stretchers
H: double row of half-brick stretchers mixed with quarter bricks
I: three adjacent rows of half-brick stretchers
J: half-brick stretchers on west or north, half-brick headers on east or south
K: half-brick stretchers on east or south, half-brick headers on west or north
L: full brick on west or north, half-brick stretcher on east or south
M: half-brick stretcher on west or north, full brick on east or south
N: within the same course sections of 3 adjacent half-brick stretchers mixed with sections with one half-brick
     stretcher and 2 half-brick headers
O: 2 full bricks
P: half-brick stretcher along one side, full brick in middle, half-brick stretcher on other side
Q: single row of full bricks on north or west or inside, 3 rows of half-brick stretchers on other side
R: single row of half-brick stretchers on north, west, or inside, with double row of full bricks on other side
S: double row of full bricks on north, west, or inside, with single row of half-brick stretchers on other side
T: single row of half-brick headers on north or west, row of full bricks on south or east
U: three rows of half-brick stretchers on north or west, single row of full bricks on south or east
V: three rows of full bricks
W: full brick on one side, double row of half-brick stretchers in the middle, full brick on the other side
X: "crazy" or haphazard pattern with full, half and quarter bricks applied without a discernible repeatable pattern
     (not illustrated)

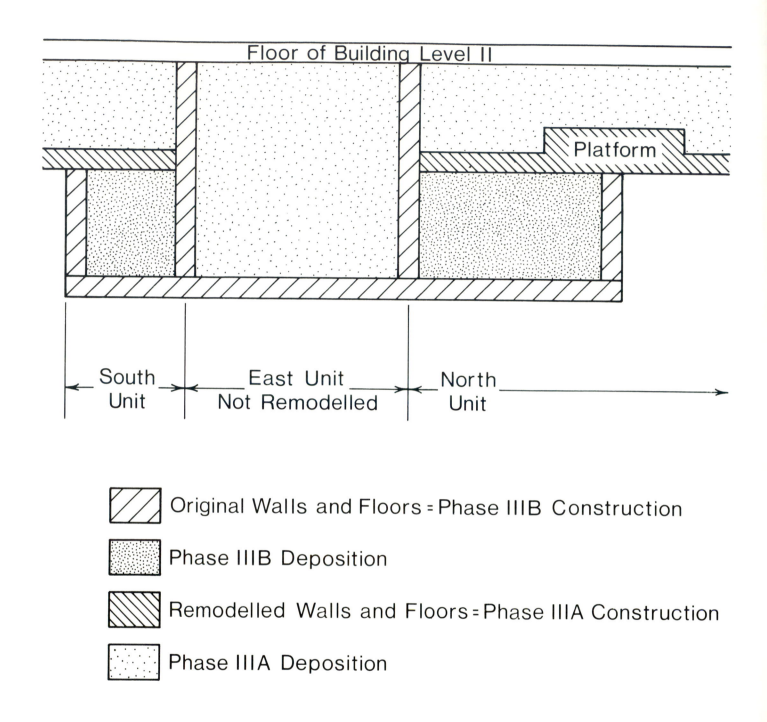

Figure 12. *Schematic diagram of B.L. III construction and deposition.*
It is important to clearly distinguish between the chronology of constructional events and the chronology of depositional events when attempting functional reconstruction.

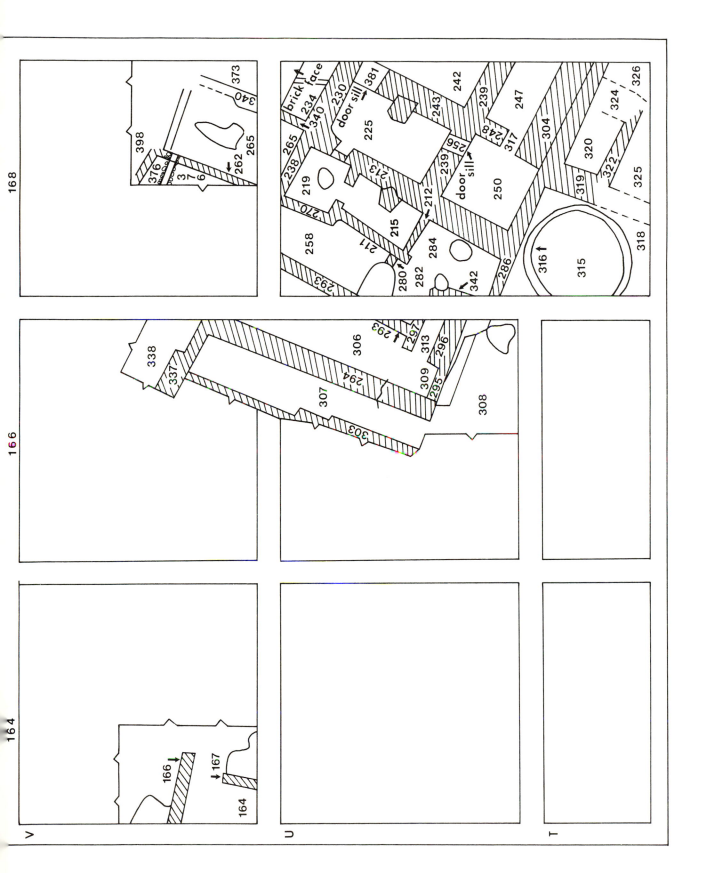

Figure 13. Plan of B.L. IIIB.
This plan shows the feature numbers assigned to walls, rooms, and areas of this level and should be used in conjunction with tables 5 and 6.

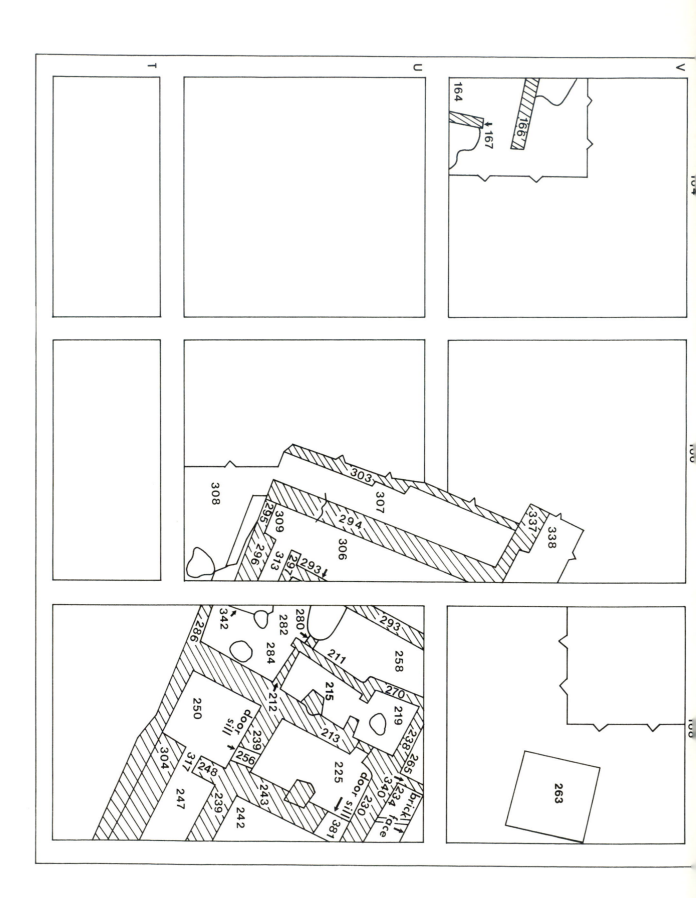

Figure 14. Plan of B.L. IIIA.
This plan shows the feature numbers assigned to walls, rooms, and areas of this level and should be used in conjunction with tables 5 and 6.

Figure 15. Plan of B.L. II.
This plan shows the feature numbers assigned to walls, rooms, and areas of this level and should be used in conjunction with tables 7 and 8.

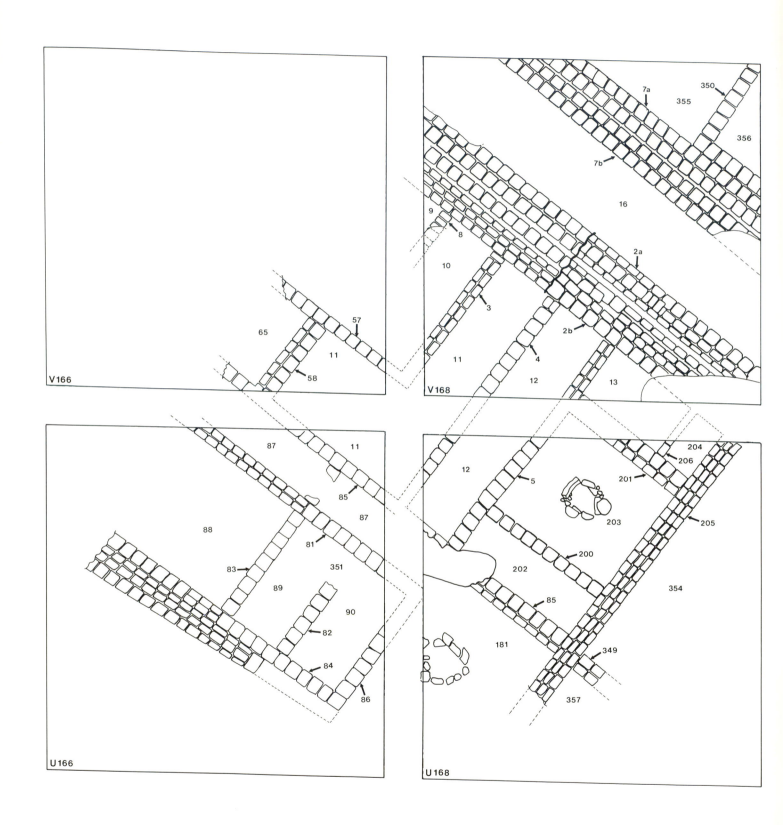

Figure 16. Plan of B.L. I.
This plan shows the feature numbers assigned to walls, rooms, and areas of this level and should be used in conjunction with tables 9 and 10.

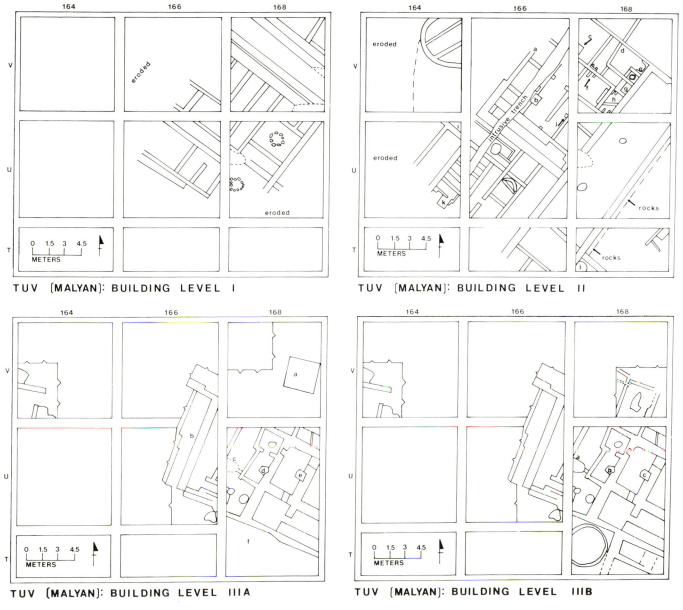

TUV (MALYAN): BUILDING LEVEL I

TUV (MALYAN): BUILDING LEVEL II

TUV (MALYAN): BUILDING LEVEL IIIA

TUV (MALYAN): BUILDING LEVEL IIIB

Figure 17. *General placement of major pyrotechnic features*[a]

B.L.	Key	Feature
I	none	
II	a	hearth 73 (type unclear)
	b	double raised-box hearth 68
	c	raised-box hearth 48
	d	domed oven 54
	e	cobble hearth 29
	f	hearth 51 (type unclear)
	g	cobble hearth 33
	h	hearth 52 (type unclear)
	i	cobble hearth 144
	j	raised-box hearth 344 (in wall 335 and balk)
	k	cobble hearth 137
	l	plastered sherd concentration 182

B.L.	Key	Feature
IIIA	a	sunken oven 223
	b	cobble hearth 305 (stratum 10)
	c	raised-box hearth 273 (largely destroyed by pit 196)
	d	domed oven 214
	e	raised hearth 227
	f	plastered sherd concentration 302 (stratum 11)
IIIB	a	raised-box hearth 273
	b	domed oven 214
	c	raised-box hearth 227

[a] This figure plots the general locations of the major pyrotechnic features discovered in the various building levels at TUV. Key letters have generally been assigned by working across the grid from west to east, beginning at the north and moving south.

Figure 18. General placement of major non-pyrotechnic features.[1]

B.L.	Key	Feature
I		
	a	pit 14 (intrusive from stratum 1)
	b	well 195
	c	pit 196 (intrusive from stratum 1)
	d	well 199
II		
	a	cobble feature 77
	b	possible foundation trench 76 (intrusive from stratum 1)
	c	bin 42
	d	pit 53
	e	plastered pit 38
	f	bin 28
	g	plastered pit 130
	h	bin 131
	i	cobble feature 353
	j	trash pit 132
	k	pit 196 (intrusive from stratum 1)
	l	well 199 (intrusive from stratum 4, B.L. I)
	m	well 195 (intrusive from stratum 4, B.L. I)
IIIA		Features on this map are from stratum 10 unless otherwise indicated.
	a	trashpit 163
	b	drainage pit 333 (stratum 9)
	c	infant burial 336
	d	trash dump 279
	e	trash dump 241
	f	infant burial 226 (stratum 9?)
	g	burial pit 257/adult burial 274
	h	cobble feature 276
	i	infant burial 278 (stratum 9)
	j	well 195 (intrusive from stratum 4, B.L. I)
	k	bin 281 (largely destroyed by pit 196)
	l	pit 196 (intrusive from stratum 1)
	m	trash dump 301
	n	trash pit 285 (stratum 9)
	o	well 199 (intrusive from stratum 4, B.L. I)
	p	child burial 221 (stratum 9)
	q	pit 220 (stratum 9)
	r	cobble feature 252 (possibly intrusive)
	s	trash pit 299
IIIB		
	a	trash pit 165
	b	drain 261
	c	well 195 (intrusive from stratum 4, B.L. I)
	d	bin 281 (largely destroyed by pit 196)
	e	pit 196 (intrusive from stratum 1)
	f	well 199 (intrusive from stratum 4, B.L. I)
	g	pit 220 (intrusive from stratum 9)
	h	cobble feature 327

---

[1] This figure plots the general locations of the major non-pyrotechnic features discovered in the various building levels at TUV. Key letters have generally been assigned by working across the grid from west to east, beginning at the north and moving south.

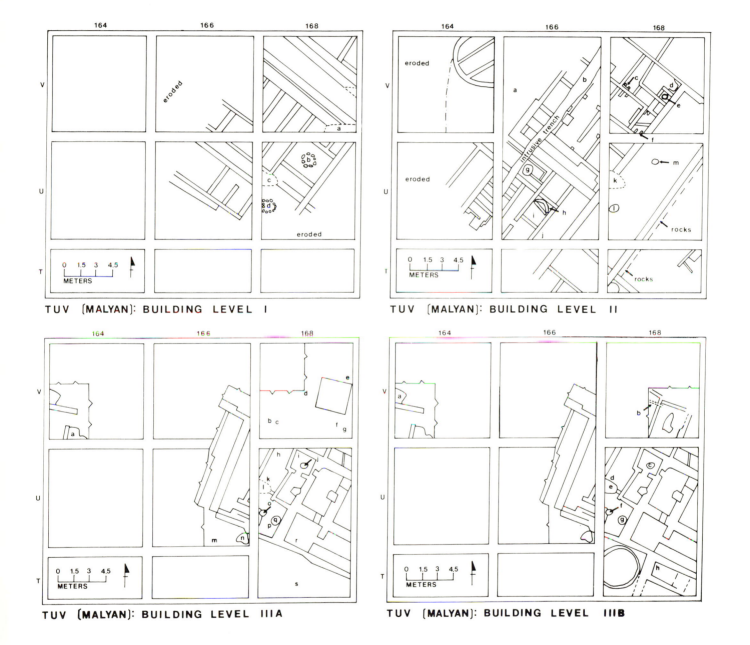

TUV (MALYAN): BUILDING LEVEL I

TUV (MALYAN): BUILDING LEVEL II

TUV (MALYAN): BUILDING LEVEL IIIA

TUV (MALYAN): BUILDING LEVEL IIIB

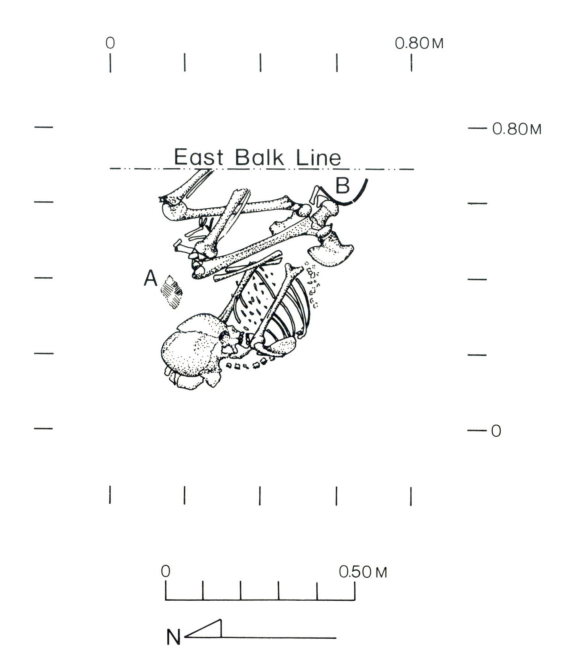

Figure 19. Burial 274, drawn at 1:10.
This adult burial was found in a B.L. IIIB stratum of V168. Item A is part of mf 3896, impressions of cloth or matting presumably constituting a burial shroud. Item B is mf 5078, a flaring-sided white limestone bowl. See also plates 12a-b and 27a.

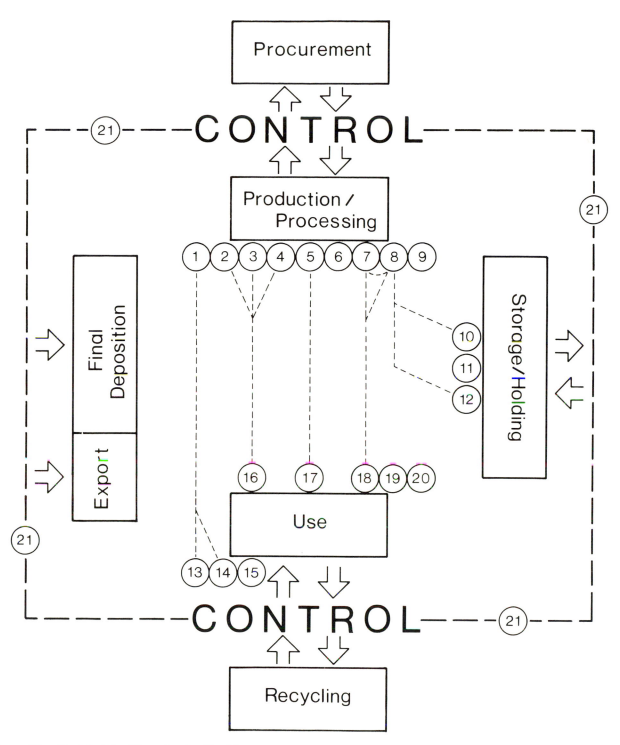

Figure 20. Model of the life cycle of utilized items.
Items are procured from "outside" and brought into a community or institutional system as raw materials, partially processed materials, or finished goods. Once in such a system, the life cycles of items are shaped by the sequence of control decisions taken by the individuals residing or working in that community or institution. Depending on the sequence of decisions made at various moments in time, individual items undergo varying combinations of production, processing, storage, consumption, use, and recycling activities. Utilized items may leave the system through loss, but normally leave when decisions are taken to discard or export the items. The functional classes used throughout this volume (see Table 21) have been keyed into this figure. The model owes an obvious intellectual debt to Schiffer's (1972:158-159) flow models representing the life cycles of durable and consumable elements. The present model has been drawn in a non-linear format to stress the importance of control decisions in shaping the life cycle of individual utilized items.

Figure 21. Distribution of items assigned to functional class 1 (manufacture of chipped stone tools) exclusive of items in tertiary context.[a]

B.L.	Key	Feature	Context[b]	Description	mf #
I	a	well 199	secondary	core	6317
				waste flake	6955
				debitage (6)	6387a,b,c
					6346 a,b,c
II	a	room 69	secondary	waste flake	11255
	b	room 43	secondary admixture	raw material	6979
	c	room 36	secondary	waste flake	6337
	d	area 39	mixed secondary	debitage	6335a
				waste flakes (3)	6335b, 6336, 6978
	e	area 32	secondary admixture	debitage	6294
				waste flakes (2)	6334, 6366
	f	alcove 25	secondary	debitage (4)	6379a,b,c,d
				waste flake	6981
	g	courtyard 30	secondary admixture	waste flake	6333
	h	room 109	secondary admixture	debitage (2)	6287a,b
	i	pit 130	secondary	raw material	6316
				waste flakes (2)	6344, 11252
	j	room 102 (U166 portion)	secondary admixture	raw material	6338
				waste flake	6342
	k	room 102 (T166 portion)	secondary admixture	waste flake	7248
	l	room 175	secondary admixture	debitage	6310
IIIA	a	room 164	secondary admixture	waste flake	6304
	b	area 375	secondary admixture	waste flake	3819
	c	trashpile 241	secondary	debitage (2)	3820a, 8572
	d	alleyway 307	secondary admixture	debitage	5154
	e	corridor 313	secondary admixture	waste flake	5206
	f	pit 285	secondary	waste flakes (2)	3976, 3980
				raw material	5053
	g	room 258	secondary admixture	debitage (2)	3840, 3844
	h	room 250	secondary	debitage	3690
				core	3715
				waste flakes (4)	3711, 3713a,b, 3714
IIIB	a	pit 165	secondary	waste flakes (5)	6352a,b, 6353, 6390, 6964
	b	room 215	secondary	debitage (38)	6226
				cores (2)	6219a, 10312

[a] This figure and the subsequent distribution maps plot the locations for registered items and large concentrations of bulk materials in the various building levels at TUV. Note that, in addition to the main stratum 10 loci, certain stratum 9 loci (area 366 and pit 285) have been included on the maps of B.L. IIIA. In general, the key letters have been entered on the distribution maps in the following order: V164 loci, V166 loci, V168 loci, U164 loci, U166-T166 loci, U168-T168 loci.

[b] Primary, secondary, and secondary admixture contexts are used in the sense defined in chapter II. In addition, the designations mixed secondary (or mixed secondary admixture) and combined sometimes appear. Mixed secondary means that the basic character of a deposit was clearly secondary in nature, but that the lot was partially mixed *during excavation* with material in an adjacent deposit of different character. A mixed secondary designation is therefore a slight downgrading of a secondary designation. "Combined" is used as a context category only when plotting areas of high concentration for bulk sherds and bone, and indicates that bulk counts were derived by pooling counts from all secondary and secondary admixture lots within each given provenience unit.

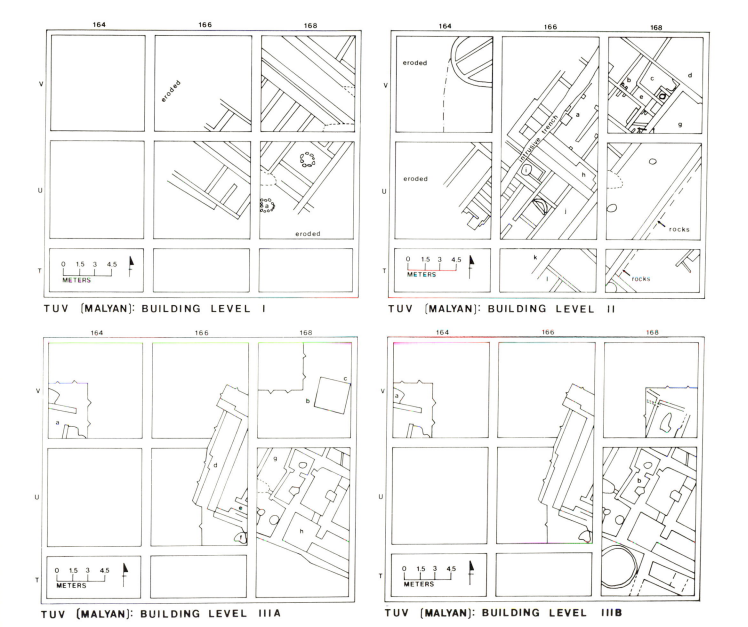

TUV (MALYAN): BUILDING LEVEL I

TUV (MALYAN): BUILDING LEVEL II

TUV (MALYAN): BUILDING LEVEL IIIA

TUV (MALYAN): BUILDING LEVEL IIIB

Figure 22. Distribution of items assigned to functional class 2 (copper-base metallurgy) exclusive of items in tertiary context.[a]

B.L.	Key	Feature	Context	Description[b]	mf #
I	a	room 88	secondary admixture	copper/slag	7115
	b	well 199	secondary	copper/slag	6929
II	a	room 45	secondary admixture	copper/slag	5977
				iron rich copper slag?	7107
	b	area 47	secondary admixture	copper/slag (2)	6947, 7105
				furnace linings (2)	1484, 6948
	c	area 39	mixed secondary	copper/slag (2)	1482, 7118
				iron rich copper slag?	7106
			secondary admixture	copper/slag	1483
				sheet metal	7099
	d	room 36	secondary	copper/slag	7113
	e	area 32	secondary admixture	copper/slag	1485
	f	courtyard 30	secondary admixture	copper/slag (2)	7112, 11244
	g	pit 130	secondary	furnace lining?	7244
	h	pit 132	secondary	copper/slag (2)	7125, 11243
				furnace lining	6951
	i	room 102	secondary admixture	copper/slag	7124
	j	room 174	secondary admixture	furnace lining	6944
IIIA	a	room 164	secondary admixture	furnace lining	6935
	b	area 366	secondary	copper/slag	6037
				furnace lining	6044
	c	area 338	secondary admixture	copper/slag (3)	6094, 6096, 6097
				furnace lining	6087
	d	area 375	secondary admixture	iron-rich copper slag?	3610
				sheet metal (2)	3611, 3811
	e	area 377	mixed secondary admixture	copper/slag	3895
	f	area 370	secondary admixture	copper/slag	3608
	g	trashpile 241	secondary	sheet metal	3581
				copper/slag (4)	3571, 3572, 3575, 3607
				furnace lining	3560
				mold	3827
	h	oven 223	secondary	copper/slag	3580
	i	area 372	secondary admixture	copper/slag	3582
	j	burial 274	(in fill of pit)	copper/slag	3908
	k	room 306	secondary admixture	copper/slag	5097
			secondary	ore? (malachite)	5222
	l	room 309	secondary admixture	sheet metal	5145
	m	area 308	secondary admixture	copper/slag (2)	5143, 5144
				furnace lining	5147
	n	trashpile 301	secondary	sheet metal	6945
				copper/slag (3)	5146, 5148, 7126
	o	pit 285	secondary	copper/slag (3)	3966, 3967, 3972
				furnace lining	3977
	p	room 258	secondary admixture	copper/slag (3)	3857, 3858, 3863
				furnace lining	3859
			secondary	copper/slag (2)	3950, 3952
	q	room 184	secondary admixture	copper/slag	7122
	r	pit 220	secondary	copper/slag	3954
	s	room 250	secondary	ingot?	3877
				copper/slag (2)	3678, 3679
IIIB	a	pit 165	secondary	bar metal	6938
				copper/slag	6936
	b	room 219	secondary	furnace lining	3536
	c	doorway 216	secondary admixture	copper/slag	7114
	d	structure 315	secondary admixture	copper/slag	5220
	e	area 325	secondary admixture	copper/slag (2)	5302, 5304
	f	area 326	secondary admixture	copper/slag	5320

[a] See caption for Figure 21 for general explanation of criteria pertaining to distribution maps.

[b] Certain finds were designated in the field register as copper slag; others were designated as copper blobs or bits of metal. Technical identification of these samples, however, is not yet complete. The designation copper/slag is therefore used here to indicate finds which fall into these categories, without attempting to discriminate absolutely between slags and small bits of metal at this stage.

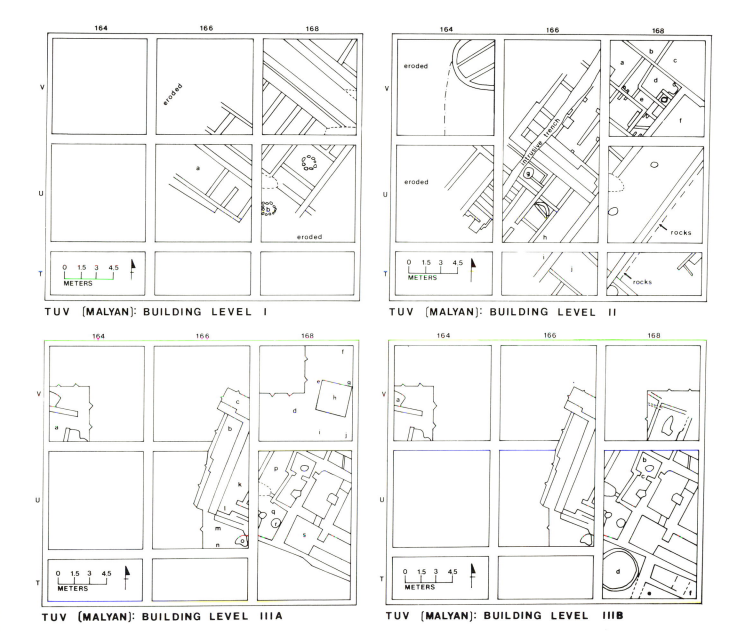

TUV (MALYAN): BUILDING LEVEL I

TUV (MALYAN): BUILDING LEVEL II

TUV (MALYAN): BUILDING LEVEL IIIA

TUV (MALYAN): BUILDING LEVEL IIIB

Figure 23. *Distribution of items assigned to class 3 (production of stone beads) and to class 4 (shell-working) exclusive of items in tertiary context.*[a]

B.L.	Key	Feature	Context	Description	mf #
I	a	room 88	secondary admixture	bivalve shell	6862
	b	well 199	secondary	unidentified shells (2)	1257, 1258
				dentalium (3)	7098 a,b,c
II	a	area 379	secondary admixture	unidentified shell	6877
	b	room 43	secondary admixture	dentalium	6886
				olive	6885
				worked shell	6887
	c	area 39	mixed secondary	dentalium	6889
				bivalve shell	6888
	d	alcove 25	secondary	bivalve shell	6890
	e	room 141	secondary	unidentified shell	6399
	f	room 109	secondary admixture	bivalve shell	6864
	g	pit 132	secondary	worked shell	6866
IIIA	a	area 338	secondary admixture	olive shell	6088
				bivalve shell	6091
	b	area 375	secondary admixture	zeolite	5075
	c	trashpile 241	secondary	loose inlay	3604
				zeolites (2)	5073, 5074
	d	area 372	secondary admixture	bivalve shell	7973
	e	room 306	secondary admixture	quartz raw material	5223
	f	area 308	secondary admixture	bivalve shell	5150
	g	trashpile 301	secondary	cone shell	5090
	h	pit 285	secondary	bivalve shell	3988
	i	room 258	secondary admixture	unidentified shell	3870
				cone shell	3871
	j	room 250	secondary	dentalium (2)	3701, 3703
				worked shell	3698
	k	room 247	secondary	cone shell	3697
IIIB	a	pit 165	secondary	bivalve shell	6874
				worked shells (2)	6873, 6963
	b	room 215	secondary	zeolite bead broken in manufacture	6229
				lapis?	6252
				quartz	6231
				possible zeolite	6230

[a] See caption for Figure 21 for general explanation of criteria pertaining to distribution maps.

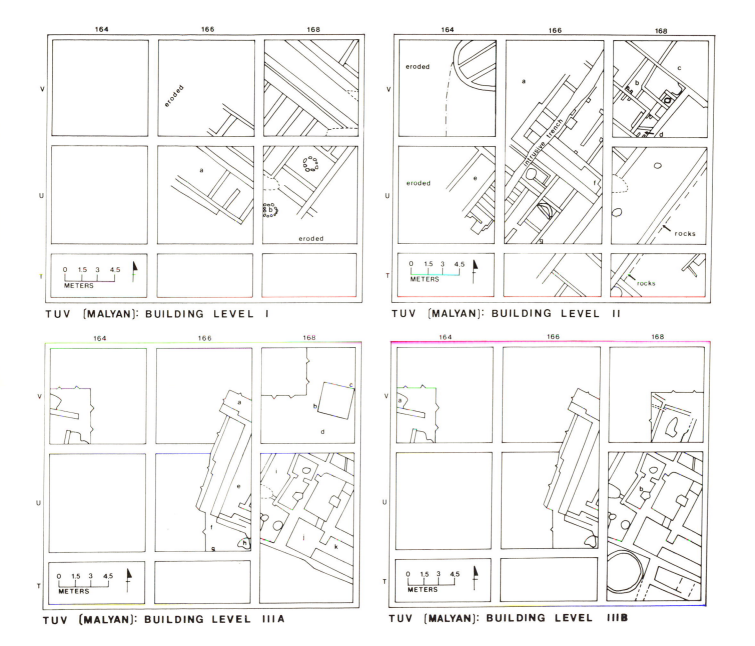

TUV (MALYAN): BUILDING LEVEL I

TUV (MALYAN): BUILDING LEVEL II

TUV (MALYAN): BUILDING LEVEL IIIA

TUV (MALYAN): BUILDING LEVEL IIIB

Figure 25. Distribution of items assigned to functional class 7 (food preparation) exclusive of items in tertiary context.[a]

B.L.	Key	Feature	Context	Description[b]	mf #
I	a	room 10	secondary	medium restricted vessel	1189
	b	alleyway 16	secondary	grill	1310
	c	pit 101	secondary	charcoal (2)	*
	d	well 195	secondary	charcoal (1)	*
	e	well 199	secondary	charcoal (7)	*
				medium restricted vessels (2)	1449, 1926
				high bone concentration	not registered
II	a	room 158	secondary admixture	high bone concentration	not registered
	b	pit 74	secondary	charcoal (1)	*
	c	room 69	secondary	charcoal (1)	*
				handstone	5975
	d	room 45	secondary admixture	charcoal (1)	*

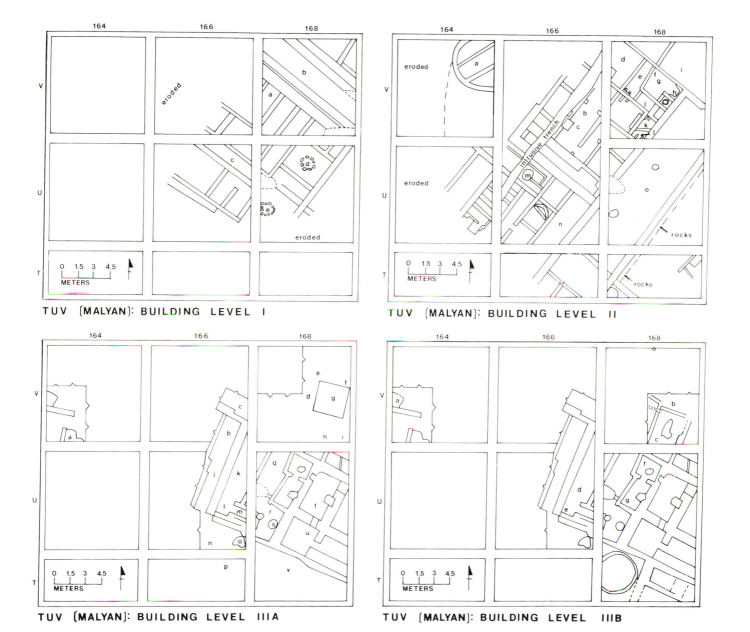

TUV (MALYAN): BUILDING LEVEL I

TUV (MALYAN): BUILDING LEVEL II

TUV (MALYAN): BUILDING LEVEL IIIA

TUV (MALYAN): BUILDING LEVEL IIIB

Figure 26. *Distribution of items assigned to functional class 10 (general storage) exclusive of items in tertiary context.*[a]

B.L.	Key	Feature	Context	Description[b,c]	mf #
I		no items of this class			
II	a	room 36	combined	high sherd concentration	not registered
	b	area 39	combined	high sherd concentration	not registered
	c	room 102	secondary admixture	seal impressions (2)	1965a,b
				high sherd concentration	not registered
	d	pit 132	secondary	sealings, no impressions (5)	1879a-c, 1881a,b
				seal impressions (15)	1878, 1879d-j, 1880, 1881c-h
	e	courtyard 30	combined	high sherd concentration	not registered
IIIA	a	room 164	secondary admixture	sealing, no impression	1785a
				seal impressions (9)	1785b, 1786a-b, 1787, 1788, 1789, 1790, 1791, 1792
	b	pit 163	secondary	sealings, no impressions (36)	1793a-f, 1935a-d, 1937a-d, 1938a-c, 1939a-c, 1940a-c, 1941a-e, 1945a-d, 1946a-d
				seal impressions (17)	1794-1797, 1936, 1937e, 1938d, 1945e-l, 1948, 1950
	c	area 338	secondary admixture	seal impressions (2)	6059, 6181
	d	trashpile 241	secondary	sealing, no impression	3828
	e	alleyway 307	secondary admixture	seal impression	5987
	f	room 309	secondary admixture	seal impressions (2)	6183, 6190
	g	pit 285	secondary	seal impression	6189
	h	room 284	secondary admixture	sealings, no impressions (2)	6202, 6204
				jar stoppers, no impressions (6)	5999a-f
				seal impressions (14)	5990, 5992, 5993, 5996-5998, 6182, 6197, 6201a-f
				high sherd concentration	not registered
	i	room 250	combined	high sherd concentration	not registered
	j	pit 299	mixed secondary	seal impressions (3)	6184, 6194, 6196
IIIB	a	pit 165	secondary	sealings, no impressions (15)	1803, 1825a-b, 1826a, 1883, 1884a, 1885a, 1886a, 1887a-c, 1947a-c, 1953a
				seal impressions (120)	1798-1802, 1804a-j, 1805-1817b, 1818-1824, 1825c-s, 1826b-n, 1882, 1884b-g, 1885b-g, 1886b-l, 1887d-n, 1944a-p, 1947d-e, 1953b
				high sherd concentration	not registered

[a] See caption for Figure 21 for general explanation of criteria pertaining to distribution maps.

[b] A high concentration of sherds of this class consists of at least 10 rim sherds.

[c] Seal impressions are also counted under class 21 (Figure 32).

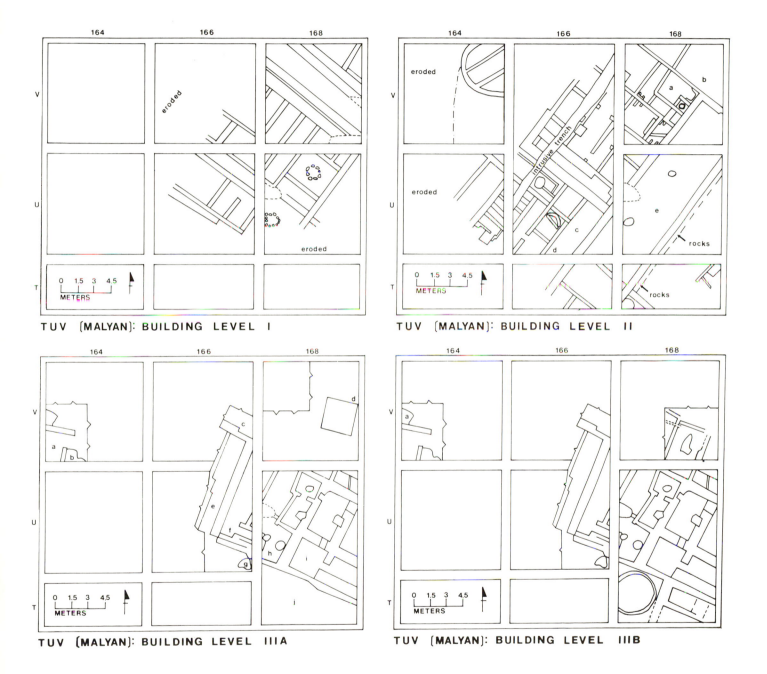

TUV (MALYAN): BUILDING LEVEL I

TUV (MALYAN): BUILDING LEVEL II

TUV (MALYAN): BUILDING LEVEL IIIA

TUV (MALYAN): BUILDING LEVEL IIIB

Figure 27. *Distribution of items assigned to functional classes 11 (basketry/matting) and 12 (special containers), exclusive of items in tertiary context.*[a]

B.L.	Key	Feature	Context	Description[b]	mf #
I		no registered items of this class; no high sherd concentrations			
II	a	room 157	secondary admixture	calcite vessel sherd	6920
	b	area 39	secondary admixture	limestone vessel sherd	5976
	c	room 36	secondary admixture	travertine vessel sherd	1453
	d	area 32	secondary admixture	limestone vessel sherd	6926
				miniature ceramic vessel	1458
IIIA	a	pit 163	secondary	bevelled-rim bowl	1725
	b	area 366	secondary	limestone vessel sherd	6034
	c	burial 336	primary	cloth/mat impression	6105
	d	trashpile 241	secondary	green marble vessel sherd	3829
	e	burial 274	primary	cloth/mat impression	3896
				limestone or plaster vessel	5078
	f	room 306	secondary	limestone vessel sherd	5230
			secondary admixture	limestone vessel sherds (2)	5205, 5295
	g	trashpile 301 (U166 segment)	secondary	high concentration of low tray and bevelled-rim bowl sherds	not registered
	h	pit 285	secondary	high concentration of low tray and bevelled-rim bowl sherds	not registered
	i	trashpile 301 (T166 segment)	secondary	high concentration of low tray, bevelled-rim bowl, and pedestal-based goblet sherds	not registered
	j	room 258	secondary	bitumen basket lining?	5394
			secondary admixture	limestone vessel sherd	5058
	k	room 284	secondary admixture	nearly complete low tray	5084
				high concentration of low tray and bevelled-rim bowl sherds	not registered
	l	room 250	secondary	bitumen basket lining?	5393
				lead bowl	3878a
IIIB	a	pit 165	secondary	bevelled-rim bowl	1724
	b	room 306	secondary	high concentration of low tray and bevelled-rim sherds	not registered

[a] See caption for Figure 21 for general explanation of criteria pertaining to distribution maps.

[b] For low trays, bevelled-rim bowls, and pedestal-based goblets, an area of high concentration refers to a locus with a minimum of *100* rim sherds of *each* type specified.

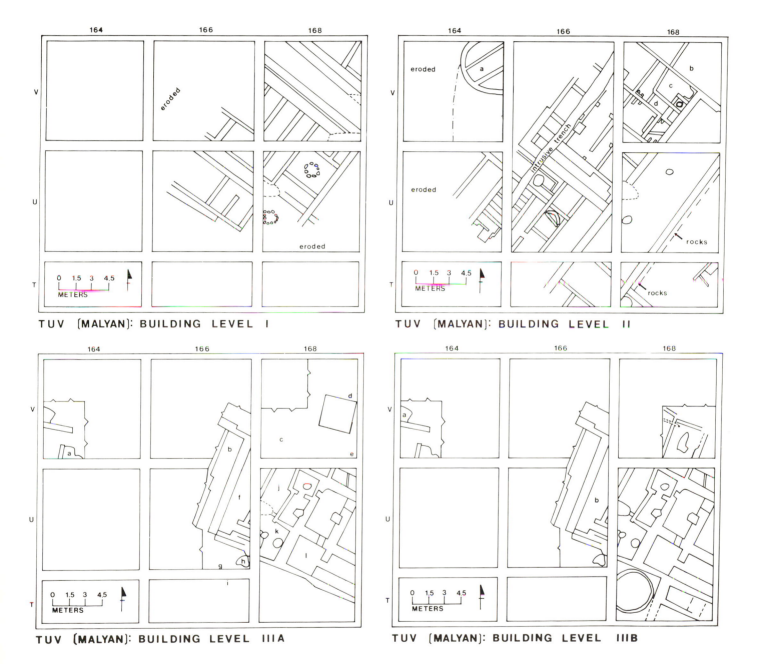

TUV (MALYAN): BUILDING LEVEL I

TUV (MALYAN): BUILDING LEVEL II

TUV (MALYAN): BUILDING LEVEL IIIA

TUV (MALYAN): BUILDING LEVEL IIIB

Figure 28. Distribution of items of classes 13 (cutting tools), 14 (diverse flaked tools), and 15 (piercing/boring tools), exclusive of items in tertiary context.[a]

B.L.	Key	Feature	Context	Description[b]	mf #
I	a	room 87	secondary admixture	blade	6280
	b	well 195	secondary	blade	6307
	c	well 199	secondary	blade segment	6392
				geometric microlith	6319
II	a	room 157	secondary admixture	possible scraper	6323
	b	area 379	secondary admixture	blades (2)	6305, 6386
	c	room 43	secondary admixture	worked flake	6307
	d	area 39	secondary admixture	worked flake	6306
	e	courtyard 30	secondary admixture	notched blade	6301
	f	room 109	secondary admixture	blade	6281
	g	room 102	secondary admixture	notched tools (2)	6309, 6339
IIIA	a	room 164	secondary admixture	blade segment	6286
	b	area 377	mixed secondary admixture	blade segment	3907
	c	area 370	secondary admixture	blade segment	3614
	d	trashpile 241	secondary	blade segment	3588
				worked flake	3820b
	e	area 372	secondary admixture	awl	7972
	f	room 306	secondary	blade segments (2)	5233, 5372
			secondary admixture	blade segment	5093
				blade	5091
	g	trashpile 301	secondary	scraper?	5153
	h	pit 285	secondary	microblade segment	3981
	i	room 258	secondary admixture	notched tool	3845
	j	room 250	secondary	blade	3687
				geometric microlith	3692
IIIB	a	pit 165	secondary	blade segment	6377
	b	room 215	secondary	blade segments (10)	6219b, 6222, 10313, 10317, 10322-10328
				diverse flake tools (10)	10310, 10311, 10314-10316, 10318-10321, 10326

[a] See caption for Figure 21 for general explanation of criteria pertaining to distribution maps.

[b] Blade, as used on this table, refers to chipped stone flakes at least twice as long as they are wide.

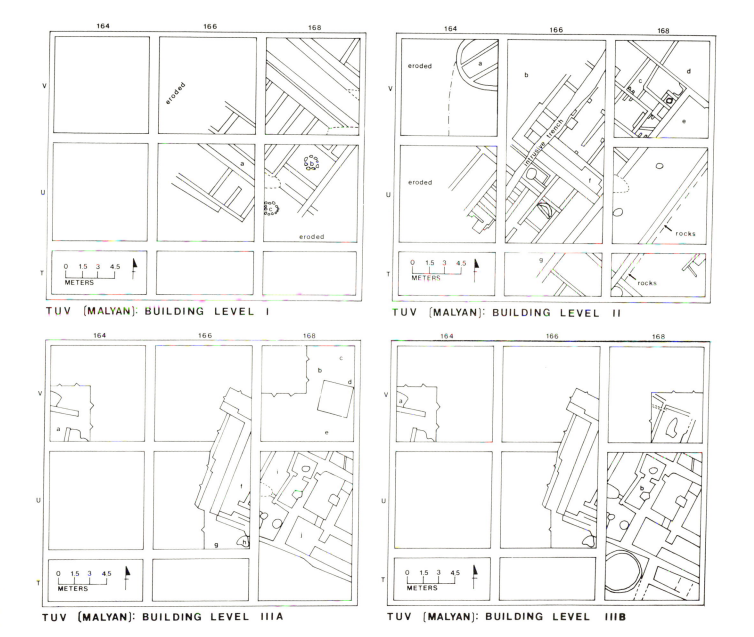

TUV (MALYAN): BUILDING LEVEL I

TUV (MALYAN): BUILDING LEVEL II

TUV (MALYAN): BUILDING LEVEL IIIA

TUV (MALYAN): BUILDING LEVEL IIIB

Figure 29. *Distribution of items of class 16 (personal ornaments) exclusive of items in tertiary context.*[a]

B.L.	Key	Feature	Context	Description	mf #
I	a	well 195	secondary	stone beads (2)	1292, 1296
	b	well 199	secondary	stone beads (2)	1297, 1299
II	a	area 379	secondary admixture	stone bead	6907
	b	room 71	secondary	pin	6937
	c	room 36	secondary	frit bead	6908
	d	courtyard 30	secondary admixture	shell bead	6905
IIIA	a	area 338	secondary admixture	stone bead	6093
	b	room 250	secondary	pin	3676
IIIB	a	pit 165	secondary	copper ring	1920

[a] See caption for Figure 21 for general explanation of criteria pertaining to distribution maps.

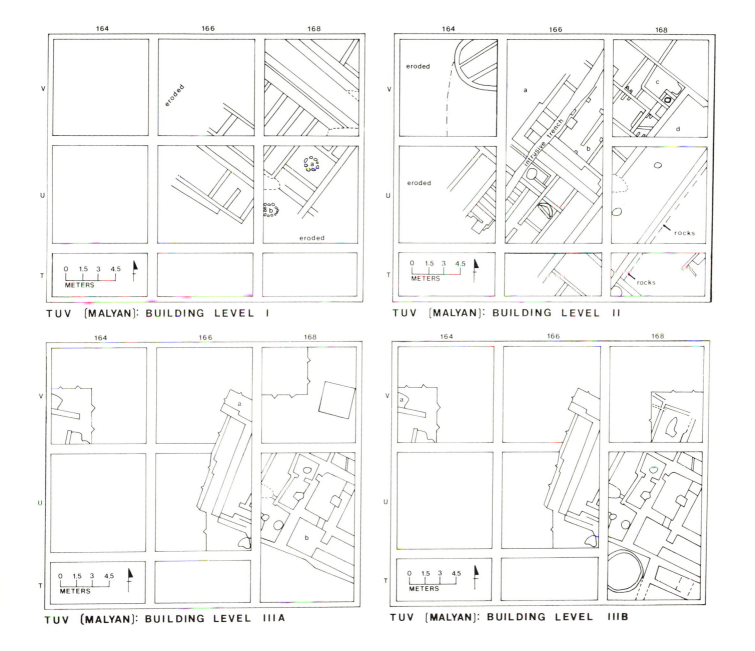

TUV (MALYAN): BUILDING LEVEL I

TUV (MALYAN): BUILDING LEVEL II

TUV (MALYAN): BUILDING LEVEL IIIA

TUV (MALYAN): BUILDING LEVEL IIIB

Figure 30. Distribution of items assigned to functional classes 17 (architecturally related items) and 19 (carpentry), exclusive of items in tertiary context.[a]

B.L.	Key	Feature	Context	Description	mf #
I	a	room 10	secondary	drain sherd	not registered
	b	well 195	secondary	wall cone	1550
	c	well 199	secondary	drain sherds (4)	not registered
II	a	area 379	secondary admixture	drain sherd	not registered
	b	area 47	secondary admixture	drain sherd	not registered
	c	courtyard 30	secondary admixture	drain sherd	not registered
	d	room 102	secondary	drain sherd	not registered
	e	courtyard 30	secondary admixture	drain sherds (2)	not registered
IIIA	a	area 375	secondary admixture	mud plaster sample	3602
	b	trashpile 241	secondary	mud plaster sample	3596
	c	area 372	secondary admixture	wall cone	3599
	d	room 306	secondary	drain	6272
				drain sherds (2)	not registered
			secondary admixture	drain sherds (6)	not registered
	e	trashpile 301	secondary	drain sherd	not registered
	f	room 250	secondary admixture	door socket	6275
			secondary	adze	5067
IIIB	a	room 265	secondary admixture	tile	3830

[a] See caption for Figure 21 for general explanation of criteria pertaining to distribution maps.

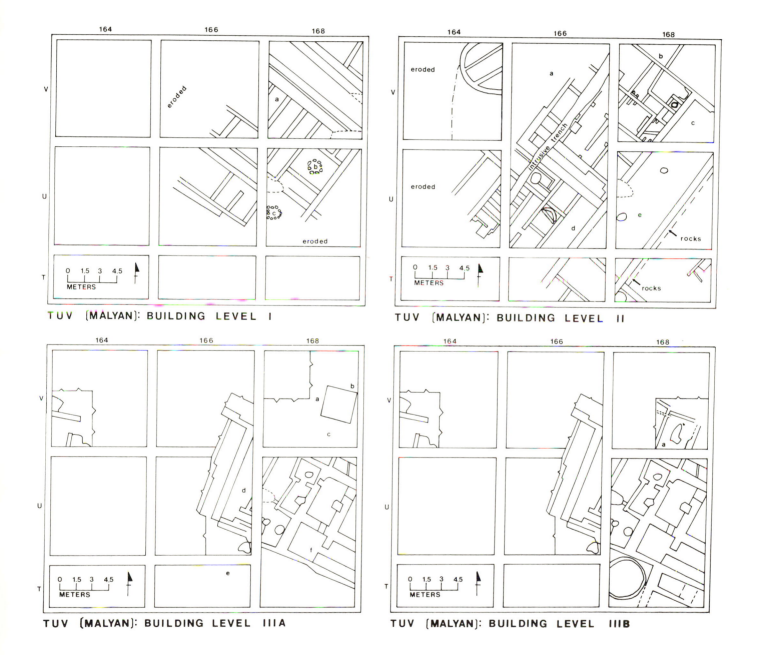

TUV (MALYAN): BUILDING LEVEL I

TUV (MALYAN): BUILDING LEVEL II

TUV (MALYAN): BUILDING LEVEL IIIA

TUV (MALYAN): BUILDING LEVEL IIIB

Figure 31.   Distribution of items assigned to functional classes 18 (food consumption) and 20 (decorated items), exclusive of items in tertiary context.[a]

B.L.	Key	Feature	Context	Description[b]	mf #
I	a	well 199	secondary	small restricted vessel	1256
II	a	area 379	secondary admixture	high sherd concentration	not registered [20]
	b	room 36	combined	high sherd concentration	not registered [20]
	c	courtyard 30	secondary admixture	flaring cup	1723
	d	room 102	secondary	flaring cup	1450
			combined	high sherd concentration	not registered [20]
	e	courtyard 30 (U168 portion)	secondary admixture	high sherd concentration	not registered [20]
IIIA	a	pit 163	secondary	relief sherd	1931
	b	area 375	secondary admixture	medium restricted vessel	3834
	c	room 306	combined	high sherd concentration	not registered [20]
	d	room 284	secondary admixture	high sherd concentration	not registered [20]
	e	room 250	secondary	high sherd concentration	not registered[20]
IIIB	a	pit 165	secondary	flaring cup	1727
				small bowl	1729
	b	room 306	secondary	high sherd concentration	not registered [20]

[a] See caption for Figure 21 for general explanation of criteria pertaining to distribution maps.

[b] High concentrations of sherds of classes 18 and 20 are defined as having at least 10 rim sherds of that class. No such high concentrations of class 18 sherds were found.

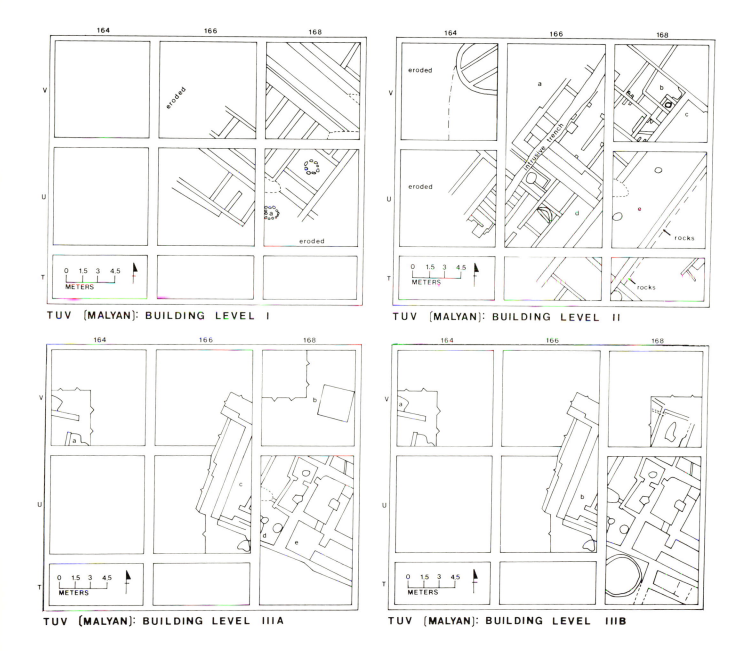

TUV (MALYAN): BUILDING LEVEL I

TUV (MALYAN): BUILDING LEVEL II

TUV (MALYAN): BUILDING LEVEL IIIA

TUV (MALYAN): BUILDING LEVEL IIIB

Figure 32. *Distribution of items in class 21 (information processing) exclusive of items in tertiary context.*[a]

B.L. Key		Feature	Context	Description[b]	mf #
I		no items of this class			
II	a	room 157	secondary admixture	small geometric ball	6961
	b	room 69 or 71[c]	secondary	Proto-Elamite tablet	1861
				Proto-Elamite tablet	1862
	c	room 102	secondary admixture	seal impressions (2)	1965a-b
	d	pit 132	secondary	seal impressions (15)	1878, 1879d-j, 1880, 1881c-h
IIIA	a	room 164	secondary admixture	seal impressions (9)	1785b, 1786a-b, 1787-1792
	b	pit 163	secondary	Proto-Elamite tablet	1860
				Proto-Elamite tablet	1691
				seal impressions (17)	1794-1797, 1936, 1937e, 1938d, 1945e-l, 1948, 1950
	c	area 338	secondary admixture	Proto-Elamite tablets (3)	4469, 4474, 4475
				seal impressions (2)	6059, 6181
	d	alleyway 307	secondary admixture	bulla interior?	5420
				seal impression (1)	5987
	e	room 306	secondary	small geometric ball	5229
			secondary admixture	small geometric ball	5094
	f	room 309	secondary admixture	bullae (7)	5452, 5453, 6046, 6176, 6177, 6179, 6180
				small geometric squat cone	5228
				seal impressions (2)	6183, 6190
	g	trashpile 301	secondary	Proto-Elamite tablet	4426
	h	pit 285	secondary	potter's marked sherd	8685
				seal impression (1)	6189
	i	room 219	secondary admixture	Proto-Elamite tablet	1859
	j	room 284	secondary admixture	Proto-Elamite tablets (7)	4435, 4476-4478, 4480-4482
				small geometric balls (2)	5065, 6959
				bulla interior(?)	6106
				seal impressions (14)	5990, 5992-5993, 5996-5998, 6182, 6197, 6201a-f
	k	room 250	secondary admixture	small geometric ovoid	3693
	l	pit 299	secondary	bulla	6178
			mixed secondary	seal impressions (3)	6184, 6194, 6196
IIIB	a	pit 165	secondary	seal impressions (120)	1798-1802, 1804a-j, 1805-1817b, 1818-1824, 1825c-s, 1826b-n, 1882, 1884b-g, 1885b-g, 1886b-l, 1887d-n, 1944a-p, 1947d-e, 1953b
				small geometric ball	6939
		doorway 216	secondary admixture	Proto-Elamite tablet	1858

[a] See caption for Figure 21 for general explanation of criteria pertaining to distribution maps.

[b] Note that seal impressions belong to both class 21 and class 10 (figure 26).

[c] These tablets were found during balk removal in 1974. The notes are unclear as to which room they were found in.

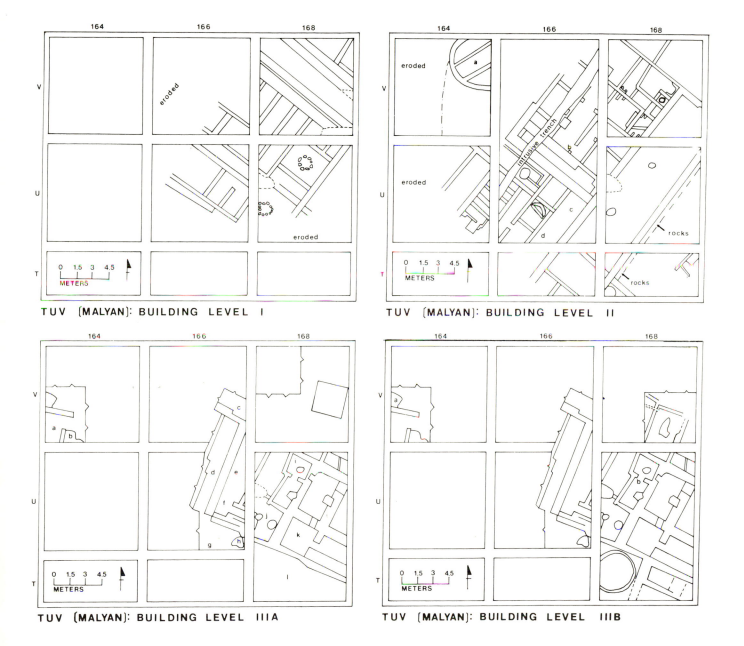

TUV (MALYAN): BUILDING LEVEL I

TUV (MALYAN): BUILDING LEVEL II

TUV (MALYAN): BUILDING LEVEL IIIA

TUV (MALYAN): BUILDING LEVEL IIIB

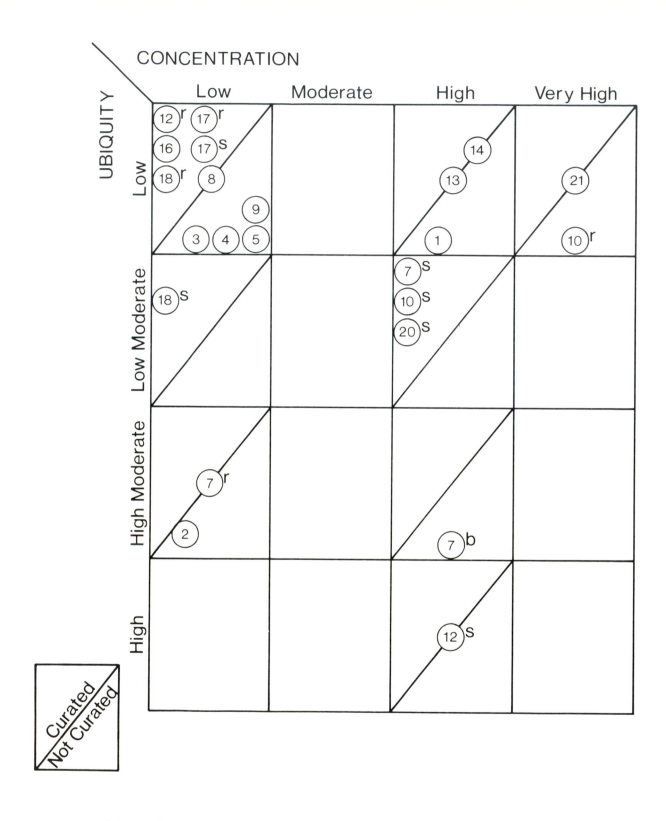

Figure 33.   Activity matrix for B.L. IIIB, based on material in primary, secondary, and secondary admixture deposits. The circled numbers are the functional classes as designated in Table 21.

Key: r = registered items
s = sherds
b = bone

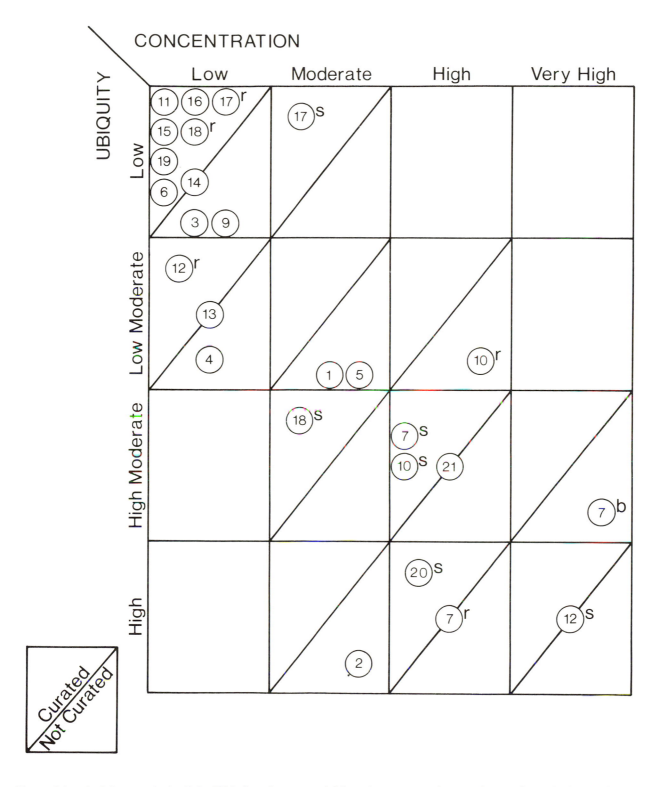

Figure 34. Activity matrix for B.L. IIIA, based on material in primary, secondary, and secondary admixture deposits. The circled numbers are the functional classes as designated in Table 21.

Key: r = registered items
      s = sherds
      b = bone

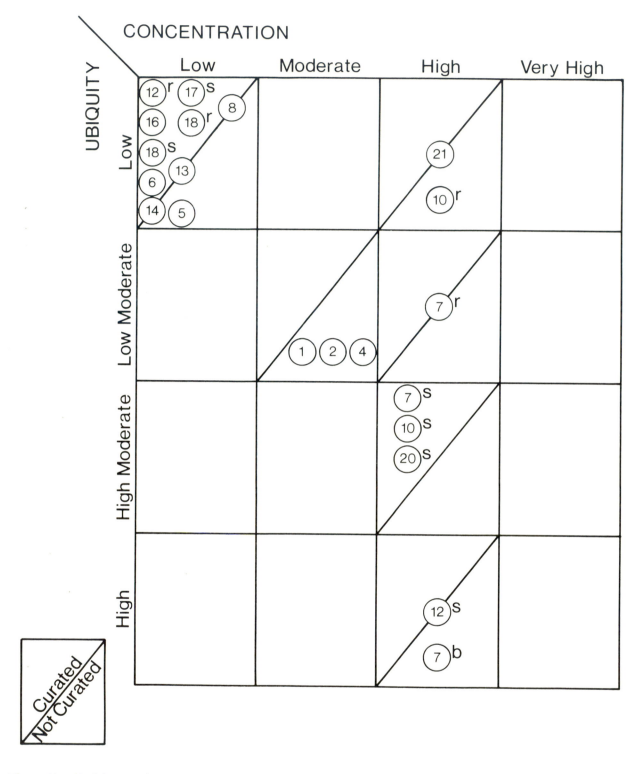

Figure 35. Activity matrix for B.L. II, based on material in primary, secondary, and secondary admixture deposits. The circled numbers are the functional classes as designated in Table 21.

Key: r = registered items
s = sherds
b = bone

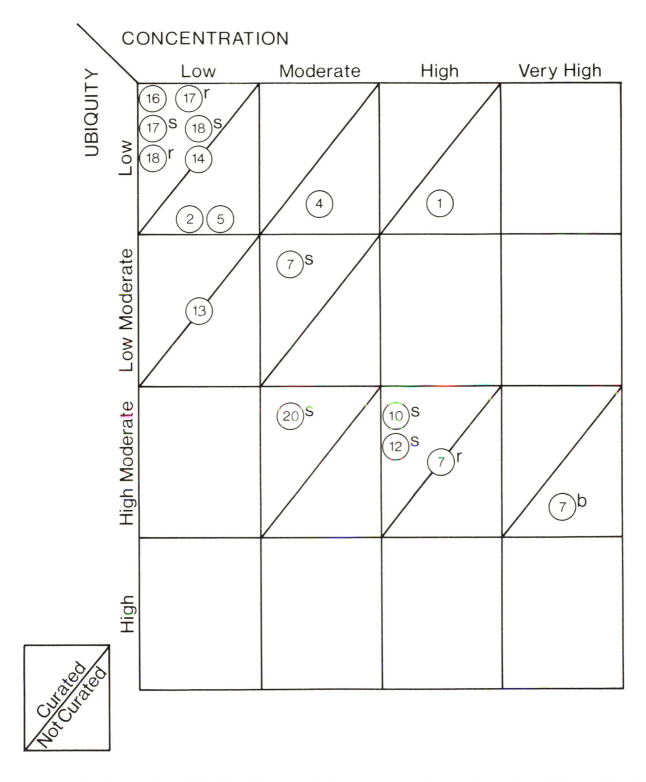

Figure 36.   Activity matrix for B.L. I, based on material in primary, secondary, and secondary admixture deposits. The circled numbers are the functional classes as designated in Table 21.

Key: r = registered items
      s = sherds
      b = bone

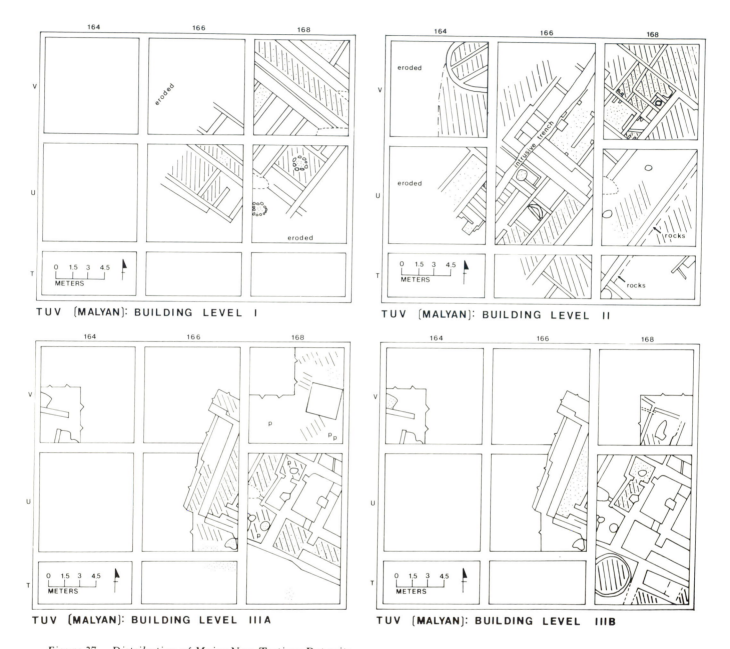

TUV (MALYAN): BUILDING LEVEL I

TUV (MALYAN): BUILDING LEVEL II

TUV (MALYAN): BUILDING LEVEL IIIA

TUV (MALYAN): BUILDING LEVEL IIIB

Figure 37. Distribution of Major Non-Tertiary Deposits.
These maps show the general locations of the major primary, secondary, and secondarily admixed deposits at TUV. Remember that many of the areas shown as having non-tertiary deposition *also* had tertiary deposition above or adjacent to the deposits shown here. Also note that some stratum 9 features have been included on the map of B.L. IIIA (compare Figure 18).

= unit in which a secondary deposit was found

= unit in which a secondarily admixed deposit was found

P = primary (burials)

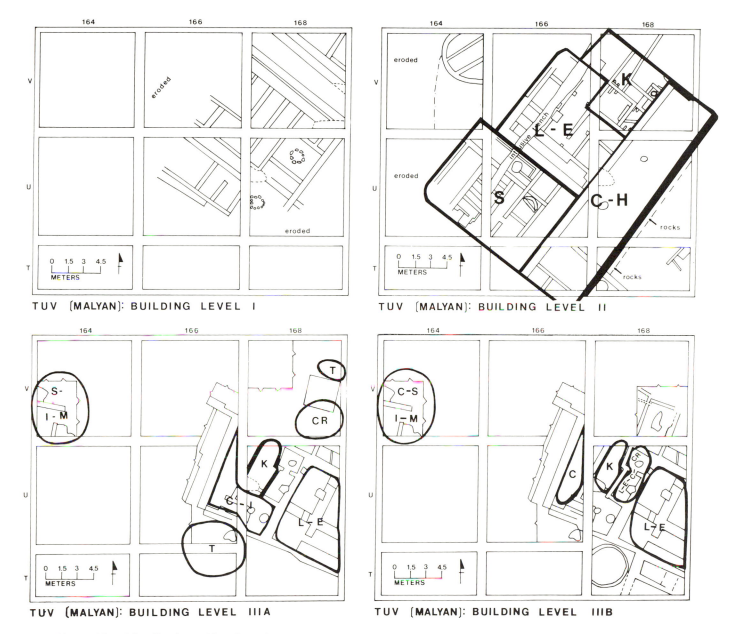

Figure 38. *Distribution of key functions.*

This figure summarizes the main functions which have been reconstructed for different sectors of TUV building levels II, IIIA, and IIIB. As explained in the text, identification of such functional sectors was not possible for B.L. I. In these plans, the key letters stand for the following uses of space:

S   = Storage area
L-E = General living/entertainment quarters
K   = Kitchen area, generally with signs of meat processing
C   = Zone with heavy use of the chaff-ware special containers (trays, goblets and/or bevelled-rim bowls)
H   = Area where short term storage or temporary holding of materials was done
I   = Information processing or control activity zone
M   = Area of meat processing activities but without preserved kitchen installations
T   = Trash dumping zone
CR   = Area of small-scale craft manufacturing

Plates

PLATE 1

Plate 1. Aerial view of the TUV operation, 1976, looking west. B.L. III architecture is visible in the foreground row of squares. In the middle row of squares areas of both B.L. II and B.L. III architecture are exposed, while B.L. II remains can be seen in the farthest row of squares. The size of a standard full grid square is 10 x 10 m. The total excavated area visible in this picture is around 900m².

PLATE 2

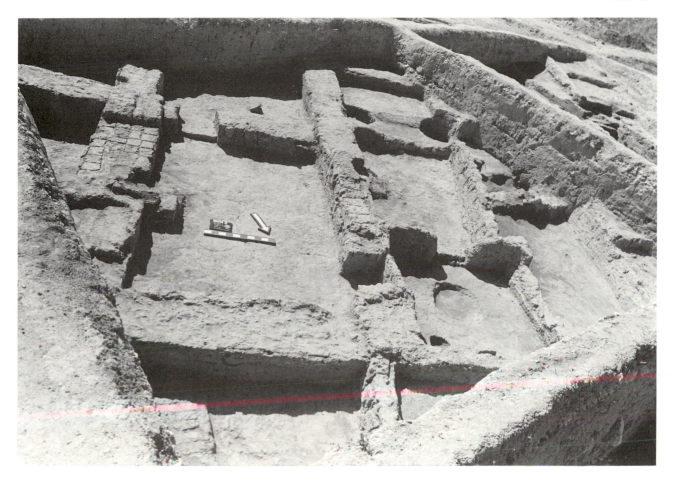

Plate 2.   Architecture of B.L. III: overview of the East and West Unit rooms in U168, looking southwest. The large room visible in the left center portion of the photograph is room 225, with hearth 227 (Plate 7a) set into its eastern wall. The rooms of the "annex" to the East Unit are visible to the immediate right of room 225. The areas in the southwest and northwest corners of the square (rooms 284 and 258 respectively) belong to the West Unit. The area in the northeast corner is part of the North Unit. The East and West Units of B.L. III were used in both the IIIB and IIIA phases of construction.

PLATE 3

Plate 3a. Architecture of B.L. III: Constructional detail of wall 294, U166, looking southeast. The picture is taken from a sounding through alleyway 307. Note the rock foundation for the wall. Wall 294 is the only wall at TUV so far demonstrated to rest on such a substantial stone footing. It forms the exterior wall of the West Unit of the main B.L. III structure and was used in both the IIIB and IIIA phases.

Plate 3b. Architecture of B.L. III: the T168 round structure (feature 315), looking east. This structure had two superimposed "cement"-like floors containing many small pebbles. The beginning of doming in the wall was observed, and the whole structure exhibited a striking red discoloration and hardness suggesting the effects of burning. Use of this structure was limited to the B.L. IIIB phase. Room 320 of the B.L. IIIB South Unit is visible in the background.

PLATE 4

Plate 4a.   Architecture of B.L. II: Room 109 of the North Unit (center of picture) and the Southwest Unit (background). U166, looking southwest. The large plastered pit (feature 130) found in area 386 of the Southwest Unit is strikingly visible.

Plate 4b.   Architecture of B.L. II: the V164 round structure (feature 169), looking south. This structure had three rooms and normal earthen floors.

PLATE 5

Plate 5.   Architecture of B.L. II: the "kitchen" area of the North Unit, V168, looking southeast. The partitioned area in the middle of the picture is room 43. Note storage bin 42 at the right end of that space (see Plate 6a for a detail). Several grinding stone fragments rest on the floor of room 43. Room 36 is the larger room in the upper left portion of the picture. The base of a large storage vessel is clearly visible resting on the floor. Alcove 38, where the base of another storage vessel was found set into a plastered pit (see Plate 9b), is the area immediately in front of the sign board. To the right of alcove 38 is feature 33, an elaborate cobble hearth.

PLATE 6

Plate 6a. Architecture of B.L. II: detail of room 43 of the North Unit, V168, looking southwest. Bin 42 and several grinding stone fragments are clearly visible. The foreground portion of the room has been cleared down to a lower floor level.

Plate 6b. Architecture of B.L. I: double wall 2, V168, looking northwest. Alleyway 16 is to the immediate right of this wall. Further to the right a small portion of double wall 7 is also visible. The square bricks visible in this picture are 36 x 36 cm and the rectangular bricks 18 x 36 cm, the standard brick sizes used throughout B.L. I at TUV.

PLATE 7

Plate 7a.   Feature 227: raised-box hearth. U168, room 225, B.L. III, looking east. This hearth, the most elaborate raised—box hearth at TUV, is built into wall 243. The photo shows the earliest construction phase of hearth 227. Note the slight channel on the top of the hearth and directly below the channel the inset crucible-like cup.

Plate 7b.   Feature 214: domed oven. U168, B.L. III East Unit, room 215, looking east. This oven, built into wall 213, covers an area of c. 66 x 68 cm. Partial doming is evident on the right side. Note the usage of sherds and mud plaster in its construction, as well as the absence of a raised box component.

PLATE 8

Plate 8a.   Feature 182: plastered sherd concentration. T168, B.L. II, looking south. The feature was excavated in 1974; this plate shows the feature as it looked in 1976, following partial sectioning.

Plate 8b.   Feature 302: plastered sherd concentration. T168, B.L. IIIA, looking south. This plate shows the feature after the top plaster layer had been removed and the roughly circular arrangement of underlying sherds was clearly visible.

PLATE 9

Plate 9a.   Feature 199: well pit. U168, B.L. I, room 181, facing southwest. This plate illustrates the stones and sherds which covered the top of the well. The well itself was circular with a diameter of c. 90 cm.

Plate 9b.   Feature 38: pot base in plastered pit. V168, B.L. II North Unit, alcove off room 36, looking southeast. A portion of cobble hearth 33 is visible on the right. For the general context of these features, see Plate 5.

PLATE 10

Plate 10a. Feature 333: drainage pit. V168, stratum 9, facing west. The feature has been partially excavated and sectioned. Note the curving packed mud partition which divides the pit into two unequally sized compartments. The cobbles in the smaller, shadowy, northern compartment have been removed. A section through the cobble fill of the deeper and larger southern compartment is visible. Over 3000 stones were used in the construction of this feature. It originates just *below* an unbroken floor of the B.L. II North Unit.

Plate 10b. Feature 76: possible robbed out foundation trench. V166, looking northeast. The 80 cm wide channel is intrusive into the architecture of the B.L. II North Unit. Note the scattered large rocks resting on the bottom surface of the feature. Erosion in this sector of the TUV mound has removed the stratum of origination for this ditch. It is not, therefore, necessarily Banesh in character.

PLATE 11

Plate 11a.   Features 353 and 131: miscellaneous cobble feature (left) and bin (right). U166, B.L. II Southwest Unit, room 103, facing northwest. Together, the two features fill the entirety of room 103. While it is possible that room 103 was in actuality a giant hearth, no signs of burning or heat were noted.

Plate 11b.   Bullae cluster *in situ*, U166 lot 82, room 309, B.L. IIIA. Bullae mfs 5452, 5453, 6046, 6179, and 6180 were found in this cluster. Both stamp and cylinder seal impressions were found on the bullae of this group.

PLATE 12

Plate 12a. Feature 274: adult burial. V168, southeast quadrant, stratum 10, looking east. The burial is in flexed position with the head oriented slightly north of west. Note the edge of mf 5078, a flaring-sided limestone or plaster bowl, protruding from the balk just to the right of the scale. This individual seems to have been buried in a shroud of cloth or matting (detail on Plate 12b).

Plate 12b. Feature 274: detail of mat or cloth impressions on the skull of the burial shown in Plate 12a.

PLATE 13   CHAFF-TEMPERED WARE: FUNCTIONAL CLASS 12

a.   Low tray. Test trench F lot 7.

b.   Low tray. Test trench F lot 7.

c.   Low tray, probable base diameter 22 cm. U166 lot 48. Room 103, B.L. II, d.c. 37 (tertiary context).

d.   Low tray, probable base diameter 26 cm. U166 lot 48. Room 103, B.L. II, d.c. 37 (tertiary context).

e.   Low tray. V166 lot 39. B.L. II, d.c. 36 (tertiary context).

f.   Low tray. U166 lot 48. Room 103, B.L. II, d.c. 37 (tertiary context).

g.   Low tray. U166 lot 48. Room 103, B.L. II, d.c. 37 (tertiary context).

h.   Low tray. U166 lot 48. Room 103, B.L. II, d.c. 37 (tertiary context).

i.   Low tray. Test trench F lot 5.

j.   Low tray. Test trench F lot 8.

k.   Bevelled-rim bowl. Mf 1725. V164 lot 24. Pit 163, B.L. IIIA, d.c. 22 (secondary context). Previously published as *Iran* XIV fig. 8d.

l.   Bevelled-rim bowl. Rim diameter 15 cm. V164 lot 21, B.L. II room 158, d.c. 37 (tertiary context).

m.   Goblet, rim diameter not measurable. T166 lot 11, B.L. IIIA, trashpile 301, d.c. 23 (secondary context).

n.   Goblet, rim diameter 13 cm. V168 lot 47, B.L. II area 47, d.c. 35 (secondarily admixed context).

o.   Goblet, rim diameter 14 cm. V168 lot 4, stratum 1, d.c. 36 (mixed context).

p.   Goblet, rim diameter 16 cm. V168 lot 6, stratum 3, d.c. 34 (tertiary context).

q.   Goblet, rim diameter 17 cm. T166 lot 13, B.L. IIIA, trashpile 301, d.c. 23 (secondary context).

r.   Goblet, rim diameter 20 cm. U166 lot 6, B.L. I, room 90, d.c. 37 (tertiary context).

s.   Goblet, rim diameter 20 cm. V164 lot 38? (tertiary context).

t.   Pinched rim of goblet. Test trench F.

u.   Base and mid-section of a pedestal-based goblet. Base diameter 6.3 cm. Test trench F.

v.   Base of pedestal-based goblet. Diameter 7 cm. V166 lot 4. Stratum 1, d.c. 32 (tertiary context).

w.   Base of pedestal-based goblet. Diameter 5 cm. T166 lot 13. Trashpile 301, B.L. IIIA, d.c. 23 (secondary context).

x.   Base of pedestal-based goblet. Diameter 6 cm. V166 lot 39. B.L. II, d.c. 36 (tertiary context).

y.   Base of pedestal-based goblet. Diameter 6 cm. V168 lot 51. Area 39, B.L. II, d.c. 35 (secondarily admixed context).

z.   Base of pedestal-based goblet. Diameter 6 cm. V166 lot 39. B.L. II, d.c. 36 (tertiary context).

aa.   Base of pedestal-based goblet. Diameter 8 cm. V168 lot 52. Room 25, B.L. II, d.c. 25 (secondary context).

bb.   Base of pedestal-based goblet. Diameter 7 cm. V166 lot 39. B.L. II, d.c. 36 (tertiary context).

PLATE 13

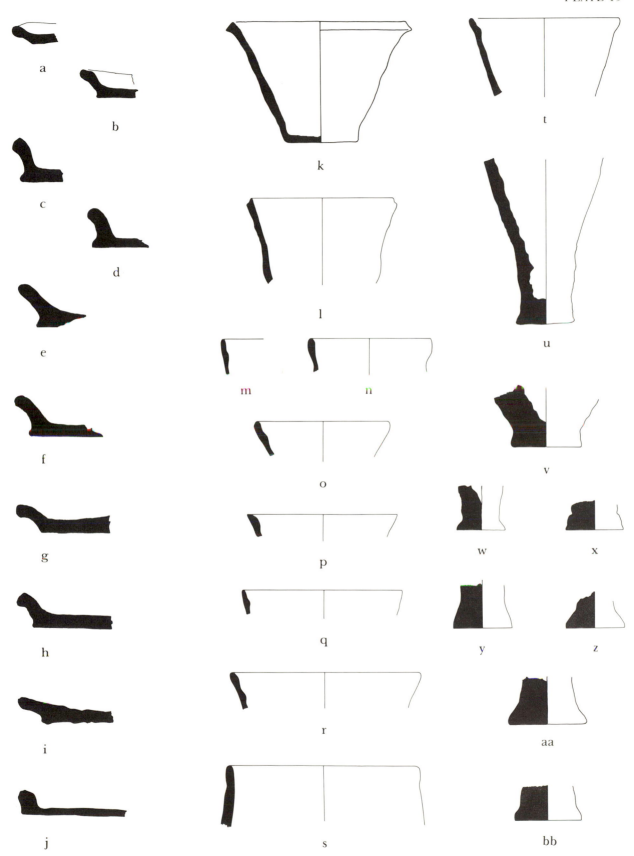

a

b

c

d

e

f

g

h

i

j

k

l

m

n

o

p

q

r

s

t

u

v

w

x

y

z

aa

bb

1:4

PLATE 14   MISCELLANEOUS REGISTERED VESSELS

a. Classes 7 and 20. Mf 1928, carinated ledge rim vessel with elaborate panel of decoration (see b on this plate). Vessel height 34.4 cm. Burnished red surface. Grit temper. Band of decoration on shoulder. U168 lot 41. Courtyard 30, B.L. II, d.c. 37 (secondarily admixed context). Previously published as *Iran* XIV fig. 9 a.

b. Detail of decoration on pot mf 1928. Relief ridge at top of panel. Below ridge, a complex design in maroon and white paint of meanders, dots, and crosses formed by triangles. Previously published as *Iran* XIV fig. 9 b.

c. Class 12. Mf 5084, nearly complete low tray. Cross-section. Straw temper. U168 lot 145. Room 284, B.L. IIIA, d.c. 35 (secondarily admixed context).

d. Plan view of mf 5084 (item c above).

PLATE 14

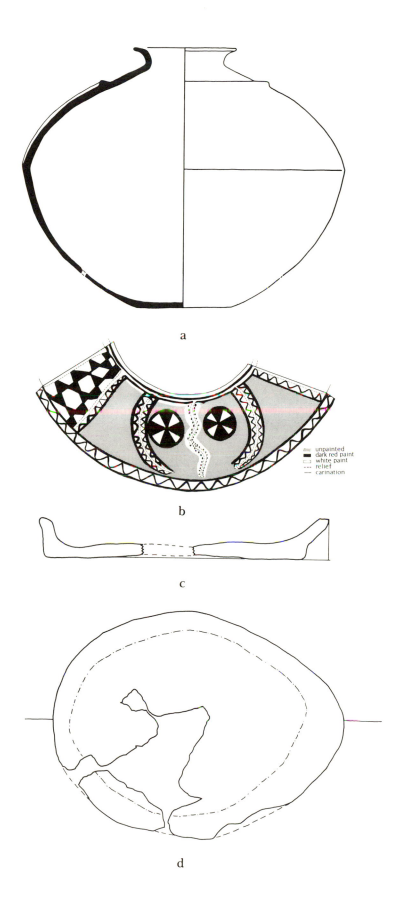

a

b

unpainted
dark red paint
white paint
relief
carination

c

d

1:4

PLATE 15   HOLE-MOUTH VESSELS AND UNRESTRICTED SPECIAL FORMS

a. Class 18. Mf 1457, restricted vessel with hole-mouth rim and small tubular spout. Rim diameter 4.2 cm. Height 8.1 cm. Base diameter 2.8 cm. Exterior slipped orange-buff. Grit temper. V168 lot 42. Room 45, B.L. II, d.c. 35 (tertiary context).

b. Class 18. Mf. 3834, hole-mouth vessel. Plain round rim, diameter 11.3 cm. Base diameter 5 cm. Burnished gray ware. White crystalline temper. V168 lots 115, 111, 118. Area 375, B.L. IIIA, d.c. 35, 36 and 51 (tertiary context).

c. Class 7. Burnished plate. Direct rounded rim, diameter 28 cm. Base diameter 13.5 cm. Specular hematite temper. V168 lot 39. Room 36, B.L. II, d.c. 35 (tertiary context).

d. Class 7. Hole-mouth vessel. Rim diameter 23 cm. Grit temper. V166 lot 60. Area 366, stratum 9, d.c. 23 (secondary context).

e. Class 10. Hole-mouth vessel. Rim diameter 35 cm. Grit temper. V166 lot 46. Cleanup, d.c. 41 (mixed context).

f. Class 7. Mf 1310, grill. Only grill found at TUV. Diameter 39 cm. Height 5 cm. A high tray with a series of circular holes punched through flat lower surface. Numerous small holes radiate from largest hole in center. Grit and straw temper. V168 lot 14. Alleyway 16, B.L. I, d.c. 25 (secondary context).

g. Class 18. Hole-mouth vessel. Rim diameter 6 cm. Grit temper. V168 lot 152. Area 374, stratum 9, d.c. 34 (tertiary context).

h. Classes 18 and 20. Mf 1455, vertical-walled cup. Direct rounded rim, diameter 6.6 cm. Height 6.9 cm. Light red to reddish yellow paste, grit temper. Entire cup gray slipped. Vertical maroon stripes over white paint or slip on exterior. U168 lot 40. Stratum 6A, d.c. 34 (tertiary context). Previously published as *Iran* XIV fig. 6 f.

i. Classes 18 and 20. Mf 1461, vertical-walled cup. Direct rounded rim, diameter 5.3 cm. Height 5.5 cm. Light red-reddish yellow paste, grit temper. Vertical maroon stripes over white slip on exterior. V168 lot 44. Room 43, B.L. II, d.c. 37 (tertiary context). Previously published as *Iran* XIV fig. 6 g.

j. Class 18. Flaring-sided cup. Direct rounded rim, diameter 12 cm. Height 7 cm. Base diameter 4.2 cm. Chaff temper. U168 lot 28. Courtyard 30, B.L. II, d.c. 35 (tertiary context). Previously published as *Iran* XIV fig. 8 e.

k. Class 18. Mf 1450, flaring-sided cup. Direct rounded rim, diameter 12.9 cm. Height 6.7 cm. Straw and grit tempered. Pits in surface. U166 lot 17. Room 102, B.L. II, d.c. 25 (secondary context). Previously published as *Iran* XIV fig. 8 f.

l. Class 18. Mf 1451, flaring-sided cup. Direct rounded rim, diameter 11.7 cm. Height 5.9 cm. Straw temper. Pits in surface. U166 lot 26. Room 103, B.L. II, d.c. 37 (tertiary context). Previously published as *Iran* XIV fig. 8 g.

m. Class 18. Mf 1723, flaring-sided cup. Direct rounded rim, diameter 12.5 cm. Height 8 cm. Straw temper. Pits in surface. V168 lot 37. Courtyard 30, B.L. II, d.c. 37 (tertiary context). Previously published as *Iran* XIV fig. 8 h.

n. Class 18. Flaring-sided cup. Direct rounded rim, diameter 11.4 cm. String-cut base, diameter 4.5 cm. Exterior light brown to light orange, somewhat smoothed. Gray core. Chaff and sparse fine grit temper. V166 lot 39. B.L. II, d.c. 36 (tertiary context).

o. Class 18. Flaring-sided cup base, diameter 4.6 cm. String-cut. Smoothed exterior, light orange through red-orange to brown. Partially gray core. Densely tempered with medium-sized grit and lime pops. V164 lot 18. Stratum 1, d.c. 32 (tertiary context).

p. Class 18. Flaring-sided cup base, diameter 3.5 cm. String-cut. Smoothed light orange exterior. Gray core. Grit tempered with lime pops. V168 lot 34. Room 36, B.L. II, d.c. 35 (secondarily admixed context).

q. Class 7. High tray. Direct rounded rim, diameter 44 cm. Handmade. Surface altered. Grit temper. Tray also shown in plan view. V168 lot 5. Room 10, B.L. I, d.c. 23 (secondary context).

Comparable registered item not illustrated: Class 7. Mf 1719, burnished plate (cf. item c above). U168 lot 38. B.L. I, d.c. 36 (mixed context).

PLATE 15

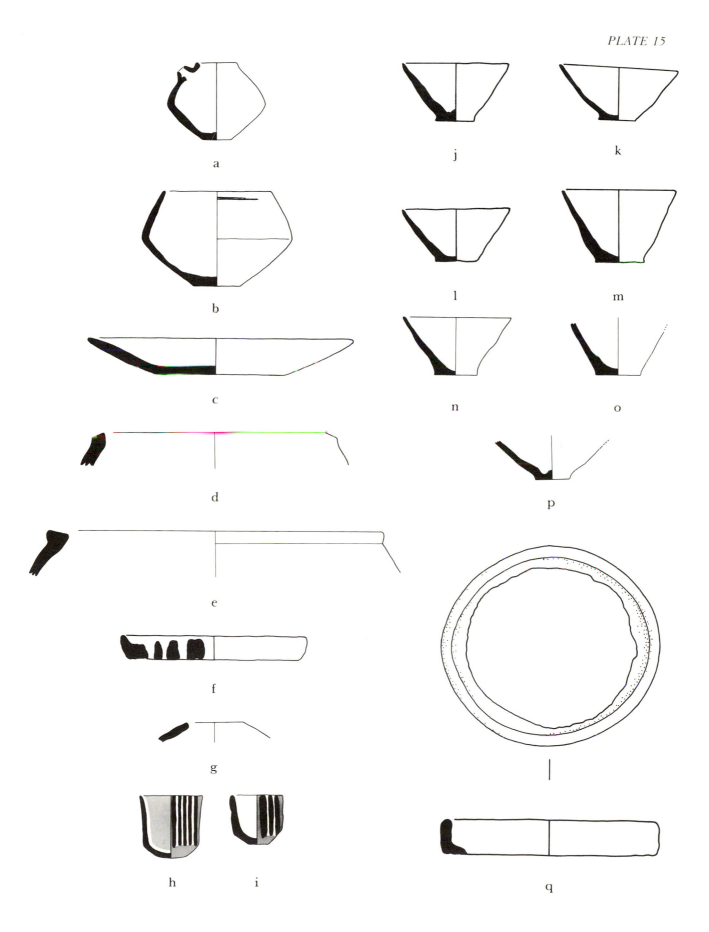

1:4

PLATE 16   RESTRICTED VESSELS WITH VERTICAL ROUNDED AND EVERTED RIMS

a. Not assigned. Vertical rounded rim, diameter unknown. Grit temper. V164 lot 23. Stratum 1, d.c. 32 (tertiary context).

b. Class 7. Vertical rounded rim, diameter 10 cm. Probably from restricted form. Multiple incised bands on neck. Grit temper. U168 lot 158. Room 258, B.L. IIIA, d.c. 35 (tertiary context).

c. Class 10. Everted rim vessel, diameter 17 cm. Light brown/orange buffware. Traces of thin black slip. Fine grit temper. V166 lot 39. B.L. II, d.c. 36 (tertiary context).

d. Class 10. Everted rim, diameter 18 cm. U166 lot 94. Area 308, B.L. IIIA, d.c. 35 (secondarily admixed context).

e. Class 10. Everted rim, diameter 20 cm. Grit temper. U168 lot 158. Room 258, B.L. IIIA, d.c. 35 (tertiary context).

f. Classes 10 and 20. Everted rim, diameter 22 cm. Maroon painted stripe over smoothed light orange buff surface. Grit temper. V166 lot 60. Area 366, stratum 9, d.c. 23 (secondary context).

g. Class 10. Everted rim, diameter 24 cm. Light orange, slightly smoothed surface. Fine grit temper. U164 lot 6. Stratum 1, d.c. 34 (tertiary context).

h. Class 10. Everted rim, diameter 29 cm. Light orange surface. Traces of thin black slip on exterior and interior. Fine to medium grit temper. V166 lot 39. B.L. II, d.c. 36 (tertiary context).

i. Class 10. Everted rim, diameter 26 cm. Grit temper. U168 lot 31. Courtyard 30, B.L. II, d.c. 35 (secondarily admixed context).

j. Class 10. Everted rim, diameter 30 cm. Incised line on neck. Grit temper. U168 lot 31. Courtyard 30, B.L. II, d.c. 35 (secondarily admixed context).

k. Class 10. Everted rim, diameter 38 cm. Grit temper. V166 lot 67. Area 338, B.L. IIIA, d.c. 42 (secondarily admixed context).

l. Class 10. Everted rim, diameter 37 cm. Grit temper. U166 lot 25. Room 102, B.L. II, d.c. 37 (secondarily admixed context).

m. Classes 10 and 20. Everted rim, diameter 55 cm. Design in maroon paint. Sloppy execution of design; meanders vary considerably in width. Grit temper. U168 lot 30. Courtyard 30, B.L. II, d.c. 35 (tertiary context).

PLATE 16

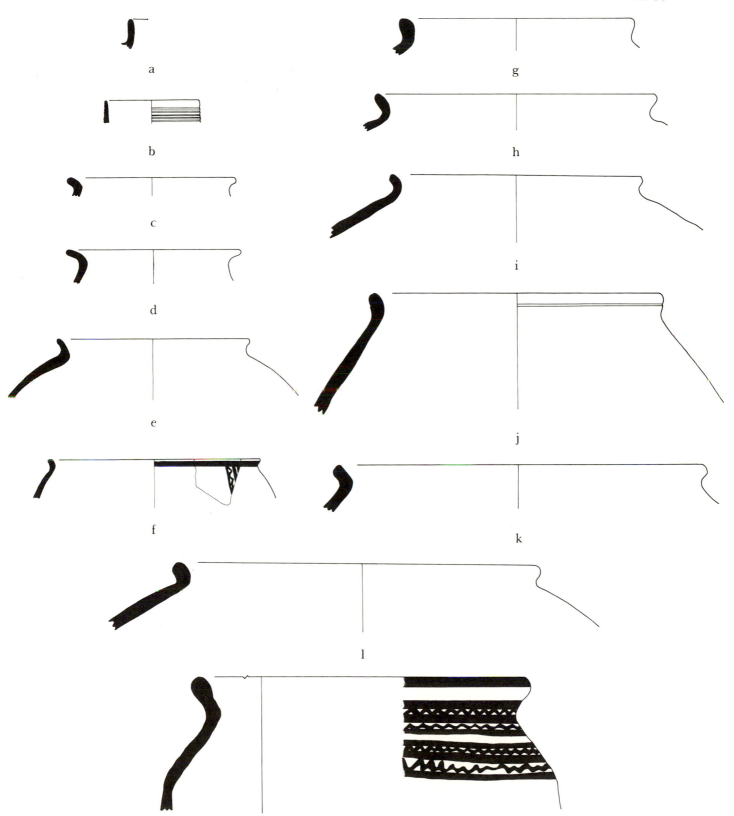

1:4

PLATE 17   VARIATION IN EVERTED RIMS

a.   Classes 18 and 20. Mf 1256, small pot. Height 7.5 cm. Flattened base with nipple on interior. Beige slip on exterior and interior. Chevron design in fugitive maroon paint on exterior between lip and carination. Grit temper. U168 lot 22. Well 199, B.L. I, d.c. 22 (secondary context).

b.   Class 7. Everted rim, diameter 8 cm. Burnished brownish-orange buff ware. Burnish extends about 1 cm over rim into interior. Black core. Fine grit temper. Two low-relief lugs appear on sherds; probably a total of four equally spaced lugs on whole pot. V168 lot 99. Trashpile 241, B.L. IIIA, d.c. 23 (secondary context).

c.   Class 7. Everted rim, diameter 12 cm. Raised spine on sherd. Grit temper. U168 lot 144. Pit 220, stratum 9, d.c. 22 (secondary context).

d.   Classes 7 and 20. Everted rim, diameter 13 cm. Dark purple paint design over a light brown to light orange surface. Gray core. Dense grit temper of varying sizes. U166 lot 1. Surface pickup, d.c. 31 (mixed context).

e.   Class 7. Simple everted rim, diameter 10 cm. Smooth chocolate-colored surface. Coarse grit temper. Test trench F lot 6.

f.   Classes 10 and 20. No registration number. Everted rim vessel, diameter 21 cm. Height 42 cm. Base diameter 42 cm. Decoration confined to shoulder zone. Four bent nose-lugs connected by relief ridge. Below lugs, a band of geometric decoration in dark red and white paint over dark gray slip. Grit and straw temper. V168 lot 48. Room 43, B.L. II, d.c. 25 (secondary context). Previously published as *Iran* XIV fig. 7 a.

g.   Class 7. Mf 1449, everted rim vessel. Height 13.3 cm. Grit temper. U168 lot 19. Well 199, B.L. I, d.c. 22 (secondary context). Previously published as *Iran* XIV fig. 7 b.

h.   Class 7. Everted rim, diameter 10 cm. Grit temper. V168 lot 152. Area 374, stratum 9, d.c. 34 (tertiary context).

i.   Class 7. Everted rim, diameter 13 cm. Dark orange buffware. Traces of burnishing. Fine grit temper. V166 lot 4. Stratum 1, d.c. 34 (tertiary context).

j.   Class 10. Everted rim, diameter 21 cm. Orange/red buffware. Traces of orange slip on exterior and interior. Medium grit temper. V166 lot 9. Stratum 1, d.c. 34 (tertiary context).

k.   Class 10. Everted rim, diameter 24 cm. Light orange buffware. Traces of black slip on rim and interior. Light gray core. Fine gray temper. V166 lot 39. B.L. II, d.c. 36 (tertiary context).

l.   Class 10. Everted rim, diameter 24 cm. Light orange paste, heavily weathered surface. Medium grit temper. U164 lot 6. Stratum 1, d.c. 34 (tertiary context).

m.   Class 10. Everted rim, diameter 27 cm. Orange buffware with gray core. Traces of thin black slip. Fine lime(?) temper. V166 lot 39. B.L. II, d.c. 36 (tertiary context).

n.   Class 10. Everted rim, diameter 26 cm. Orange buffware. Traces of thin black slip on exterior and interior. Fine to medium grit temper. V166 lot 39. B.L. II, d.c. 36 (tertiary context).

o.   Class 10. Everted rim, diameter 25 cm. Orange buffware with gray core. Smoothed surface. Fine to medium grit temper. V166 lot 39. B.L. II, d.c. 36 (tertiary context).

Comparable registered items not illustrated: Class 7. Mf 1927, everted rim vessel. Plain everted rim, globular body, rounded base. The vessel has a broken tubular spout standing nearly straight up above the shoulder. U166 lot 61. B.L. II, d.c. 35 (tertiary context).

Classes 7 and 20. Mf 1930, everted rim vessel. Height 32.1 cm. Egg-shaped pot with narrow part of egg at flat base. Broad part of egg is at top with a small opening of about 11 cm where the short neck and rim join pot. Surface covered with dark red slip/paint. Three black bands on shoulder. U168 lot 61. Room 284, B.L. IIIA, d.c. 35 (secondarily admixed context).

PLATE 17

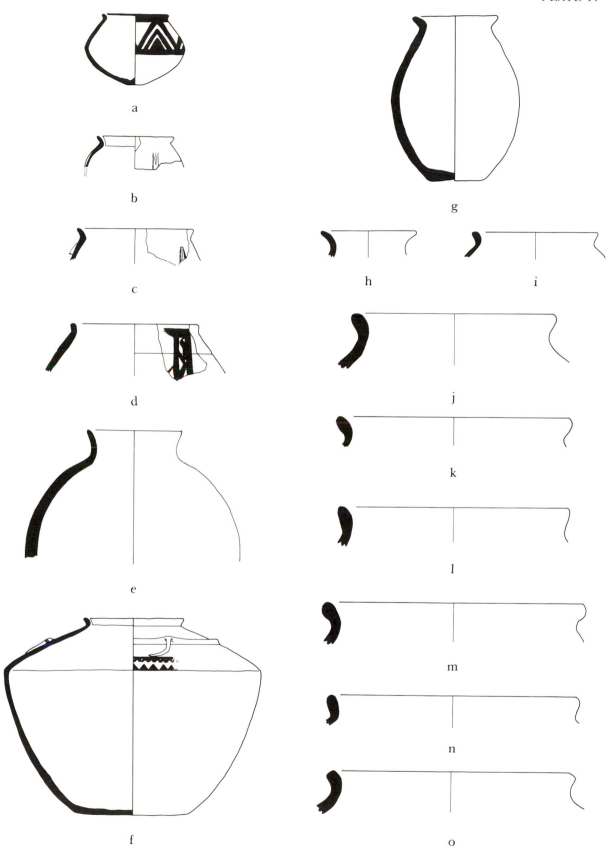

a

b

c

d

e

f

g

h

i

j

k

l

m

n

o

1:4

PLATE 18   RESTRICTED VESSELS, PRIMARILY WITH EXPANDED AND FOLDED RIMS

a. Class 7. Square everted rim, diameter 11 cm. Light brown-buff surface. Medium to coarse grit temper. U166 lot 148. Room 103, B.L. II, d.c. 37 (tertiary context).

b. Classes 7 and 20. Expanded rim, diameter 12.5 cm. Two painted bands on shoulder. Grit temper. V166 lot 56. Stratum 8c, d.c. 36 (tertiary context).

c. Classes 7 and 20. Mf 1189, expanded rim vessel, diameter 13 cm. Height 16.1 cm. Ring base. A white band of paint or slip from rim to below carination. Design of bands, chevrons, and a meander in maroon paint superimposed over this band. Grit temper. V168 lot 13. Room 10, B.L. I, d.c. 23 (secondary context). Previously published as *Iran* XIV fig. 7 d.

d. Classes 18 (and 20?). Expanded rim, spouted vessel form. Orange buff ware. Buff slipped, possible traces of painted bands at carination. V168 lot 42. Room 45, B.L. II, d.c. 35 (tertiary context). Previously published as *Iran* XIV fig. 6 a.

e. Class 10. Expanded rim, diameter 26 cm. Grit temper. U168 lot 19. Well 199, B.L. I, d.c. 22 (secondary context). Previously published as *Iran* XIV fig. 8 j.

f. Class 7. Folded rim, diameter 13 cm. Light orange to brown smoothed surface. No visible temper. V166 lot 9. Stratum 1, d.c. 34 (tertiary context).

g. Class 10. Folded rim, diameter 23 cm. Light orange, slightly smoothed surface. Fine to medium grit temper. U164 lot 6. Stratum 1, d.c. 34 (tertiary context).

h. Class 10. Folded rim, orange buff ware with gray core. Smoothed surface. Dense, coarse grit temper. V166 lot 39. B.L. II, d.c. 36 (tertiary context).

i. Class 10. Folded rim, diameter may be greater than shown (32 cm). Grit temper. V166 lot 16. Area 67, B.L. II, d.c. 35 (tertiary context).

j. Class 10. Folded rim, diameter 34 cm. Grit temper. V168 lot 86. B.L. II, d.c. 36 (tertiary context).

k. Class 10. Folded rim, diameter 38 cm. Grit temper. V168 lot 41. Area 39, B.L. II, d.c. 35 (secondarily admixed context).

l. Class 10. Folded rim, diameter 43 cm. Grit temper. U166 lot 69. Pit 285, stratum 9, d.c. 22 (secondary context).

PLATE 18

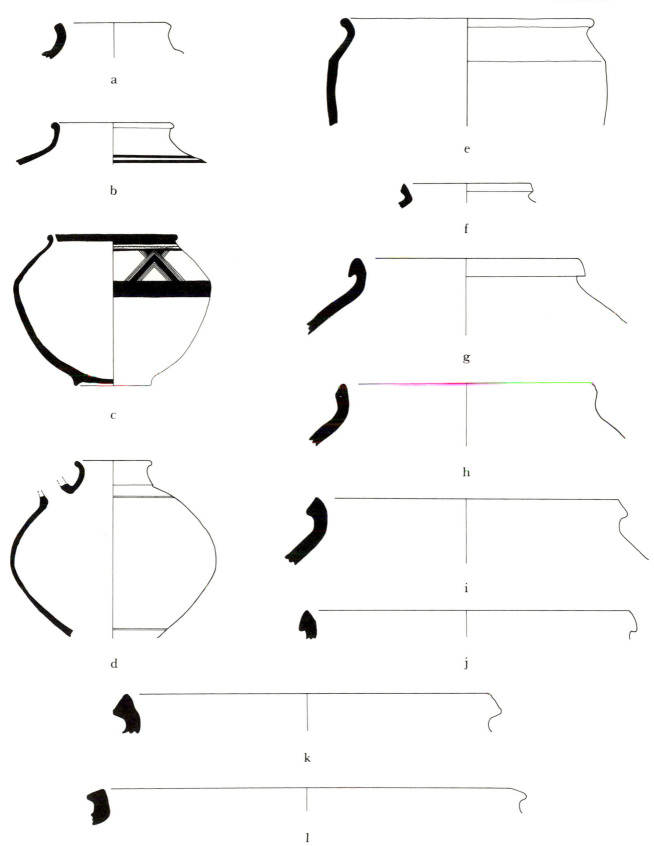

a

b

c

d

e

f

g

h

i

j

k

l

1:4

a.   Class 12. Mf 1458, miniature ledge rim vessel. Height 7.7 cm. Flat base. Gray slip on exterior and interior. White paint/slip applied over gray slip from below rim to carination. Grit temper. V168 lot 38. Room 32, B.L. II, d.c. 35 (secondarily admixed context). Previously published as *Iran* XIV fig. 6 b.

b.   Class 18. Ledge rim, diameter 6 cm. Grit temper. U166 lot 93. Trashpile 301, B.L. IIIA, d.c. 23 (secondary context).

c.   Classes 7 and 20. Mf 5055, ledge-rim pot. Rim diameter 8.6 cm. Height 11.8 cm. Base flat on exterior, but has an interior bump. Three stripes in black paint on upper body. Traces of two reddish brown bands on inside flare of rim. Heavy grit temper. V168 lot 143. Burial 274, B.L. IIIB, d.c. 13 (primary context).

d.   Class 10. Ledge rim, diameter 18 cm. Grit temper. U166 lot 25. Room 102, B.L. II, d.c. 37 (secondarily admixed context).

e.   Class 10. Ledge rim, diameter 18 cm. Grit temper. U166 lot 25. Room 102, B.L. II, d.c. 37 (secondarily admixed context).

f.   Class 10. Drooping ledge rim, diameter 19 cm. Grit temper. U168 lot 85. Room 234, B.L. IIIA, d.c. 35 (tertiary context).

g.   Classes 7 and 20. Mf 1453, ledge rim vessel. Diameter 12 cm. Height 19 cm. Beige slip with band of white paint on shoulder crossed by four maroon horizontal bands. Flat top surface of rim is also painted white with maroon bands across it. Grit temper. U168 lot 39. Courtyard 30, B.L. II, d.c. 35. Previously published as *Iran* XIV fig. 7 c.

h.   Class 7. Ledge rim, diameter 8 cm. Slightly smoothed light orange to light brown surface. Tiny holes visible in paste. U164 lot 6. Stratum 1, d.c. 34 (tertiary context).

i.   Class 7. Vessel with "incipient" ledge rim (intermediate between everted and ledge rim form). Rim diameter 9 cm. Grit temper. U168 lot 152. Well 199, B.L. I, d.c. 22 (secondary context).

j.   Class 7. Ledge rim, diameter 9 cm. Smoothed orange surface. Band of dark brown slip or paint inside rim. Fine grit temper. V166 lot 4. B.L. I, d.c. 34 (tertiary context).

k.   Class 7. Ledge rim, diameter 13 cm. V168 lot 101. Trashpile 241, B.L. IIIA, d.c. 23 (secondary context).

l.   Class 7. Ledge rim, diameter 12 cm. Buffware with orange slip. Grit temper. T166 lot 13. Courtyard 30, B.L. II, d.c. 35 (tertiary context).

m.   Class 7. Ledge rim, diameter 12 cm. Grit temper. U168 lot 94. Area 183, B.L. II, d.c. 29 (tertiary context).

n.   Class 7. Ledge rim, diameter 12 cm. Red-orange, slightly smoothed surface. Gray core. Fine to medium grit temper. U166 lot 6. Room 90, B.L. I, d.c. 37 (tertiary context).

o.   Class 7. Ledge rim, diameter 13 cm. Orange buffware. Remnants of dark slip on exterior and inside rim. Fine grit temper. V166 lot 4. Stratum 1, d.c. 34 (tertiary context).

p.   Class 7. Ledge rim, diameter 13 cm. Light orange, slightly smoothed surface. Fine grit temper. V166 lot 4. Stratum 1, d.c. 34 (tertiary context).

q.   Class 7. Ledge rim, diameter 13 cm. Grit temper. U166 lot 48. Room 103, B.L. II, d.c. 37 (tertiary context).

r.   Class 7. Ledge rim, diameter 12 cm. Grit temper. U168 lot 39. B.L. I, d.c. 36 (tertiary context).

s.   Class 7. Ledge rim, diameter 11.5 cm. Orange slip on exterior. Incised line on shoulder. Tubular spout. Grit temper. V168 lot 118. Area 375, B.L. IIIA, d.c. 51 (tertiary context).

t.   Classes 7 and 20. Ledge rim, diameter 13 cm. Orange slip on light orange to light brown body. Cream slip on shoulder, with two bands of dark brown or light black paint. Traces of light black streaking on neck. Grit temper. V168 lot 152. Area 374, stratum 9, d.c. 34 (tertiary context).

Comparable registered item not illustrated: Class 7. Mf 1926, partial vessel with ledge rim, diameter 11.4 cm. Globular vessel with base missing. Red slip on exterior, with remnants of two black painted stripes at base of neck and wider black band above shoulder. Probably a further design in black on shoulder below wider band, but pattern is no longer understandable. Grit temper. U168, well 199, B.L. I, d.c. 22 (secondary context).

PLATE 19

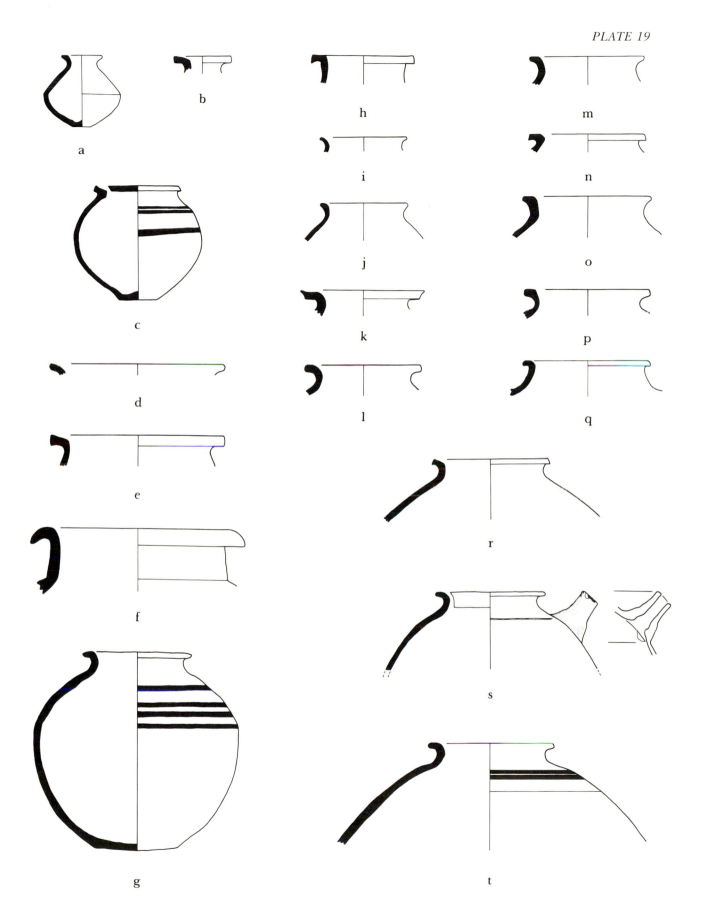

PLATE 20 BOWLS WITH DIRECT AND LEDGE RIMS

a. Class 18. Mf 1729, bowl with square direct rim. Height 3.3 cm. Rim diameter 4.5 cm. Base diameter 3 cm. Smoothed surface. Grit temper. V164 lot 131. Pit 165, B.L. IIIB, d.c. 22 (secondary context). Previously published as *Iran* XIV fig. 6 h.

b. Class 18. Mf 1721, bowl with truncated direct rim. Height 3.8 cm. Rim diameter 8.2 cm. Base diameter 3.5 cm. String-cut base. Paste shows lime pops and small holes. V166 lot 9. Stratum 1, d.c. 34 (tertiary context). Previously published as *Iran* XIV fig. 6 c.

c. Class 18. Direct rounded rim, diameter 15 cm. Grit temper. V166 lot 60. Area 366, stratum 9, d.c. 23 (secondary context).

d. Class 18. Direct rounded rim, diameter 15 cm. Black painted stripes. Grit temper. U168 lot 118. Room 247, B.L. IIIA, d.c. 26 (secondary context).

e. Class 7 or 18. Incised direct rounded rim, diameter unknown. Incised sides. Orange slip on light orange grit tempered ware. Angle of stance may be slightly distorted by rim incisions. V166 lot 1. Surface pickup, d.c. 32 (mixed context).

f. Class 7. Direct rounded rim, diameter 22 cm. Grit temper. U168 lot 63. Clean-up, d.c. 41 (mixed context).

g. Class 10. Direct rounded rim, diameter 34 cm. Incised sides. Grit temper. V168 lot 158. Feature 333, stratum 9, d.c. 36 (tertiary context).

h. Classes 18 and 20. Mf. 1459, carinated ledge rim bowl. Height 5.5 cm. Rim diameter 11.9 cm. Base diameter 2 cm. Gray slip on exterior and part of rim. Maroon stripes on rim. Grit temper. U168 lot 39. B.L. I, d.c. 36 (mixed context). Previously published as *Iran* XIV fig. 6 d.

i. Class 18. Ledge rim, diameter 16 cm. Maroon stripe. Grit temper. V168 lot 109. Area 370, B.L. IIIA, d.c. 35 (secondarily admixed context).

j. Classes 7 and 20. Direct rounded rim, diameter 25 cm. Light brown exterior surface, light orange interior surface. Grit temper of medium density and mixed coarseness. Faint indications of painted bands on exterior and interior. U166 lot 1. Surface pickup, d.c. 32 (mixed context).

k. Class 7. Direct rounded rim, diameter 26 cm. Mixed straw and grit temper. V168 lot 104. Trashpile 241, B.L. IIIA, d.c. 23 (secondary context).

l. Class 10. Incised direct rounded rim, diameter 31 cm. Light orange ware with encrusted surface and gray core. Coarse grit temper of medium density with lime pops. V166 lot 12. Stratum 1, d.c. 34 (mixed context).

m. Class 10. Ledge rim, diameter 35 cm. Light orange ware, slightly smoothed surface. Grit temper with some straw. V166 lot 39. B.L. II, d.c. 36 (tertiary context).

n. Classes 10 and 20. Ledge rim, diameter 41 cm. Maroon painted design. U168 lot 31. Courtyard 30, B.L. II, d.c. 35 (secondarily admixed context).

PLATE 20

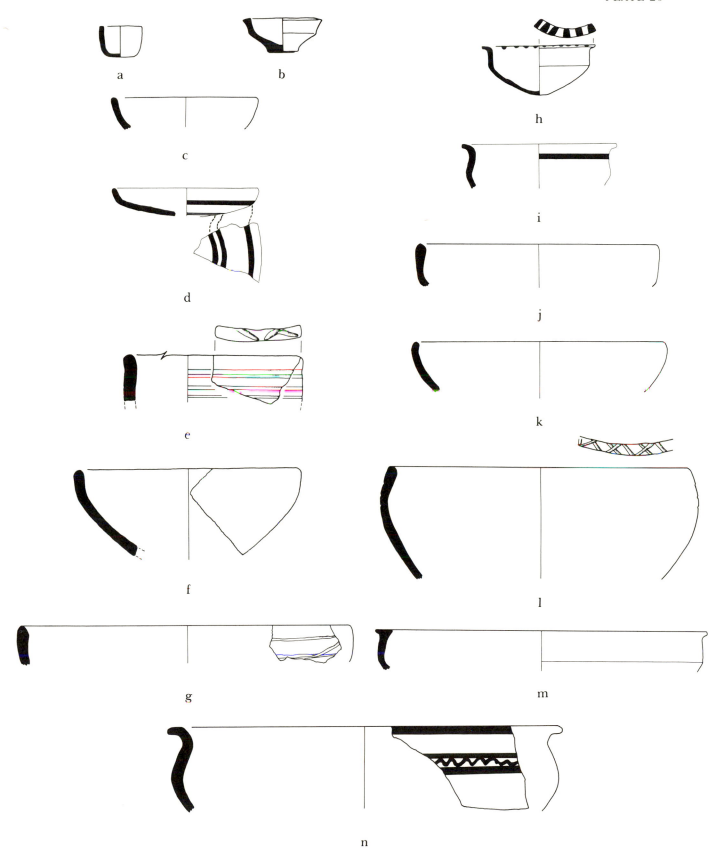

1:4

PLATE 21   EXPANDED RIM BOWLS

a. Class 18. Exteriorally expanded rim, diameter 11 cm. Grit temper. U166 lot 93. Trashpile 301, B.L. IIIA, d.c. 23 (secondary context).

b. Classes 18 and 20. Exteriorally expanded rim, diameter 15 cm. Two black painted bands on slightly smoothed orange surface. Slightly gray core. Fine grit temper. V164 lot 23. Stratum 1, d.c. 32 (tertiary context).

c. Class 18. Exteriorally expanded rim, diameter 16 cm. Grit temper. T168 lot 24. Pit 299, B.L. IIIA, d.c. 22 (mixed secondary context).

d. Classes 18 and 20. Exteriorally expanded rim, diameter 18 cm. Maroon band on exterior. Grit temper. V168 lot 123. Area 376, B.L. IIIB, d.c. 35 (tertiary context).

e. Class 18. Exteriorally expanded rim, diameter 20 cm. Grit temper. V166 lot 46. Cleanup, d.c. 41 (tertiary context).

f. Class 7. Exteriorally expanded rim, diameter 22 cm. Grit temper. U168 lot 89. Room 225, B.L. IIIA, d.c. 51 (tertiary context).

g. Class 7. Exteriorally expanded rim, diameter 26 cm. Brown, slightly smoothed surface. Fine grit temper. V168 lot 51. Area 39, B.L. II, d.c. 35 (secondarily admixed context).

h. Class 10. Exteriorally expanded rim, diameter 33 cm. Grit temper. U166 lot 69. Pit 185, stratum 9, d.c. 22 (secondary context).

i. Class 7. Exteriorally expanded rim, diameter 23.5 cm. Grit and straw temper. Pits in surface. V168 lot 24. Stratum 1, d.c. 36 (tertiary context). Previously published in *Iran* XIV fig. 8 b.

j. Class 7. Mf 1452, bilaterally expanded rim vessel, maximum diameter 29 cm. Height nearly 11 cm. Flat base diameter 6 cm. Rough exterior and interior surfaces. Grit temper. U166 lot 17. Room 102, B.L. II, d.c. 25 (secondary context). Previously published as *Iran* XIV fig. 8 c.

k. Class 7. Bilaterally expanded rim, diameter 25 cm. Orange surface; gray core. Grit temper. V168 lot 37. Courtyard 30, B.L. II, d.c. 37 (tertiary context).

l. Class 7. Bilaterally expanded rim, interior diameter 27 cm. Light orange smoothed surface. Gray core. Medium grit temper with scattered lime pops. V168 lot 34. Room 36, B.L. II, d.c. 35 (secondarily admixed context).

m. Class 7. Exteriorally expanded rim, diameter 27 cm. Grit temper. U168 lot 31. Courtyard 30, B.L. II, d.c. 35 (secondarily admixed context).

PLATE 21

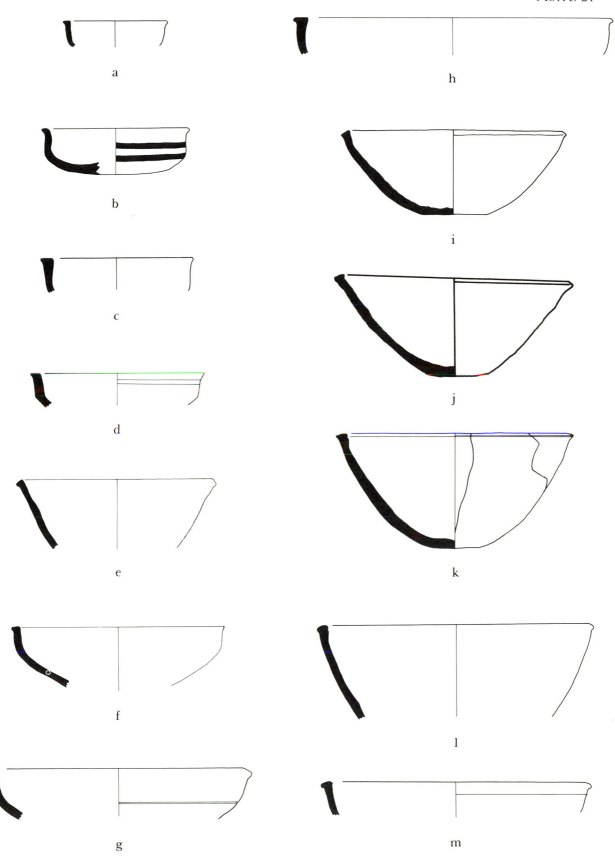

a

b

c

d

e

f

g

h

i

j

k

l

m

1:4

PLATE 22   BASE SHERDS*

a. Class 12. Probable straight-sided goblet base. Diameter 6 cm. Chaff temper. U166 lot 93. Trashpile 301, B.L. IIIA, d.c. 23 (secondary context).

b. Class 12. Possible straight-sided goblet base. Base diameter 7 cm. Rough exterior, light orange to light brown; some gray in core. Straw temper. V164 lot 23?

c. Class 12. Probable straight-sided goblet base, diameter 7.5 cm. U166 lot 69. Pit 285, stratum 9, d.c. 22 (secondary context).

d. Not assigned. Flat base, diameter 4 cm. Medium orange smoothed surface. Light gray core. Medium gray temper. V164 lot 23. Stratum 1, d.c. 32 (tertiary context).

e. Class 18. Flat base, possibly flaring-sided cup. Diameter 5 cm. Light orange slightly smoothed surface; gray core. Straw temper. V164 lot 23. Stratum 1, d.c. 32 (tertiary context).

f. Class 18. Probable cup base. Diameter 4 cm. T168 lot 48. Cleanup, d.c. 41 (tertiary context).

g. Not assigned. Base diameter 7 cm. V168 lot 142? Area 377, B.L. IIIA, d.c. 35 (secondarily admixed context).

h. Not assigned. Flat base, diameter 12 cm. Slightly smoothed brown surface. Traces of slip or paint. Medium grit temper. Single depression on one side just as it joins the base. V164 lot 23. Stratum 1, d.c. 32 (tertiary context).

i. Not assigned. Flat base, diameter 11 cm. Orange to brown smoothed exterior surface; gray core. Straw temper with some very fine grit inclusions. U166 lot 48. Room 103, B.L. II, d.c. 37 (tertiary context).

j. Not assigned. Ring base, diameter 10 cm. Traces of paint or slip on undersurface of base. Grit temper. V166 lot 60. Area 366, stratum 9, d.c. 23 (secondary context).

k. Not assigned. Flat base, diameter 10 cm. Brown to orange smoothed surface. Medium grit temper. V164 lot 23. Stratum 1, d.c. 32 (tertiary context).

l. Not assigned. Flat base on carinated form. Base diameter 6 cm. U166 lot 147. Area 308, B.L. IIIB, d.c. 40 (tertiary context).

m. Not assigned. Slightly rounded base, diameter 9 cm. Medium brown slightly smoothed surface. Coarse ware. Chaff temper. V166 lot 39. B.L. II, d.c. 36 (tertiary context).

n. Not assigned. Flat base, diameter 15 cm. Light brown surface. Very fine grit temper. U166 lot 48. Room 103, B.L. II, d.c. 37 (tertiary context).

o. Not assigned. Basin with straight sides on ring base, diameter 18 cm. U166 lot 133. B.L. II, d.c. 36 (tertiary context).

p. Not assigned. Flat base, diameter 9 cm. U166 lot 25. Room 102, B.L. II, d.c. 37 (secondarily admixed context).

q. Not assigned. Straight-sided basin. Base diameter at least 40 cm. U166 lot 93. Trashpile 301, B.L. IIIA, d.c. 23 (secondary context).

* In most instances base sherds cannot be assigned to a functional class.

PLATE 22

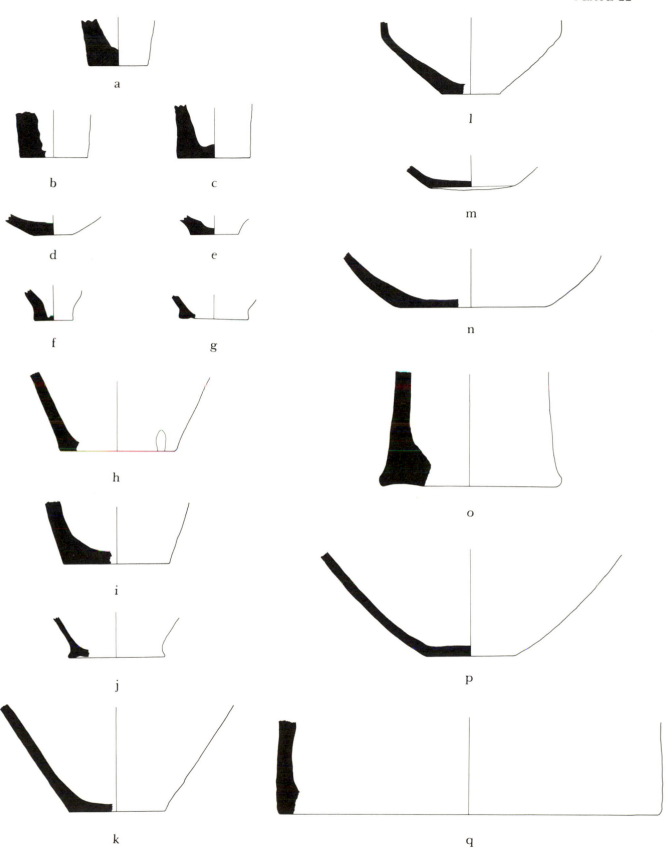

a

b

c

d

e

f

g

h

i

j

k

l

m

n

o

p

q

a. Class 20. Body sherd with bas-relief step design and possible remnants of dark red paint on reddish surface. Grit temper. V168 lot 27. Area 18, stratum 6A, d.c. 34 (tertiary context).

b. Class 20. Body sherd with raised rope decoration and two light black/gray painted stripes on smoothed medium orange surface. Very fine grit temper. Holes visible in paste. U168 lot 7. Room 203, B.L. I, d.c. 37 (secondarily admixed context).

c. Not assigned. Trough spout. Grit temper. U166 lot 93. Trashpile 301, B.L. IIIA, d.c. 23 (secondary context).

d. Not assigned. Godin-IV style rim sherd, diameter 12 cm. Unrestricted vessel form with square direct rim. Only example found at TUV. Slightly burnished exterior of light brown to grayish brown; grayish brown smoothed interior. Light gray core. Compact paste with fine grit temper. Remnants of white substance found in stippled wedges indicated on drawing. V164 lot 23. Stratum 1, d.c. 32 (tertiary context).

e. Class 20. Body sherd with incised line crossed by finger nail impressions. Grit temper. V168 lot 118. Area 375, B.L. IIIA, d.c. 51 (tertiary context).

f. Not assigned. Loose round handle. Grit temper. U168 lot 116. Room 247, B.L. IIIA, d.c. 42 (secondarily admixed context).

g. Class 20. Mf 1738, sherd with snakelike relief decoration. Traces of dark brown or black paint on yellowish-orange buff ware. Fine grit temper. U168 lot 53. Stratum 9, d.c. 34 (tertiary context).

h. Class 20. Mf 1931, relief sherd with wheat sheaf decoration. Grit temper. V164 lot 34. Pit 163, B.L. IIIA, d.c. 22 (secondary context).

i. Class 21. Mf 8685, flat base sherd incised with potter's mark. Grit temper. U166 lot 69. Pit 285, stratum 9, d.c. 22 (secondary context).

j. Class 20. Mf 5190, body sherd with painted relief decoration in scale pattern. Grit temper. T168 lot 31. Area 395, B.L. IIIA, d.c. 34 (tertiary context).

k. Not assigned. Large straight nose lug. Undersurface shown on left. May have been cream slipped originally. Medium orange to medium brown surface. Medium grit temper. V168 lot 24. B.L. I, d.c. 36 (tertiary context).

l. Class 20. Banesh monochrome painted ware sherd with rope impression and small nose lug. Gray paint over white slipped buff ware. Grit temper. Test trench F. Previously published as *Bastan Chenassi* fig. 4 j and as *Iran* XII fig. 4 h.

m. Class 20. Mf 3600, carinated body sherd with relief dots. Grit temper. U168 lot 63. Cleanup, d.c. 41 (tertiary context).

n. Not assigned. Large Banesh bent nose lug on body sherd. Grit temper. U166 lot 25. Room 102, B.L. II, d.c. 37 (secondarily admixed context).

o. Class 20. Mf 3993, base sherd with archlike relief decoration, painted white and black. Grit temper. U166 lots 74 and 81. B.L. II, d.c. 36 (tertiary context) and stratum 9, d.c. 34 (tertiary context), respectively.

p. Not assigned. Square ledge handle on sherd with everted rim. Gray buff ware. Black grit temper. V166 lot 13. Stratum 1, d.c. 34 (tertiary context).

PLATE 23

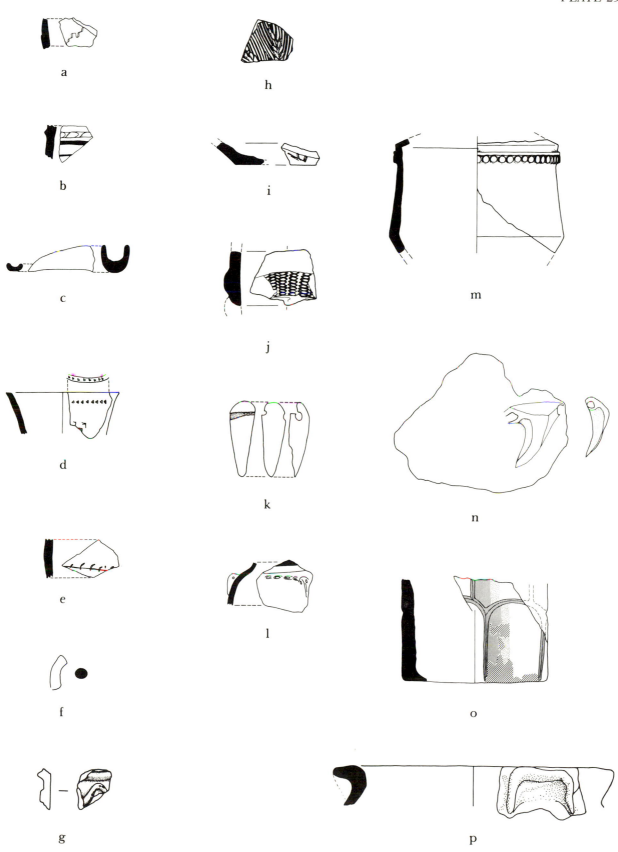

a

h

b

i

c

m

d

j

e

k

n

f

l

g

o

p

PLATE 24   PAINTED SHERDS

a. Class 20. Unique painted sherd. Monochrome red paint on smoothed light orange surface. Compact ware. Gray core. Fine holes visible in paste. Casually painted stripes (wavy and of uneven width) in triangle pattern. Possibly from shoulder of small globular pot. V166 lot 27. Area 379, B.L. II, d.c. 35 (secondarily admixed context).

b. Class 20. Unique painted sherd. Black paint on light brown smoothed surface. Compact ware. Very fine grit temper. V166 lot 1. Surface pickup (tertiary context).

c. Class 20. Unique painted sherd. Faded black paint on light orange surface. Compact ware. Fine grit temper with some straw. W168 lot 5. Pit 191, stratum 1, d.c. 22 (secondary context).

d. Class 20. Unique painted sherd. Black paint on smoothed, lightly burnished dark red exterior surface. Gray interior surface. Compact paste. Brownish-gray core. Very fine grit temper. V166 lot 9. Stratum 1, d.c. 34 (tertiary context).

e. Class 20. Checkerboard design in reddish-brown paint on smooth cream to very light brown surface. Very hard compact paste. No visible temper, but some holes. W168 lot 5. Pit 191, stratum 1, d.c. 22 (secondary context).

f. Class 20. Grit temper. T168 lot 48. Cleanup, d.c. 41 (tertiary context).

g. Class 20. Grit temper. U168 lot 171. Room 215, B.L. IIIB, d.c. 37 (secondarily admixed context).

h. Class 20. Black and white bichrome (W) over maroon slip (M). Grit temper. U166 lot 111. Room 306, B.L. IIIB, d.c. 26 (secondary context).

i. Class 20. Grit temper. U166 lot 69. Pit 285, stratum 9, d.c. 22 (secondary context).

j. Classes 18 and 20. Direct rounded rim, bowl form. Rim diameter 18 cm. Gray paint on red slip. Grit temper. V168 lot 75. Area 371, stratum 9, d.c. 34 (tertiary context).

k. Class 20. Black paint on white slip. Grit temper. U168 lot 110. Room 250, B.L. IIIA, d.c. 23 (secondary context).

l. Class 20. Black paint on white slip. Grit temper. Test trench F lot 7. Previously published as *Bastan Chenassi* Fig. 4 L.

m. Class 20. Dark red paint over light orange slip over a pink slip on orange buff ware. Lime pops in surface. Fugitive paint. V168 lot 68. Clean up, d.c. 41 (mixed context).

n. Class 20. Black painted teardrops. Grit temper. V168 lot 165. B.L. II, d.c. 36 (tertiary context).

o. Class 20. Black paint over white slip. Grit temper. U168 lot 110. Room 250, B.L. IIIA, d.c. 23 (secondary context).

p. Class 20. Black paint. Grit temper. V166 lot 50. Area 366, stratum 9, d.c. 23 (secondary context).

q. Class 20. Darkened maroon paint over light orange to light brown surface. Grit temper.

r. Class 20. Black paint over white slip. Grit temper. U168 lot 110. Room 250, B.L. IIIA, d.c. 23 (secondary context).

s. Classes 10 and 20. Ledge rim bowl form with painted rim and side. Rim diameter 47 cm. Maroon paint over light orange buff slip. Grit temper with pits in surface. V168 lot 18. Area 355, B.L. I, d.c. 23 (secondary context). Previously published as *Iran* XIV fig. 8i.

t. Class 20. Base sherd, diameter 32 cm. Fugitive black paint over white slip. No remaining paint or slip on stippled areas. Lower surface of base covered with black paint. Grit temper. U168 lot 110. Room 250, B.L. IIIA, d.c. 23 (secondary context).

PLATE 24

a. Class 2. Mf 3977, top of furnace lining fragment. U166 lot 69. Pit 285, stratum 9, d.c. 22 (secondary context).

b. Class 2. Mf 3831, possible ingot mold. 10 x 4.5 x 2.2 cm. Depression in mold has slightly rounded ends. V168 lot 118. Area 375, B.L. IIIA, d.c. 51 (tertiary context).

c. Class 2. Mf 3827, possible ingot mold. Oval shape; broken at one end. Existing fragment 9.5 x 5.5 x 2.4 cm. Depression in mold has rounded end. V168 lot 99. Trashpile 241, B.L. IIIA, d.c. 23 (secondary context).

d. Class 2. Mf 3905, possible ingot mold. Fragmentary, 7 x 4.5 x 2.6 cm. Depression in mold is shallow (0.06 cm) and possibly triangular. V168 lot 22. Alleyway 16, B.L. I, d.c. 35 (secondarily admixed context).

e. Class 16. Mf 1487, copper pin. U166 lot 30. B.L. I, d.c. 36 (mixed context).

f. Class 16. Mf 3585, copper pin. V168 lot 71. B.L. II, d.c. 36 (tertiary context).

g. Class 16. Mf 5160, copper pin. T168 lot 22. Area 395, B.L. IIIA, d.c. 34 (tertiary context).

h. Class 16. Mf 3677, copper pin. U168 lot 86. Stratum 9, d.c. 34 (tertiary context).

i. Class 16. Mf 5060, copper pin. U168 lot 120. Room 258, B.L. IIIA, d.c. 35 (tertiary context).

j. Class 16. Mf 3676, copper pin. U168 lot 110. Room 250, B.L. IIIA, d.c. 23 (secondary context).

k. Class 16. Mf 3583, copper bar/pin? V168 lot 100. Area 371, stratum 9, d.c. 34 (tertiary context).

l. Class 2. Mf 3612, copper bar. V168 lot 111. B.L. IIIA, d.c. 36 (tertiary context).

m. Class 6. Mf 3813, copper needle. V168 lot 84. Stratum 9, d.c. 36 (tertiary context).

n. Class 2. Mf 5389, copper sheet stock bent into hook. V166 lot 42. Alleyway 307, B.L. IIIA, d.c. 51 (tertiary context).

o. Class 16. Mf 1920, copper ring. Diameter 3.2 cm. V164 lot 31. Pit 165, B.L. IIIB, d.c. 22 (secondary context).

Comparable registered item not illustrated: Class 2. Mf 3838, possible ingot mold fragment (cf. mf 3827, item c on this plate). A small piece of copper was found adhering to this artifact. V168 lot 130. Hearth 266, stratum 14, d.c. 28 (secondary context).

PLATE 25

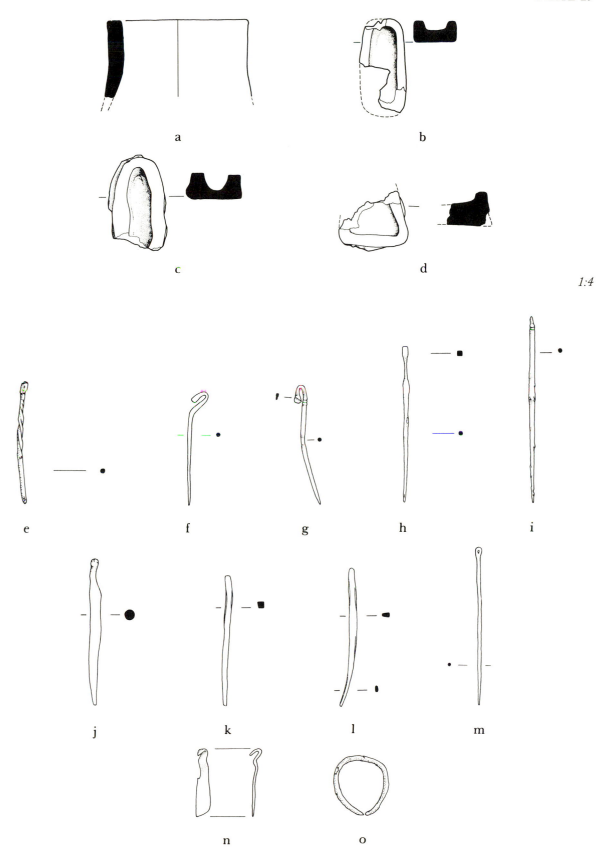

a

b

c

d

1:4

e

f

g

h

i

j

k

l

m

n

o

1:2

PLATE 26   MISCELLANEOUS ARTIFACTS

a. Not assigned. Mf 3694, ground stone tool of undetermined function. 3.2 x 2.3 cm. U168 lot 98. Hearth 227, B.L. IIIB, d.c. 36 (tertiary context).

b. Class 19. Mf 5067, stone adze. U168 lot 111. Room 250, B.L. IIIA, d.c. 26 (secondary context).

c. Class 21. Mf 5228, small clay geometric object. Squat cone shape. U166 lot 97. Room 309, B.L. IIIA, d.c. 37 (secondarily admixed context).

d. Class 21. Mf 1912, small clay geometric object. Squat cone shape. U164 lot 5. Room 141, B.L. II, d.c. 37 (tertiary context).

e. Class 21. Mf 3601, small clay geometric object. Squat cone shape. V164 cleanup (tertiary context).

f. Class 6. Mf 3597, unbaked clay spindle whorl. V168 lot 98. Area 39, B.L. II, d.c. 29 (tertiary context).

g. Class 6. Mf 6950, unbaked clay spindle whorl. W168 lot 19. Stratum 1, d.c. 34 (tertiary context).

h. Not assigned. Mf 1741, white plaster object. Circular depressions appear to have been pressed when material was soft. Semicylindrical area on right view is similar to a depression that might be left by a mounting rod of some sort. V164 lot 27. Pit 165, B.L. IIIB, d.c. 22 (secondary context).

i. Class 14. Mf 3841, chipped stone tool. U168 lot 128. Well 195, B.L. I, d.c. 41 (tertiary context).

j. Class 13. Mf 3846, chipped stone blade. U168 lot 136. Pit 196, stratum 1, d.c. 49 (tertiary context).

k. Class 13. Mf 3847, chipped stone blade. Twin to item h above. U168 lot 136. Pit 196, stratum 1, d.c. 49 (tertiary context).

l. Class 13. Mf 3507, chipped stone blade. U168 lot 86. Stratum 9, d.c. 34 (tertiary context).

m. Class 13. Mf 3689, chipped stone blade. U168 lot 100. Stratum 1, d.c. 22 (tertiary context).

n. Class 13. Mf 3501, chipped stone tool. U168 lot 73. Room 225, B.L. IIIA, d.c. 51 (tertiary context).

o. Class 16. Mf 1295 a and b, lapis lazuli beads. U166 lot 5. Room 89, B.L. I, d.c. 37 (secondary admixture).

p. Class 16. Mf 6907, lapis lazuli bead. V166 lot 31. Area 379, B.L. II, d.c. 35 (tertiary context).

q. Class 16. Mf 1299, lapis lazuli bead. U168 lot 23. Well 199, B.L. I, d.c. 22 (secondary context).

r. Class 16. Mf 6906, frit bead. V166 lot 13. B.L. I, d.c. 34 (tertiary context).

s. Class 16. Mf 6908, pale blue-green frit bead. V168 lot 49. Room 36, B.L. II, d.c. 25 (secondary context).

t. Class 16. Mf 6901, black limestone bead. U166 lot 11. B.L. I, d.c. 35 (tertiary context).

u. Class 16. Mf 1292, red marble bead. U168 lot 10. Well 195, B.L. I, d.c. 22 (secondary context).

v. Class 16. Mf 1309, carnelian bead. V166 lot 3, B.L. I, d.c. 32 (tertiary context).

w. Class 16. Mf 6903, white banded chalcedony bead. U166 lot 13, B.L. I, d.c. 35 (tertiary context).

x. Class 16. Mf 1914, dentalium shell bead. U168 lot 42. Area 183, B.L. II, d.c. 37 (tertiary context).

PLATE 26

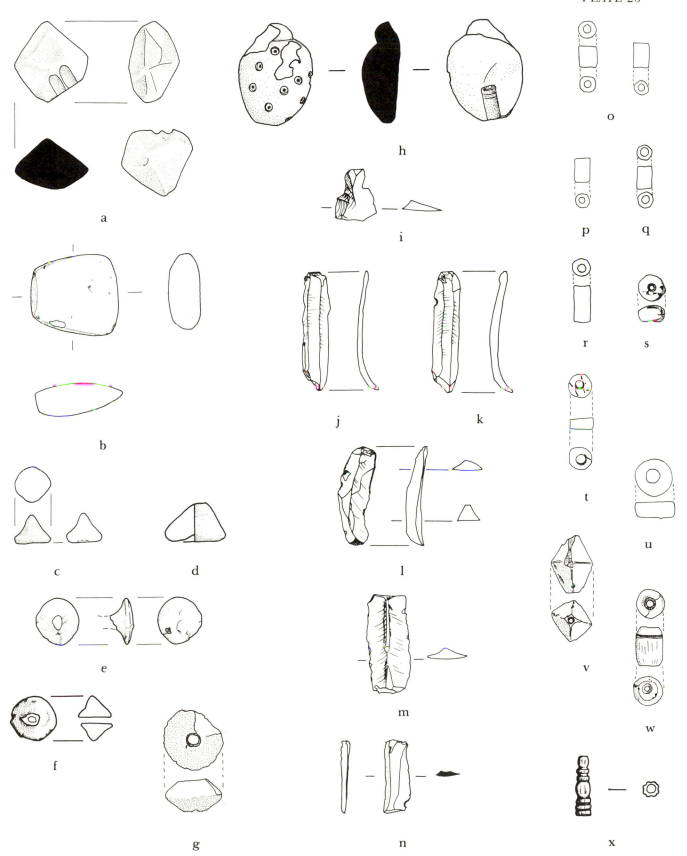

a

b

c

d

e

f

g

h

i

j

k

l

m

n

o

p

q

r

s

t

u

v

w

x

1:2

PLATE 27   MISCELLANEOUS ARTIFACTS

a.   Class 12. Mf 5078, complete limestone or plaster vessel. Recut rim. V 168 lot 143. Burial 274, B.L. IIIB, d.c. 13 (primary context).

b.   Class 12. Mf 6104, rim sherd from white limestone vessel. V 166 lot 51. Area 366, stratum 9, d.c. 51 (tertiary context).

c.   Class 12. Mf 5058, rim sherd from limestone vessel. (Mf 1120, 3829, 5062, and 5202, not illustrated here, are similar in form.) U 168 lot 133. Room 258, B.L. IIIA, d.c. 35 (secondarily admixed context).

d.   Class 12. Mf 5295, rim sherd from stone vessel. Incised side (Mf 5230, not illustrated here, is comparable in rim form.) U 166 lot 113. Room 306, B.L. IIIA, d.c. 35 (secondarily admixed context).

e.   Class 12. Mf 1124, rim from stone vessel. W 168 lot 13. Stratum 1, d.c. 34 (tertiary context).

f.   Class 12. Mf 1121, base of stone vessel (Mf 5205, not illustrated here, is similar.) V 168 lot 3. Stratum 2, d.c. 17 (the pebble/cobble stratum).

g.   Class 17. Mf 1312, door socket made from heavy grit-tempered pot sherd. Roughly circular. Diameter of about 11.2 cm. Thickness of 3.3 cm. U 168 lot 16. Courtyard 30, B.L. II, d.c. 37 (secondarily admixed context).

h.   Class 12. Mf 3878a, lead bowl. U 168 lot 111. Room 250, B.L. IIIA, d.c. 26 (secondary context).

i.   Not assigned. Mf 3685, small boot-shaped piece of lead. U 168 lot 93. Room 219, B.L. IIIB, d.c. 26 (secondary context).

j.   Class 7. Mf 6274, stone mortar. Found set into floor. V 168 lot 58. Alcove 26, B.L. II, d.c. 37 (but mortar itself was still in primary context).

k.   Not assigned. Mf 3878b, two lead discs. Found inside bowl 3878a. U 168 lot 111. Room 250, B.L. IIIA, d.c. 26 (secondary context).

l.   Class 17. Mf 1313, drain spout. Light orange buff surface; gray core. Black grit and straw temper. Finger-scrape marks in channel. U 166 lot 10. B.L. I, d.c. 35 (secondarily admixed context).

m.   Class 17. Mf 6272, drain spout (reconstructed view). U 166 lot 114. Room 306, B.L. IIIA, d.c. 21 (secondary context).

PLATE 27

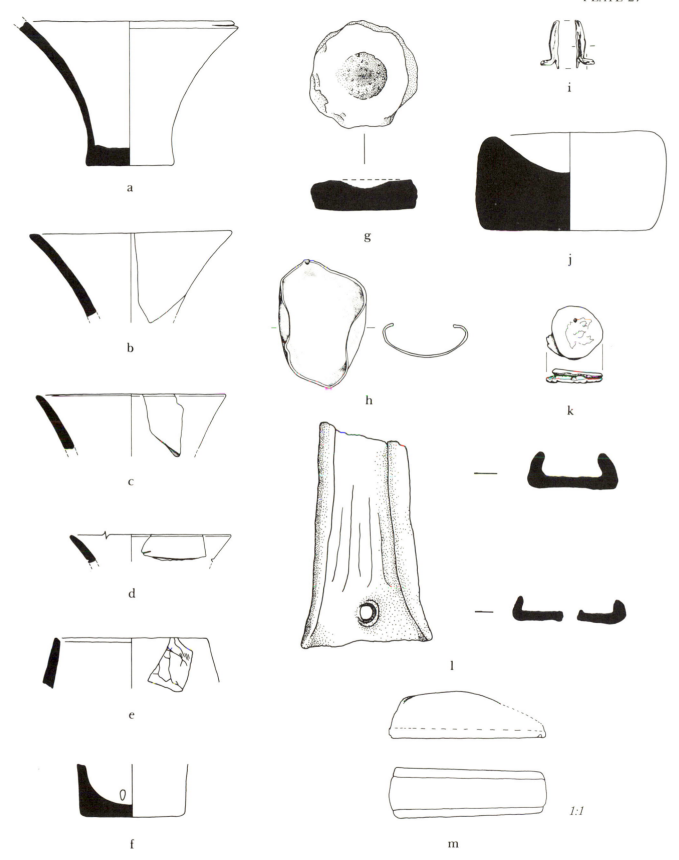

a

b

c

d

e

f

g

h

i

j

k

l

m

1:1

1:4

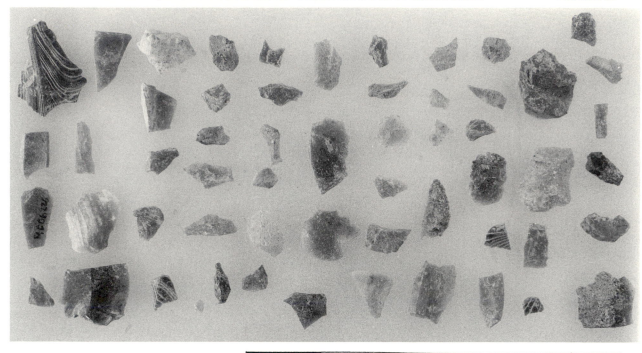

2:1

0   5 cm

The collection of debitage and tools shown here was registered under one number, Mf 6226. These items were found in a very secure secondary context (U168 lot 172, d.c. 21) on lower floor of room 215 of B.L. IIIB East Unit, sealed over by upper floor 13a. Collection would thus seem to represent a fairly discrete moment of flint knapping activity.

FUNCTIONAL CLASSES 2 AND 12   PLATE 29

1:2.5

0   5 cm

A. Large piece of copper sheet stock. Mf 3613: V168 lot 108, d.c. 36, B.L. IIIA stratum 11.

B. Fragmentary mold, low-fired, high density chaff-tempered ware. 9.5 x 5.5 x 2.4 cm. Mf 3827: V168 lot 99, d.c. 23, trashpile 241, B.L. IIIA northern periphery.

C. Iron-rich copper or copper slag, with an ingotlike appearance. Weight: 165 gm. 9.2 x 4.0 cm. Rounded on one end; appears broken on other. One surface flattish; other convex. Mf 3953: U168 lot 149, d.c. 35 (tertiary context), room 284, B.L. IIIA West Unit.

D. Lead bowl, functional class 12, special containers, plus 2 tightly joined lead discs found inside bowl. Bowl apparently formed from circular sheet raised to form irregular sides. Length of bowl 13.5 cm. Mf 3878a and b: U168 lot 111, d.c. 26, room 250, B.L. IIIA East Unit.

PLATE 30   DIVERSE FUNCTIONAL CLASSES

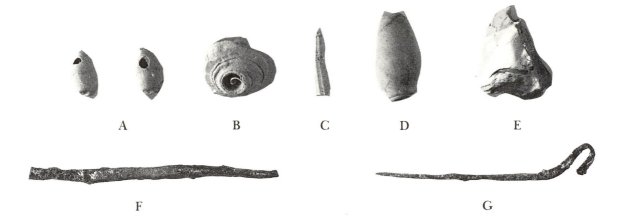

A   B   C   D   E

F   G

A. 2 cowrie shells, functional class 4, shell-working. Mf 3555: U168 lot 84, d.c. 35 (tertiary), room 234, B.L. IIIA East Unit.

B. Cone shell, functional class 4, shell-working. Mf 3696: U168 lot 116, d.c. 42 (secondary admixture), room 247, B.L. IIIA East Unit.

C. Dentalium, functional class 4, shell-working. Mf 3701: U168 lot 110, d.c. 23, room 250, B.L. IIIA East Unit.

D. Olive shell bead, functional class 16, personal ornaments. Mf 3557: V168 lot 80, d.c. 36, removal of a B.L. II feature.

E. Mother of pearl material, functional class 4, shell-working. Mf 3605: V168 106, d.c. 36, B.L. IIIA.

F. Copper pin, functional class 16, personal ornament. Mf 3583: V168 lot 100, d.c. 34, area 371, stratum 9.

G. Copper pin, functional class 16, personal ornament. Mf 3585: V168 lot 71, d.c. 36, removal of a B.L. II feature.

H   I

1:1

H. Perforated sherd disc of chaff-tempered ware, assigned to functional class 6, cloth manufacture. Disc pierced from both sides. 7.4 x 1.3 cm. Mf 5179: U166 lot 93, d.c. 35 (tertiary), alley 307. B.L. IIIA.

I. Unperforated sherd disc of grit tempered ware, assigned to functional class 8, possible pottery manufacture. Mf 5180: U166 lot 103, d.c. 35 (secondary admixture), alley 307, B.L. IIIB stratum 13d.

0   5 cm

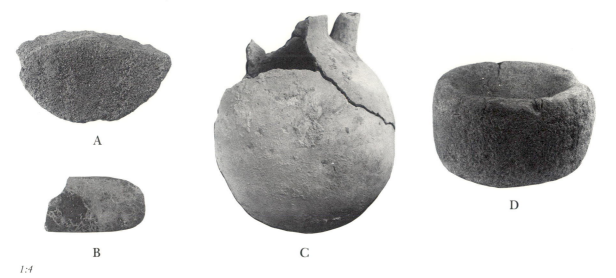

1:4

A. Fragmentary quern, coarse jasper sandstone. 8.7 x 18.7 x 4.7 cm. Mf 3723: U168 lot 105, d.c. 22, stratum 1 (mixed).

B. Fragmentary handstone with a flattened oval cross-section, sandstone or siltstone. At least 10 x 5.7 x 2.2 cm. Mf 3721: U168 lot 111, d.c. 26, room 250, B.L. IIIA East Unit.

C. Spouted jar with everted rim. Plain everted rim, globular body and rounded base. Broken tubular spout above shoulder. Height 24.9 cm. Mf 1927 (M 1214): U166 lot 61, d.c. 35 (tertiary context), B.L. II.

D. Mortar. Sandstone type 3, 18.5 x 9.7 cm, depth of central depression 4.4 cm. Mf 6274: V168 lot 58, d.c. 37 (but the mortar itself was in primary context), room 26, B.L. II North Unit.

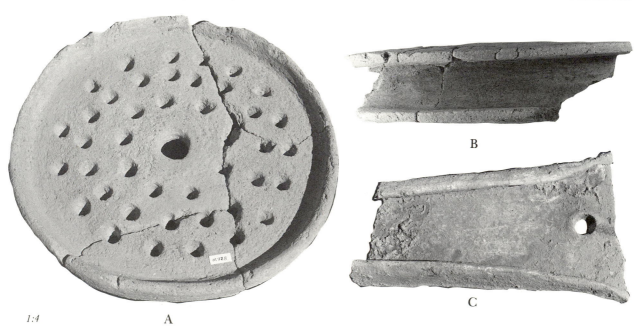

1:4

A. Grill, functional class 7, food preparation. Diameter 39 cm, height 2.5 cm. Mf 1310: V168 lot 14, d.c. 25, alley 16, B.L. I.

B. Drain pipe of low fired chaff-tempered ware, functional class 17, architecturally related items. Mf 6247: V168 lot 168, d.c. 34, area 397, B.L. IIIA northern periphery.

C. Drain pipe, black grit and straw temper, functional class 17, architecturally related items. 22.5 x 14.0 x 4.0 cm. Mf 1313: U166 lot 10, d.c. 35 mixed (secondarily admixed), B.L. I stratum 4.

0   5cm

PLATE 33   FUNCTIONAL CLASS 12, SPECIAL CONTAINERS

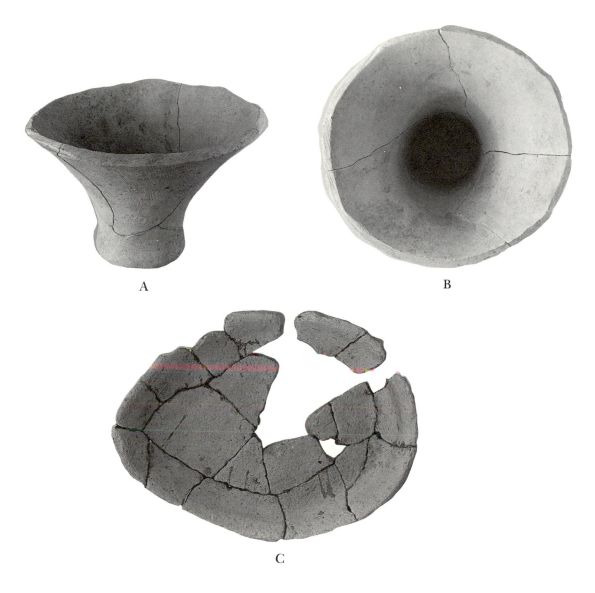

A

B

C

1:4

A. Limestone vessel. 14.9 cm tall, 22.7 cm rim diameter. Mf 5078: V168 lot 143, d.c. 13, burial 274, B.L. IIIA northern periphery.

B. Top view of vessel. Mf 5078.

C. Teardrop shaped Banesh low tray, chaff-tempered ware. Length 30.8 cm. Mf 5084: U168 lot 145 (secondarily admixed), d.c. 35, room 284, B.L. IIIA West Unit.

0   5 cm

1:2.5

A.-D. Sherds with potter's marks, functional class 21, information processing.

A. Mf 6244: V166 lot 66, d.c. 34, area 367, B.L. IIIA stratum 9.

B. Mf 6246: U168 lot 158 (tertiary), d.c. 35, room 258, B.L. IIIA West Unit.

C. Mf 6243: U166 lot 132 (tertiary), d.c. 35, alley 307, B.L. IIIA exterior.

D. Mf 6245: V168 lot 153, d.c. 36, drainage pit 333, B.L. IIIA stratum 9.

E. Sherds bearing relief decoration, all evidently from the same vessel. Functional class 20, decorated items. Relief beading, black paint or slip on orange buff grit-tempered ware. The sherds come from two lots and were registered under two numbers. Mf 3600: U168 lot 63, d.c. 41 mixed. Mf 3957: U168 lot 143, d.c. 29 mixed, courtyard 30, B.L. II stratum 8c.

PLATE 35   FUNCTIONAL CLASS 21, INFORMATION PROCESSING

1:1

(A.-F. also reflect class 10, storage.)
A. Seal impression. Mf 1819: V164 lot 27, d.c. 22, pit 165, B.L. IIIB.
B. Reverse of sealing Mf 1819.
C. Seal impression. Mf 1882: V164 lot 32, d.c. 22, pit 165, B.L. IIIB.
D. Reverse of sealing Mf 1882.
E. Seal impression. Mf 6195: U168 lot 149 (tertiary), d.c. 35, room 284, B.L. IIIA West Unit.
F. Reverse of sealing Mf 6195.
G. Small geometric cylinders. Mf 5182: U166 lot 100, d.c. 42 (tertiary), alley 307, B.L. IIIA exterior.
H. Small geometric ball. Mf 3598: V168 lot 69 mixed, d.c. 29, courtyard 30, B.L. II East Unit.

0   5 cm

A

B

1:1

A. Proto-Elamite tablet. 7.4 x 4.0 x 2.2 cm. Writing only on obverse; no seal impressions. Mf 4469: V166 lot 64, d.c. 42 (secondarily admixed), area 336, B.L. IIIA.

B. Bulla (interior core and exterior envelope). Outer shell fragmentary and bears faint traces of cylinder seal impression. Thickness of envelope varies from 0.3 to 1.7 cm. Mf 6176: U166 lot 82, d.c. 35 (secondarily admixed), room 306, B.L. IIIA West Unit.

0   5 cm

PLATE 37   CLASS 21 AND UNCLASSIFIED OBJECTS

A

B

C

D

E

1:1

A. Naturalistic cylinder seal and impression, fragmentary, functional class 21, information processing. Soft white stone, deeply carved. Height of fragment 2.0 cm, width 1.9 cm. Mf 5056: U166 lot 72, d.c. 36, B.L. II stratum 8c.

B. Geometric cylinder seal and impression, functional class 21, information processing. Claystone or ceramic. 3 cm hole drilled through length. Mf 5057: V168 lot 68, d.c. 41 mixed.

C. Unusual object of white plaster, not assigned to functional class under present model of TUV activities. Circular depressions appear to have been made when material was soft. 5.5 x 4.0 x 1.9 cm. Mf 1741: V164 lot 27, d.c. 22, pit 165, B.L. IIIB.

D. Reverse of object Mf 1741. Semi-cylindrical area similar to depression that might be left by mounting rod of some sort.

E. Unusual multifaceted object of ground sandstone, not assigned to functional class under present model of TUV activities. 3.2 x 2.3 cm. One facet has 2 adjacent grooves, each 0.6 cm wide. One groove is 1.5 cm long and the other 1.7 cm long. Mf 3694: U168 lot 98, d.c. 36, incorporated in matrix of hearth 227, B.L. IIIB stratum 13c.

0   5 cm